Ohio and the War of 1812

A Collection
of
Lists, Musters and Essays

Eric Eugene Johnson

Society of the War of 1812
in the
State of Ohio

HERITAGE BOOKS
2013

HERITAGE BOOKS
AN IMPRINT OF HERITAGE BOOKS, INC.

Books, CDs, and more—Worldwide

For our listing of thousands of titles see our website
at
www.HeritageBooks.com

Published 2013 by
HERITAGE BOOKS, INC.
Publishing Division
5810 Ruatan Street
Berwyn Heights, Md. 20740

Copyright © 2013 Society of the War of 1812 in the State of Ohio

Heritage Books by the Society of the War of 1812 in the State of Ohio:
American Prisoners of War Held at Bermuda, Cape of Good Hope and Jamaica During the War of 1812
American Prisoners of War Held at Barbados, Newfoundland and New Providence During the War of 1812
American Prisoners of War Held at Quebec During the War of 1812, 8 June 1813–11 December 1814
American Prisoners of War Held at Halifax, During the War of 1812, Volume I and II
Ohio and the War of 1812: A Collection of Lists, Musters and Essays

All rights reserved. No part of this book may be reproduced or transmitted in any form or by any means, electronic or mechanical, including photocopying, recording or by any information storage and retrieval system without written permission from the author, except for the inclusion of brief quotations in a review.

International Standard Book Numbers
Paperbound: 978-0-7884-5495-0
Clothbound: 978-0-7884-6812-4

Table of Contents

Introduction v
Ohio Militia 1
   Ohio's lost militia companies 3
   Three militiamen were killed at the Battle of Copus' Hill 9
   Ohio's odd battalions 10
   John Chapman's Amazing Call to Arms 11
   Tuscarawas County's militia officers 12
   Coshocton County's 2nd Militia Battalion 17
   Court-Martial of Brigadier General Reasin Beall 22
   Ohio women also served in the War of 1812 26
   Camp Avery 27
Regular Army 29
   Regular army muster rolls found in Ohio 31
   America's greatest disaster during the War of 1812 42
   Ohioans who served as army officers during the War of 1812 43
   Regular Army enlistments and discharges in Ohio 50
   Ohio's forgotten military cemeteries 57
   The War of 1812 pensioners in the Pension List of 1818 59
   History of the 17th Regiment of U.S. Infantry 65
   History of the 19th Regiment of U.S. Infantry 71
   Captain George Sanderson and the Battle of the Thames 80
   History of the 26th Regiment of U.S. Infantry 81
   Blankets for the dead 85
   History of the 27th Regiment of U.S. Infantry 86
   History of the other Ohio army units 92
   The Old Guard 96
   Some Ohio soldiers and militiamen who were captured during the War of 1812 97
   List of Ohio officers in the Regular Army 101
Essays 103
   The Battle of Marblehead Peninsula 105
   Gunboats on the Cuyahoga: Lake Erie's Lost Squadron 111
   Making sense of the Roster of Ohio Soldiers in the War of 1812 119
   The case of the missing records: 125
   Everything you ever wanted to know about obtaining service records 128
   Forts, Stockades and Blockhouses 136
   Ohio's militia laws during the War of 1812 145
   A War of 1812 roster which has a unique tie to history 153
   This once mighty army 155
   Regimental reorganizations during the War of 1812 159
   The Invasion of Upper Canada: Harrison's Amphibious Assault 165
   Captain Stanton Sholes and the Ohio Militia 176
   U.S. Schooner Ohio 177
   How many men served in America's land forces during the War of 1812? 179
Dictionary of the War of 1812 181
Charts 197
   Militia divisions as organized under the Federal Militia Act of 1792 199
   Militia regiments as organized under the Federal Militia Act of 1792 201
   Ohio Militia Regiments as organized during the War of 1812 203

Ohio Militia Odd Battalions as organized during the War of 1812 205
Ohio's Regular Army Infantry Regiments Lineage 207

Introduction

The War of 1812 is long gone and largely forgotten by the American public. It was a little war, which has been overshadowed by the Revolution, the Civil War, and the wars of the 20th century. Americans do remember bits and pieces of this war. Perry defeated the British on Lake Erie. Jackson won the Battle of New Orleans. A man named Key wrote our national anthem during the Battle of Fort McHenry. Ask for dates and the names of other battles which are associated with this war, and you will see many blank stares.

For Ohio, this was an important war. The state was invaded four times, three by land and once by water, and each time, we defeated the enemy. Ohioans participated in many of the battles in this war, and our men, both militia and regular army soldiers, are buried where they were killed or died. Cemeteries in Ohio, Michigan, Indiana, Illinois, Missouri, Louisiana, Alabama, Pennsylvania and New York contain the bodies of many of these fallen soldiers. Ohioans also died in Canada, across the rivers from both Detroit and Niagara Falls, and in the prison camps in Montreal, Quebec and Halifax.

Ohio's militia was formed when the state was still part of the Northwest Territory. Upon statehood, the militia came under the control of the governor, as the commander in chief, and the state's general assembly. The militia was an involuntary military organization which would be replaced by the voluntary National Guard during the Civil War.

Ohio was a frontier state when the war began in 1812 having only been admitted to the union in 1803. The state had a 400% increase in population going from approximately 70,000 people in 1803 to 227,843 in 1810, a period of only seven years. By the start of the war, Ohio would have approximately 240,000 citizens and even during the war more people would be moving into the state from the east. Throughout the war, the state's general assembly would create new counties to administer to the needs of its citizens.

Ohio's contributions in the War of 1812 have been over shadowed by Kentucky in the amount of men and support used to defend this country during the war. In Henry Adams' *The War of 1812* he states, "except [for] New York, Kentucky, Tennessee, and perhaps Ohio, no state gave to the war the full and earnest cooperation it needed." The state contributed approximated 20,000 militiamen to the war effort and another 2,500 men for the army. The 1812 state militia rolls had 34,726 men listed.

Preparations for the war begin on 26 February 1812 when Ohio's Governor Return J. Meigs, Junior, received a letter from Secretary of War William Eustis requesting him to raise 1,200 volunteer militiamen to be used in the defense of Fort Detroit, Territory of Michigan, and for a possible invasion of Upper Canada once war was declared against Great Britain. The secretary cited the Congressional Act of 6 February 1812 asking the states for volunteers. The war would last for three long years.

The War of 1812 did not end on 14 December 1814 when the Treaty of Ghent was signed but it would continue well into 1815. Because of the slowness of ocean travel, most of America, both the United States and the colonies of Canada, would not know of the signing of the treaty until early February 1815. The war ended when the governments of Great Britain and the United States exchanged ratified treaties on 17 February 1815.

On June 15, 1815, the terms of the peace treaty went into effect and the armies from both sides returned to their own borders. It was also on this date that the regular army was reduced to a peacetime strength and the last of the militia companies on federal duty were sent home.

Ohio started the war in good position as a lead state in the northwest but lost out to Kentucky after Brigadier General William Hull's surrender. The three Ohio militia regiments under General Hull gave a very good account of themselves and had there been a better leader than General Hull, Ohio would have had a more prominent role during the war. General Hull's poor leadership greatly hurt the morale of, and the respect for, the Ohio militia.

Two of the Ohio's colonels under General Hull, Duncan McArthur and Lewis Cass, would both command regular army regiments in 1813, and McArthur, as a general, would later take over command of the Army of the Northwest from Major General William Henry Harrison in 1814. Ohio produced many good military leaders throughout the war.

General Harrison would use two brigades of Ohioans in his first military campaign of the war but he preferred his own regular army regiments plus the militia from Kentucky to do most of the fighting. Kentuckians were well represented at the Battle of Tippecanoe under General Harrison in 1811 and they would spearhead his army at the Battle of the Thames in 1813. They were General Harrison's preferred troops. Illinois, Indiana, Michigan, Pennsylvania and Virginia would also play backseat roles to the Kentuckians.

There were three massive call-ups of Ohio militia during the war. The first call up was for 1,200 men, which was used to form the nucleus of the first Army of the Northwest. The second massive call up occurred after General Hull surrendered his army at Fort Detroit. Approximately 10,000 men took up arms and headed to Ohio's frontier to repel any invasion by the British and the Indians. The final massive call up took place in May 1813 when Governor Meigs asked for volunteers to help lift the first siege of Fort Meigs. Between 5,000 to 6,000 men responded to this call up.

Throughout the war Gov. Meigs would tap one of his commanders to organize a brigade in support of the Army of the Northwest. These call ups would normally involve around 1,000 men.

One of the biggest misconceptions about the war is that men from the same community or general area banded together to form companies and then marched off to fight the British and the Indians. In actuality, there were little differences between the militia during the Revolutionary War and the War of 1812 in the way they were called to duty and how they fought.

The Ohio militia evolved from the militia forces of the Northwest Territory and the military structure and militia laws were well in place long before the War of 1812 started. Once the governor issued a "call to arms," runners were sent to each division commander and in turn each brigade, regiment, battalion and company commander was ordered to activate their commands. Every area of the state was affected.

Ohio was divided into four militia divisions and each division was divided into brigades and then regiments. Each township in each county had at least one militia company serving as part of that county's regiment. The larger populated counties had up to six regiments.

Every able-bodied man between 18 and 45 was a member of the militia, except those exempted by law. At least half of the men were armed and although training may have been sub-standard, the officer corps knew what to do in time of crisis or war. The militia companies from the frontier immediately began to construct blockhouses for the defense of frontier communities. Other companies from the non-frontier areas of Ohio were then sent forward to assist in this defense.

Ohioans were reluctant to serve on a tour of duty that lasted more than three months at a time. The federal Militia Act of 1792 set into law that the federal government could only call up the state's militia for three months in any given year and that the militia could only be used within the borders of the United States. The federal government preferred to have all militia forces serve for a year on a voluntary basis but the government accepted the services of many of the states' regiments for six-month duties. The militia forces from Kentucky had no problem serving a 6-month or a year-long tour of duty.

Since most of the fighting in the northwest was on or near Ohio soil, the militia companies from within this state did not have to travel far to see action during the war. Kentuckians, on the other hand, had to travel anywhere from 200 to 500 miles, one way, to Ohio, depending on which area of Kentucky they were from. Kentuckians tended to accept longer tours of duty than Ohioans because of the distances involved.

Kentuckians were also better armed and equipped than most of their counterparts in the Ohio militia. This is only because most of the militia of Kentucky passed through Newport, Kentucky, on their way to Ohio, where they drew arms and equipment from the federal arsenal at the Newport Barracks. Most Ohio companies did not have this opportunity to draw arms from a federal arsenal so a larger percentage of our men were not armed.

Another misconception is that a lot of militiamen did not own firearms and that is why these men reported for duty without muskets or rifles. In reality most men did own a weapon but these weapons were of a smaller caliber that were designed for shooting birds and small game, not men. These weapons were left behind in the care of teenage sons so that they could continue to provide food for the family tables.

Many men brought to the field the muskets of their fathers that were used during the revolution. Many of these muskets were of the proper caliber but they were old and worn, and many were in need of repairs. Other men simply showed up for their tour of duty without firearms in hopes of being issued a new musket or rifle, which they assumed that they would be able to keep once their tour of duty was over.

As a member of a number of hereditary societies, I have helped many men and woman in researching their military ancestors. I am amazed that many of these individuals totally overlook the fact that their ancestors may have served in the army and not the militia. The U.S. Army kept far better records than the state militia, which is a genealogical plus if an ancestor had served in the army.

Approximately one out of five Ohioans who served during the War of 1812 actually served in the U.S. Army and not in the militia. Ohio took an active role in the recruiting of army soldiers and these men not only served in the old northwest but also at New Orleans and in New York. Many Ohioans fought at the Battle of New Orleans, the Battle of Chippewa and the Battle of Lundy's Lane.

In 1812, the old northwest and Kentucky were assigned the raising of two companies of light artillery, three troops of light dragoons, a battalion and a half for the 2nd Region of Artillery, the 1st Regiment of Infantry, the 17th Regiment of Infantry, the 19th Regiment of Infantry and four companies of rifles. It is doubtful that the two companies of light artillery were raised and the old northwest only raised one troop for the light dragoon regiment and only one company for the artillery regiment.

By the end of the war the old northwest had also been assigned the task of raising the 26th, 27th and 28th Regiments of Infantry plus part of the 2nd Regiment of Rifles. Additionally, the old northwest raised most of the ranger companies for the U.S. Army during the war. Two of the ranger companies were raised in Ohio. The 1st Ranger Company, under the command of Captain James Manary, operated in western Ohio. The 2nd Ranger Company, under the command of Captain William Perry, operated out of Vincennes, Indiana.

The 19th Regiment of Infantry was raised throughout Ohio. This regiment saw considerable action in the northwest before most of the regiment was transferred to Sackets Harbor, New York, in the fall of 1813. This regiment also had men from Michigan and Indiana serving among its ranks. On 12 May 1814 this regiment was disbanded and the men were transferred to the new 17th Regiment of Infantry.

The 26th Regiment of Infantry was raised in western Ohio. Most of this regiment was transferred to Sackets Harbor in the fall of 1813. This regiment merged with the 27th Regiment of Infantry on 14 May 1814 to form the new 19th Regiment of U.S. Infantry. The 27th Regiment of Infantry had been raised in eastern Ohio.

Captain Daniel Cushing raised an artillery company of Ohioans for the 2nd Regiment of Artillery, which was stationed at Fort Meigs, Ohio, during most of 1813 before it was reassigned to Fort Detroit, Michigan. A battalion of four companies was raised for the 1st Regiment of Rifles in Kentucky and Ohio. By the time the battalion was formed, the war in the old northwest was over and the battalion was transferred to Sackets Harbor in the fall of 1813.

Although the 7th Regiment of Infantry was primarily raised in Kentucky, the unit did recruit in Ohio and Tennessee. The 7th Infantry maintained two recruiting stations in Ohio early in the war, one at Cincinnati and the other at Lebanon. This regiment had three captains from Ohio: Enos Cutler, Thomas S. Jesup and Michael McClelland. McClelland would be killed on 23 December 1814 during the First Battle of New Orleans, Louisiana.

The new 17th Regiment of Infantry was formed on 12 May 1814 with the merger of the old 17th and 19th Infantries. The command structure was made up of Ohioans and the headquarters was moved from Kentucky to Chillicothe, Ohio. This regiment continued to recruit men from both states. The new 19th Regiment of Infantry was formed on 12 May 1814 with the merger of the 26th and 27th Infantries plus some of the men from the old 17th Infantry. This regiment recruited primarily in Ohio.

Captain Samuel Hopkins of Kentucky raised a company of light dragoons for the 2nd Regiment of Light Dragoons. First Lieutenant James Hedges of Ohio recruited troopers from Ohio. The majority of the men, however, were from Kentucky. The company was involved in most of the conflicts in the northwest before it was transferred to Sackets Harbor in the fall of 1813.

The 2nd Regiment of Rifle was raised in 1814 in the states of Kentucky, Ohio and Tennessee. This regiment was stationed at Fort Detroit during the last year of the war and it saw no action during this conflict.

This book is divided into three major sections, which highlight the Ohio militia, the Ohioans who enlisted in the U.S. Army, and essays on a number of important events along with some genealogical aids. The book is a mixture of history and genealogical information. But, it is still only a snapshot of the information on Ohioans who served in the War of 1812.

As stated in my title, this is a collection of lists, musters and essays on the War of 1812 as it pertains to Ohio. It is the result of twenty years of research and twelve years of writing articles for various magazines. There are also a number of previously unpublished works in this book.

Eric E. Johnson
May 2013

Ohio Militia

Ohio's lost militia companies

The primary source for research in identifying militiamen who served during the War of 1812 from the State of Ohio has been the *Roster of Ohio Soldiers in the War of 1812* (herein referred to as the *Roster*).[1] The *Roster* contains the listing of most of the militia companies and headquarters' staffs that were activated for state or federal service in Ohio during the war.

Twelve militia companies are missing from the *Roster* and they are also missing from the militia rosters stored at the Ohio Historical Society (OHS). The Society has copies of the actual militia rosters which were copied from the National Archives in Washington, D.C., during the 1870's.[2] These militia rosters were incorporated into the *Roster of Ohio Soldiers in the War of 1812* in 1916.

Eleven of these lost companies are included in the muster rolls stored at the Western Reserve Historical Society[3] (WRHS) in Cleveland, Ohio. The WRHS's archive library also has a copy of the musters for the War of 1812 which it obtained from the National Archives during the 1870's. The final lost muster role is listed in the WHRS's publication called the *Tracts* from the 1870's.[4]

Between the two sets of rosters stored at these societies, there are numerous errors in the spelling of militiamen's names, dates copied incorrectly, and missing information about the militiamen.

In the *Roster*, Captain Grove Case's Company is listed as a company from the 27th Regiment of U.S. Infantry. His company is listed in the militia rosters from the WRHS as a mounted infantry company in the Ohio militia from Licking County and not a regular army company.

Captain George Sanderson's company from the 27th Regiment of U.S. Infantry is listed in the *Roster* but the information from the OHS for this company was obtained from William Alexander Taylor's book, *Centennial History of Columbus and Franklin County, Ohio.*[5] The Ohio Historical Society does not have a copy of this muster roll for Captain Sanderson's regular infantry company.

Copies of all of the musters listed in this article can be obtained by writing to the Western Reserve Historical Society. The society has a website which contains the fee and ordering information. With each request you will need the name of the commander of each company, the dates that the company served plus the container number and box number.

Western Reserve Historical Society
ATTN: Reference Division
10825 East Boulevard
Cleveland, OH 44106
(216) 721-5722

Muster Rolls Arranged Alphabetically by the
Commanding Officer's Surname.
MSS 660 - Container 2 – Folder (number needed)

---

[1] **Roster of Ohio Soldiers in the War of 1812**, The Adjutant General of Ohio 1916, (Heritage Books, Inc., Bowie, Maryland: 1995).

[2] **Rosters of Ohio Militia, War of 1812**, Series 110, microfilm number GR9273 Index and microfilm number GR9274 Lists of Militia Companies & Members, Adjutant General's Records, Ohio Historical Society, Columbus, Ohio.

[3] **War of 1812, Collection of Papers 1791-1876**, MSS 660, Container 2, Muster Rolls & Newspaper Clippings, Western Reserve Historical Society Library, Cleveland, Ohio.

[4] Western Reserve Historical Society, Cleveland, Ohio, **Historical and Archaeological Tracts**, number three, page 2, muster roll of Captain John D. Seely's Company

[5] **History of Franklin and Pickaway Counties, Ohio**, (Williams Brothers, Evansville, Indiana: 1880), chapter XIX Military Record, Captain George Sanderson's Company of the 27th Regiment of U.S. Infantry, muster roll, December 1813, pp. 107-108.

Ohio and the War of 1812

Captain William Barbee's Company [6]
Colonel Adams' Regiment, for relief of Fort Wayne
From 25 August to 12 September 1812
(Miami County)

Captain William Barbee	Lieutenant James Orr	Sergeant Daniel McClung
Sergeant William Barbee, Jr	Sergeant Benjamin Bennett	Sergeant James Youart

Privates

Brown, William	Kerns, John	Petit, Amos
Cox, John	Kerris, Henry	Price, John
Culbertson, Joseph	Machy, Samuel	Reed, Samuel
Gerard, Charles	McGrunsy, Robert	Sewell, John R.
Gerard, Moses	Miller, Jesse	Teuery, Joseph L.
Jones, Jonas	Moor, Samuel	Tod, John

Captain William Beard's Company [7]
Colonel Charles Williams' Regiment
Ordered on the Frontiers of Knox and Richland Counties
From 26 August to 26 September 1812
(Coshocton County)

Captain William Beard	Lieutenant Richard Fowler	Ensign Solomon Vail
Sergeant Lewis Vail	Sergeant Isaac Meredith	Sergeant Thomas P. James
Sergeant William Biggs	Corporal Samuel Elson	Corporal Abraham Fry
Corporal Thomas Workman	Corporal Sem Flahearty	

Privates

Addy, Hugh	Hartley, John	Miller, Nicholas
Addy, Robert	Hawkins, William	Miller, Stephen
Ammory, George	Hill, John	Mulvane, John
Beatty, Robert	Horton, Thomas	Musgrove, Moses
Beckworth, Joseph	Hull, Henry	Norris, Samuel
Bowen, Courtant	John, Thomas	Oglesby, James
Cantwell, Thomas	Jones, William	Preston, Henry
Clark, James	Kearlos, John	Rolling, William
Clark, William	Lisk, James	Severn, Joseph
Coe, Martin	Maples, David	Shaw, Elijah
Darling, Jonathan	Mason, George	Smith, Reuben
Darling, William	McFarlin, Samuel	Titus, George
Elson, John	McLean, Daniel	Varris, John
Evans, Gabriel	Meredith, Obed	Waggoner, John
Evans, Thomas	Miller, Henry	Willis, James
Griffin, Robert	Miller, James	Willis, Richard
		Wisecarver, Abraham

---

[6] **Muster Rolls Arranged Alphabetically by the Commanding Officer's Surname**, MSS 660, Container 2, Folder 6, T-Z - Militia Rosters, Western Reserve Historical Society, Reference Division, Cleveland, OH.

[7] **Ibid**, Folder 1, A-C - Militia Rosters, Western Reserve Historical Society, Reference Division, Cleveland, OH.

Sergeant John Cartright, Junior's Company [8]
Paymaster McDongal, Major R. Harper
From 28 July to 18 August 1813
(Ross County)

Sergeant John Cartright, Jr. Musician John Ortman

Privates
Boblets, John	Dolahan, Hugh	Jones, Zachariah
Cartright, Abraham	Dunn, Silas	McClure, James
Cartright, Henry	Epey, Thomas	Neff, George
Cartright, Nathaniel	Ferguson, Isaac	Pemelton, William
Coe, Thomas	Gates, John	Shreaklugust, George
		Yeakey, Peter

Roll of Captain Adam Johnston's Rifle Company [9]
Colonel Charles Williams' Regiment
Ordered on Frontier of Richland and Knox Counties
From 26 August to 26 September 1812
(Coshocton County)

Captain Adam Johnston	Lieutenant William Morrison	Ensign Abraham Miller
Sergeant Thomas Foster	Sergeant John M. Miller	Sergeant Frederick Markley
Sergeant Robert Culbertson	Corporal John H. Miller	Corporal Zebedee Baker
Corporal John M. Bantham	Corporal John D. Moore	

Privates
Arnold, George	McFarland, Joseph	Miller, Windle
Baker, John	McKearn, John	Moore, Allen
Boner, Mathew	Miller, Daniel	Morrison, Samuel
Bucklew, James	Miller, Edward	Neff, Joseph
Carr, Henry	Miller, Isaac G.	Steerman, John
Howland, Isaac	Miller, Isaac M.	Williams, Mathew
Lybarger, Andrew	Miller, John G,	Winders, James
McCullock, George	Miller, Michael	Workman, Benjamin

Captain Robert Nelson's Mounted Company [10]
Ralph Osborn, Paymaster
From 26 July to 26 August 1813
(Pickaway County)

Captain Robert Nelson	Ensign John B. Johnson	Sergeant Richard W. Owings **
Sergeant Thomas Roberts **	Sergeant Peter Tills	Sergeant David Bradley **
Corporal Reubin Parish	Corporal Joseph Powell	Corporal Joseph Lawford **
Corporal Benjamin Chenowith	Trumpeter Daniel Sinks	

** Deserted 10 August 1813

---

[8] **Muster Rolls Arranged Alphabetically by the Commanding Officer's Surname**, MSS 660, Container 2, Folder 1, A-C - Militia Rosters, Western Reserve Historical Society, Reference Division, Cleveland, OH.

[9] **Ibid,** Folder 3, H-K - Militia Rosters, Western Reserve Historical Society, Reference Division, Cleveland, OH.

[10] **Ibid,** Folder 4, L-O - Militia Rosters, Western Reserve Historical Society, Reference Division, Cleveland, OH.

Privates

Aog, Jacob	Filbery, John **	Martin, John
Bailey, James **	Frakes, Henry **	Merion, William
Bailey, Mathew	Horrington, Peter **	Milled, Gilbert
Bassett, Alexander	How, Peter	Mills, Joseph **
Coffman, Henry	Hughey, Nathan **	Parish, John
Coonrad, Woolery	James, Dawson	Perringes, John
Droddy, Charles	Lisle, James	Price, James
Elsworth, Daniel **	Lynn, John	Rudinour, Matthew
		Shrynour, Peter

** Deserted 10 August 1813

Captain Nathan Newsom's Mounted Company [11]
By order of Governor Meigs, defense of the frontier (Gallia County)
From 1 August to 4 September 1813

Captain Nathan Newsom	Lieutenant Cushing Shaw	Ensign George Burris
Sergeant Jesse Hubbell	Sergeant Qernire Wells	Sergeant Alvin Rothburn
Sergeant Cyrus Heighley	Corporal Philip Jones	Corporal Moses Gillarpie
Corporal Benjamin Long	Corporal Abijah Hubbell	Trumpeter Isaac Hawkins

Privates

Aleshire, Abraham	Hale, John	Lyman, Samuel
Aleshire, David	Hawk, Isaac Sr.	McCarty, David
Aleshire, John	Hill, Jacob	Montgomery, David
Aleshire, Peter	Hoffis, George	Prickerman, John
Bailey, David	Humphries, William	Ray, Martin
Bailey, John	Hyne, Francis	Saxton, John
Benedick, Hubbell	Hysel, Leonard	Scott, Charles
Brown, James	Jones, Thomas	Skurlock, High
Bucher, John	Keaton, David	Smith, William
Durst, David	Keaton, George	Stow, Erastus
Ewing, William	Keaton, William	Swin, John
Gastiu, Jonathan	Long, Elisha	Tarr, George
Hacket, Jeremiah	Lotts, Abraham	Thomas, Jason

Captain Joel Paines' Company [12]
(Geauga County)

Names of individuals who served in Capt. Joel Paines' Company of Volunteers, Mounted men, at the urgent request of Brig. Gen. Simon Perkins, commanding the drafted and volunteer militia at Camp Avery in the autumn of A.D. 1812.

Captain Joel Paine	Lieutenant James A. Harper	Ensign I. F. Atkins
1st Sergeant John M. Austin	2nd Sergeant Samuel W. Phelps *	3rd Sergeant Isaac H. Phelps **
1st Corporal Jedediah Beard	2nd Corporal Roger Nettleton	3rd Corporal Anson Sisson

---

[11] **Muster Rolls Arranged Alphabetically by the Commanding Officer's Surname**, MSS 660, Container 2, Folder 4, L-O - Militia Rosters, Western Reserve Historical Society, Reference Division, Cleveland, OH.

[12] **Ibid**, Folder 8, Miscellaneous Copies of Muster Rolls, Western Reserve Historical Society, Reference Division, Cleveland, OH.

Privates

Bartholomew, Abraham	Gaylord, Levi	Montgomery, Levi
Bartholomew, Samuel J.	Gregory, Eli	Morecraft, James
Beckwith, Samuel	Harper, Archibald	Paine, Edward J. ***
Blakeslee, John G.	Harper, Robert	Potter, William
Bond, Eli	Hendry, Samuel	Rockwell, Caleb
Brackman, John	Hubbard, Matthew	Rockwell, Joshua
Calhoon, Reynolds	Jackson, Walter	Waters, Winthrop
Cowles, Alpheus	Miller, William	Woodworth, Ezekiel
French, Squire B.	Mixer, Phineas Jr	

* Discharged 17 October 1812
** Discharged 19 October 1812
*** Discharged 14 October 1812

Captain Elnathan Scofield's Dragoon Company [13]
By order of Governor Meigs and General Harrison
(Fairfield County)

Captain Elnathan Scofield	From 8 May to 18 May 1813
Lieutenant Hugh Boyle	From 8 May to 18 May 1813
Sergeant Daniel Smith	From 8 May to 23 May 1813

Privates

Abrams, John	From 8 May to 4 May 1813
Canode, George	From 8 May to 18 May 1813
Cloud, Robert	From 8 May to 18 May 1813
Durry, John	From 8 May to 23 May 1813
Foster, Samuel	From 8 May to 23 May 1813
Goodwin, James	From 8 May to 18 May 1813
McElby, Thomas	From 8 May to 18 May 1813
Osenbach, Henry	From 8 May to 23 May 1813
Reem, Jacob	From 8 May to 23 May 1813
Sheaffer, Jacob	From 8 May to 14 May 1813
Shullenberger, Samuel	From 8 May to 23 May 1813
Weaver, Christian	From 8 May to 18 May 1813

Roll of Captain Nicholas Shaver's Rifle Company [14]
For the defense of the frontier, 2nd regiment
From 20 August to 27 September, 1812
(Licking County)

Captain Nicholas Shaver	Lieutenant John Switzer	Ensign George Waggoner
Sergeant John Arput	Sergeant Elisha L. Bonham	Sergeant George Black
Sergeant William Vance		

Privates

Armstrong, George	Gaylor, William	Parr, Samuel
Beard, John Jr.	Gizer, Anthony	Rathbone, Gideon
Beard, Joseph	Harter, George	Rees, Thomas

---

[13] **Muster Rolls Arranged Alphabetically by the Commanding Officer's Surname**, MSS 660, Container 2, Folder 5, P-S - Militia Rosters, Western Reserve Historical Society, Reference Division, Cleveland, OH.

[14] **Ibid**, Folder 5, P-S - Militia Rosters, Western Reserve Historical Society, Reference Division, Cleveland, OH.

Brewer, Peter	Horkinson, John	Ruble, Abraham
Carsin, Isaac	Horksinson, Andrew	Rush, Jacob
Dispenny, George	Kite, Michael	Sutton, Levi
Edgell, Daniel	McInturf, John	Switzer, Frederick
English, George	Miers, Lewis	Switzer, Jacob
Foulk, Jacob	Nehen, Adam	Trout, Nicholas
Gaylor, Daniel	Orput, Richard	Trumbo, Andrew

Captain James Sloan's Company [15]
Cincinnati Light Dragoons, Colonel Duval
From 1 July to 30 September 1812
James Taylor, Paymaster
(Hamilton County)

Captain James Sloan	Lieutenant Christopher Walker	Cornet William Waring
Sergeant Daniel Walker	Sergeant Samuel Littel	Sergeant Thomas Carter
Sergeant Charles Hasson	Corporal Moses Robinson	Corporal Elijah Carter
Corporal James McCauley	Corporal Henry Luster	Trumpeter David Wilson

Privates

Allen, Robert	Kauts, David	Ridde, William
Avery, Samuel	Kelsimer, Francis	Saunders, William
Boteler, Edward S.	King, Thomas D.	Sayre, Annanias
Campbell, David	Lofleud, William	Scoggins, Joel
Case Lewis H.	McCauley, Nicholas	Shane, John
Emiley, James (died)	McFerrau, John (died)	Spiers, James H.
Gilliard, James M.	Misuer, Demarcus	Stall, George W.
Haine, Daniel S.	Petatt, Thomas	Stewart, John
Hasson, William	Pierson, John	Wall, William
Hatton, William (killed 8 Aug)	Preston, Patrick	Williams, Benjamin
Hole, Samuel	Pugh, Joseph	Williamson, George
		Woolf, John

Captain Christopher Wood's Company of Spies [16]
Colonel Williams' Regiment, General Tupper's Brigade
From 4 September 1812 to 2 March 1813
Those marked with * were discharged in October or November 1812
(Champaign County)

Captain Christopher Wood	Lieutenant John Fillis Jr.	Lieutenant William Scott
Sergeant Benjamin Cheney *	Sergeant William Bay	Sergeant James Suit *
Sergeant Joseph Sutton		

Privates

Blalark, George Jr. *	Fillis, John Sr.	McLeod, Colin
Blalark, George Sr. *	Franks, John	Myers, Isaac
Bridges, William (discharged 27 Sep)	Franks, Robert	Pearce, Thomas
	Gilliland, Nathan *	Pittijohn, William
Brince, Nathanial *	Gilliland, Samuel *	Robins, Vincent

---

[15] **Muster Rolls Arranged Alphabetically by the Commanding Officer's Surname**, MSS 660, Container 2, Folder 5, P-S - Militia Rosters, Western Reserve Historical Society, Reference Division, Cleveland, OH.

[16] **Ibid**, Folder 6, T-Z - Militia Rosters, Western Reserve Historical Society, Reference Division, Cleveland, OH.

Cheney, Ebenezer *	Grayum, Joseph	Ross, Joseph W.
Cheney, Jonathan *	Hulse, John	Shaw, Henry *
Cheney, William *	Humble, James (discharged 27 Sep)	Stuart, Archibald
Cochran, John	Humble, James *	Suit, John *
Colison, Robert	Kendle, James *	Sutton, Eli
Cor, Joseph	Knight, John *	Tatman, Joseph *
Crukfield, Arthur	Martin, Asel *	Tharp, Levi *
Davis, William	Martin, Thomas	Tucker, Jeremiah
Donaldson, E.	Mathews, Henry	Wood, Isaac *
Drunnan, Charles	McDonald, William	Wood, John
Entzminger, John	McHenry, Isaac	

Captain John W. Seely's Company, U.S. Voluntary Corps [17]

12 June 1812

(Huron, Cuyahoga, Geauga, Ashtabula, Portage and Trumbull Counties)

Captain John W. Seely	Ensign James Kerr	1st Sergeant Samuel Bill
3rd Sergeant Zadock Bowell	1st Corporal John Cherry	

Privates

Anderson, James	Fowler, Daniel	Netterfield, Joseph
Blackley, Miller	Hayes, Alexander	Newman, Eathen
Brewer, Robert	Kiddle, David	Rathburn, Amos
Buell, Ezra	Knafe, Conrad	Scroggs, Aaron
Burnett, Urial	Lane, Asa	Slavin, Barnabas
Chalpin, James	Lanterman, Peter	Stanley, Nathanel
Crawford, William	Markee, Andrew Junior	Strader, William
Crumrine, Michael	Markee, Hugh	Strain, John
Dobbins, Matthew	Martin, William	Tid, Martin Junior
Fitch, David	Mears, James	Walker, Joseph
Fobes, Justin	Meeker, William	Wartrous, Solomon
		Yatman, Peter

Three militiamen were killed at the Battle of Copus' Hill

A detachment of militiamen from Captain Absalom Martin's militia company from Guernsey County stopped for the night at the home of James Copus on 14 September 1812. Copus' homestead, now in Mifflin Township, Ashland County, was about nine miles east of Mansfield. The militiamen had torched the deserted Indian village of Greentown near Mansfield during the day.

The next morning four of the men went to the spring unarmed to wash up when Indians ambushed them. George Shipley, John Tedrick and Robert Warnick were killed and scalped while a fourth militiamen, Robert Dye, made it back to the cabin with a wound in his thigh. The Indians then attacked the cabin and in this assault James Copus was killed and his daughter, Nancy, was wounded. George Launtz, another militiaman, was also wounded. A musket ball had broken his arm.

This skirmish lasted for five hours before the Indians withdrew. It is believed that 45 Indians took part in this assault since 45 small campfires were found near the cabin. The Indians had been roasting corn the night before the attack. A monument was erected to the fallen men on 15 September 1882 on the site of their burial. The battle is also called the "Battle at Copus' Farm."

---

[17] Western Reserve Historical Society, Cleveland, Ohio, **Historical and Archaeological Tracts**, Number 3, page 2, muster roll of Captain John D. Seely's Company.

Ohio's odd battalions

One of the more interesting terms to come out of the War of 1812 was Ohio's "odd battalions." This was a unique term for a military unit which appears to have been used only in Ohio during the early 1800s. There was nothing "odd" about these battalions or "odd" about the men who served in these units.

The amendment to the Ohio's Militia Act of 1803, which was passed in 1805, created "odd battalions." Basically, if there weren't a sufficient number of militia companies in any one county within the state to form a regiment, the commanding officer of the brigade, usually a brigadier general, could form these companies into an odd battalion. As new companies were formed in a county due to population growth, they were added to the odd battalions. When the number of companies within an odd battalion reached eight, then the odd battalions became a regiment.

The majors of the odd battalions were permitted to have a regimental staff. In short, odd battalions were mini-regiments. The majors could appoint adjutants and other staff officers.

The brigade commanders could attach an odd battalion to any existing regiment. Regiments were divided into two battalions of four companies each under the command of a lieutenant colonel. With the added odd battalions, these regiments would then have three battalions in their structure.

Odd battalions were permitted to have a band made up of a chief musician, one assistant musician and a clerk. The musicians had to furnish their own instruments. A two-man band doesn't sound too exciting even for the military.

Under the Militia Act of 1814, odd battalions could raise a company of riflemen, light infantry or grenadiers bringing the total minimum number of companies to five as long as the number of privates in each of the infantry companies did not fall below 40 men each. Under the Militia Act of 1814, the clerks in odd battalions were required to keep the same records as the clerks in regiments.

The total number of odd battalions created in Ohio may never be known. The records of Ohio's Adjutant General's Department, which are located at the Ohio Historical Society in Columbus, are not complete. The list below are the known odd battalions found in the *Roster of Ohio Soldiers in the War of 1812* and the National Archives' compiled military records for the War of 1812.

These are the odd battalions that were called to duty during the war and whose soldiers were paid by the federal government.

Commander	Organization	County
Major George P. Torrence	1st Division, 1st Brigade, Odd Battalion	Hamilton County
Major Daniel Kain	1st Division, 4th Brigade, Odd Battalion	Greene-Clark County
Major Isaac Dawson	2nd Division, Odd Battalion	Ross County
Major Benjamin Daniels	2nd Division, 2nd Brigade, Odd Battalion	Ross County
Major William Renick	2nd Division, 4th Brigade, Odd Battalion	Pickaway County
Major Samuel Connell	3rd Division, Odd Battalion	Fairfield County
Major Joseph Rhodes	4th Division, 2nd Brigade, Odd Battalion	Columbiana County
Major George Darrow	4th Division, 4th Brigade, Odd Battalion	Portage County

Odd battalions were independent militia battalions. Other states also had independent battalions but they did not use the term "odd battalion." However, Illinois, after the War of 1812, passed a law requiring that the first militia unit to be formed after the creation of a new county, would be called an "odd battalion."

Bibliography

Acts of the State of Ohio, Passed and Revised, First Session of the Third General Assembly begun and held at the Town of Chillicothe, December 3, 1804, and in the Third Year of said State. N. Willis, printer, Chillicothe, Ohio: 1804, (reprinted The Laning Company, Norwalk, Ohio: 1901), Militia Act Amendment of 1805, Chapter XLIV, Sections 1, 2 and 16.

Acts Passed at the First Session of the Seventh General Assembly of the State of Ohio, begun and held in the Town of Chillicothe, December 5, 1808, and in the Seventh Year of the Said State, (J. S. Collins, Chillicothe, Ohio: 1809), Militia Act of 1809, Chapter 1, Section 13.

Acts Passed at the First Session of the Twelfth General Assembly of the State of Ohio, begun and held in the Town of Chillicothe, December 6, 1813, and in the Twelfth Year of Said State, volume XII, (John Bailhache, Chillicothe, Ohio: 1814), Militia Act of 1814, Chapter XXIII, Section 16.

Laws passed by the Fourth General Assembly of the State of Illinois, at their Second Session, Commenced at Vandalia, January 2, 1826, and Ended January 28, 1826, (Robert Blackwell, Printer to the State: Vandalia, IL 1826).

National Archives and Records Administration. **Index to the Compiled Military Service Records for the Volunteer Soldiers Who Served During the War of 1812**. Washington, D.C.: National Archives and Records Administration. M602, 234 rolls.

Roster of Ohio Soldiers in the War of 1812, The Adjutant General of Ohio 1816, (Heritage Books, Inc., Bowie, Maryland: 1995).

John Chapman's Amazing Call to Arms

Paul Revere has been immortalized by Henry Wadsworth Longfellow's poem entitled "Paul Revere's Ride" but in fact his 'call to arms' was a total failure since Revere was captured by the British long before he was able to warn the militiamen at Lexington and Concord. Boston's Committee of Safety actually sent three patriots into the countryside on that night in April 1775 to warn the colonists that "the British are coming!" The three men were Revere, William Dawes and Samuel Prescott. Dawes got lost in the darkness, but Prescott made it to Lexington, and the rest is history.

Thousands of men in America's past have made similar attempts to warn their fellow countrymen in order to call out the militia during the time of war. This was the standard method of notifying the militiamen so that they could form up at their designated rendezvous. Sorry to say that the names of only a handful of these men are known today.

During the War of 1812 John Chapman of Richland County, Ohio, made an amazing "call of arms" in which he traveled from Mansfield in Richland County to Mount Vernon in Knox County, a distance of 30 miles. He accomplished this feat by running bare-footed the whole way in a single night and then returning the next day with the men that he was able to assemble. He had traveled a total of 60 miles on foot within a 24-hour period. All along the way he had stopped at every cabin warning the settlers to hasten to the nearest blockhouse because on a pending Indian attack.

After Brigadier General William Hull had surrendered his American army to the British at Fort Detroit on 16 August 1812, the British armed and then unleashed a number of Indian raiding parties into northern Indiana and northern Ohio. One party was sighted in late August near Mansfield and Chapman volunteered to go for help. Richland County was sparsely settled and the nearest large settlement was at Mount Vernon. Chapman saved the day by returning with reinforcements, and Mansfield was spared from an Indian attack. Later, the Indians did kill a number of settlers in the eastern part of the county.

Although John Chapman has not been immortalized by his amazing feat in August 1812, he has been made into one of America's most beloved folk heroes. John Chapman is also known as Johnny Appleseed.

Tuscarawas County's militia officers

Tuscarawas County was a frontier county in 1812. The county was only four years old in 1812 and in those four short years both the population had grown and the area of county had been increased by 50%. The county militia, which consisted of only two companies in 1807, had grown by 1811 to eight companies of infantry and one of cavalry.

The Ohio Historical Society has the early Adjutant General's records of the Ohio militia. Among these holdings are the militia officer's election results for the years between 1803 and 1857. Copies of the officer's elections results were required to be sent to the Adjutant General's Office in Columbus. The surviving elections results are on microfilm and can be viewed by the public.

Militia officers were elected to a five year term. In order to obtain a promotion to the next rank, an officer ran for next available position for the higher rank. As men died, moved away or turned 45 years of age, officer positions became vacant and elections were scheduled.

No militia records have been found prior to 1807 in the Ohio Adjutant General's records at the Ohio Historical Society for companies formed in the area that would become Tuscarawas County. The officer's election returns for 6 October 1807 for Muskingum County show that three new militia companies were formed in the districts of New Philadelphia, Gnadenhutten and White Eye's for the 1st Brigade of the 3rd Division of the Ohio Militia.[18]

The present day Coshocton and Tuscarawas Counties made up the township of Salem in Muskingum County in 1807. This township was divided into three company (militia) districts with the New Philadelphia District consisting of today's northern Tuscarawas County and the Gnadenhutten District constituting the rest of today's Tuscarawas County. The White Eye's District consisted of today's Coshocton County and may have included a part of the southwestern corner of Tuscarawas County.

Prior to 6 October 1807 there was probably only one militia company in Salem Township. The settlement of this area of Ohio began in earnest during this time period which brought about the need for the formation of new militia companies. Most likely, three of the nine men listed below were officers in the original militia company. The officers for these new companies were:

New Philadelphia company district
   Isaac Deardorff, Captain
   Frederick Torrance, Lieutenant
   Daniel Harbough, Ensign

Gnadenhutten company district
   Benjamin Callan (Walton), Captain
   James Clark, Lieutenant
   Russell Engler, Ensign

White Eye's company district
   James McClure, Captain
   David Vulgenot, Lieutenant
   Joseph Mulvean, Ensign

---

[18] **Militia officer's election returns 1803-1857**, Ohio Adjutant General's Department, State Archives Series 9, GR6956, Muskingum County, Series 9, Box 2, Folder 21, 3rd Division, 1st Brigade, 6 October 1807, Ohio Historical Society's Archives, Columbus, Ohio.

Tuscarawas County began to operate as a county on 15 March 1808 and on 13 August 1810 the seventh and eighth militia companies were formed.[19] Six new companies had been formed since 1807 each with approximately 77 men.

The militia companies at the time when the county was organized were probably grouped into an 'odd battalion' commanded by a major. Odd battalions operated as a regiment with a regimental staff and half the number militia companies. In August 1810 the battalion probably became a regiment with Robert Bay as the commanding officer. This regiment was the 3rd Regiment of the 4th Brigade of the 3rd Division of the Ohio Militia.

The two new militia companies were formed on 13 August 1810. Major Peter Cribbs was the commander of the 1st Battalion in which these new companies were assigned. The officers were:

3rd Division, 4th Brigade, 3rd Regiment, 1st Battalion, 7th Company
George Richardson, Captain
John Gard, Lieutenant
Jacob Winkleplank, Ensign

3rd Division, 4th Brigade, 3rd Regiment, 1st Battalion, 8th Company
John Crawford, Captain
William Casey, Lieutenant
Jacob Ross, Ensign

On 22 January 1811 David Casebeer was elected lieutenant and George Sluthover was elected ensign in the first company of the first battalion.[20] Godfrey Westhaver was elected lieutenant in the third company of the second battalion on 30 March 1811.[21] Major James Vanator signed the officer's election returns. All of these men filled vacancies.

John Snelbaker was elected captain of the second company of the first battalion while John Cline was elected ensign of the third company of the second battalion on 18 June 1811.[22] Major Peter Cribbs was the commanding officer of the second battalion.

The last militia company formed for the 3rd Regiment before the War of 1812 was the cavalry company. By law a regiment could have from eight to sixteen infantry companies, one cavalry company and two rifle companies. Most regiments in Ohio contained eight infantry companies and either a cavalry company or a rifle company. It is doubtful that Tuscarawas County had rifle companies although some men within each infantry company may have been armed with a rifle instead of a musket.

Colonel Robert Bay signed the officer's election return on 1 October 1811 creating the cavalry company.[23] The officers of this new company were:

Cavalry Company
Alexander McConnell, Captain
Nathan Wyant, Lieutenant
William Henderson, Ensign

---

[19] **Militia officer's election returns 1803-1857**, Ohio Adjutant General's Department, State Archives Series 9, GR6958, Muskingum County, series 9, box 5, folder 30, 13 August 1810, Ohio Historical Society's Archives, Columbus, Ohio.

[20] **Ibid**, GR6959, Tuscarawas County, Series 9, Box 7, Folder 13, 22 January 1811, Ohio Historical Society's Archives, Columbus, Ohio.

[21] **Ibid**, Muskingum County, Series 9, Box 7, Folder 11, 30 March 1811, Ohio Historical Society's Archives, Columbus, Ohio.

[22] **Ibid**, Muskingum County, Series 9, Box 7, Folder 11, 18 June 1811, Ohio Historical Society's Archives, Columbus, Ohio.

[23] **Ibid**, Muskingum County, Series 9, Box 7, Folder 11, 1 October 1811, Ohio Historical Society's Archives, Columbus, Ohio.

It is extremely doubtful that the cavalry company was a true cavalry company. Most likely the company operated as a mounted infantry company. It was very expensive to outfit a cavalry company with the proper sabers, pistols, horses and mounts. The men would have to have purchases their own arms and equipment. They also supplied their own horses and saddles.

Mounted infantry used horses for transportation. Once these men arrived at a battle site they would dismount and fight on foot. During the war the mounted company was used as a dispatch service in notifying militiamen of militia call ups and for regimental formations.

On 12 December 1811 three officers' positions were filled by elections in the fifth company. It is not known if this was a new company or that there were actually three officer vacancies in this company.[24] The fifth company was apart of the second battalion under the command of Major James Vanator. The officers were:

3rd Division, 4th Brigade, 3rd Regiment, 2nd Battalion, 5th Company
  Robert H. Caples, Captain
  Jack Enos, Lieutenant
  George Henry, Ensign

Daniel Humel was elected captain in the first company of the first battalion on 29 February 1812.[25] This battalion was commanded by Major Robert Cribbs. Four positions in the second battalion were filled on 19 November 1812.[26] Colonel Robert Bay signed this officer's election return. These officers were:

2nd Battalion, 4th Company
  James Davis, Lieutenant
  John Shepherd, Ensign

2nd Battalion, 1st Company
  Benjamin Waggoner, Captain

2nd Battalion, 2nd Company
  David Edmonds, Ensign

The brigade commander, Brigadier General Lewis Cass, accepted a volunteer colonel's position in the Army of the Northwest in the spring of 1812 under Brigadier General William Hull. Colonel Cass commanded a regiment made up of men from the 3rd Division including men from Tuscarawas County. This regiment fought at Detroit during the summer of 1812.

Robert Bay became the acting brigadier general and commanded the militia forces from Coshocton, Guernsey, Muskingum and Tuscarawas Counties. Bay remained the colonel of the Tuscarawas County militia during this time. On 18 March 1814 he was elected as the colonel of the 5th Regiment in Guernsey County.[27] He signed his own officer's election return as the commanding officer of the brigade. Also on this election return, the second company of the second battalion received a new commander on 22 April 1814. He was Captain Elijah Moore.

George Richardson became the new commander of the 3rd Regiment. The date of his election is not known but he did sign the next surviving officer's election return for Tuscarawas County. On 23 June

---

[24] **Militia officer's election returns 1803-1857**, Ohio Adjutant General's Department, State Archives Series 9, GR6959, Muskingum County, Series 9, Box 7, Folder 11, 12 December 1811, Ohio Historical Society's Archives, Columbus, Ohio.

[25] **Ibid**, 29 February 1812, Ohio Historical Society's Archives, Columbus, Ohio.

[26] **Ibid**, GR6960, Tuscarawas County, Series 9, Box 9, Folder 13, 19 November 1812, Ohio Historical Society's Archives, Columbus, Ohio.

[27] **Ibid**, GR6961, Roll 6, 18 March 1814, Muskingum County, Ohio Historical Society's Archives, Columbus, Ohio.

1815 James Crawford was elected major of the second battalion replacing James Vanator who had moved from the county.[28] On the next day Henry Laffer was elected major to replace Peter Cribbs who had resigned his position as a battalion commander.[29] This occurred on 24 June 1815.

The officer's election return for 11 July 1815 lists five men who were elected captains.[30] The report does not show to which companies these men were assigned. The men were:

Abraham Shaw, Captain
John Snelbaker, Captain
Nathan McGrew, Captain
Henry Laffer, Captain
James Crawford, Captain

The final officer's election return which closed out this county's participation in the War of 1812 occurred on 29 August 1815.[31] Two men were elected to officer's positions in two companies but the report does not show the rank for either man. Major Henry Laffer signed the report. They were:

3rd Regiment, 1st Battalion, 4th Company
John Miller, Junior

3rd Regiment, 1st Battalion, 2nd Company
John Butt

Ohio militia regiments rarely had more than eight infantry companies although the regiments were authorized to have 16 infantry companies. Each regiment had two battalions with four companies a piece. Each battalion was also authorized to have one rifle company for a total of five companies. A regiment could also have one cavalry company which was not assigned to a battalion. Each regiment had a regimental staff and two battalion staffs. There were approximately 795 men in each regiment.

Below is a re-constructed officer's rank roll for the 3rd Regiment from Tuscarawas County during the War of 1812. The names of the missing officers are not known at this time.

---

[28] **Militia officer's election returns 1803-1857**, Ohio Adjutant General's Department, State Archives Series 9, GR6962, Tuscarawas County, Roll 7, 1815-1816, 23 June 1815, Ohio Historical Society's Archives, Columbus, Ohio.

[29] **Ibid**, 24 June 1815, Ohio Historical Society's Archives, Columbus, Ohio.

[30] **Ibid**, 11 July 1815, Ohio Historical Society's Archives, Columbus, Ohio.

[31] **Ibid**, 29 August 1815, Ohio Historical Society's Archives, Columbus, Ohio.

Ohio and the War of 1812

3rd Regiment Officer's Rank Roll
(Re-constructed)

Organization	Name and Rank	Date Elected
Regimental Commander	1) Colonel Robert Bay	Prior to 1812
	2) Colonel George Richardson	By 23 Jun 1815
1st Battalion	1) Major Peter Cribbs	Prior to 1812
	2) Major Henry Laffer	24 Jun 1815
1st Company	Captain Daniel Humel	29 Feb 1812
	Lieutenant David Casebeer	22 Jan 1811
	Ensign George Sluthover	22 Jan 1811
2nd Company	Captain John Snelbaker	18 Jun 1811
	Captain John Butt	29 Aug 1815
	Lieutenant (unknown)	
	Ensign (unknown)	
3rd Company	Captain (unknown)	
	Lieutenant (unknown)	
	Ensign John Cline	18 Jun 1811
4th Company	Captain John Miller Junior	29 Aug 1815
	Lieutenant (unknown)	
	Ensign (unknown)	
7th Company	Captain George Richardson	13 Aug 1810
	Lieutenant John Gard	13 Aug 1810
	Ensign Jacob Winkleplank	13 Aug 1810
8th Company	Captain John Crawford	13 Aug 1810
	Lieutenant William Casey	13 Aug 1810
	Ensign Jacob Ross	13 Aug 1810
2nd Battalion	1) Major James Vanator	Prior to 1812
	2) Major James Crawford	23 Jun 1815
1st Company	Captain Benjamin Waggoner	19 Nov 1812
	Lieutenant (unknown)	
	Ensign (unknown)	
2nd Company	Captain (unknown)	
	Lieutenant (unknown)	
	Ensign David Edmonds	19 Nov 1812
3rd Company	Captain (unknown)	
	Lieutenant Godfrey Westhaver	30 Mar 1811
	Ensign (unknown)	
4th Company	Captain Elijah Moore	22 Apr 1814
	Lieutenant James Davis	19 Nov 1812
	Ensign John Shepherd	19 Nov 1812
5th Company	Captain Robert H. Caples	12 Dec 1811
	Lieutenant Jack Enos	12 Dec 1811
	Ensign George Henry	12 Dec 1811
Calvary Company	Captain Alexander McConnell	1 Oct 1811
	Lieutenant Nathan Wyant	1 Oct 1811
	Ensign William Henderson	1 Oct 1811

Coshocton County's 2nd Militia Battalion

The record book of the 2nd battalion of the Coshocton County militia fills in a missing piece in this county's early history. This record book logs the activity of this battalion starting in 1809 and ending in 1819. It has valuable information on the men who served from this county during the War of 1812.

The record book contains the correspondences, rank rolls, class rolls, detachment listings, muster rolls, court of enquiry reports, strength and equipment lists, and numerous other documents pertaining to the 2nd battalion. This book is in the militia collection of the Western Reserve Historical Society in Cleveland, Ohio.

The record book is not as complete as it should be. Not all of the rolls and rosters generated by the companies of the 2nd battalion were recorded in this book. The class rolls of 1812 only show the first four companies. The class rolls of 1813 are missing. There were two sets of class rolls in 1814 for the 1st, 4th and 5th companies, none for the 2nd company or the rifle company, and only one for the 3rd company. The record book does list the majority of men who were assigned to the 2nd battalion and who served during the War of 1812.

Coshocton County was a part of the 3rd division of the Ohio militia, which included the counties in the southeastern portion of Ohio. This division was divided into four brigades. The 4th brigade included the counties of Coshocton, Guernsey, Muskingum and Tuscarawas.

The 4th brigade was made up of six militia regiments. Muskingum County had the 1st, 5th and 6th regiments while Coshocton County had the 2nd regiment, Tuscarawas County had the 3rd regiment and Guernsey County had the 4th regiment. Each of the regiments had two battalions consisting of a minimum of four infantry companies. By law there may have been a rifle company assigned to each of the battalions, and a cavalry and an artillery company assigned to each of the regiments.

This list of 370 men represents those militiamen who served during the War of 1812 in the Ohio militia. Most of the men lived in the southeastern quarter of Coshocton County. Some of the men may be listed twice if they had been transferred from one company to another. Not all of these men were called up to serve a Tour of Duty in other parts of the state.

The list also represents only half of the men from Coshocton County who served in the militia during this time frame. The location of the record book for the 1st battalion is not known.

Name	Rank	Company	Name	Rank	Company
Achlin, Alex.	Private	2nd Comp.	Mason, George	Private	3rd Comp.
Addy, Hugh	Private	5th Comp.	Mattingly, William	Private	1st Comp.
Addy, James	Private	5th Comp.	McBride, John	Private	1st Comp.
Addy, Robert	Sergeant	4th Comp.	McCauly, Alex	Private	2nd Comp.
Addy, Thomas	Corporal	5th Comp.	McClain, Andrew	Private	5th Comp.
Ammons, Joshua	Private	2nd Comp.	McClane, Daniel	Private	5th Comp.
Amory, George	Private	1st Comp.	McClane, David	Private	5th Comp.
Ansbaugh, George	Lieutenant	4th Comp.	McClauly, Alex	Private	1st Comp.
Arbuckle, David	Private	5th Comp.	McCune, George	Private	5th Comp.
Arbuckle, John	Private	5th Comp.	McCune, James	Private	5th Comp.
Arnold, William	Private	1st Comp.	McCune, John	Sergeant	5th Comp.
Baker, Bazebel	Private	4th Comp.	McDonald, Stephen	Private	2nd Comp.
Baker, Benjamin	Private	4th Comp.	McFarlin, Andrew	Private	4th Comp.
Baker, Edward	Private	5th Comp.	McFarlin, Ezekiel M.	Private	4th Comp.
Baker, Isaac	Private	4th Comp.	McFarlin, Joseph	Private	4th Comp.
Baker, Isiah	Private	5th Comp.	McFarlin, Robert	Sergeant	4th Comp.
Baker, Luke	Private	5th Comp.	McFarlin, Samuel	Private	4th Comp.
Baker, Reason	Private	5th Comp.	McGuire, Francis	Corporal	1st Comp.

Ohio and the War of 1812

Name	Rank	Company	Name	Rank	Company
Balentine, Hugh	Sergeant	2nd Comp.	McLane, Andrew	Private	5th Comp.
Bauman, Ignatuis	Private	1st Comp.	McLane, David	Private	4th Comp.
Beam, David	Private	2nd Comp.	McLane, James	Private	5th Comp.
Beard, William	Captain	2nd Comp.	Meridith, David	Lieutenant	3rd Comp.
Beaty, Robert	Private	3rd Comp.	Meridith, Isaac	Captain	3rd Comp.
Beaty, Seavey	Private	3rd Comp.	Merydeth, Obed	Sergeant	3rd Comp.
Beckwith, Thomas	Private	3rd Comp.	Middleton, Nathaniel	Private	3rd Comp.
Beckworth, Joseph	Private	3rd Comp.	Miller, Charles	Major	2nd Reg.
Bennington, Oliver	Private	3rd Comp.	Miller, David	Private	4th Comp.
Biggs, James	Private	3rd Comp.	Miller, Henry	Private	3rd Comp.
Biggs, William	Ensign	3rd Comp.	Miller, Isaac	Private	4th Comp.
Bilman, Andrew	Private	3rd Comp.	Miller, Jacob	Private	4th Comp.
Bird, William	Private	1st Comp.	Miller, James	Private	3rd Comp.
Bookler, William	Private	2nd Comp.	Miller, Nicholas	Private	1st Comp.
Boothe, Daniel	Private	4th Comp.	Miller, Stephen	Private	3rd Comp.
Bower, Constant	Private	4th Comp.	Mills, John	Captain	4th Comp.
Bryam, Moses	Private	3rd Comp.	Mills, Stephen	Private	4th Comp.
Bryson, Benjamin	Sergeant	4th Comp.	Miskimins, James	Private	4th Comp.
Burrell, Joseph	Private	1st Comp.	Miskimons, William	Private	5th Comp.
Butler, James	Private	3rd Comp.	Mohhalin, John	Private	4th Comp.
Butler, Jonathan	Private	3rd Comp.	Moore, Charles	Private	2nd Comp.
Butler, Joseph	Private	3rd Comp.	Moore, Elijah	Private	2nd Comp.
Butler, Thomas	Private	3rd Comp.	Moore, Jared	Private	1st Comp.
Byers, Samuel	Private	1st Comp.	Moore, Thomas	Private	2nd Comp.
Cain, Aaron	Private	4th Comp.	Morrison, William	Captain	1st Comp.
Calder, James	Private	2nd Comp.	Mulford, James	Private	4th Comp.
Cantwell, Barne	Private	2nd Comp.	Mulhallon, John	Private	4th Comp.
Cantwell, James	Private	2nd Comp.	Mulvain, John	Private	4th Comp.
Cantwell, Nathaniel	Private	1st Comp.	Mulvain, Joseph	Private	4th Comp.
Cantwell, Samuel	Corporal	1st Comp.	Mulvain, Junkins	Private	4th Comp.
Cantwell, Thomas	Private	1st Comp.	Mulvain, William	Private	4th Comp.
Carmill, Nath	Private	2nd Comp.	Murphey, William	Private	4th Comp.
Carpenter, Thomas	Private	1st Comp.	Musgrove, John	Private	4th Comp.
Casey, Peter	Private	1st Comp.	Musgrove, Moses	Private	1st Comp.
Clark, Gabriel	Corporal	1st Comp.	Nash, David	Private	4th Comp.
Clark, James	Private	1st Comp.	Nash, Urich	Private	4th Comp.
Clark, Richard	Corporal	2nd Comp.	Neighhart, Samuel	Private	4th Comp.
Clark, Samuel	Private	2nd Comp.	Nelden, John	Private	3rd Comp.
Clark, William	Private	2nd Comp.	Nelson, Elijah	Corporal	2nd Comp.
Cline, John	Private	1st Comp.	Nelson, John	Corporal	2nd Comp.
Cline, Phillip	Private	1st Comp.	Newcomb, Elijah	Lieutenant	1st Comp.
Cochrin, Edward	Corporal	1st Comp.	Newell, Thomas	Private	1st Comp.
Consor, David	Private	4th Comp.	Nolan, Peirce	Private	4th Comp.
Corbet, Robert	Private	4th Comp.	Norman, Abraham	Private	4th Comp.
Cosler, William	Private	4th Comp.	Norman, Benjamin	Corporal	1st Comp.
Coulter, William	Private	3rd Comp.	Norman, Daniel	Private	1st Comp.
Cox, David	Private	3rd Comp.	Norman, Jabis	Private	1st Comp.
Cox, Martin	Private	3rd Comp.	Norman, John	Corporal	4th Comp.
Cox, Michael	Private	3rd Comp.	Norris, John	Corporal	5th Comp.

Ohio and the War of 1812

Name	Rank	Company	Name	Rank	Company
Cox, Thomas	Private	4th Comp.	Norris, Samuel	Sergeant	4th Comp.
Crager, Daniel	Private	4th Comp.	Norris, William	Private	4th Comp.
Crager, Jacob	Corporal	4th Comp.	Nowles, James	Private	1st Comp.
Crager, John	Private	4th Comp.	Nowles, John	Private	1st Comp.
Craig, John	Private	5th Comp.	Nowles, Moses	Private	1st Comp.
Darling, Abraham	Private	3rd Comp.	Nowles, Peter	Private	1st Comp.
Darling, William	Private	3rd Comp.	Oglesbie, James	Private	1st Comp.
Davis, Matthew	Private	3rd Comp.	Oliver, Robert	Private	2nd Comp.
Dean, Enos	Sergeant	1st Comp.	Parker, Ezekiel	Sergeant	3rd Comp.
Delong, Edward	Private	3rd Comp.	Parker, Joshua	Private	3rd Comp.
Desmes, Thomas	Private	5th Comp.	Patterson, Robert M.	Private	5th Comp.
Devore, Daniel	Private	3rd Comp.	Peachey, Moses	Private	4th Comp.
Devore, John	Private	5th Comp.	Peterson, John G.	Sergeant	1st Comp.
Douglass, David	Private	4th Comp.	Phillips, George	Private	5th Comp.
Douglass, James	Private	4th Comp.	Phillips, John	Private	5th Comp.
Draper, Isaac	Private	3rd Comp.	Pigman, Daniel	Private	3rd Comp.
Duncan, Mathew	Private	3rd Comp.	Poulson, Conrad	Private	5th Comp.
Edger, James	Private	5th Comp.	Preston, Henry	Private	1st Comp.
Elder, John	Ensign	1st Comp.	Rates, Nicholas	Private	4th Comp.
Elson, Archabald	Private	5th Comp.	Raw, Nicholas	Private	4th Comp.
Elson, John	Private	4th Comp.	Rice, Thomas L.	Clerk	2nd Reg.
Elson, Samuel	Ensign	5th Comp.	Roberts, Eli	Private	1st Comp.
Evans, Henry	Private	4th Comp.	Roberts, William	Private	4th Comp.
Evans, Isaac	Captain	4th Comp.	Robinson, William	Private	5th Comp.
Evens, Gabriel	Sergeant	5th Comp.	Robison, William	Private	4th Comp.
Evens, Henry	Private	4th Comp.	Rodrick, John	Private	5th Comp.
Farquhar, Benjamin	Corporal	3rd Comp.	Rollins, Wm. V.	Private	2nd Comp.
Farquhar, Enoch	Private	3rd Comp.	Roop, Jacob	Corporal	4th Comp.
Forby, Benjamin	Private	1st Comp.	Roully, Samuel	Private	3rd Comp.
Fowler, Richard	Captain	5th Comp.	Sampson, Henry	Private	4th Comp.
Frey, Cristley	Private	4th Comp.	Schwetzer, Samuel	Private	5th Comp.
Fry, Abraham	Sergeant	1st Comp.	Sells, David	Private	4th Comp.
Fry, Isaac	Private	1st Comp.	Sells, Jonathan	Private	4th Comp.
Fuller, John	Private	5th Comp.	Shaw, Elijah	Private	2nd Comp.
Futhy, Isaac	Private	2nd Comp.	Shaw, Enos	Private	2nd Comp.
Gellyland, John	Private	2nd Comp.	Shay, John	Private	4th Comp.
Giffin, Robert	Private	3rd Comp.	Sills, David	Private	4th Comp.
Gilman, Samuel	Private	1st Comp.	Sills, Jonathan	Private	4th Comp.
Ginn, Charles	Private	2nd Comp.	Simmons, Casper	Private	4th Comp.
Graham, James	Private	2nd Comp.	Simpson, Henry	Private	4th Comp.
Greger, Jacob	Corporal	4th Comp.	Smith, Francis	Private	4th Comp.
Gross, John	Private	2nd Comp.	Smith, James	Private	4th Comp.
Hagney, Frederick	Private	4th Comp.	Smith, James	Sergeant	5th Comp.
Haines, Henry	Private	3rd Comp.	Smith, John Junior	Private	5th Comp.
Haines, John	Private	3rd Comp.	Smith, John Senior	Private	5th Comp.
Hair, Joseph	Sergeant	4th Comp.	Smith, Reubin	Private	2nd Comp.
Haney, Frederick	Private	4th Comp.	Smith, William	Corporal	5th Comp.
Hangman, Frederick	Private	4th Comp.	Smith, William Senior	Private	5th Comp.
Hankins, Jonathan	Private	1st Comp.	Soverns, John	Private	3rd Comp.

Ohio and the War of 1812

Name	Rank	Company	Name	Rank	Company
Hankins, Wm.	Corporal	3rd Comp.	Soverns, Joseph	Private	3rd Comp.
Hartly, John	Corporal	4th Comp.	Soverns, Samuel	Sergeant	3rd Comp.
Haskins, William	Corporal	3rd Comp.	Srimpin, Samuel	Private	3rd Comp.
Haslett, Jos.	Private	5th Comp.	Srimplin, Abraham	Private	3rd Comp.
Hawkins, George W.	Private	5th Comp.	Stonelawker, Michael	Private	1st Comp.
Helms, Nicholas	Private	3rd Comp.	Stootzman, Jonas	Private	4th Comp.
Hershman, Jacob	Private	2nd Comp.	Stootzman, Powel	Corporal	4th Comp.
Hide, Thomas	Private	3rd Comp.	Stringer, Moses M.	Private	4th Comp.
Highger, Martin	Private	4th Comp.	Switzer, Jacob	Private	5th Comp.
Highhart, Jacob	Private	4th Comp.	Switzer, Samuel	Private	5th Comp.
Hill, John	Private	1st Comp.	Thomas, Samuel	Private	1st Comp.
Hill, Samuel	Private	5th Comp.	Thompson, Joshua	Sergeant	1st Comp.
Hirshman, William	Private	4th Comp.	Thomson, James	Sergeant	2nd Comp.
Holt, John	Private	3rd Comp.	Thomson, Jonathan	Sergeant	1st Comp.
Horton, David	Private	3rd Comp.	Tilton, Elijah	Private	3rd Comp.
Horton, Thomas	Corporal	3rd Comp.	Tipton, Solomon	Private	3rd Comp.
Hull, Henry	Sergeant	3rd Comp.	Trimble, Josiah	Private	3rd Comp.
Hull, William	Private	3rd Comp.	Usher, John	Private	2nd Comp.
Humphrey, William	Private	3rd Comp.	Vail, James	Private	1st Comp.
Humphreys, Squire	Private	3rd Comp.	Vail, Jonathan	Sergeant	1st Comp.
Ison, Christopher	Private	4th Comp.	Vail, Joseph	Private	1st Comp.
James Butler	Private	3rd Comp.	Vail, Lewis	Private	4th Comp.
James, Elias	Private	3rd Comp.	Vail, Lewis	Lieutenant	5th Comp.
James, Thomas P.	Lieutenant	2nd Comp.	Vail, Solomon	Captain	1st Comp.
Jeffers, James	Sergeant	4th Comp.	Vansky, Moses	Private	2nd Comp.
Jeffers, Thomas	Private	5th Comp.	Waggoner, Jacob	Private	4th Comp.
John, David	Private	3rd Comp.	Waggoner, John	Private	4th Comp.
John, Thomas	Corporal	3rd Comp.	Wagner, Jacob	Ensign	4th Comp.
Johnston, Adam	Clerk	2nd Reg.	Wagner, John	Private	4th Comp.
Johnston, Thomas	Sergeant	5th Comp.	Wagner, Phillip	Corporal	4th Comp.
Johnston, William	Private	5th Comp.	Wagon, Daniel	Private	3rd Comp.
Jones, James	Private	4th Comp.	Walker, Joseph	Private	3rd Comp.
Jones, Jesse	Private	5th Comp.	Wallis, Thomas	Private	5th Comp.
Jones, Joseph	Private	3rd Comp.	Warden, Benjamin	Private	2nd Comp.
Jones, Levi	Private	2nd Comp.	Wardin, Benjamin	Private	1st Comp.
Jones, William	Corporal	5th Comp.	Warner, Wright	Private	2nd Comp.
Jonson, Richard	Private	4th Comp.	West, Jonathan	Private	2nd Comp.
Jonson, Thomas	Private	4th Comp.	Wiggans, Edward	Private	5th Comp.
Junkins, David	Private	4th Comp.	Wiggins, Edward	Private	4th Comp.
Junkins, John	Private	4th Comp.	Wiggins, Francis	Private	5th Comp.
Kerr, Peter	Private	2nd Comp.	Wiggins, Job	Private	5th Comp.
Kerr, William	Private	5th Comp.	Williams, Abr.	Private	1st Comp.
Kesler, John	Private	3rd Comp.	Williams, Abraham	Private	1st Comp.
Kimberly, Ira	Private	1st Comp.	Williams, Benjamin	Private	5th Comp.
Lawrence, John	Private	4th Comp.	Williams, Charles	Colonel	2nd Reg.
Lawrence, Thomas	Private	5th Comp.	Williams, James	Private	5th Comp.
Laylor, William	Private	1st Comp.	Williams, John	Private	5th Comp.
Leighinger, George	Private	4th Comp.	Williams, William	Private	5th Comp.
Lelon, William	Private	1st Comp.	Willis, James	Private	1st Comp.

Name	Rank	Company	Name	Rank	Company
Lemons, John	Private	5th Comp.	Willis, James	Sergeant	3rd Comp.
Lockard, William	Clerk	Regiment	Willis, Richard	Private	3rd Comp.
Lose, John	Private	4th Comp.	Wilson, James	Private	1st Comp.
Luke, George	Private	4th Comp.	Wilson, John P.	Private	1st Comp.
Luke, John	Private	4th Comp.	Wilson, John T.	Private	1st Comp.
MacClain, Daniel	Private	4th Comp.	Wise, Christian	Private	4th Comp.
Macvey, Henry	Private	3rd Comp.	Wisecarver, Abm.	Private	2nd Comp.
Magness, Levi	Private	5th Comp.	Wolf, Phillip	Sergeant	4th Comp.
Maple, David	Private	5th Comp.	Wolford, Jerimiah	Private	3rd Comp.
Maple, Jacob	Private	4th Comp.	Wolgamott, Jacob	Private	1st Comp.
Maple, Jacob Junior	Private	5th Comp.	Wolgamuth, John	Corporal	4th Comp.
Markley, Amos	Corporal	1st Comp.	Wolgomote, Jacob	Private	4th Comp.
Markley, John	Private	1st Comp.	Wolgomots, Isaac	Private	4th Comp.
Markley, Martin	Private	1st Comp.	Wood, Joshua	Private	3rd Comp.
Markley, William	Private	1st Comp.	Wood, Joshua	Private	1st Comp.
Marlett, Abraham	Corporal	5th Comp.	Wood, Peter	Private	3rd Comp.
Marlett, John	Private	5th Comp.	Woolford, Jeremiah	Private	3rd Comp.
Marsh, Cyrus	Private	5th Comp.	Workman, Thomas	Private	1st Comp.
Marsh, Lemuel	Private	5th Comp.	Young, Cornelius	Private	3rd Comp.
Marshal, Thomas	Private	2nd Comp.	Youther, Christian	Private	4th Comp.

Bibliography

MSS-2396 - Ohio Militia, 2nd regiment 1809-1819 (Coshocton County), Record book of the 2nd battalion of the 2nd regiment of the 4th brigade of the 3rd division of the Ohio Militia., Captain Isaac Evens, Captain Isaac Meridith, Captain William Beard, Captain Adam Johnston, Captain Solomon Vail, Captain Richard Fowler, and Captain John Mills; Western Reserve Historical Society, Cleveland, Ohio.

Court-Martial of Brigadier General Reasin Beall

Brigadier General Reasin Beall wasn't the only Ohio militia officer to be court-martialed during the War of 1812, and he wasn't the only general to be brought up on charges of disobeying orders during this same conflict. General Beall (pronounced BELL) was the victim of receiving conflicting orders from two of his superiors: Brigadier General William Henry Harrison, the commander of the U.S. Army's Army of the Northwest, and Major General Elijah Wadsworth, the commander of the 4th Division of the Ohio Militia.

Court-martial proceedings contain very little genealogical information. but they can be useful in order to fill in the missing pieces of a soldier's military career during this time period. It may be important for a researcher to find out why an ancestor was charged with a crime or why the ancestor was forced to leave the military service due to a court-martial. On a grimmer note, finding the reason why a soldier was executed as a result of a court-martial may bring peace to the current generation.

Many officers demanded court-martials during their military careers, not because they committed crimes, but because someone accused them of wrong-doing. A trial was a way of proving your innocence and clearing your name.

Graves of Reasin and Rebecca Beall

Beall Home, Wooster, Ohio

The court-martial proceedings will list the names of the men serving on the court and the names of all of the witnesses. This may seem insignificant, but if you are building a service record of an ancestor who was court-martialed, then the date, place, and the names of all involved can be important.

Both the Ohio Historical Society and the Western Reserve Historical Society have court-martial proceedings for both officers and enlisted men in their military collections for the Ohio militia.

To continue with General Beall's trial, we must first step back a bit to the events that led to his court-martial.

To put it mildly, all "hell" broke loose across Ohio when word was received in the state that Brigadier General William Hull had surrendered an American army, the Army of the Northwest, on 16 August 1812 to the British at *Fort Detroit* without a good fight. Panic swept across the state as rumors spread that the British would be unleashing their hoards of Indians onto the frontier settlements. The northern counties of the state also feared a British invasion of red coats since the British had warships on the upper Great Lakes and the United States did not.

Ohio's governor, Return Jonathan Meigs, Junior, called upon his four division commanders to handle the situation as best they could. Each major general called up the militiamen from their divisions, and they marched them towards the frontier areas of the state in order to repel any impending invasion.

Brigadier General James Winchester, second in command of the Army of the Northwest, was raising a new regular army but it would be a while before the regulars would be ready to fight again. For now, the Ohio militia would have to stand tall and defend their state.

General Beall received his marching orders from General Wadsworth in late August 1812. Beall commanded the 2nd Brigade of the 4th Division, which covered the counties of Columbiana, Stark and Wayne (as they existed in 1812). The 4th Division consisted of the counties in the Western Reserves (including the Firelands) plus Columbiana, Stark, Wayne and Jefferson Counties.

General Beall organized a new brigade which was made up of one regiment from the 1st brigade, headquartered in Jefferson County, and the other regiment from his own 2nd brigade from Columbiana County. The two regiments met in Canton, Stark County, where they were joined by a detachment from that county.

A second brigade was organized from the remaining counties of the 4th Division, and this brigade was under the command of Brigadier General Simon Perkins. General Perkins would march his brigade to Huron County in order to set up defenses against the British and the Indians.

From Canton, General Beall's brigade pushed on to Wooster in Wayne County where the brigade erected a blockhouse and established a camp called *Camp Christmas*. General Beall then sent his militia companies to the various settlements within this county where they built additional blockhouses for the protection of the settlers. Along the way, the companies either built new roads or improved existing roads so that wagons could pass. Two forward operating bases were also established, one near Jeromesville, called *Camp Musser*, and another at Olivesburg, called *Camp Whetstone*.

General Beall received orders from General Wadsworth on 6 September 1812 to bring his brigade to Wadsworth's headquarters in Cleveland. General Beall declined to obey this order since he had new orders from the governor of Ohio and General Harrison to construct a road between Wooster and Mansfield and then onwards to what is now Upper Sandusky. From Upper Sandusky the road would be extended to the Maumee River just south of today's Toledo.

General Harrison had issued orders to Brigadier General Richard Crooks of the Pennsylvania Militia to bring his 2nd Pennsylvania Brigade to the Maumee River. General Crooks' brigade would be using General Beall's new military road. A company from the 2nd Regiment of U.S. Artillery under the command of Captain Daniel Cushing accompanied the Pennsylvania Brigade. This force brought with them 20 pieces of artillery and a large quantity of military stores and baggage which would be used to build a new fort. This fort would be called *Fort Meigs*.

General Beall would receive two more orders from General Wadsworth (September 30th and October 14th) ordering him to march his brigade to Cleveland. It is assumed that General Beall did notify General Wadsworth of his new orders from General Harrison, but there is no documentation to this effect in his court-martial papers.

Captain James Doud, under orders from General Wadsworth, arrested General Beall on October 26th. General Beall surrendered his sword to Captain Doud and Colonel John Andrews, the second in command of Beall's brigade, marched the brigade to *Camp Avery* which was three miles north of present day Milan in Erie County. At that time, *Camp Avery* was in Huron County.

On November 7th General Beall was formally charged with four accounts of disobedience and the trial was set to start at *Camp Avery* on November 11th. The first three charges were for disobeying General Wadsworth's three orders while the fourth charge was for repeatedly ignoring these orders.

The members of the court-martial court were Brigadier General Simon Perkins, president of the court, Colonel William Rayen, Colonel John Andrews, Colonel John Hindman, Major John Shannon, Major Samuel Frasor, Major George Darrow, Captain Thomas Latta, Captain William Stokes, Captain David Perk, Captain Amos Lusk, Captain John R. Rud, Captain Harvey Murray, Captain John Alexander and Captain Aaron Allen.

Major William W. Cotgreave was appointed the judge advocate while Adjutant James Mackey was appointed the provost marshal. The witnesses were Hugh Baird, Doctor McGraham, Colonel Andrews, and Russell Strom.

The trial lasted six days and General Beall was found not guilty on all charges. His sword was returned to him on November 16th. He was then ordered to take his brigade to the River Raisin in the Territory of Michigan in order to support Brigadier General James Winchester of the regular army. Upon reaching the Sandusky River, General Beall received new orders to return to *Camp Avery* and to disband his brigade. Word had arrived stating that General Winchester's brigade had been defeated during the Battle of the River Raisin.

While at *Camp Avery* volunteers from both General Beall's and General Perkins' brigades merged to form the 2nd Ohio Brigade under General Perkins. This brigade was federalized and they were then ordered to the Rapids of the Maumee River as part of Brigadier General William H. Harrison's right wing of the Army of the Northwest.

Beall served on Ohio's militia duty during the War of 1812 between 8 September 1812 and 23 November 1812. After his brigade merged with General Perkins' brigade, he resigned his militia commission and returned home. He was later elected as a Republican to the Thirteenth Congress to fill the vacancy caused by the death of John S. Edwards. He served in Congress from 20 April 1813 until his resignation on 7 June 1814. He became the registrar of the land offices at Canton and later Wooster from 1814 to 1824.

Reasin Beall was born in Maryland on 3 December 1769 and he died in Wooster on 20 February 1843. He is buried in the Wooster Cemetery. When Beall was a young boy his parents and family moved to Washington County, Pennsylvania. He married Rebecca Johnson on 4 November 1794 in Allegheny County, Pennsylvania. Rebecca was born on 8 October 1777 and she died on 30 August 1840. She was the daughter of Richard Johnson and Elizabeth Nash. Beall remarried to Nancy McNamee on 4 November 1841 in Richland County, Ohio. Nancy died around 1880.

Beall was commissioned an ensign in the U.S. Army on 7 March 1792, and he served in the Regiment of Infantry in Captain William Faulkner's Company. On 4 September 1792 this regiment became a part of the Legion of the United States, and Beall was assigned to the 3rd Sub-Legion along with his company. He served as the adjutant and later as the quartermaster for the sub-legion. On 1 March 1793 Beall was transferred Captain Richard Sparks' company. Beall resigned from the army on 3 January 1793, and he returned home to Pennsylvania. While in the army, Beall served in the Northwest Territory.

In 1801 Beall and his family moved to Steubenville, Jefferson County, Northwest Territory, with his in-laws. In the fall of 1803, he moved to New Lisbon in Columbiana County. Beall served as the clerk of the supreme and common pleas courts between 1803 and 1810, county treasurer between 1803 and 1806, and county recorder between 1803 and 1813 for Columbiana County. By 1806 Beall had been elected lieutenant colonel in command of the 1st regiment of the 2nd brigade of the 4th division of the Ohio militia. Before the War of 1812, Beall was elected to the brigadier general's position in the 2nd Brigade.

General Beall's widow received a widow's military pension for the general's military services before and during the War of 1812, pension numbers WO-34272 and WC-19614. She also received 160 acres of land for the general's early war service, warrant number 21840-160-50. This land was sold to Reuben H. Gilson and the land was located in Paulding County, Ohio.

The children of Reasin and Rebecca were:

Elizabeth Johnson Beall, born 9 February 1796
Keziah Beall, born 29 November 1797
Nancy Campbell Beall, born 30 March 1801
Harriet Beall, born 27 November 1803
Mariah Stibbs Beall, born 20 February 1806
Rebecca Beall, born 19 July 1809
Margaret Ann Beall, born 21 January 1814
Mary Jane Beall, born 6 December 1816
Reasin Stibbs Beall, born 17 April 1819

Bibliography

Barth, Harold B., **History of Columbiana County, Ohio**, volume 1, (Topeka-Indianapolis: Historical Publishing Company, 1926), chapter XXII, County Officials, page 336.

Court-Martial Papers of Brigadier General Reasin Beall, **War of 1812: Collection of Papers, 1810-1820**, manuscripts collection, call number MS 3133, Western Reserve Historical Society Library, Cleveland, Ohio.

"Declaration of Nancy Beall, widow of Reasin Beall," widow's pension number WO-35272 and WO-19614, War of 1812, Records of the Veterans Administration, Record Group 15, National Archives and Record Administration, Washington, D.C.

Gateway to the West, Volume VI, Number II, April-June 1973, (Arcanum, Ohio), pp. 59-60.

Graham, A.A., **History of Richland County, Ohio**, (Mansfield, Ohio: A.A. Graham & Co., Publishers, 1880), pp. 286-291.

Heitman, Francis B., **Historical Register and Dictionary of the United States Army From Its Organization, September 29, 1789, to March 2, 1903**, Volume I, (Baltimore, Maryland: Genealogical Publishing Company, 1994), page 202, Reazin Beall.

History of Columbiana County, Ohio, (Philadelphia, Pennsylvania: D. W. Ensign & Company, 1879), pp 55-56, chapter XX, Military History, Militia, and page 58, Chapter XXI, Militia Militant, last war with England.

Montgomery, Thomas Lynch, **Pennsylvania Archives**, 6th Series, Volume VIII, (Harrisburg Publishing Company, State Printers, Harrisburg, Pennsylvania: 1907), Pennsylvania Volunteers, War of 1812-1814 Soldiers, Part I, Troops commanded by Generals William H. Harrison and Richard Crooks, pp. 141-261.

Ohio Genealogical Society Report, volume 22, Fall 1982, pp. 145-150, Reasin Beall, Ohio Pioneer, (Mansfield, Ohio: Ohio Genealogical Society).

Ohio Records and Pioneer Families, Volume XXXIII, Number 4, pp. 151-152, (Mansfield, Ohio: Ohio Genealogical Society), Court Records – Journal of Reasin Beall.

U.S. Department of the Interior, Bureau of Land Management, General Land Office Records, Defiance Land Office (Ohio), military warrant number 21840-160-50, 1 December 1853, Nancy Beall, widow of Reason Beall to Reuben H. Gilson.

Western Pennsylvania Genealogical Society Quarterly, volume 21, number 2, page 31, Joseph Becket J.P. Marriages 1792-1815 from Elizabeth, PA, Newspapers, Bazel Bell and Rebecca Johnson, 3 November 1794, (Pittsburgh, Pennsylvania).

Ohio women also served in the War of 1812

We tend to overlook the role that women played during the War of 1812 in support of our military. Women were used in the "cottage" industries sewing uniforms and rolling cartridges for our boys in blue. They also made buckskin jackets for the militia and prepared rations. A hand-full of women actually served with our troops on the battle lines during the war. They were not camp followers, but they were members of regular army's companies.

Under the Congressional Act of 16 March 1802 [32] up to four women could be hired to serve as washerwomen in each of the army's companies. Although they were in fact contract workers, they were permitted to receive one army ration per day and were "entitled" to bedding straw, medical care and payment for their work. Most of these women were the wives of soldiers. They were treated on the same level as a private, and they were invaluable in the day-to-day operation of a company.

During the first siege of Fort Meigs in May of 1813, there were six infantry, one artillery and one light dragoon companies of the U.S. Army stationed at this fort. There could have been up to 32 women within this fort serving as washerwomen at the time of the siege. During this siege the women were probably assisting in the fort's hospital, or they were carrying food and water to the men who were manning the walls, blockhouses and artillery ramparts.

A general order, issued at Fort Meigs on 1 August 1813 states "Any married woman who has or shall abandon her husband and be found strolling about camp or lodging in the tents of other men shall be drum'd out of camp." [33] Although women may not have been present during the two sieges of Fort Meigs, there were women serving with the army at this fort during the summer of 1813.

Most company musters and rosters don't list the names of these women who were hired to do the laundry of the men. Three recruiting rosters, however, do list the names of some of these women who served in Ohio. On a roster of recruits being sent to Chillicothe from Zanesville on 9 August 1812 two women are listed as washerwomen: Polly Waters and Betsey Laurence.[34] Chillicothe was the recruiting rendezvous for the 19th Regiment of U.S. Infantry where recruits were organized into companies and then sent to the front to join the rest of the regiment.

On 18 September 1812 another detachment of recruits was sent to Chillicothe from Zanesville.[35] On this roster two more women are listed: Susannah Bright, the wife of George Bright, and Fanny Stultz, the wife of Adam Stultz. Adam Stultz would be killed on 5 May 1813 during the first siege of Fort Meigs. Fanny Stultz may have been with her husband at Fort Meigs and she may have witnessed his death. The Stultz's were from Muskingum County.

Captain Daniel Cushing of Ohio commanded the artillery company from the 2nd Regiment of U.S. Artillery, which was stationed at Fort Meigs. Mrs. Aaron Haning is listed on a recruiting detachment listing for this company that rendezvoused at Chillicothe on 29 October 1812.[36]

---

[32] **Public Statutes at Large of the United States of America**, Volume I, (Boston: Charles C. Little and James Brown, 1845), Seventh Congress, Session I, Chapter IX, pp. 132-137, 16 March 1802, "An act fixing the military peace establishment of the United States."

[33] Lindly, Harlow, **Fort Meigs and the War of 1812**, (The Ohio Historical Society, Columbus, Ohio: 1975), page 55.

[34] Compete muster roll of a detachment of recruits," 9 August 1812, **George Tod Papers 1783-1834**, Western Reserve Historical Society Archives Library, Cleveland, Ohio, manuscript section, call number MS-3202, container 2a.

[35] "Compete muster roll of a detachment of recruits," 18 September 1812, **George Tod Papers 1783-1834**, Western Reserve Historical Society Archives Library, Cleveland, Ohio, manuscript section, call number MS-3202, container 2a.

[36] "List of artillery men sent to Chillicothe," 29 October 1812, **George Tod Papers 1783-1834**, Western Reserve Historical Society Archives Library, Cleveland, Ohio, manuscript section, call number MS-3202, container 2a.

Camp Avery

One of the obscure and forgotten military outposts of the War of 1812 in northern Ohio was Camp Avery. This wooden stockade was situated above what is now Milan in Erie County just north of the Ohio Turnpike along the eastern bank of the Huron River. In 1812, Erie County was still a part of Huron County.

Between September 1812 and February 1813 this fort defended the Western Reserve from Indian attacks and against a possible British invasion of northern Ohio. The fort was replaced by Fort Meigs and Fort Stephenson after the U.S. Army took control of northern Ohio in early 1813. This facility was also called Camp Huron and Camp Perkins.

When word reached Major General William Wadsworth, commander of the 4th Ohio militia division in the northeastern part of the state on August 22, 1812, that Brigadier General William Hull had surrendered his American army at Detroit without a fight, General Wadsworth activated his 7,500-man division. After seeing that only half the men had weapons and only a tenth had bayonets, he ordered half the division home, and the general reorganized the remaining men into two provisional brigades; one under Brigadier General Simon Perkins and the other under Brigadier General Reasin Beall.

General Perkins was ordered to take half his men to the Huron River to set up defenses against any possible invasion while the remaining men in his brigade remained at Cleveland to defend the village. General Beall took his brigade to Wooster in Wayne County to set up defenses there, and then he took his brigade on to Mansfield in Richland County.

General Perkins had his men build Fort Huron three miles east of the Huron River along the lake shore. Realizing that the fort was undefendable from both the lake and the land, he ordered the fort abandoned, and the brigade moved ten miles up the Huron River where they built a second fort called Camp Avery. Fort Huron had been dubbed "Fort Nonsense" by the brigade.

The new fort was built in Avery Township, which would later become Milan Township. The township was the population center of Huron County with other settlements on the Marblehead Peninsula and at the mouth of the Huron River. Most of the citizens had fled east towards Cleveland once word was received that Detroit had fallen to the enemy. Avery Township alone had approximately 275 inhabitants.

Camp Avery became the headquarters of the 4th Division in the western area of the Western Reserve. It was probably a wooden stockade with one least one blockhouse. During September and October 1812 there were approximately 500 militiamen stationed at this facility and nearly half of men were sick during this time. Most of the men probably slept in tents or in lean-tos outside of the fort.

Two local militia companies were dismissed and ordered home to their families. Captain Joseph Quigley and his company were from what is now northern Lorain County while Captain David Barrett and his company were from the local area in and around Avery Township.

Once the camp had been constructed, General Perkins sent two expeditions to scout the area north and west of Camp Avery. The first militia party headed west to occupy the abandoned camp on the lower Sandusky River. This camp was called Camp Sandusky, and it was built by the forces of General Hull as a supply post along the supply line between Cleveland and Detroit. This fort would be taken over by the army in the early spring of 1813. It was rebuilt and then renamed as Fort Stephenson.

A second militia expedition was sent to Cunningham's Island (now Kelley's Island) where the men found a beached British schooner. The vessel was stripped and then burnt. Part of the men crossed over to the Marblehead Peninsula, and they were ambushed by the Indians on September 10th and two militiamen were killed.

By September 28th a third expedition was launched to attack the Indians on the peninsula. Captain Joshua Cotton formed a provisional company of militiamen from the five companies stationed at Camp Avery. The company arrived on Marblehead Peninsula the next day, and they were ambushed twice by the Indians. During those medleys, eight militiamen were killed as well as approximately 40 Indians. The Battle of Marblehead Peninsula on September 29, 1812, has been termed as the 'first battle site' in Ohio during the War of 1812.

In October the brigade under General Beall was ordered to Camp Avery where Brigadier General William Henry Harrison combined the two provisional brigades of the 4th division and federalized them. General Perkins was appointed the commander of this new brigade, and General Beall and half of the men were released from duty and sent home.

General Perkins and his new brigade were ordered to improve the road between Camp Avery and Fort Meigs. The section between Fort Meigs and Camp Sandusky crossed the Great Black Swamp of northwestern Ohio. The brigade spent its remaining days at Fort Meigs until released from duty in later February 1813. It is believed that some of the men were involved in a minor skirmish with the Indians just north of Fort Meigs during the winter.

It is doubtful that Camp Avery was occupied after the winter of 1813. Camp Sandusky, renamed Fort Stephenson, became the principal army post for north central Ohio. Camp Avery was probably used as a overnight rest area for both the army and the militia on the military road between Cleveland and Fort Meigs, and was probably dismantled by the returning settlers and its timbers used to build and repair the settler's cabins.

A two-story log cabin had been built in 1811 near the site of Camp Avery. This building was Huron County's first courthouse and jail. It was probably used by the militia stationed at the nearby camp. In 1818 the county seat was moved to Norwalk.

In 1930. the Martha Pitkin Chapter of the Daughters of the American Revolution dedicated a monument to Camp Avery, and the early county seat. On the monument is written:

> Camp Avery – One-fourth mile southwest from this site on the brow of the hill overlooking the eastern bend of the Huron River, General Simon Perkins, commanding the Ohio militia, built the fortifications and blockhouse of Camp Avery for the protection of early settlers from the British and Indians.
>
> County Seat – 1811 - On this site was located Avery, the first county seat of Huron County. Here stood the two story log house used as a courthouse and jail.
>
> 1818 – County seat moved from here to Norwalk
>
> 1838 – Erie County was established from the northern part of Huron County.
>
> This locality was frequented by tribes of Indians: Ottawas, Miamis, Chippewas, and Senecas.
>
> Erected by Martha Pitkin Chapter, Daughters of the American Revolution 1930

Beside the monument are two smaller stones dedicated to Gideon Bradley and David Barrett. Bradley was a Revolutionary soldier who served in the 12th regiment from Massachusetts while David Barrett was the captain of the Huron Rangers, the first military company formed in the Firelands, now Erie and Huron Counties.

Regular Army

Regular army muster rolls found in Ohio

Muster roll of Capt. James Heron's company under the command of Col. John Miller of the 19th Regiment of U.S. Infantry in the service of the United States from the 31st of August 1813. The last muster to the 31st of October 1813 inclusive.[37]

War = enlisted for the duration of the war

Name	Rank	Date of appointment or enlistment	To what time enlisted	Remarks
Herron, James	Captain	14 Mar 1812		
Campbell, James	1st Lieut.	14 Mar 1814		
Atchison, James	2nd Lieut.			On command at Detroit
McKnight, Thomas	Ensign			On command
Jones, Wm.	Sergeant	24 Aug 1812	18 mos	Sick absent
Parcel, Jas. H.	"	17 Nov 1812	5 yr	
Blakeman, Nathan	"	16 Dec 1812	18 mos	Sick absent
Young, Alex.	"	3 Aug 1812	18 mos	
Barlow, Wm. A.	"	8 Jun 1813		
Walker, Joseph	Corporal	15 Sep 1812	18 mos	Sick absent
Bartlett, Wm.	"	26 Oct 1812	18 mos	Sick absent
Kiger, John	"	9 Aug 1812	18 mos	
Doughty, Daniel	"	7 Jul 1812	18 mos	Sick absent
Manett, Lewis	"			Sick absent, date or enlistment not known
Fulk, Abram	"	31 Oct 1812		
Ashly, Jeremiah	Private	3 Oct 1812	18 mos	Sick absent
Boon, John	"	6 Aug 1812	18 mos	
Bannon, John	"	2 Oct 1812	18 mos	Sick absent
Buckles, Robt.	"	6 Oct 1812	18 mos	
Brown, Solomon	"	13 Oct 1812	18 mos	Sick
Blanchard, Labin	"	3 Oct 1812	18 mos	Sick absent
Bennett, Archibald	"	28 Aug 1812	18 mos	Sick absent
Bennett, Paul	"	1 Sep 1812	18 mos	Sick absent
Best, Georg	"	30 Oct 1812	5 yr	Sick absent
Bonvill, Lewis	"			Date or enlistment not known
Belvill	"			Sick absent, date or enlistment not known
Chick, Nathaniel	"	11 Aug 1812	5 yr	Sick in hospital
Clark, James	"	13 Sep 1812	5 yr	
Cooder, Jonathan	"	3 Dec 1812	5 yr	Sick absent
Creighton, Hugh	"	21 Nov 1812	5 yr	Sick absent
Duncan, Joseph	"	16 Nov 1812	5 yr	Sick absent
Fisher, Peter	"	29 Aug 1812	18 mos	Sick absent
Fitzpatrick, James	"	4 Aug 1812	18 mos	Sick absent

---

[37] "Muster roll of Captain James Herron's company," 31 August 1813 to 31 October 1813, **George Tod Collection**, Western Reserve Historical Society Archives Library, Cleveland, Ohio, manuscript section, call number MS-3202, Container 2, Folder 3.

Name	Rank	Date of appointment or enlistment	To what time enlisted	Remarks
Fover, Philip	"	30 Oct 1812		Sick absent, enlistment not known
Goodrain, John R.	"			In the hospital, date or enlistment not known
Gubby, John R.	"			Sick absent, date or enlistment not known
Gordan, Thomas	"	27 Apr 1813	War	
Henson, George	"	17 Aug 1813	18 mos	
Hood, Henry	"	13 Oct 1813	18 mos	Sick absent
Helms, Stephen	"	27 Jun 1813	War	Sick absent
Hide, Charles W.	"			Sick absent, date or enlistment not known
Hamilton, James	"	14 Sep 1812	5 yr	
Insnogle, David	"			Date or enlistment not known
Johnston, Wm.	"	3 Oct 1812	18 mos	Sick absent
Jamison, Wm.	"	Aug 1812		Enlistment not known
Jeremy, ---	"			Sick absent, date or enlistment not known
Knight, Fielding	"	21 Nov 1812	5 yr	Sick absent
Littleton, John	"	11 Aug 1812	5 yr	Sick absent
Lewis, Solomon	"	29 Aug 1812	18 mos	Sick absent
Little, Alexander	"	8 Nov 1812	18 mos	Sick absent
Lowens, Hiett	"	11 Dec 1812	18 mos	
Lampher, Benjamine	"	31 Mar 1813	War	Sick absent
Lepalm, Neil	"			Sick absent, date or enlistment not known
McGonegal, Charles	"	19 Aug 1812	18 mos	
Martin, Robt.	"	31 Aug 1812	18 mos	Sick absent
Martin, Samuel	"			Died 22 Oct 1813, date or enlistment not known
Martin, Alex.	"	30 Oct 1812	5 yr	
Moslander, Sheron	"	26 Sep 1812	18 mos	Sick absent
Moor, Nathaniel	"	26 Sep 1812	18 mos	Waiter at Buffalo
Miller, Peter	"	17 Sep 1812		Sick absent
Muller, Charles	"	17 Dec 1812	5 yr	Sick in hospital
Mahan, Archibald	"	18 Sep 1812	18 mos	Sick absent
Mitchel, James	"	29 Oct 1812		Enlistment not known
Mayer, Francis	"			Date or enlistment not known
Mayer, George	"			Date or enlistment not known
Mantany, Isaac	"			Date or enlistment not known
Mercil, John	"			Date or enlistment not known
Montgomery, Wm.	"	14 May 1814	War	
Morison, Robt.	"			Sick in hospital, date or enlistment not known
Marsac, Lewis	"			Sick absent, date or enlistment not known

Name	Rank	Date of appointment or enlistment	To what time enlisted	Remarks
Marsac, John B.	"	Sept	War	Sick absent, date or enlistment not known
Meloy, Seth	"	30 Apr 1813	War	Sick absent
Nante, John B.	"			Sick absent, date or enlistment not known
O'Neil, John	"			Sick absent, date or enlistment not known
Patten, Thomas	"	17 Sep 1812	18 mos	Sick absent
Purl, John	"	22 Dec 1812	18 mos	Sick absent
Peters, Thomas	"			Date or term not known
Pangburn, Wm.	"			Date or term not known
Petit, Charles	"			Sick absent, date or enlistment not known
Quck, Aron	"	13 Sep 1812	18 mos	Sick absent
Randle, Benjamin	"	17 Sep 1812	18 mos	Sick absent
Reed, Frederick	"	16 Sep 1812	18 mos	
Price, John	"	16 Dec 1812	5 yr	Died 5 Oct 1813
Russle, Joshua	"			Sick hospital, date or enlistment not known
Shoemaker, Thos.	"	15 Sep 1812	18 mos	Sick absent
Strawbrige, John	"	15 Sep 1812	18 mos	Sick absent
Sheets, Wm.	"			Date or enlistment not known
Shaver, Thomas	"	14 May 1813	5 yr	Sick absent
Sloan, Samuel	"			Sick absent, date or enlistment not known
Taylor, Hastings	"	29 Aug 1812	18 mos	Sick absent
Thompson, John	"	30 Apr 1813	5 yr	Sick absent
Thompson, John	"	28 Aug 1812	18 mos	Sick absent
Tanner, Wm.	"	Oct 1812	18 mos	Sick absent
Vince, James	"	Nov 1812		Sick absent
Whitehed, James	"	15 Sep 1812	18 mos	Sick absent
Worthington, Joshua	"	1 Dec 1812	18 mos	
Willis, John	"	5 Nov 1812		Confined, sick absent, enlistment not known
Wood, Benjamin	"	10 Jul 1812	War	
Williams, Charles	"	27 Jun 1812	5 yr	
Williams, Remembrance	"	27 Apr 1812	War	Sick absent
Young, Philip	"	22 May 1812	18 mos	
Dunevin, James L.	Musician	25 Jul 1812	5 yr	Sick absent, reduced to the ranks
Power, Thomas	"	6 Aug 1812	18 mos	Sick absent

Captain Alexander Hill's Company [38]

Captain Alexander Hill
1st Lt Charles L. Cass / 2nd Lt John Carrel / 3rd Lt Alexander Patterson
Ensign Nathan Reeves
1st Sergeant John Elliot / 2nd Sergeant Stephen Worthington / 3rd Sergeant Allen Lowry
4th Sergeant Elijah Adams / 5th Sergeant Ambrose A. Ford
Corporal Manna Root / 2nd Corporal John Franks / 3rd Corporal William Wallace
4th Corporal Daniel Moore / 5th Corporal Cyrus Baily / 6th Corporal John L. Gordon
Christian B. Smith, musician / William Spurgon, musician

Privates

James Armstrong	Matthias Gates	Stephen Mowry
William Arnold	John Gates	George Osborn
Abraham Badgly	Jesse Graham	Benjamin Patrick
Nicholas Bumgarner	Thomas Grey	Hira Pettee
James Brooks	James Garner	James Pritchett
John Barker	Joseph Heaton	John Potts
Adam Bair	John Hill	Daniel Paine
John Bowman	Elisha Heitt	John Ridingour
Ebenezer Buckly	James Hillyard	William Reynolds
Jacob Brosius	Samuel Higley	Gabriel Root
Thomas Clark	Samuel Henning	John Swift
Nathan Cross	John Johnston	Oliver Stockings
Israel Cross	David Johnston	John D. Smith
John Cox	W. M. Lockhart	John W. Smith
Lewis Clapper	William Lyons	John Stanley
Shirley Callogg	John Lyons	John Silvers
Samuel Cooper	John Loveland	Christian Standsburg
Henry Crown	Ephraim Lucas	Philip Swagert
Joseph Dean	Jacob Monteith	Benjamin Snyder
Jehu Dealy	Samuel Morfoot	William Snyder
Noah Demster	William Morgan	William A. Strong
William Elliot	John McCombs	Jesse Spalding
John Fishback	Nehemiah Morse	Nicholas Teel
Samuel Fisher	John McMullen	John Taylor
Ira L. Foster	John Mowry	Daniel Trumble
Joseph Fisher	Andrew Millburn	

---

[38] Andrews, Martin R., M.A., **History of Marietta and Washington County, Ohio, and Representative Citizens**, (Biographical Publishing Company, Chicago, Illinois: 1902), page 560.

Ohio and the War of 1812

Combination of two musters of Lt. John McElvain's Company [39]

Discharge muster roll of Lt. John McElvain's company of the 19th Regiment of Infantry commanded by Lieutenant Colonel J. B. Van Horne, 28 February 1815 to 31 May 1815.

Payroll of Lt. John McElvain's company of the 19th Regiment of Infantry for July, August, September, October, November, December 1814 and January, February, March, April and May 1815.

Captain Carey A. Trimble
1st Lt John Carroll   2d Lt Alexander Patterson   2d Lt John McElvain
3rd Lt William Griffith
Sergeant Elyah Adams   Sergeant Allen Lowry   Sergeant Manna Root
Sergeant Samuel Walker   Sergeant John Dyer   Samuel Lynch, Clerk
Corporal William Howell   Corporal John Totten   Corporal John Lyons
Corporal Jehu Daley   Corporal John Franks   Corporal William Lyons
Noah Downs, fifer   William Spurgeon, fifer

<u>Privates</u>

Anway, George	Harper, Clayton	Ramsbottom, Simeon
Baley, Cyrus	Hoff, Benjamin	Smith, John D.
Barker, John	Hutcheson, William	Stockings, Oliver
Brooks, James	Heaton, Joseph	Simmons, Ira
Brosius, Jacob	Johnson, John (1)	Silvers, John
Brown, Frederick	Johnson, John (2)	Swagart, Philip
Benson, John	Jones, Joshua	Snyder, William
Ballard, Evan	Jackson, Robert C.	Sullivan, William
Burk, John	Johnson, David	Steth, John
Bridges, William	Lucas, Ephram	Scott, Joseph
Buley, Nathan	Likens, John	Shipley, Peter
Clark, Stephens B.	Lincicum, David	Siberal, William
Curtis, John	Lycgrell, Thomas	Shrose, Emanuel
Culberson, Samuel	Lefoc, Peter	Shaw, John
Cross, Israel	Lott, William	Stephens, John
Crone, Henry	McCombs, John *	Simons, Faulkner
Dean, Joseph	Morse, Nehemiah	Trader, Moses
Exline, Edward	McMullen, John	Taylor, John
Exline, Daniel	Milburne, Andrew	Teel, Nicholas
Elliott, William	Mellin, Levi	Tennis, John
Foster, Ira L.	McTuney, Samuel	Terrill, Roswell
Frederick, Henry	McGowen, Levi	Vulgermett, Joseph
Fisher, Samuel	Nicewinter, Joseph	White, John
Cottles, Daniel	Oneal, John	White, Matthew
Davis, Elias	Pettu, Hira	Weir, James
Ford, Ambrose A.	Prichart, James	Wallace, Allen
Groves, Lawrence	Potts, John	Wilcox, Daniel
Gates, Matthias	Porter, Randall	Welshons, Jacob
Hill, John	Pettitt, Jonas	Wilmuth, Benson
Hillard, James	Patrick, Benjamin	Wilson, William
Higby, Samuel	Ragan, William	Watson, John
Hemming, Samuel	Riggle, Abraham	Wilt, George
Hall, Benjamin	Rogers, Hugh	Young Andrew

---

[39] "Discharge muster and payroll muster of Lieutenant John McElvain's Company, 19th Regiment of Infantry," **Adjutant General's Militia Records**, Series 88, Payroll, Folder 2, Ohio Historical Society's Library, Columbus, Ohio.

Hood, William Runden, Daniels Herrington, Charles
Hardy, Joseph Rankins, James Taylor, Townly, waiter
* Left sick at Buffalo, 23 November 1814

Pay roll of Captain Richard C. Talbott's Company
19th Regiment of Infantry
March, April and May 1815 [40]

Captain Richard C. Talbott
1st Lt John Goode 2d Lt John Hall 2d Lt O. Grander
Sergeant Colston Payton Sergeant Jacob Shank Sergeant James Moon
Sergeant Samuel Greyhain Sergeant James McAuly Sergeant Jacob Wolff
Corporal William Duncan Corporal James Blackburn Corporal Joseph H. Farrer
Harris Catterline, musician Daniel Stuterman, musician

Privates
Adams, James Haines, William Rymeanous, Joakina
Amery, James Jones, William Roberson, John
Birch, Daniel Kelley, John Rhoads, Sanford
Bernett, Robert Lucky, Abiel Rhoads, Conway
Bryan, Farren W. Lovey, Daniel Sterret, Alexander
Carlisle, Robert McKnight, Anthony Salleday, Samuel
Danbury, Philip McGuire, Thomas Shields, Patrick
Evans, Robert McLaughlin, David Scott, John
Fletcher, Jacob Newkirk, John Shiely, David
Fires, Thomas Oxly, Henry Sanders, Isaac
General, Lewis Pratt, Joseph Strickland, William
Harper, Alexander Peeples, Alexander Whittlesey, Joseph
Harrison, William B. Reed, Charles Wilkerson, Thomas B.
Hook, Henry Redding, Elijah Wyant, John
Hugh, Levi Ropell, Meshack Walker, H.V.

Pay roll of Captain William Gill's Company
19th Regiment of Infantry
March, April and May 1815 [41]

Captain William Gill
1st Lt Wyncoop Warner 1st Lt James Blair
Sergeant John Elliott Sergeant George Elliott Sergeant Benjamin Gassway
Sergeant James Douglass Sergeant John Parrish
Corporal John Huttinhour Corporal Daniel Moore Corporal John Clark
Corporal Thomas Baxter Corporal William Wallace Corporal Aaron Robison
Christian Crow, musician Abraham Badley, musician Lewis Farer, musician

Privates
Ambler, Peter Furgerson, John Otterman, Lewis
Alexander, Ezekiel Gladman, Michael Osburne, Lewis
Armstrong, James Gunn, John Palmer, Richard

---

[40] "Payroll Muster of Captain Richard C. Talbott's Company, 19th Regiment of Infantry," **Adjutant General's Militia Records**, Series 88, Payroll, Folder 2, Ohio Historical Society's Library, Columbus, Ohio.

[41] "Payroll Muster of Captain William Gill's Company, 19th Regiment of Infantry," **Adjutant General's Militia Records**, Series 88, Payroll, Folder 2, Ohio Historical Society, Columbus, Ohio.

Blue, Frederick	Gilman, Daniel	Radcliff, John
Brown, John	Gordon, John L.	Ridgway, Paul
Buckley, Cornelius	Handcock, Daniel	Risher, Daniel
Brady, James	Hyet, Elsey	Russell, John
Brewan, Enoch	Hooper, John	Robison, John
Boucher, John	Hutcheson, Samuel	Ranking, John
Brown, Joseph	Hapleton, Joseph	Stewart, James
Brown, John	Huffman, John	Smith, John
Beach, William	Huston, James M.	Smith, Joseph D.
Black, William	Hodge, William	Smith, Wilson
Burris, James	Harvey, Peter	Smith, John W.
Buckley, Ebenzer	Johnston, John	Smith, Ecelston
Benedict, Elvin	Jones, Thomas	Sanburn, John
Bird, Johnston	Kersey, Archabold	Taggert, Samuel
Collins, John	Kerlogge, Shirley	Thompson, Lewis
Caster, Charles	Kingsland, John	Tish, Peter
Cahall, Isaac	Moore, William	Vail, Samuel
Connett, Henry	Morse, Amos	Vanverson, John
Cissna, Stephen	Murphey, Patrick	Vantile, Isaac
Cooper, Samuel	Moone, Thomas	Walking, Thomas
Davis, William	McWilliam, Alexander	Wertcoat, James
Davison, William	McGill, James	Williamson, John
Davis, William	Meeks, John	Williams, Linzar
Devore, Peter	Merryon, James	Walker, James
English, George	Marfoot, Samuel	Wesley, Archabald
Echart, William	Maurnon, William	Wert, David
Fisher, Peter	Morris, Zadock	Writson, Joseph
Falkner, John	Monteath, Jacob	Crumer, Peter
		Crumer, Hiram

Captain George Sanderson's Company Muster Roll
December 1813 [42]

Name	Enlisted	Notes
Captain George Sanderson	9 April 1813	
1st Lieutenant Abner P. Pinney		
2nd Lieutenant Audory Buttler		
2nd Lieutenant Andrews Bushnell	4 May 1813	
2nd Lieutenant John H. Mefford	28 May 1813	
2nd Lieutenant Abraham J. Fisk	15 Aug 1813	
Ensign William Hall	2 May 1813	
1st Sergeant Linus Williams	5 May 1813	Appointed Sergeant Major 4 July 1813
1st Sergeant John Vanmeter	3 Jun 1813	Appointed 1st Sergeant 4 July 1813
2nd Sergeant Chauncey Miller	4 May 1813	
3rd Sergeant Robert Sanderson	28 Apr 1813	
4th Sergeant Joshua Pierce	24 May 1813	
5th Sergeant John Neibling	23 Apr 1813	
1st Corporal John Dugane	10 Apr 1813	
2nd Corporal John Collins	12 Apr 1813	

---

[42] **History of Franklin and Pickaway Counties, Ohio**, (Williams Brothers, Evansville, Indiana: 1880), chapter XIX Military Record, George Sanderson's Company, pp. 107-108.

Ohio and the War of 1812

Name	Enlisted	Notes
3rd Corporal Luther Edson	26 Apr 1813	
4th Corporal Peter Gray	Apr 1813	Absent sick
5th Corporal Smith Headly	8 Jun 1813	
6th Corporal Daniel I. Bartholomew	8 May 1813	
Drummer Jonathan C. Shupe	8 May 1813	
Fifer Abraham Deeds	28 Apr 1813	

Privates
Allways, Joseph	22 Jun 1813	
Anderson, Joseph	27 Apr 1813	Sick at Upper Sandusky
Anderson, William	29 May 1813	Sick at Put-in-Bay
Atkins, John	31 May 1813	
Baker, Daniel	24 May 1813	On command
Bartholomew, Abram	31 May 1813	
Bartholomew, John	18 Jun 1813	
Bartholomew, Samuel	8 Jun 1813	
Batteese, John	4 Jun 1813	
Beaty, John	15 Apr 1813	
Bebee, Sheldon	28 Apr 1813	
Benjamin, Daniel	27 Apr 1813	
Berryman, John	19 Jun 1813	Sick at Put-in-Bay
Billings, Thomas	3 Jun 1813	
Bixler, Henry	27 May 1813	
Boyle, Thomas	16 Apr 1813	
Braden, James	23 Jul 1813	Sick
Brady, Eli	7 Jul 1813	
Brown, James	27 Apr 1813	
Burdinoo, Charles	8 May 1813	
Bussey, John	26 Apr 1813	
Cady, William	12 May 1813	Died 20 Nov 1813
Cady, William	12 May 1813	Sick at Seneca
Caneley, Peter	1 Jun 1813	
Canway, Jacob	19 Apr 1813	Sick
Canway, Lewis	28 Apr 1813	Died 27 Oct 1813
Carleton, Almon	17 Jun 1813	Died 28 Nov 1813
Case, Henry	28 Apr 1813	Sick at Put-in-Bay
Case, Nathan	29 Apr 1813	Waiter for Lieutenant Pinney
Clark, Chaney	27 Apr 1813	
Clark, Joseph	18 May 1813	Sick at Put-in-Bay
Cole, Chester P.	12 May 1813	
Collins, Holdon K.	5 Jun 1813	Sick in camp
Cook, Stephen	5 Jul 1813	Died 8 Nov 1813
Cremenes, Baldes	19 Apr 1813	Sick at Put-in-Bay
Crosby, David	30 Jun 1813	Sick
Daily, Benjamin	18 Jun 1813	Discharged 12 Jul 1813
Davis, Jesse	20 May 1813	Appointed sergeant May 20th
Devore, Enos	31 May 1813	
Draper, Asa	28 Jun 1813	
Dunham, Walter	1 May 1813	
Ellinger, Joseph	16 Apr 1813	
Evans, John	14 Jun 1813	
Faid, John	22 Apr 1813	Discharged 23 Nov 1813
Filkall, Daniel	1 May 1813	
Forsythe, John	28 Apr 1813	Sick at Put-in-Bay

Name	Enlisted	Notes
Fulk, Peter	26 Apr 1813	
Gates, Wilson L.	6 July 1813	
Gause, Samuel	25 Jun 1813	Sick at Put-in-Bay
Gibson, Joseph	5 Jun 1813	Died 28 Aug 1813
Gregory, Elnathan	21 Jun 1813	
Grimes, Ephraim	14 May 1813	
Haberson, John	19 Jul 1813	
Hagerty, James	22 Jun 1813	
Hall, John	30 May 1813	
Harter, John	27 Apr 1813	
Hartman, Frederick	30 Apr 1813	Died at Zanesville
Headley, Jacob	27 Apr 1813	Sick at Put-in-Bay
Hinkley, Josiah	17 Apr 1813	Died 5 Sep 1813
Holcomb, Perlin	18 Apr 1813	
Hughes, David	26 May 1813	
Hunt, John	12 Jun 1813	
Jackson, James	19 May 1813	Discharged (no date)
Jee, John	16 Apr 1813	Sick
Johnston, John	1 May 1813	Sick
Johnston, John, 2nd		On furlough
Joice, Ambrose	22 Jun 1813	
Jones, James	4 Jul 1813	
Kincaid, Jonas	9 Jun 1813	
Kiniman, Samuel	30 May 1813	
Kisler, John	17 Apr 1813	
Kissinger, George	23 Jun 1813	Sick
Kittsmiller, Jonathan	5 May 1813	
Larimore, Joseph	24 Apr 1813	
Lathere, Frederick	27 Apr 1813	
Leonard, Amos	28 May 1813	
Lief, Henry	31 May 1813	
Louther, William	21 Jun 1813	
Loveland. Marinas M.	27 Apr 1813	
Mains, Henry	13 Jun 1813	Sick
Mapes, Thomas	28 Jun 1813	Sick
McBride, John	28 Jun 1813	Sick at Put-in-Bay
McClain, William	16 Jun 1813	Sick at Put-in-Bay
McCloud, Francis	14 Jun 1813	
McClung, John	28 Apr 1813	
McClung, Joseph	17 Jun 1813	Sick
McConkey, John	31 May 1813	
McConnell, John	15 Jun 1813	
McCord, Alexander	8 Jun 1813	
McElwayne, John	1 Jun 1813	
McGarvy, Morris	1 Jun 1813	
Mellow, Joshua	4 May 1813	
Merril, Hosea	13 Aug 1813	
Miller, Andrew	5 Jun 1813	
Mose, James	9 Apr 1813	Shot at Seneca 2 Aug 1813
Naper, William	19 May 1813	
Nickerson, Isachar	19 Jun 1813	
Osborn, George	26 Apr 1813	
Paine, Roswell	6 Jun 1813	

Ohio and the War of 1812

Name	Enlisted	Notes
Palmer, Luther	29 Apr 1813	Sick
Parkhurst, Benjamin	5 Jun 1813	
Parks, George	26 May 1813	Died 28 Nov 1813
Pierce, Arzel	3 May 1813	
Prat, Lemuel	29 Apr 1813	On recruiting service
Ray, John	28 Apr 1813	
Reed, William	16 May 1813	Sick at Put-in-Bay
Ridinour, David	30 Apr 1813	
Rogers, Elijah	25 May 1813	
Rophy, George	27 Apr 1813	Died 2 Dec 1813
Rose, Asa	15 Jul 1813	
Sardon, Jonathan	27 Apr 1813	
Severs, David	19 May 1813	Sick at Put-in-Bay
Severs, John	9 Jun 1813	Sick at Put-in-Bay
Shadley, Henry	8 Jun 1813	Died at Fort Ball
Shadwick, George	25 Sep 1813	
Sharp, Thomas	4 Jul 1813	
Sheanor, Soloman	4 Jul 1813	
Sheers, Mynder	19 May 1813	
Shroup, Jacob	22 May 1813	
Shyhawk, Christian	17 Jun 1813	Died 18 Nov 1813
Siner, Adam	23 Jun 1813	
Skills, Henry	22 May 1813	Sick at Put-in-Bay
Smith, Charles	20 Apr 1813	
Smith, Christian B.	28 Jun 1813	
Smith, John	4 Jul 1813	
Spry, Perry	4 Jun 1813	
Strait, Henry C.	17 Apr 1813	
Stratler, Joseph	22 May 1813	
Summers, Ephraim	23 Apr 1813	Sick at Seneca
Sunderland, John	5 Jun 1813	
Taylor, David	9 Jun 1813	
Tester, Frederick	27 Apr 1813	
Thorp, Benjamin	19 Apr 1813	Sick
Thorp, John	10 May 1813	
Trovinger, Jacob	2 Jun 1813	
Tucker, Frederick	21 May 1813	Sick
Twaddle, Joseph	16 Apr 1813	Sick
Tyler, Seymour	29 Jul 1813	
Walker, Alexander	15 May 1813	Sick
Wallace, William	4 Jun 1813	On command
Walters, David	27 Apr 1813	
Watson, William	28 Apr 1813	
Weaver, Jacob	28 May 1813	
Welshaus, John	25 May 1813	
Wheatley, Thomas	12 Apr 1813	
Wheeler, Jacob	25 May 1813	
White, Ansel	20 Apr 1813	Sick
Williams, Flavel	31 May 1813	
Wilson, Archibald		On command
Wilson, Joseph	19 Jun 1813	Discharged 15 Sep 1813
Wolfley, Coonrod	31 May 1813	
Wright, Joseph	30 Jun 1813	Sick
Zimmerman, Henry	7 Jun 1813	Sick

Zipler, Daniel   6 Jul 1813

Captain Daniel Cushing's Company [43]
2nd Regiment of U.S. Artillery
2 July 1812 – 31 May 1813

Captain Daniel Cushing
1st Lieutenant Joseph H. Larwill   2nd Lieutenant Alexander A. Meek

1st Sergeant Thomas Morgan   2nd Sergeant Jeremiah Mead   3rd Sergeant Jacob Kelley
4th Sergeant John Melchum

1st Corporal Joshua Warman   2nd Corporal William D. Powers   3rd Corporal Patrick Devling
4th Corporal Michael Spiceman   5th Corporal Enoch Bowman   6th Corporal Joseph Tinsley
6th Corporal Archibald Armstrong

Musician Moses Blanchard   Musician Richard Cheney   Musician William Cisna

Arnold, John	Hannah, Robert	Oldham, George
Arwin, Joseph	Hart, David	Parsons, Robert
Boner, William	Heaton, Samuel	Patterson, Joseph
Briney, John	Jones, Thomas	Pearson, Robert
Bucey, Jesse	Kelley, John	Pelham, Bine
Buchanan, John	Lawrence, Andrew	Pove, James
Campbell, Alexander	Leddle, John	Reed, John
Campbell, John	Leonard, Caleb	Rude, Felix
Craegen, John	Lewis, Fielding	Shields, William
Dedgear, Coonrad	Lewis, Joseph	Shiller, Samuel
Donahy, Samuel	Louis, Louis	Simmonds, Joseph
Dutton, Jonas	Marker, Benjamin	Simson, Isaac
Faircloth, James	Mason, Jacob	Slaughter, Jonathan
Faulker, James	McConky, Alexander	Smoot, Jeremiah
Feddeman, Henry	McConky, Samuel	Swaney, Frederick
Ferguson, James	McCordy, James	Teal, Nicholas
Fig, James	McCullock, John	Thompson, James
Goudling, Thomas	McGuffin, George	Toline, Anthony
Grossman, Samuel	Munsey, Jesse	Turk, Ephraim
Gwin, Richard	Murray, William	Waggoner, Ephraim
Hackley, Richard	Nicholson, Andrew	Wastimber, Francis
Haning, Aaron	Norton, John	Welch, James

---

[43] Lindley, Harlow, **Fort Meigs and the War of 1812, Orderly Book of Cushing's Company, 2nd U.S. Artillery April 1813 – February 1814**, (The Ohio Historical Society, Columbus, Ohio: 1975), pp. 80-82.

America's greatest disaster during the War of 1812

The greatest American disaster during the War of 1812 did not occur on any battlefield with the enemy. Instead, a cholera-like disease struck Major General William Henry Harrison's Army of the Northwest between December 1813 and January 1814 at Fort Shelby, Territory of Michigan. This fort had previously been named Fort Detroit.

Before the epidemic had run its course, 700 soldiers had died, and they were buried in a make-shift cemetery just west of the fort. Many of these men were buried in mass graves after the coffin makers could not keep up with the demand. The epidemic struck down both regular soldiers and militiamen.

Out of approximately 1,400 soldiers who had been stationed at this facility, or in the nearly area, only 300 soldiers were well enough to guard the fort during and after the epidemic. Militia companies from both Kentucky and Ohio were called up to help protect Detroit while the army recruited and rebuilt its forces.

The military never maintained or marked the cemetery that interned the soldiers who had died during this epidemic. After the war the cemetery was used as a parade ground and later as a billeting area to house soldiers in tents. The cemetery was destroyed as buildings were constructed to form downtown Detroit during the mid-1800's.

A good percentage of soldiers who had died during this sickness came from Ohio. The other soldiers were from Kentucky, Pennsylvania, Indiana, Michigan and Tennessee.

Another major disaster had hit the troops stationed at Buffalo, New York, the previous winter. These deaths were due to disease, starvation, and a harsh winter. About 300 American soldiers died in winter camp, and they were buried in a meadow that is now the Delaware Park in Buffalo. The remains of these men have not been disturbed and there is a monument in the meadow honoring their spirit.

Ohioans who served as army officers during the War of 1812

The *Historical Register and Dictionary of the United States Army From Its Organization, September 29, 1789, to March 2, 1903 (Historical Register)*[44] lists all of the men who were commissioned officers in the army between 1789 and 1903. Among these men were 222 Ohioans who served as officers during the War of 1812. The book is divided into two volumes with the first volume concentrating on regimental lineages and short biographies of each of the army officers. Volume two deals with listings of army officers by categories, including Civil War, prisoners of war, generals, etc. It also gives a chronological listing of all the battles with regimental participation.

The majority of Ohio's officers served in Army of the Northwest from before the fall of Fort Detroit to the British on 16 August 1812 through the Battle of the Thames on 5 October 1813. After the Battle of the Thames, half of this army was transferred to the Army of the North in New York where some of our men were involved in the major battles in 1814 along the Niagara River. One regiment, which had been a part of the Army of the Northwest, was transferred to the Army of the Southwest and they participated in the Battle of New Orleans on 8 January 1815.

Before the War of 1812 the 1st Regiment of Infantry had been assigned to the Northwest Territory where this regiment participated in the various Indian wars of the 1790's. The regiment was originally raised in the Middle Atlantic States, but by 1812 a large percentage of the men that had been recruited from Kentucky and the Northwest Territory to replace the original men whose enlistments had expired.

On 12 April 1803 the Regiment of Rifle was created and four companies of soldiers were recruited from Kentucky, Ohio and the Territory of Indiana. This regiment was renamed the 1st Regiment of Rifle on 10 February 1814 after three more rifle regiments were authorized by Congress. The 7th Regiment of Infantry was authorized under the act of 12 April 1808 and it was raised primarily in Kentucky. A number of Ohioans were recruited for this regiment.

The 17th Regiment of Infantry was organized in Kentucky and Ohio under the Congressional Act of 11 January 1812. There were actually two 17th regiments organized during war. The first 17th regiment was created on 11 January 1812, and it was disbanded under the act of 3 March 1814. The second 17th Regiment of Infantry was authorized under the act of 3 March 1814 when the 17th and 19th Regiments of Infantry merged to form this new regiment on 12 May 1814. The "17" designation was reused for this regiment. The new regiment was made up of men from Kentucky, Ohio, and the Territories of Indiana and Michigan.

The 19th Regiment of Infantry was organized in Ohio and in the Territory of Michigan under the Congressional Act of 26 June 1812. Like the 17th regiment there were two entirely different regiments organized during the war using the "nineteenth" designation. The first 19th regiment was created on 26 June 1812, and it was disbanded under the act of 3 March 1814 then this regiment merged with the 17th regiment to form a new 17th Regiment of Infantry. The second 19th Regiment of Infantry was authorized under the act of 3 March 1814 then the 26th and 27th Regiments of Infantry along with two companies from the original 17th Regiment of Infantry merged to form this second regiment on 12 May 1814. None of the officers from the first 19th regiment were transferred to the second 19th regiment.

The 24th Regiment of Infantry was organized under the Congressional Act of 26 June 1812. The Secretary of War assigned the raising of this regiment to the State of Tennessee and the Territory of Mississippi[45]. Under an Act of Congress, dated 29 January 1813, the raising of two infantry regiments

---

[44] Heitman, Francis B., **Historical Register and Dictionary of the United States Army From Its Organization, September 29, 1789, to March 2, 1903**, (Genealogical Publishing Company, Baltimore, Maryland: 1994).

[45] **Tennessee State Library and Archives, Historical and Genealogical Information**, Regimental Histories of Tennessee Units during the War of 1812, Nashville, Tennessee.

was assigned to Ohio and another to Kentucky. The 26th Regiment of Infantry was raised in western Ohio while the 27th Regiment of Infantry was raised in eastern Ohio. The 28th Regiment of Infantry was raised in Kentucky.

The 2nd Regiment of Rifle was organized under the act of 10 February 1814. This regiment was raised in Kentucky, Ohio and Tennessee. The 2nd Regiment of Light Dragoons was organized under the act of 11 January 1812. One company of light dragoons was raised in Kentucky and Ohio. The 2nd Regiment of Artillery was organized under the act of 11 January 1812. Ohio raised one company for this regiment. Six companies of rangers were organized under the act of 2 January 1812, and by the act of 1 July 1812 an additional company was authorized. Ohio was assigned the raising of two of these ranger companies.

Congress authorized the creation of the infantry regiments that served during the War of 1812 while the President and Secretary of War delegated which state or territory would raise a particular regiment. Most infantry regiments were raised in one or more states or territories. The light dragoons, artillery and rifle regiments were recruited nationally in which each area of the country would raise a company or companies. These later regiments never operated as a single unit during the war. Ranger companies were assigned to an individual state or territory for their raising, and they were not organized into regiments but were attached to infantry regiments. The majority of ranger companies operated with the 1st and 7th Regiments of Infantry.

Each regiment maintained its own recruiting service throughout the war. One field grade officer was assigned to head the recruiting efforts for the regiment and most of the company grade officers not assigned to a company became recruiting officers. When the number of recruits reached 100 men, a new company would be formed, and they would then be sent into the field to join the rest of the regiment. Many officers in a new regiment would be temporality assigned to an existing regiment for training. Once trained they would report back to their regiments and take command of a new company.

Other officers were transferred into a new regiment to form a nucleus of experienced officers and to help train the inexperienced officers. This gave many officers a chance to be promoted. When the 17th, 19th, 26th and 27th regiments merged to reform the 17th and 19th regiments, twelve junior officers from the 17th and 19th regiments were transferred to either the 24th regiment or the 28th regiment.

The listing of Ohio's army officers begins with the name of the individual, his highest rank obtained during the war, the regiments or units in which he was a member of during the war, his commissioning date, his date of discharge from the army and his residence as listed in the *Historical Register*. In most cases the *Historical Register* lists the birthplace and the residence at the time of commissioning. Only the place of residence is included in this listing since very few officers were born in Ohio. Three men had their place of residence listed as the 'Northwest Territory' and they are included in this listing. They may not be Ohio residences but residences in the Territories of Indiana, Illinois or Michigan.

William Henry Harrison is included in this listing since he was an Ohio resident for the majority of the war. He had maintained a residence in Ohio while serving as the Territorial Governor of Indiana between 1800 and 1812. After he accepted a brigadier general's commission in the army, he moved his family back to Ohio. The *Historical Register* lists his residence as Indiana. James Manary, Senior, was Ohio's first captain of a United States ranger company. He was not included in the *Historical Register*.

Abbreviations used in the Listing of Officers

MG	Major General	1LT	First Lieutenant			S	Surgeon
BG	Brigadier General	2LT	Second Lieutenant			SM	Surgeon's Mate
Lt Col	Lieutenant Colonel	3LT	Third Lieutenant			JA	Judge Advocate
Capt	Captain						
Asst AG		Assistant Adjutant General		Dist PM		District Paymaster	
Asst Dep QG		Asst. Deputy Quartermaster General		Dep CP		Deputy Commissioner of Purchasing	
Asst Dist PM		Assistant District Paymaster		Dep QG		Deputy Quartermaster General	
Asst IG		Assistant Inspector General		Top Eng		Topographical Engineer	
Dep CO		Deputy Commissioner of Ordinance		QG		Quartermaster General	

1, etc	Numbers represent infantry regiments	CA	Corps of Artillery
2LD	2nd Regiment of Light Dragoons	1RR	1st Regiment of Rifle
1RA	1st Regiment of Artillery	2RR	2nd Regiment of Rifle
2RA	2nd Regiment of Artillery	Rangers	United States Rangers

Listings of Ohio's regular army officers during the War of 1812

Name	Highest Rank	Units	Commissioning Date	Discharge Date	Residence
Abbott, James	3LT	26	20 May 1813	1 Mar 1814	Ohio
Anderson, Charles M.	Captain	1RA	25 Mar 1812	2 Jul 1812 Died	Ohio
Anderson, Robert	1LT	26	20 May 1813	1 Jun 1814	Ohio
Applegate, James	Captain	27	20 May 1813	16 Oct 1813	Ohio
Armstrong, Daniel D.	Ensign	19	12 Mar 1812	18 Nov 1812	Ohio
Armstrong, William	2 LT	1RR	19 Jan 1813	1 Oct 1816	Ohio
Avery, John C.	3LT	26	20 May 1813	1 Jun 1814	Ohio
Baird, William	Captain	26 19	29 May 1813	15 Jun 1815	Ohio
Baskerville, Edward B.	Ensign	19	4 Jun 1812	9 Nov 1813	Ohio
Benedict, Ebenezer	1LT	27	20 May 1813	12 May 1814	Ohio
Blair, James	1LT	27 19	29 May 1813	15 Jun 1815	Ohio
Booker, Samuel	Captain	19	12 Mar 1812	1 Jun 1814	Ohio
Booten, John	2LT	27 19	20 May 1813	15 Jun 1815	Ohio
Bradford, Harry C.	S	24	9 Aug 1813	14 Apr 1815	Ohio
Brady, Josiah	1LT	26	20 May 1813	12 May 1814	Ohio
Brown, John	2LT	26	20 May 1813	1 Jun 1814	Ohio
Bryan, George S.	2LT	26	1 Jun 1813	15 Aug 1813	Ohio
Bryan, Peter	2LT	28 19	31 Mar 1814	31 Jan 1815	Ohio
Bushnell, Andrew	1LT	27 19	20 May 1813	15 Jun 1815	Ohio
Buttles, Avery	2LT	27	20 May 1813	1 Jun 1814	Ohio
Cairns, Joseph	Captain	27	20 May 1813	18 Feb 1814	Ohio
Campbell, Caleb B.	Ensign	19	24 Oct 1813	27 Aug 1814	Ohio
Campbell, James	1LT	19 17	6 Jul 1812	15 Jun 1815	Ohio
Carney, David L.	2LT	19 17	6 Apr 1813	15 Jun 1815	Ohio
Carr, Robert	3LT	19	6 Apr 1813	1 Jun 1814	Ohio
Carroll, John	1LT	27 19	20 May 1813	15 Jun 1815	Ohio
Cass, Charles Lee	1LT	27 19	20 May 1813	15 Jun 1815	Ohio
Cass, Lewis	BG		20 Feb 1813	1 May 1814	Ohio
Cissna, Charles[46]	2LT	26 19	20 May 1813	15 Jun 1815	Ohio
Clarkson, Charles S.	Asst Dist PM		21 Sep 1814	15 Jun 1815	Ohio
Clendenin, David	Asst Dist PM		10 Apr 1814	18 Dec 1814	Ohio
Cole, Leonard	Ensign	26	7 Aug 1813	12 May 1814	Ohio
Coleman, Samuel	1LT	27 19	20 May 1813	15 Jun 1815	Ohio
Collins, Jeremiah	2LT	27	20 May 1813	1 Jun 1814	Ohio
Collins, Joel	Captain	26 19	20 May 1813	15 Jun 1815	Ohio
Crawford, Bratton	2LT	Rangers	5 May 1813	15 Jun 1814	Ohio
Cushing, Daniel	Captain	2RA CA	2 Jul 1812	24 Mar 1815 Drown	Ohio
Cutler, Enos[47]	Major	7 38	3 Sep 1810	30 Nov 1839	Ohio
Danielson, Timothy E.	1LT	24	12 Mar 1812	Sept 1813 Died	Ohio
Delerae, Alexander	1LT	26	20 May 1813	17 May 1814	Ohio
Dougherty, William	3LT	2RR	17 Mar 1814	15 Jun 1815	Ohio

---

[46] Lieutenant Cissna was brevetted a 2nd Lieutenant on 15 August 1814 for distinguished service in defense of Fort Erie, Upper Canada.

[47] Major Cutler served as an assistant adjutant general between 15 February 1813 and 18 March 1813 holding the rank of major and then he served as an assistant inspector general between 18 March 1813 and 1 May 1814.

Ohio and the War of 1812

Name	Highest Rank	Units	Commissioning Date	Discharge Date	Residence
Drennan, Samuel	1LT	27	20 May 1813	1 Jun 1814	Ohio
Eagan, John	2LT	27	20 May 1813	27 Apr 1814	Ohio
Edwards, Abraham[48]	Captain	17	12 Mar 1812	15 Mar 1814	Ohio
Elliott, Wilson	Captain	19	12 Mar 1812	12 May 1814	Ohio
Finley, James B.	2LT	19 28	30 Mar 1814	15 Jun 1815	Ohio
Fisk, Abraham James	2LT	27 19	10 May 1813	30 Sep 1814	Ohio
Flinn, James	1LT	Rangers	13 Mar 1812	1814	Ohio
Forbes, Caleb G.	1LT	24	12 Sep 1812	24 Apr 1814 Died	Ohio
Frederick, Henry	1LT	19	12 Mar 1812	1 Jun 1814	Ohio
Gano, Aaron G.[49]	3LT	CA	2 Mar 1815	1 Oct 1817	Ohio
Gill, William	Captain	27 19	20 May 1813	15 Jun 1815	Ohio
Gillfillan, John	3LT	7	13 Jun 1814	15 Jun 1815	Ohio
Gilman, Samuel	1LT	27	20 May 1813	18 May 1814	Ohio
Gilmore, Andrew	3LT	2RR	17 Mar 1814	15 Jun 1815	Ohio
Goode, John	2LT	26 19	20 May 1813	15 Jun 1815	Ohio
Granger, Orrin	2LT	27 19	20 May 1813	15 Jun 1815	Ohio
Gregory, Nehemiah	1LT	27 19	20 May 1813	15 Jun 1815	Ohio
Guthridge, William	Ensign	26	20 May 1813	1 Jun 1814	Ohio
Gwynne, David	Major	19 2RR	12 Mar 1812	17 May 1815	Ohio
Hall, John	2LT	26 19	20 May 1813	15 Jun 1815	Ohio
Hall, William	Ensign	27	20 May 1813	1 Jun 1814	Ohio
Halm, Michael	3LT	27	20 May 1813	1 Jun 1814	Ohio
Hamm, John	S	27 19	16 Apr 1813	6 Jul 1814	Ohio
Harper, James A.	Captain	27	20 May 1813	1 Jun 1814	Ohio
Harrison, Batteal	Captain	19 2RR	12 May 1812	15 Jun 1815	Ohio
Harrison, William H.	MG		22 Aug 1812	31 May 1814	Indiana (Ohio)
Harvey, John	2LT	28	31 Mar 1814	21 Jan 1815	Ohio
Hays, Michael C.	Captain	1RR	1 Jun 1811	30 Nov 1813	Ohio
Hedges, James	Captain	2LD 46	21 Apr 1814	15 Jun 1815	Ohio
Herron, James	Captain	19 17	12 Mar 1812	15 Jun 1815	Ohio
Hill, Alexander	Captain	27 19	20 may 1813	11 Nov 1814	Ohio
Hoffman, Adam E.	1LT	19 17	6 Apr 1813	4 Jan 1815	Ohio
Hopkins, John	1LT	Rangers	20 Jan 1812	15 Jun 1815	Ohio
Howell, Lewis	1LT	19	12 Mar 1812	20 Mar 1813	Ohio
Hughes, Joseph L.	Chaplin		20 May 1813	5 Aug 1813	Ohio
Hunt, Jesse	Dist PM		22 Sep 1812	15 Jun 1815	Ohio
Huntington, Samuel	Dist PM		3 Oct 1812	31 Mar 1815	Ohio
Huston, William	2LT	26	20 May 1813	1 Jun 1814	Ohio
Jackson, George W.	Captain	19 17	12 Mar 1812	9 Jul 1814	Ohio
Jenkinson, Joseph	Major	26	19 Feb 1813	1 Jun 1814	Ohio
Jesup, Thomas S.	Major	7 19	1 Dec 1089	19 Apr 1814	Ohio
Johns, Abijah	Ensign	26 19	20 May 1813	1 Sep 1814	Ohio
Jolly, John	Ensign	19	19 Jul 1813	10 May 1814	Ohio
Kercheval, Samuel	1LT	7	10 Feb 1812	20 Jun 1813 Died	Ohio
Kesling, George	Captain	26 19	20 May 1813	15 Jun 1815	Ohio
Knox, John	1LT	Rangers	6 Jul 1812	14 Jun 1814	Ohio
Langham, Angus L.	Captain	19	12 Mar 1812	15 Aug 1813	Ohio
Langham, Elias T.	2LT	19	12 Mar 1812	17 Mar 1814	Ohio
Larwill, Joseph H.	1LT	2RA CA	12 Mar 1812	15 Jun 1815	Ohio
Leavitt, William	3LT	19	6 Apr 1813	1 Jun 1814	Ohio

---

[48] Captain Edwards served as a deputy quartermaster general between 15 March 1814 and 15 June 1815 holding the rank of major.

[49] Lieutenant Gano was a graduate of the military academy.

Ohio and the War of 1812

Name	Highest Rank	Units	Commissioning Date	Discharge Date	Residence
Leslie, Jacob C.	2LT	26 19	20 May 1813	13 Sep 1814	Ohio
Lindsay, Andrew	3 LT	1RR	29 Jun 1813	10 Feb 1814	Ohio
Lindsley, Stephen	Chaplin		29 Jul 1813	15 Jun 1815	Ohio
Lockhart, Josiah	Captain	26	20 May 1813	1 Jun 1814	Ohio
Looker, Alison C.	3LT	19 2RR	19 Jul 1813	15 Jun 1815	Ohio
Lucas, John	Captain	26	20 May 1813	1 Jun 1814	Ohio
Lucas, Robert [50]	Captain	19	14 Mar 1812	10 Feb 1813	Ohio
MacDonald, William [51]	Captain	26 19	20 May 1813	17 May 1815	Ohio
Maltbie, Benjamin	1LT	26	20 May 1813	2 Aug 1813	Ohio
Manary, James Junior	1LT	Rangers	6 Jul 1812	15 Jun 1815	Ohio
Manary, James Senior	Captain	Rangers	5 Aug 1813	15 Jun 1815	Ohio
Martin, Absalom	Captain	27	20 May 1813	1 Jun 1814	Ohio
Marvin, Charles	SM	19 26 1RR	12 Mar 1812	15 Jun 1815	Ohio
Mason, John	Captain	28	20 May 1813	15 Jun 1815	Ohio
McArthur, Duncan	BG		20 Feb 1813	15 Jun 1815	Ohio
McClain, Joseph	1LT	26 2RR	20 May 1813	30 Sep 1814	Ohio
McClelland, Michael [52]	Captain	7	10 Feb 1812	23 Dec 1814 Killed	Ohio
McCormick, Samuel	Captain	Rangers	17 Mar 1812	15 Jun 1815	Ohio
McDonald, James	Lt Col	1RR	1 Aug 1812	17 Sep 1814	Ohio
McDonald, John	Captain	26	20 May 1813	7 Aug 1813	Ohio
McElvain, John	2LT	26 19	20 May 1813	15 Jun 1815	Ohio
McFadden, Neal	Ensign	27 19	20 May 1813	15 Jun 1815	Ohio
McFarland, Daniel	1LT	26	20 May 1813	1 Jun 1814	Ohio
McGuire, James	Ensign	19 17	15 Aug 1813	15 Jul 1814	Ohio
McKeehan, Samuel	S	18	29 Jul 1813	18 Jan 1815	Ohio
McKnight, Thomas R.	3LT	19 17	14 Jun 1814	15 Jun 1815	Ohio
McLeod, Collin	2LT	26 19	20 May 1813	17 May 1815	Ohio
McMillan, William	Lt Col	17	12 Mar 1812	1 Jun 1814	Ohio
Meek, Alexander A.	2LT	2RA	8 May 1812	31 May 1813	Ohio
Meek, John	1LT	7	10 Feb 1812	30 Sep 1814	Ohio
Meldrum, John	3LT	26	7 Aug 1813	1 Jun 1814	Ohio
Milford, John	2LT	27	20 May 1813	1 Jun 1814	Ohio
Miligan, John	2LT	19	12 Mar 1812	1 Jun 1814	Ohio
Miller, Edward W.	3LT	2RR	17 Mar 1814	15 Jun 1815	Ohio
Miller, John	Colonel	19 17	12 Mar 1812	7 May 1815	Ohio
Miller, Joseph	Capt Asst Dep QG		1 Sep 1813	1814 Died	Ohio
Monroe, Thomas J. C.	GSM	6	12 Sep 1811	15 Jun 1815	Ohio
Moore, Hugh	Captain	19	12 May 1814	12 Oct 1814	Ohio
Moore, John	Captain	26	20 May 1813	1 Jun 1814	Ohio
Moore, Robert	S	19	6 Jul 1814	15 Jun 1815	Ohio
Morgan, John E.	Ensign	19	12 Mar 1812	4 Dec 1812	Ohio
Morris, David	2LT	19	8 May 1812	20 Jan 1813	Ohio
Morrison, Robert	Lt Col	27	9 Apr 1813	12 Dec 1813 Died	Ohio
Munson, Jeremiah R.	Major	27	18 Mar 1813	1 Jun 1814	Ohio
Murray, Harvey	2 LT	1RR	17 Oct 1812	4 Sep 1813 Died	Ohio
Neville, Robert	3LT	26 19	20 May 1813	16 Jun 1814	Ohio
Niswonger, Christian	3LT	19	19 Jul 1813	1 Jun 1814	Ohio

---

[50] Captain Lucas was commissioned a lieutenant colonel on 20 February 1813, and then he resigned on 30 June 1813 without having been assigned to a regiment.

[51] Captain MacDonald was brevetted a major on 25 July 1814 for distinguished service during the Battle of Lundy's Lane, Upper Canada.

[52] Captain McClelland was killed during the first Battle of New Orleans, Louisiana.

Ohio and the War of 1812

Name	Highest Rank	Units	Commissioning Date	Discharge Date	Residence
Nixon, James	1LT	27 19	20 May 1813	15 Jun 1815	Ohio
Noel, John	Ensign	26	20 May 1813	1 Jun 1814	Ohio
Northup, Henry	Captain	27 19	20 May 1813	11 Nov 1814	Ohio
Norton, Carlos A.	1LT	26 19	20 May 1813	6 Jul 1814	Ohio
Patterson, Alexander	2LT	2719	20 May 1813	15 Jun 1815	Ohio
Patterson, John	3LT	2719	20 May 1813	15 Jun 1815	Ohio
Paull, George	Colonel	19 27	9 Apr 1813	12 May 1814	Ohio
Perrine, James	SM	19	29 Jun 1814	15 Jun 1815	Ohio
Perry, William	Captain	Rangers	1812	1813	Ohio
Phillips, Asher	2LT	19 17	12 Mar 1812	17 May 1815	Ohio
Piatt, John H.	Dep CP		18 Sep 1812	15 Jun 1815	Ohio
Pickett, James C.	2LT	2RA CA	14 Aug 1813	15 Jun 1815	Ohio
Pigman, John G.	Ensign	27	20 May 1813	1 Jun 1814	Ohio
Pinney, Abner P.	1LT	27 19	20 May 1813	27 May 1814	Ohio
Price, Clarkson	2LT	26	20 May 1813	1 Jun 1814	Ohio
Price, Philip P.	1LT	1917	12 Mar 1812	1 Oct 1815	Ohio
Prosser, William	1LT	7	10 Feb 1812	28 Sep 1814 Died	Ohio
Puthuff, William H.	Major	26 2RR	20 May 1813	17 May 1815	Ohio
Ramsay, Thomas	Captain	1RR	31 Jul 1812	15 Jun 1815	Ohio
Rees, Jonathan	1LT	1917	12 Mar 1812	15 Jun 1815	Ohio
Reeves, John D.	2LT	19	1 May 1812	11 May 1813	Ohio
Reeves, Nathan L.	2LT	2719	20 May 1813	15 Jun 1815	Ohio
Reynolds, James [53]	SM		6 Jul 1812	16 Aug 1812 Killed	Ohio
Richardson, Robert D.	Dep CO		5 Aug 1813	8 Feb 1814	Ohio
Richardson, Thomas H. [54]	1LT	7	10 Feb 1812	11 Oct 1813 Killed	Ohio
Riddle, Thomas	3LT	27 19	20 May 1813	15 Jun 1815	Ohio
Rieley, Isaac M.	1LT	7	8 May 1812	15 Jun 1815	Ohio
Rogers, Levi	S	19	28 Jan 1813	30 Sep 1813	Ohio
Rowland, Thomas	Major	27 19	29 Jun 1813	17 May 1815	Ohio
Rue, Benjamin S.	3LT	17 24	12 May 1814	15 Jun 1815	Ohio
Sanderson, George	Captain	27	20 May 1813	1 Jun 1814	Ohio
Seaman, Ebenezer	Ensign	Rangers	5 Aug 1813	15 Jun 1815	Ohio
Servess, William G.	2LT	Rangers	1 Oct 1813	15 Jun 1815	Ohio
Shane, Abraham	1LT	27	20 May 1813	1 Jun 1814	Ohio
Shannon, James	2LT	19	12 May 1814	15 Jun 1815	Ohio
Shannon, John	Ensign	27	20 May 1813	12 May 1814	Ohio
Shannon, Samuel	1LT	2719	20 May 1813	15 Jul 1815	Ohio
Shannon, Thomas	Ensign	19	12 May 1814	27 May 1814	Ohio
Shaug, William H.	3LT	19 17	30 Mar 1814	15 Jun 1815	Ohio
Shields, Thomas C.	1LT	27 19	20 May 1813	15 Jun 1815	Ohio
Sidney, Thomas S. [55]	Major	25	18 Apr 1814	17 May 1815	Ohio
Simmons, John	3LT	19 17	19 Jul 1813	13 Aug 1814	Ohio
Simons, John H.	2LT	27 19	20 May 1813	15 Jun 1815	Ohio
Smith, Daniel Junior	SM	2RR	17 Mar 1814	15 Jun 1815	Ohio
Smith, Robert	3LT	26 19	20 May 1813	15 Jun 1815	Ohio
Spencer, Anderson	2LT	26	20 May 1813	1 Jun 1814	Ohio
Spencer, John	Captain	27	20 May 1813	1 Jun 1814	Ohio
Spenck, Peter Junior	SM	26 19	26 Apr 1813	15 Jun 1814	Ohio
Stall, George W.	1LT	19 17	12 Mar 1812	15 Jun 1815	Ohio

---

[53] Surgeon's Mate Reynolds was killed at Fort Detroit, Territory of Michigan.

[54] Lieutenant Richardson was killed in a duel.

[55] Major Sidney was brevetted a lieutenant colonel for gallantry during the Battle of Chippewa, Upper Canada, on 5 July 1814.

Ohio and the War of 1812

Name	Highest Rank	Units	Commissioning Date	Discharge Date	Residence
Steele, David	3LT	Rangers	5 Aug 1813	15 Jun 1815	Ohio
Stephenson, John	2LT	Rangers	20 Jan 1813	15 May 1813	Ohio
Stockton, John	1LT	19 2RR	31 Dec 1812	15 Jun 1815	Ohio
Stockton, Robert	1LT	26 19	20 May 1813	13 Mar 1815	Ohio
Struthers, Alexander	1LT	27	20 May 1813	18 Dec 1813 Died	Ohio
Swearingen, James	Colonel QG		17 Mar 1813	15 Jun 1815	Ohio
Swearingen, John	1LT	26 19 2RR	20 May 1813	15 Jun 1815	Ohio
Swearingen, Samuel	Captain	26	20 May 1813	9 Apr 1814	Ohio
Symmes, John Cleeves	Captain	1	29 Jul 1807	15 Jun 1815	NW Territory
Talbott, John G.	3LT	26	20 May 1813	1 Jun 1814	Ohio
Talbott, Richard C.	Captain	26 19	20 May 1813	15 Jun 1815	Ohio
Tiffin, Clayton	SM	17	11 Mar 1814	15 Jun 1815	Ohio
Tod, George	Lt Col	19 17	12 May 1812	15 Jun 1815	Ohio
Townsley, William [56]	1 LT	1RR	15 May 1813	11 Jan 1814	Ohio
Trimble, Carey A.	Captain	26 19	20 May 1813	15 Jun 1815	Ohio
Trimble, David	2LT	1	19 Apr 1814	14 May 1814	Ohio
Trimble, William A.	Lt Col	26 19 1	18 Mar 1813	17 May 1815	Ohio
Tullass, John J.	Ensign	27	7 Aug 1813	1 Jun 1814	Ohio
Turney, Daniel	SM	19 2RR	31 Dec 1812	15 Jun 1815	Ohio
Van Horne, Isaac Junior [57]	Captain	27 19	20 May 1813	4 Aug 1814 Killed	Ohio
Van Horne, Thomas B.	Lt Col	26 19	9 Apr 1813	17 May 1815	Ohio
Wadsworth, Edward	Captain	1RR	12 May 1812	15 Jun 1815	Ohio
Warner, Wynkoop	1LT	27 19	20 May 1813	15 Jun 1815	Ohio
Watson, Joseph	Dist PM		25 Jul 1812	15 Jun 1815	Ohio
Watson, Simon Z.	Major Top Eng		20 Aug 1813	1 Feb 1814 Died	Ohio
Watson, William	Ensign	26	20 May 1813	1 Jun 1814	Ohio
Whistler, William	Captain	1	4 Mar 1807	17 May 1815	NW Territory
Whitlock, Ambrose	Captain Dist PM		13 Jun 1805	17 May 1815	NW Territory
Will, George	Captain	19	12 May 1814	15 Jun 1815	Ohio
Williams, Biram	3LT	19 28	15 Apr 1814	15 Jun 1815	Ohio
Williby, John	Ensign	27	20 May 1813	1 Jun 1814	Ohio
Wills, John S.	JA		7 May 1813	15 Jun 1815	Ohio
Wood, Christopher	Captain	26	20 May 1813	1 Jun 1814	Ohio
Young, Robert	3LT	26 19	20 May 1813	15 Jun 1815	Ohio

---

[56] Lieutenant Townsley served as the assistant deputy quartermaster general between 11 January 1814 and 30 April 1814 holding the rank of captain.

[57] Captain Van Horne was killed during the Battle of Mackinaw Island, Territory of Michigan.

Regular Army enlistments and discharges in Ohio

Little attention has been given to the approximately 2,500 Ohioans who served in the U.S. Army during the War of 1812. The Ohio militiamen have taken the limelight since the majority of the men from this state served in this militia organization. However, approximately one out of every ten Ohioans who served during the war served in the U.S. Army.

Ohio raised the 19th, 26th and the 27th Regiments of Infantry plus one company of artillery and two companies of rangers for the army. The state also participated in the raising of the 1st, 7th and 17th Regiments of U.S. Infantry, the 2nd Regiment of U.S. Rifles, plus a company of light dragoons and another four companies of riflemen for the 1st Regiment of U.S. Rifles.

Lieutenant Colonel George Tod of Youngstown, Ohio, has the distinction of serving as a senior recruiter during the war in three different infantry regiments: the 17th Regiment of U.S. Infantry, the 19th Regiment of U.S. Infantry and finally in the reorganized 17th Regiment of U.S. Infantry.

George Tod's military papers are located in the archives of the Western Reserve Historical Society in Cleveland, Ohio.[58] The various weekly, monthly and quarterly recruiting reports used in this article were found in the manuscript series MS-3202 along with three discharge reports. The collection also contains numerous types of military papers generated by these three regiments including muster rolls, clothing reports and official correspondences. The collection is not complete. It contains only the reports in the possession of Colonel Tod at the time when he was discharged from the army.

The 17th Regiment of Infantry was organized under the Congressional Act of 11 January 1812.[59] On paper, this regiment contained two battalions with nine 110-man companies each.[60] One battalion was headquartered in Kentucky while the other battalion was headquartered in Chillicothe, Ohio. On 28 April 1812, Brigadier General James Winchester ordered Colonel Tod (then a major) to Lexington, Kentucky, to receive instructions in order to form a recruiting service in Ohio.[61] Tod's official orders were dated 9 May 1812.[62]

Ohio was divided into two recruiting districts with Chillicothe serving as the headquarters for the first district in western Ohio and Zanesville as the headquarters for the second district in eastern Ohio. Both of these centers would serve as rendezvous points where recruits would be organized into new companies. After the two districts became operational, Colonel Tod's took command of the 2nd Recruiting District, also known as the District of Zanesville.[63]

---

[58] **George Tod Collection**, Western Reserve Historical Society Archives Library, Cleveland, Ohio, manuscript section, call number MS-3202: container 1B, folders 3 and 9; container 2, folders 4, 5 and 6; container 2A, folders 2 and 3.

[59] Heitman, Francis B., **Historical Register and Dictionary of the United States Army From Its Organization, September 29, 1789, to March 2, 1903**, Volume I, (Genealogical Publishing Company, Baltimore, Maryland: 1994), page 113, Seventeenth Regiment.

[60] Mahon, John K. and Romana Danysh, **Infantry Part 1: Regular Army**, Army Lineage Series, (Office of the Chief of Military History, United States Army, Washington, DC: 1972), page 14, History of the Organization of the Infantry: *Through the Second War with England*.

[61] **Western Reserve and Northern Ohio Historical Society,** Tract Number 15, April 1873, (Cleveland, Ohio: 1877), page 2, Letter from Brigadier General James Winchester to Major George Tod, 28 April 1812.

[62] **Ibid**, page 1, Letter from Brigadier General James Winchester to Major George Tod, 9 May 1812.

[63] "2nd Recruiting District, 17th Regiment of Infantry," 14 June 1812, **George Tod Collection**, Western Reserve Historical Society Archives Library, Cleveland, Ohio, manuscript section, call number MS-3202, container 2A.

On 26 June 1812, the army reorganized its regimental structures and standardized the manpower strengths for its infantry regiments.[64] The 17th Infantry was downsized into ten 109-man companies with an authorized manning level of 1,070 men. At the same time, the second battalion was split off to become 19th Regiment of U.S. Infantry with the same structure and manning as the 17th Infantry.[65] Ohio was assigned the raising of this new regiment.

Although the recruiting service in Ohio was fully functional by June 1812, it appears that no company of Ohioans was activated for the 17th Infantry. The recruiting service in Ohio, with all of its officers and men plus the new recruits, was transferred to the 19th Regiment of U.S. Infantry. Colonel Tod would spend the next two years as the senior recruiter for the 19th Infantry.

Under the Act of 3 March 1814, the 19th Infantry was consolidated with the 17th Infantry to create the new 17th Regiment of U.S. Infantry. Once the merger took effect on 12 May 1814 Colonel Tod was ordered to take up the duties as the senior recruiter for this new regiment. It was his responsibility to merge the existing recruiting services of the 17th and 19th Infantries into a single service.

The U.S. Army kept far better records than the militia. Personal information was kept on each soldier in the form of descriptive reports, which were required to be maintained by each company and regiment. Recruiting reports and discharge musters also contained the same personal information.

Three tables have been constructed using the various recruiting and discharge reports found in the George Tod collection. Only the data with genealogical information is listed. The recruiting officer's name, bounty information and other non-relevant information has been left off these tables. The names of the men from Kentucky were purposely left on these tables since many Kentuckians would settle in northern Ohio after the war ended.

Both regiments were authorized to enlist men for five years, 18 months or "during the war". The men enlisting for five years or during the war were entitled to a full benefits package upon discharge, while those men who enlisted for 18 months received a much smaller package.

Not all of the information was annotated for each man. The age of the soldier is the age when that soldier enlisted. "Where Enlisted" does not show residency only where the enlistment occurred. The soldier could have been living in the same city or county or in one of the surrounding counties at the time of his enlistment. A soldier's trade before the war was extremely important to the army since posts and forts were operated as mini-cities and many of the 'civilian' trades were needed to operate these facilities. If your ancestor was a teamster, he could have been detached from his company in order to help haul supplies from the depots to his post.

These tables only represent a faction of the men who served in the 17th and 19th Regiments of U.S. Infantry during the War of 1812.

```
18 mos – 18 mosnths      Corp – Corporal      Cty - County
5 yr – 5 years           Sgt – Sergeant
DW – During the War      Mus - Musician
```

19th Regiment of U.S. Infantry Enlistments

Name	Age	Height	Birth	Enlisted	Period	Where Enlisted
Alberry, John	19	6' 2 1/2"	Allegeny Cty, MD	22 Jul 1812	18 mos	Zanesville, OH
Armer, Robert				10 May 1813	DW	Cincinnati, OH
Arnold, John	26	5' 8"	Allegeny Cty, MD	6 Jul 1812	5 yr	St. Clairsville, OH
Arthurs, John				10 May 1813	DW	Cincinnati, OH
Arwin, Joseph **						

---

[64] Heitman, Francis B., **Historical Register and Dictionary of the United States Army From Its Organization, September 29, 1789, to March 2, 1903**, Volume II, (Genealogical Publishing Company, Baltimore, Maryland: 1994), pp. 572-573, Organization of the Army under the Act of June 26, 1812.

[65] **Ibid**, Volume I, page 116, Nineteenth Regiment.

Ohio and the War of 1812

Name	Age	Height	Birth	Enlisted	Period	Where Enlisted
Ball, Edward	43	5' 11"	Fauquier Cty, VA	2 Sep 1812		
Blair, Daniel	26	5' 7"	Morris Cty, NJ	16 Jul 1812	18 mos	
Bourn, William				10 April 1813	18 mos	Cincinnati, OH
Bright, George	27	6'	Augusta Cty, VA	2 Aug 1812	18 mos	
Bryan, Cornelius	37	5' 10 1/2"	Rockingham Cty, VA	1 Jul 1812	5 yr	
Bullman, Jonathan	39	5' 8"	Morris Cty, NJ	18 Aug 1812	18 mos	
Burnet, Nehemiah *	21	6' 1 1/2"	Luzerne Cty, PA	24 Jun 1812	5 yr	
Cain, John	30	5' 8"	Trenton Cty, NJ	4 Jul 1812	5 yr	
Calder, Daniel	27	5' 8 1/2"	Scotland	6 Jul 1812	5 yr	
Campbell, Joseph Jr	17	5' 5"	Shenandoah Cty, VA	18 Jul 1812	5 yr	
Campbell, Joseph Sr	43	5' 10"	Ireland	18 Jul 1812	5 yr	
Cavaller, Thomas, Sgt	30	5' 9"	CT	9 Jul 1812	5 yr	
Chapman, Soloman, Corp	22	5' 9 1/2"	Cumberland Cty, PA	6 Jul 1812	18 mos	
Childs, Isaac	42	5' 9"	Burlington Cty, NJ	1 Jul 1812	5 yr	
Cramer, Richard	36	5' 10 1/2"	Baltimore Cty, MD	10 Jul 1812	5 yr	St. Clairsville, OH
Crosser, Jacob	21	5' 8 1/2"	MD	7 Jul 1812	5 yr	
Crum, Abraham	21	5' 9"	Loudoun Cty, VA	1 Sep 1812		
Cunningham, Benjamin	26	5' 10 1/2"	Orange Cty, NY	20 Aug 1812		
Currant, James, Sgt	26	5' 11"	Alleghany Cty, PA	4 Aug 1812	18 mos	Warren, OH
Dalson, James				2 Jun 1813	DW	Cincinnati, OH
Daugherty, Mathew	18	5' 7"	Cumberland Cty, PA	10 Sep 1812	18 mos	
Davis, Benjamin	21	6' 1"	PA	8 Sep 1812		
Davis, Jacob	24	6'	Loudoun Cty, VA	25 Aug 1812	5 yr	
Devault, Edward	18	5' 7"	Prince Georges Cty, MD	22 Jun 1812	5 yr	
Donahaue, David	43	6' 1"	New Castle Cty, DE	4 Aug 1812		
Doughty, Daniel	31	6'	Sussex Cty, NJ	7 Jul 1812	5 yr	
Dunseath, David				6 May 1813	18 mos	Cincinnati, OH
Duval, Presberry *	32	5' 7 3/4"	RI	4 Aug 1812		
Dyar, Conrad **	18	5' 5 3/4"		22 Aug 1812		
Edgin, Martin	18	5' 7"	MD	18 Jul 1812	5 yr	
Edminson, William	32	5' 10"	Ireland	6 Jul 1812	5 yr	St. Clairsville, OH
Enimans, Elisha	23	5' 11"	Monmouth Cty, NJ	30 Jul 1812	18 mos	
Fairhurth, David	23	5' 11"	Loudoun Cty, VA	10 Jul 1812	5 yr	St. Clairsville, OH
Fisher, Thomas, Sgt	23	5' 11"	PA	20 Jul 1812	18 mos	
French, John, Sgt	26	5' 9"	NH	1 Jul 1812	5 yr	
Fryman, Frederick	24	6' 2"	Shenandoah Cty, VA	7 Jul 1812	18 mos	St. Clairsville, OH
Fulton, Edward	22	5' 7"	PA	26 Jul 1812	18 mos	
Gibson, John	27	5' 7 1/2"	Fayette Cty, PA	1 Jul 1812	5 yr	
Gordon, Thomas				27 Apr 1813	DW	Cincinnati, OH
Grant, William	38	5' 8"	Worcester Cty, MA	27 Aug 1812		
Haning, Aaron **	29	5' 8"	NJ	26 Aug 1812		
Hannah, Robert **	17	5' 5"	Washington Cty, PA	12 Jul 1812		
Harvey, William	19	5' 6"	Great Britain	2 Jul 1812	5 yr	
Haughey, Jacob	33	5' 9"	New Castle Cty, DE	20 Aug 1812		
Haukpal, Conrad	18	5' 5"	Allegany Cty, MD	13 Jul 1812	5 yr	
Higgins, Daniel	42	5' 7"	County Derry, Ireland	8 Aug 1812		
Hill, William	23	5' 6 1/2"	Otsego Cty, NY	17 Aug 1812		
Jackman, Barnard				24 Apr 1813	DW	Cincinnati, OH
Lamb, Richard	25	6'	Washington Cty, PA	11 Jul 1812	5 yr	St. Clairsville, OH
Lawrence, Andrew **	25	5' 8"	DE	26 Aug 1812		
Leavitt, William, Sgt	30	5' 10"	Suffield, Hartford Cty, CT	9 Jul 1812	5 yr	
Love, James H.	32	5' 6"	Ireland	27 Jul 1812	5 yr	
Lufft, Frederick				14 Apr 1813	5 yr	Cincinnati, OH
Madden, James	23	5' 6 1/2"	Ireland	28 Jul 1812		
Madden, Thomas	23	5' 6 1/2"	Ireland	28 Jul 1812	5 yr	
Malony, Samuel	26	5' 6"	Philadelphia Cty, PA	27 Jul 1812	18 mos	
Marrs, James				10 May 1813	18 mos	Cincinnati, OH
Marshall, William	23	5' 5 1/2"	Frederick Cty, VA	22 Jun 1812	5 yr	
McCallaster, Walter	21	5' 9"	PA	30 Jul 1812	18 mos	
McConken, Samuel **			NJ			
McCoy, James, Corp	20	5' 11"	Shenandoah Cty, VA	22 Jun 1812	5 yr	
McKinsey, John	30	5' 6 1/2"	Allegany Cty, MD	2 Jul 1812	5 yr	
McKnight, Alpheus	18	5' 8"	Suffield, Hartford Cty, CT	14 Jul 1812	5 yr	
McMahon, James **	31	5' 8 1/2"	Ireland	11 Jul 1812	5 yr	

Name	Age	Height	Birth	Enlisted	Period	Where Enlisted
Mead, Jeremiah **		5' 9 1/2"	CT	30 Jun 1812		
Meddles, Joseph	22	5' 9"	PA	22 Jul 1812	18 mos	
Meek, Samuel	21	5' 8"	PA	7 Jul 1812	5 yr	St. Clairsville, OH
Mick, James	21	5' 8"	Washington Cty, PA	7 Jul 1812	5 yr	
Montgomery, William				14 May 1813	DW	Cincinnati, OH
Moore, John	22	6' 1"	Washington Cty, PA	11 Jul 1812	5 yr	
Moore, John	21	5' 10"	MD	8 Aug 1812	18 mos	
Murphy, William				16 Apr 1813	DW	Cincinnati, OH
Nicholson, George	19	5' 5 1/4"	Fayette Cty, PA	27 Jul 1812	5 yr	
Oliver, Robert	30	6' 1 1/4"	Chester Cty, PA	1 Jul 1812	5 yr	
Patch, Joshua	21	5' 7"	Hillsborough Cty, NH	25 Jul 1812	5 yr	Zanesville, OH
Patch, Samuel Sgt	23	5' 8"	Hillsborough Cty, NH	1 Jul 1812	5 yr	
Patterson, Joseph **	22	5' 8 3/4"	Washington Cty, PA	24 Aug 1812		
Paulin, David	44	5' 11"	NJ	21 Jul 1812	5 yr	
Pearson, Robert **	19	5' 7 1/2"	Hardy Cty, VA	22 Aug 1812		
Peters, Ebenezer				8 May 1813	DW	Cincinnati, OH
Pew, James	24	5' 10"	NY	18 Jul 1812	18 mos	
Prophet, James				9 Apr 1813	5 yr	Cincinnati, OH
Robinson, Thomas				26 Apr 1813	5 yr	Cincinnati, OH
Routh, Joseph				30 Mar 1813	18 mos	Cincinnati, OH
Saltsgiver, Jacob	21	5' 7"	Adams Cty, PA	27 Jul 1812	5 yr	Warren, OH
Serow, Leonard				3 May 1813	DW	Cincinnati, OH
Sheller, Samuel **		5' 5 1/2"	Lancaster Cty, PA	5 Jul 1812		
Shriver, James	22	5' 7"	Georgetown, Prince Georges Cty, MD	25 Jul 1812	5 yr	Zanesville, OH
Smith, John	19	5' 9"	PA	3 Apr 1813		Mt. Vernon, OH
Smith, Richard	21	5' 5"	Queen Anne's Cty, MD	18 Jul 1812	5 yr	
Stackpole, Conrad	18	5' 5"	Allegany Cty, MD	13 Jul 1812	5 yr	
Stewart, John				26 Mar 1813	18 mos	Cincinnati, OH
Strupple, John	18	5' 6"	PA	30 Jul 1812	5 yr	
Stultz, Adam	28	5' 8"	Northhampton Cty, PA	19 Jun 1812	5 yr	
Swaney, Frederick **		5' 5 1/2"	Washington Cty, PA	10 Jul 1812		
Teal, Nicholas **	49	6'	Baltimore Cty, MD	19 Aug 1812		
Thompson, John	36	5' 6"	Somerset Cty, England	3 Apr 1813		Mt. Vernon, OH
Thompson, John				29 Apr 1813	DW	Cincinnati, OH
Tyroder, James	37	5' 7"	Guernsey, England	15 Jul 1812	5 yr	
Vance, Daniel	18	5' 7 1/2"	Green Cty, KY	31 Jul 1812	18 mos	
Walters, Henry	24	5' 8 1/2"	MD	30 Jul 1812	5 yr	
Wartember, Francis **			NJ	30 Aug 1812		
Weaver, Adam				1 May 1813	DW	Cincinnati, OH
Wellington, Thomas	20	5' 9"	VA	30 Jul 1812	18 mos	
Wells, James	19	5' 3"	Allegany Cty, MD	26 Jul 1812	5 yr	
Wells, Thomas, Sgt	36	5' 10"	VA	15 Jul 1812	18 mos	
Whetsone, Jasper				16 Apr 1813	5 yr	Cincinnati, OH
Wiley, James	28	5' 10"	Fayette Cty, PA	27 Jul 1812	5 yr	
Wiley, John	28	5' 10"	Fayette Cty, PA	27 Jul 1812	5 yr	Zanesville, OH
Wilson, James	19	5' 10 1/2"	Allegheny Cty, PA	3 Sep 1812		
Windel, James				30 Jan 1813	18 mos	Cincinnati, OH

* Deserted after enlisting
** Enlisted in the 2nd Regiment of U.S. Artillery

17th Regiment of U.S. Infantry Enlistments

Name	Enlistment	Period	Where Enlisted
Baily, Benjamin	15 Jun 1814	DW	Lexington, KY
Ball, Edward	2 Sep 1812	18 mos	
Banfill, Enoch	18 Dec 1814	DW	West Union, OH
Bays, Francis	31 Mar 1814	18 mos	Lexington, KY
Brown, James	27 Apr 1814	DW	Lexington, KY
Cameron, William	4 Jan 1815	5 yr	West Union, OH
Cash, John	6 Jan 1815	DW	Xenia, OH
Collins, James	15 Jan 1815	5 yr	Xenia, OH

Ohio and the War of 1812

Name	Enlistment	Period	Where Enlisted
Cornwell, David	22 Apr 1814	DW	Lexington, KY
Covington, Benjamin	12 Jan 1815	5 yr	West Union, OH
Crum, Alexander	1 Sep 1812	5 yr	
Cryssett, Samuel	4 Jan 1814	18 mos	Lexington, KY
Curren, Robert	21 Dec 1814	DW	West Union, OH
Davis, Benjamin	8 Sep 1812	18 mos	
Davison, Jabe L.	8 Dec 1814	5 yr	West Union, OH
Davison, Samuel	16 Jan 1815	DW	West Union, OH
Eghew, Samuel	15 May 1814	DW	Lexington, KY
Forrester, Robert	30 Dec 1813	DW	Lexington, KY
Hall, Joseph	4 Jan 1815	DW	West Union, OH
Haughey, Jacob	13 Jun 1814	DW	Lexington, KY
Higgins, Daniel	31 Aug 1812	18 mos	
Hughey, J. H.	25 May 1814	DW	Lexington, KY
Marsh, William	15 Apr 1814	5 yr	Lexington, KY
McKee, Jonathan	8 Aug 1812	18 mos	
Miller, Isaac A.	15 Jan 1815	DW	Xenia, OH
Mills, Samuel	17 Dec 1814	5 yr	West Union, OH
Morehead, Obed	16 Jan 1815	DW	West Union, OH
Morrison, T. L.	6 Feb 1814	18 mos	Lexington, KY
Robinson, Otis	5 Jan 1814	18 mos	Lexington, KY
Schooley, James	14 Jan 1815	5 yr	Xenia, OH
Shelhour, Jacob	12 Jan 1815	5 year	West Union, OH
Smith, William	1 Dec 1814	DW	Xenia, OH
Snodgrass, James	13 Jan 1815	5 yr	Xenia, OH
Steelman, James	13 Jan 1815	5 yr	Xenia, OH
Stewart, James	22 Apr 1814	DW	Lexington, KY
Sturdevail, Iris	5 Jan 1814	18 mos	Lexington, KY
Taylor, L. H.	27 Jan 1814	DW	Lexington, KY
Willson, Earl	22 Dec 1814	DW	Xenia, OH
Wilson, James	3 Sep 1812	18 mos	

17th Regiment of U.S. Infantry
Honorable Discharges – During the War Enlistments

Name	Rank	Age	Height	Birth	Trade	Enlisted	Where Enlisted
Aiso, Morris	Pvt	22	5' 6"	PA	Farmer	5 Jun 1814	
Alridge, Thomas	Pvt	37		RI	Carpenter	15 Jul 1814	Portsmouth, OH
Armstrong, William	Sgt	36	5' 6"	Ireland	Laborer	24 May 1814	
Baldwin, John	Pvt	44	5' 11"	Albermarle Cty, VA	Laborer	17 Feb 1814	
Blickman, Nathanial	Pvt	32	5' 9"	Morristown, NJ	Bricklayer	2 Apr 1814	Detroit, MI
Boothe, John	Pvt	5	6' 1/2"	VA	Hatter	12 Jun 1814	
Brinkley, Alex.	Pvt	18	5'	Halifax Cty, NC	Laborer	22 Apr 1813	Logan County, KY
Brinkley, William	Pvt	45	5' 7 1/2"	NC	Laborer	22 Apr 1813	Logan County, KY
Brown, Hugh	Pvt	25	5' 6 1/2"	Northumberland Cty, PA	Shoemaker	25 Jun 1814	New Lisbon, OH
Brown, Samuel	Pvt	26	6' 1"	Washington Cty, VA		3 May 1813	
Brownfield, John	Pvt	46	5' 11"	Berkeley Cty, VA	Laborer	25 Aug 1813	
Buck, John	Pvt	22	5' 9"	PA	Farmer	24 May 1814	
Buck, Joseph	Pvt	16	5' 4"	OH	Farmer	9 Jun 1814	
Burns, John	Pvt	22	5' 9"	Nelson Cty, KY	Laborer	10 May 1814	
Byard, John	Pvt	35	6' 1"	PA	Laborer	29 Apr 1814	
Cecil, B. Henry	Pvt	31	5' 10"	Frederick, MD	Laborer	4 Apr 1814	Detroit, MI
Chalfin, Robert	Pvt	23		VA	Carpenter	22 Jun 1814	Cincinnati, OH
Chambers, Jonathan	Pvt	22	5' 9"	NY	Nailer		Portsmouth, OH
Champ, Nathaniel	Sgt	21		Hardy Cty, VA	Farmer	7 Jun 1813	Circleville, OH
Chartwright, George	Pvt	19	5' 8"	MI	Laborer	3 May 1814	Detroit, MI
Cleming, James	Pvt	22	6'	Charles Cty, MD	Farmer	16 Jun 1814	
Clendennings, John	Pvt	34	5' 9 1/2"	Franklin Cty, PA	Farmer	30 Jun 1814	Franklinton, OH
Cook, Solomon	Pvt	20		Ralland Cty, VT	Laborer	13 Mar 1813	Franklinton, OH
Courtney, Nicholas	Pvt	21	5' 7"	VA	Farmer	30 May 1814	
Crow, Edward	Corp	20	5' 6 1/2"	Baltimore Cty, MD	Tanner	2 Mar 1814	Franklinton, OH

Ohio and the War of 1812

Name	Rank	Age	Height	Birth	Trade	Enlisted	Where Enlisted
Davis, Daniel	Sgt	23		Washington Cty, PA	Laborer	12 Mar 1814	Hamilton, OH
Decher, John	Pvt	35	5' 1"	Germany	Farmer	25 May 1814	
Denningsburgh, William	Pvt	23	5' 4 1/2"	Baltimore, MD	Wheelwright	1 Apr 1814	Detroit, MI
Dolson, Nathan	Pvt	27		Northumberland Cty, PA	Laborer	16 May 1813	Franklinton, OH
Dougherty, James	Corp	20	5' 9"	Jefferson Cty, TN	Farmer	15 May 1814	Limestone, KY
Doughty, Zachaniah	Pvt	20		Paris Cty, KY	Farmer	3 Jul 1813	Cincinnati, OH
Dummand, Robert	Pvt	18	6' 1/2"	Mason Cty, KY	Farmer	31 May 1814	Limestone, KY
Ellis, William	Pvt	25	5' 6"	Liverpool, England	Blacksmith	12 May 1814	Detroit, MI
Fry, Jacob	Pvt	35		York Cty, PA	Miller	22 mar 1813	Chillicothe, OH
Gable, Abraham	Pvt	21	5' 8"	Shanadoah Cty, VA	Laborer	7 Mar 1813	Franklinton, OH
Green, George	Pvt	38	6'	Louisa Cty, VA	Carpenter	21 Jul 1814	Franklinton, OH
Green, Samuel	Pvt		5' 11"	Hamphire Cty, VA	Hatter	21 Jul 1813	Chillicothe, OH
Hattfield, William	Pvt	37	5'	Berkley Cty, VA	Farmer	20 Jun 1814	
Helsley, Jacob	Pvt	23	5' 9"	Shanadoah Cty, VA	Laborer	6 Jul 1813	
Houghley, Jacob	Sgt	34	5' 10"	New Castle Cty, DE	Farmer	23 Jun 1814	Chillicothe, OH
Hoyte, Lewis	Sgt	32		Fairfield Cty, CT	Hatter	22 Jun 1814	New Lisbon, OH
Hull, Jesse	Pvt	35	5'	NJ	Farmer	15 Apr 1814	
Hull, Samuel	Pvt	25	5' 7"	PA	Blacksmith	29 Apr 1814	Detroit, MI
Hutchings, Henry	Pvt	22		Hampshire Cty, MA	Hatter	25 Jul 1813	Portsmouth, OH
Irwin, Benjamin	Pvt	33	5' 7 1/2"	Rockbridge Cty, VA	Laborer	31 May 1814	
Isabeart, Jacob	Pvt	27	5' 5"	Northhampton Cty, PA	Carpenter	7 Apr 1814	
Jackman, Bernard	Corp	20	5' 7"	Brownsville, PA	Laborer	24 Apr 1813	Cincinnati, OH
Jones, Benjamin	Pvt	22	5' 8"	Philadelphia, PA	Tanner	21 Apr 1814	Detroit, MI
Kelly, John	Pvt	55		Ireland	Laborer	27 Jul 1813	Chillicothe, OH
Kerns, Richard	Pvt	30	5' 11 1/2"	Ireland	Carpenter	13 May 1814	
Kerr, William	Pvt	18	5' 4"	Allegheny Cty, PA	Laborer	7 May 1814	
King, James	Sgt	22	5' 10 1/2"	Jefferson Cty, KY	Laborer	22 Jul 1815	Louisville, KY
Lane, Elhaneth	Sgt	26	5' 11"	Swanney, Cheshire Cty, NH	Laborer	24 Mar 1814	Hamilton, OH
Lapping, Robert	Pvt	33	5' 10"	PA	Distiller	11 Jun 1814	
Lasher, Jacob	Pvt	19	5' 11"	PA	Laborer	20 May 1814	
Lee, Thomas	Pvt	45		Ireland	Laborer	8 Mar 1813	Franklinton, OH
Lewis, William T.	Pvt	19	5' 11 1/2"	Bracken Cty, KY	Laborer	26 Mar 1814	Limestone, KY
Loar, John	Mus	26	5' 10"	Allegany Cty, MD	Stone mason	7 Mar 1813	
Marr, James	Pvt	22	5' 5"	PA	Laborer	2 Apr 1814	Detroit, MI
Matto, Joshua	Pvt	26	5' 10"	Summersett Cty, MD	Laborer	2 Apr 1814	Detroit, MI
McCord, James	Pvt	17	5' 3"	Nicholas Cty, KY	Wagon maker	31 Mar 1814	Limestone, KY
McCormack, Valentino	Pvt	25	5' 7"	Allegheny Cty, PA	Hatter	15 Dec 1813	Frankford, KY
McCullen, Sheldon	Pvt	20	5' 3"	VA	Laborer	24 Jun 1814	
McGinnis, John	Pvt	35	5' 11"	Ireland	Laborer	4 Mar 1814	
McLeonold, Shase	Pvt	34	5'	Ireland	Laborer	22 Apr 1814	
McMurray, Samuel	Pvt	25		Lincoln Cty, KY	Shoemaker	17 Feb 1184	Chillicothe, OH
McNeil, Alexander	Pvt	22	5' 11 1/2"	NY		5 Jan 1814	
Miller, Jacob	Pvt	33	5' 11"	New Haven, CT	Blacksmith	7 Sep 1813	
Montgomery, John	Pvt	28	5' 10"	PA	Laborer		
Moore, Joseph	Pvt	35	5'	Fayette Cty, PA	Laborer	10 May 1814	Limestone, KY
Morton, Washington	Pvt	21	5' 10"	Cincinnati, OH	Tanner	3 Feb 1813	Cincinnati, OH
Murr, Thomas	Pvt	26		Frederick Cty, VA	Laborer	5 Mar 1813	Franklinton, OH
Nida, Philip	Pvt	28	5' 11"	PA	Laborer	28 Apr 1814	
Northrup, Asa	Sgt	29	5' 10"	Lower Canada	Carpenter	5 Mar 1814	Brookville, OH
Otlinger, Meschesba	Sgt	40	6'	MD	Blacksmith	1 Oct 1813	
Palmer, Jesse W.	Pvt	21		CT	Distiller	17 Aug 1814	Cleveland, OH
Park, James	Corp	21	5' 11"	Adams Cty, PA	Farmer	7 Jun 1814	Limestone, KY
Peoples, Laymous	Pvt	26	5' 9"	Chester Cty, PA	Carpenter	30 Mar 1814	Franklinton, OH
Ray, Aaron	Pvt	20	5' 9"	Madison Cty, KY	Blacksmith	11 Dec 1813	
Reed, Robert	Pvt	24	5' 8 3/4"	Jefferson Cty, KY	Laborer	25 Jun 1814	Limestone, KY
Rheam, Adam	Corp	21	5' 10"	Dauphin Cty, PA	Hatter	13 Jan 1813	Portsmouth, OH
Risley, Charles	Pvt	38	5' 8"	PA	Laborer	23 Aug 1813	
Rook, James	Pvt	23	5'	MD	Laborer	14 Jun 1814	
Rudulph, ?	Pvt	21	5' 10"	MD	Shoemaker	21 May 1814	Warren, OH
Ruggles, Nicholas	Pvt	25	6'	KY	Laborer	1 Jul 1814	Chillicothe, OH
Rumsey, Samuel A.	Pvt	31	5' 11"	NJ	Brick maker	4 May 1814	Warren, OH

Ohio and the War of 1812

Name	Rank	Age	Height	Birth	Trade	Enlisted	Where Enlisted
Ryan, Patrick	Pvt	18		Ireland	Laborer	28 Jan 1814	Steubenville, OH
Sayer, Joseph	Pvt	38	5' 6"	Somerset Cty, NJ	Laborer	14 Feb 1814	
Scott, James	Pvt	36	5' 11"	York, York Cty, PA	Clerk	17 May 1814	
Scudder, Thomas	Pvt	19		NJ	Laborer	27 Apr 1814	Hamilton, OH
Severs, John	Pvt	23	5' 9"	NJ	Laborer	27 Apr 1814	Detroit, MI
Seward, John L.	Sgt		5' 7 1/2"	Fayette Cty, PA	Laborer	22 Jul 1813	Lebanon, OH
Shoemaker, Henry	Pvt	21	5' 9"	Beaver Cty, PA	Blacksmith	14 Jan 1813	
Shultz, Henry	Pvt	17	5'	Bedford, Bedford Cty, PA	Laborer	21 Nov 1813	
Sickman, Presley	Pvt	25	5' 9"	PA	Laborer	18 Jun 1814	
Simmans, Thomas	Pvt	21	5' 6"	Frederick Cty, VA	Laborer	14 Mar 1814	Franklinton, OH
Simpson, John	Sgt	27		Ireland	Sailor	7 Jun 1814	Cincinnati, OH
Smartsfeller, Adam	Pvt	28		PA	Carpenter	29 Jun 1814	Cincinnati, OH
Smith, John	Pvt	30	5' 10"	Hawkins Cty, TN	Laborer	3 Apr 1814	Cleveland, OH
Snyder, Jacob	Pvt	21		VA	Laborer	22 Jun 1814	Cincinnati, OH
Starnes, Luther	Pvt	27		Addison Cty, VT	Laborer	4 Jun 1813	Cleveland, OH
Steward, Edward	Pvt	31	6' 1/2"	Charles Cty, MD	Cooper	18 May 1814	Limestone, KY
Sturgeon, Thomas	Pvt	19	5' 6"	Mason Cty, KY	Laborer	21 Mar 1812	
Summers, Frederick	Pvt	21	5' 9"	Washington Cty, MD	Laborer	23 May 1814	Limestone, KY
Suthern, Levin	Pvt	28	5' 6"	Hartford Cty, VA	Miller	6 Feb 1814	Limestone, KY
Sutton, Mariah	Pvt	20	5' 5"	PA	Laborer	30 Apr 1814	Detroit, MI
Swartwood, Abraham	Pvt	47	5' 10"	PA	Laborer	23 Jan 1814	Erie, PA
Symonds, Daniel	Pvt	22	5' 8 3/4"	Montgomery Cty, MD	Laborer	9 Jun 1814	Limestone, KY
Thompson, John	Pvt	30	5' 8"	NJ	Bricklayer	29 Apr 1813	Cincinnati, OH
Tompson, William	Pvt	22		Lancaster Cty, PA	Laborer	22 Jun 1813	Hamilton, OH
Trowbridge, Amia K.	Pvt	19	5' 7"	Allegheny Cty, PA	Laborer	9 Jun 1814	Limestone, KY
Tuttle, Jabez	Pvt	28	5' 8"	Morris, Morris Cty, NJ	Tanner	27 Apr 1814	Detroit, MI
Waggoner, Michael	Pvt	26	5' 10"	Bergen Cty, NJ	Laborer	2 Apr 1814	Detroit, MI
Walk, John D.	Sgt	23	5' 10"	Franklin Cty, PA	Chair Maker	7 Mar 1814	Franklinton, OH
Wallace, William	Sgt	35	5' 10"	VA	Taylor	25 Jul 1814	Cincinnati, OH
Watraut, William	Pvt	27	5' 10"	CT	Laborer	10 Apr 1814	Marietta, OH
Whitman, William	Sgt	20		Philadelphia Cty, PA	Laborer	17 Jan 1814	Warren Cty, OH
Wilcox, William	Sgt	28	5' 8"	MA	Laborer	26 Feb 1814	Hamilton, OH
Willey, Frederick	Pvt	35		Germany	Laborer	21 May 1813	Cleveland, OH
Willson, Thomas	Pvt	21		Fayette Cty, KY		9 Jun 1814	Cincinnati, OH
Wingard, James	Sgt					11 May 1813	
Young, William	Pvt	22	5' 9"	Warren Cty, SC	Laborer	9 Sep 1813	

Ohio's forgotten military cemeteries

The nation's military cemeteries were not created in this country until the end of the American Civil War. Very few cemeteries have survived for those veterans who had died in the early wars of our country, particularly, the Revolutionary War and the War of 1812. Thousands of gravestones are marked for those veterans who were fortunate enough to have survived a war and who had later died at home. Those who fell on the battlefield or who had died by disease are less likely to have a known location for their burial let alone a gravestone or a marker.

From the Indian wars of the 1790's to the end of the War of 1812, Ohio was a main battleground for the conflicts with the Indians and later the British. At most of the battlefields, forts and posts located within the state, cemeteries were established to bury the dead. These cemeteries were never maintained after the end of each of these conflicts and today the majority of these cemeteries are lost and forgotten.

Samuel R. Brown was a militiaman in the Pennsylvania militia who served in Ohio during the War of 1812. After the war he wrote the *Views of the Campaigns of the North-Western Army*. This book is a history of the American military campaign in the northwest, and it is also a diary of his personal experiences during the war.

Brown writes in his book, "I went frequently to the burying grounds to count the fresh graves and mark the progress of death. My heart sickened at the sight. By inspecting those of Detroit, Fort Meigs, Portage, Sandusky, Erie, Buffalo and Eleven Mile Creek, and by ascertaining the loss sustained by different corps, I was enabled to form a pretty correct estimate of the number of deaths by sickness. The aggregate was alarming."[66]

Detroit, Michigan, had two military cemeteries, one started by the French and used by both the British and the Americans and another cemetery just west of Fort Detroit in which 700 American soldiers from the War of 1812 were buried. These two cemeteries are long gone because of the development of downtown Detroit.

Fort Meigs is in Perrysville, Ohio, while Camp Portage is in present day Port Clinton, Ohio. Sandusky is Fort Stephenson in Fremont, Ohio, while Fort Erie is in Ontario, Canada, across from Buffalo, New York. Buffalo had a cemetery in what is now downtown Buffalo while Eleven Mile Creek is in Williamsville, New York, just northeast of Buffalo, where there was an army barracks and a hospital.

Brown's statement is significant since he was able to determine how many men from the different army regiments and militia units were buried at each of these locations. It shows that the army had maintained the graves and that each grave had a marker, probably of wood, in which the soldier's name, date of death and the unit's name were inscribed. After the war these cemeteries were neglected, the markers rotted away and nature reclaimed the location of the graves.

Brown used the Petersburgh Volunteers, a volunteer militia company from Virginia, as an example for his estimates on the number of deaths per company. He said that the company came to Ohio with 101 men and that 22 had died from disease and four were killed in battle. Four men were still in hospitals when the company was discharged from military duty, and he doubted that the remaining 70 men would all make it home to Virginia. "From what I have heard and seen, I am induced to believe that the loss by disease, sustained by the northern army, is in the same proportion,"[67] he said.

Using these observations, Brown concluded that approximately one third of the men who served in the Army of the Northwest in the War of 1812 died on the battlefield or by disease. This estimate is probably too high since many companies, both regular army and militia, never participated in a battle or were in an area plagued by diseases. But, for every soldier who was killed in the war there were probably two or three men who died from disease or illness.

---

[66] Brown, Samuel R., **Views of the Campaigns of the North-Western Army,** (Philadelphia, Pennsylvania: Griggs and Dickinson, Printers, 1815), page 115.

[67] **Ibid,** page 116.

In the *Historical Register and Dictionary of the United States Army From Its Organization, September 29, 1789, to March 2, 1903*,[68] it is stated that 65 officers and 1,235 enlisted men in the regular army were killed during the war and that 577 militiamen were killed. This book does not mention the thousands of deaths and injuries caused by disease, accidents, and weather related illnesses. These other casualties were inflected upon both the regular forces and the militia on both sides of the battle line.

William Jay published a listing of the number of men who were killed during the War of 1812 in a table organized by location and event.[69] He states that 149 Americans and 15 British soldiers were killed at Fort Meigs. Multiply these numbers by three for the men who died at or near the fort then there may have been 500 men or more who were buried at the fort's cemetery or near by. Jay also states that 194 men were wounded at Fort Meigs. Of these men, many would have died from wounds days or months after the conflict. Days after the first siege was over, parties of soldiers were sent from the fort to bury the dead and to look for survivors. Across the river from the fort the remains of the men killed when Colonel Dudley's militia from Kentucky was ambushed by the Indians were located and the men were buried where they fell.

Fort Stephenson had a total of 17 Americans killed, and 25 British soldiers were killed or died from wounds during the course of the war. The Battle of Lake Erie saw 24 Americans and 70 British soldiers, marines and sailors killed in action, and they were buried 'at sea' off Middle Sister Island. Three American officers and three British officers were buried in a common grave at Put-in-Bay, South Bass Island. There was probably an enlisted men's cemetery located at Put-in-Bay also. Brown stated that there was a regular soldier who was shot for desertion at Put-in-Bay on 24 September 1813, and other soldiers probably died there during the war.[70]

A short distance down the Maumee River from Fort Meigs was the remains of an old British fort, which became the British headquarters during both of the sieges. After the first siege, the Americans found fresh graves at this old fort. and apparently they had been marked since the men knew which were British and which were the American graves.

Up the river within sight of Fort Meigs was the site of the Battle of Fallen Timbers. There were 30 American soldiers killed during this battle on 20 August 1794, and they were buried on this battle site.[71] A total of 632 Americans were killed by Indians during St. Clair's Defeat on 4 November 1791 in western Ohio. These men were also buried at this battle site.

Between the American Revolution and the end of the War of 1812, there may have been as many as three to four thousand American soldiers and militiamen who died and are buried in Ohio. Add to this number the British and Indians killed and this number multiplies. We can only estimate the number of men who died during this time period, and we leave it up to the Almighty to know where they are all buried.

---

[68] Heitman, Francis B., **Historical Register and Dictionary of the United States Army From Its Organization, September 29, 1789, to March 2, 1903**, Volume II, (Genealogical Publishing Company, Baltimore, Maryland: 1994), Part II, chronological list of battles, page 281.

[69] **Collections of the New York Historical Society**, second series, Volume II, (New York: 1849), Table of the Killed and Wounded in the War of 1812, by William Jay.

[70] Brown, Samuel R., **Views of the Campaigns of the North-Western Army**, (Philadelphia, Pennsylvania: Griggs and Dickinson, Printers, 1815), page 58.

[71] Gillett, Mary C., **The Army Medical Department 1775-1818**, (Washington, D.C.: U.S. Government Printing Office, 1981), Chapter 6, Between Wars 1783 to June 1812.

The War of 1812 pensioners in the Pension List of 1818

The book, *Revolutionary Pensioners of 1818*, is actually a misnomer for it deals with both the military pensioners of the Revolutionary War and the recently ended War of 1812. The list, also called the Pension List of 1818, is divided into two parts. Part A is sub-divided into the *List of Invalid Pensioners of the United States* (Revolutionary War service) and the *List of Half-pay Pensioners of the United States* (War of 1812). Part B, entitled *Statement showing the Widows and Orphans*, lists only the War of 1812 pensioners. This article will only deal with the War of 1812 pensioners.

The 1818 pension list was compiled during 1817 and published by the United States Senate on 28 March 1818. It lists all of the pensioners by state, territory and district. Ohio had 99 men on the pension roll from the Revolutionary War and 194 men from the War of 1812. All of Ohio's Revolutionary War pensioners had served from other states.

This is by no means a complete list of Ohioans who were entitled to a pension by the federal government. This list has only the men who were injured on duty or wounded in action and the heirs of the men who had died on duty or were killed in action who had applied and were approved for a pension by 1817. Many pension applications were still pending approval. This is actually an invalid pension list.

Service pensions, those given to veterans or their widows, would be issued years after 1818 based upon the number of days that a veteran served. Many pension applications were rejected for one reason or other. More veterans or their heirs would apply for a pension years after the War of 1812 was over. One sad note is that single men who died during the war did not receive an invalid pension since they left no heirs, widows or children.

Widows only received a pension for five years or until they remarried. Veterans who were injured or wounded received a pension only until a doctor certified that a veteran no longer needed a pension. Pensions during this time period only helped the veterans or their heirs to get back on their feet. It was not intended to be a long-term benefit.

Half-pay Pensioners from the 1818 Pension Rolls (War of 1812) [72]

This is a list of heirs who elected to receive half pay for five years instead of land bounties for compensation for the loss of their husbands or fathers who served in the regular army. All of these men had a child or children and it was required to have guardianships for these heirs. Check the local courthouse where the family lived in order to obtain the guardianship papers for the children.

Soldier	Guardian of the Heirs	Rank	Per annum
Hallman, Stephen	Anthony Ritzer	Private	$48.00
Rice, John	Rosanna Rice	"	48.00
Timmons, Eli	Naomi Timmons	"	48.00
Everhart, Samuel	Harris, Amos	"	48.00
March, William	George Foglesong	"	48.00
North, Zachariah	John Marks	Corporal	60.00
Oliver, Robert	Robert Taylor	Private	48.00
Fryman, Henry	David Jennings	"	48.00
Dodds, Joseph	Samuel Hearn	"	48.00
Davis, Jacob W.	Peter Grubb	Sergeant	66.00
Landsdown, William	Henry H. Evans	Private	48.00
Morrison, Robert	Davis, Nicholas	"	48.00
Gaston, Hugh	Moses Crist	"	48.00

---

[72] **Pensioners of the U.S., 1818, Invalids & Half Pay Pensioners, Widows & Orphans**, (Washington, D.C.: E. De Krafft, 1818), Half-Pay Pensioners, Ohio, page 209.

Pensioners from the 1818 Pension Rolls (War of 1812) [73]

For the most part, this listing is for the heirs of militiamen who had died or were killed during the war. The "Paid Started" is the first day in which the pension started which is also the date of death. The remarks column shows which widows remarried and the date of their remarriage before 1818. Many widows would have remarried after 1818.

Nbr	Soldier	Heirs W=Widows W&C = Widows & children	Rank	Paid started (Date of death)	Per annum	Remarks
1120	Anderson, William	W	Private	22 Nov 1813	$48.00	
1121	Allebaugh, John	"	"	27 Sep 1813	48.00	
1122	Asbel, Robert	"	"	25 Dec 1813	48.00	
1123	Boulebough, Abraham	W & C	"	28 Feb 1814	48.00	Widow intermarried 15 Oct 1814
1124	Ball, Isaiah	W	"	1 Jan 1814	48.00	Widow intermarried 3 Aug 1815
1125	Beason, James	"	"	7 Apr 1814	48.00	Widow intermarried 17 Oct 1815
1126	Briney, Frederick	"	"	29 Jul 1813	48.00	
1127	Bryant, John	"	"	20 Jul 1813	48.00	
1128	Bigham, Alexander	"	"	20 Jul 1813	48.00	
1129	Brown, Clayton	"	"	9 Nov 1813	48.00	
1130	Baldwin, Caleb	W & C	First Lieutenant	9 Mar 1813	180.00	Widow intermarried 5 Jun 1816
1131	Britton, Apollo	W	Private	20 Dec 1813	48.00	
1132	Beans, Moses	W & C	"	16 Dec 1813	48.00	Widow intermarried 14 Aug 1815
1133	Berryman, John	W	"	17 Nov 1813	48.00	
1134	Borden, George	"	"	11 Jul 1812	48.00	
1135	Boots, George	"	Corporal	22 Nov 1812	43.92	
1136	Baily, Thomas Z.	"	Private	29 Jul 1813	48.00	Widow intermarried 30 Nov 1815
1137	Brozier, Peter	"	"	24 Aug 1814	48.00	
1138	Boatman, George	"	"	5 Apr 1814	48.00	Widow intermarried 18 Jan 1817
1139	Bowman, Gilbert	"	"	8 Nov 1813	48.00	
1140	Brandlebury, Jacob	"	"	23 Feb 1813	48.00	
1141	Boerstler, Jacob	"	Captain	5 Aug 1812	240.00	
1142	Clark, Stephanus	"	Corporal	23 Mar 1814	60.00	
1143	Cooksey, Josiah	"	Private	5 Aug 1813	48.00	Widow intermarried 27 May 1815
1144	Chance, William	"	"	10 Dec 1813	48.00	
1145	Colby, Samuel	W & C	"	21 May 1813	48.00	Widow intermarried 23 Jun 1814
1146	Carpenter, Joseph	W	Captain	20 Feb 1814	240.00	
1147	Cassin, Thomas	"	Private	30 Sep 1814	48.00	
1148	Cushing, Daniel	"	Captain	24 Mar 1815	240.00	
1149	Cochran, Andrew	"	Private	20 Feb 1814	48.00	
1150	Campton, Robert	W & C	"	5 Aug 1812	48.00	Widow intermarried 7 Apr 1814

---

[73] **Pensioners of the U.S., 1818, Invalids & Half Pay Pensioners, Widows & Orphans**, (Washington, D.C.: E. De Krafft, 1818), Pensioners, Ohio, pp. 310-326.

Ohio and the War of 1812

Nbr	Soldier	Heirs W=Widows W&C = Widows & children	Rank	Paid started (Date of death)	Per annum	Remarks
1151	Campbell, Andrew	W	"	4 Apr 1814	48.00	
1152	Craig, John	"	"	7 Aug 1813	48.00	
1153	Clark, Isaac	"	"	15 Sep 1812	48.00	
1154	Culp, Jacob	"	"	5 Mar 1813	48.00	
1155	Carmene, Blades	W & C	"	31 Dec 1813	48.00	Widow intermarried 1 Jan 1815
1156	Douthit, Jacob	W	"	9 Oct 1813	48.00	
1157	Deibler, George	"	"	24 Sep 1812	48.00	
1158	Devore, Nathan	"	Corporal	7 Dec 1812	43.92	
1159	Doty, William	W & C	Private	14 Nov 1813	48.00	
1160	Day, Lewis	W	Sergeant	26 Aug 1812	48.00	
1161	Dever, Benjamin	"	Private	5 Aug 1812	48.00	
1162	Danford, William	"	"	23 Oct 1813	48.00	
1163	Dollarhide, William	"	"	15 May 1813	48.00	
1164	Denton, Jonathan	"	"	22 Nov 1812	48.00	
1165	Denny, David	"	"	4 Sep 1812	48.00	
1166	Davis, William	"	"	21 May 1813	48.00	
1167	Edwards, Josias	"	Ensign	23 Mar 1814	120.00	
1168	Farner, Michael M.	"	Private	9 Sep 1813	48.00	
1169	Fulk, Peter	W & C	"	23 May 1814	48.00	Widow intermarried 13 Jun 1815
1170	Ford, William	"	"	7 Jul 1813	48.00	
1171	Foreman, Isaac	"	"	25 Mar 1813	"	Widow intermarried 21 Mar 1816
1172	Frees, Adam	"	"	10 Jun 1813	48.00	
1173	Flynn, Hugh	W & C	Captain	15 Aug 1813	240.00	Widow died 9 May 1814
1174	Gaston, John	W	"	16 Nov 1812	48.00	
1175	Grey, Mathew	"	Private	8 Sep 1812	48.00	
1176	Griffith, James	"	Sergeant	7 Nov 1813	66.00	
1177	Guntridge, John	"	Private	9 Sep 1813	48.00	
1178	Gee, William	"	"	1 Jan 1814	48.00	
1179	Gillaspy, Thomas	"	"	14 Feb 1814	48.00	
1180	Garrison, Jesse	"	"	4 Jan 1814	48.00	
1181	Green, Charles	"	"	17 Oct 1813	48.00	
1182	Gilchrist, Robert	"	Captain	5 Aug 1812	240.00	
1183	Harr, Isaiah	"	Corporal	10 May 1813	60.00	
1184	Holston, William	"	Private	23 Dec 1814	48.00	
1185	Hale, Samuel	"	"	1 Nov 1813	48.00	Widow intermarried 30 Nov 1815
1186	Hammett, Joseph	"	"	5 Jan 1814	48.00	
1187	Hollow, Philip	"	"	5 Nov 1813	48.00	
1188	Holt, James	"	"	1 Sep 1813	48.00	
1189	Hall, John	"	"	1 Dec 1814	48.00	
1190	Ice, John	"	"	12 Feb 1814	48.00	Widow intermarried 30 Jul 1816
1191	Johnson, William	"	"	6 Aug 1814	48.00	
1192	Jacob, Gilson	"	"	1 Sep 1813	48.00	
1193	Johnson, Thomas	"	"	9 Aug 1812	48.00	Widow intermarried 30 Jul 1813
1194	Jacobs, Jacob	W & C	First Lieutenant	14 Apr 1813	180.00	Widow intermarried 1 May 1815

Ohio and the War of 1812

Nbr	Soldier	Heirs W=Widows W&C = Widows & children	Rank	Paid started (Date of death)	Per annum	Remarks
1195	Jackson, Gideon	W	Corporal	5 Aug 1812	43.92	
1196	King, Robert	"	Private	3 May 1813	48.00	
1197	Kincaid, Samuel	"	"	5 May 1813	48.00	
1198	Kirkpatrick, Charles	W & C	"	20 Sep 1812	48.00	Widow intermarried 19 Aug 1813
1199	Kilgour, William	W	Captain	14 Apr 1814	240.00	
1200	King, John	"	Private	6 Oct 1814	48.00	
1201	Kerr, William	"	"	28 Feb 1814	48.00	Widow intermarried 27 Feb 1816
1202	Kirk, George	"	"	22 Apr 1814	48.00	
1203	Kestor, William	"	"	10 Apr 1814	48.00	
1204	Lemunyan, Stephen	"	"	21 Apr 1814	48.00	
1205	Linton, William	"	"	5 Apr 1814	48.00	
1206	Little, Robert	"	Corporal	8 Sep 1813	60.00	
1207	Lampson, Eleazer	W & C	Private	4 Dec 1812	48.00	Widow intermarried 15 Mar 1815
1208	Lamont, Robert	W	"	2 Feb 1813	48.00	Widow intermarried 2 Aug 1815
1209	Lancaster, William	"	"	1 Jun 1813	48.00	
1210	Laforce, Robinson	"	"	4 Mar 1813	48.00	
1211	Moses, Thomas	"	"	16 Mar 1814	48.00	Widow intermarried 16 Nov 1816
1212	Mullin, William	"	Sergeant	12 Jan 1814	66.00	
1213	Mitten, Isaias	"	Private	1 Feb 1814	48.00	Widow intermarried 28 Oct 1816
1214	McBride, John	"	"	4 Apr 1814	48.00	
1215	Millikan, John	W & C	First Lieutenant	25 Mar 1814	180.00	Widow intermarried 8 Jun 1816
1216	McKnight, John C.	W	Private	4 Nov 1813	48.00	
1217	McClurg, David	"	"	1 Nov 1813	48.00	
1218	McFall, Malcolm	"	"	6 Nov 1812	48.00	
1219	Murphy, Samuel	"	"	4 Sep 1812	48.00	
1220	Mecker, Peter	"	"	7 May 1814	48.00	
1221	McDill, Thomas	"	"	13 Jun 1813	48.00	
1222	McNeal, Samuel	"	"	10 Jan 1814	48.00	
1223	Michael, Paul	"	Sergeant	20 Nov 1813	66.00	
1224	Mount, John	"	Private	27 Oct 1813	48.00	
1225	Musterson, Jeremiah	"	"	28 Dec 1813	48.00	
1226	Miller, Isaac	"	Sergeant	1 Oct 1813	66.00	
1227	McCune, Thomas	"	Corporal	26 Mar 1814	60.00	
1228	McPherson, John	"	Private	11 Nov 1813	48.00	
1229	Mathers, Daniel	"	"	20 Aug 1813	48.00	
1230	Mingers, Calvin	W & C	"	19 Nov 1813	48.00	Widow intermarried 18 Aug 1814
1231	Moore, Thomas	W	"	16 Dec 1813	48.00	
1232	Moreland, John	"	"	29 Sep 1813	48.00	
1233	Mershon, Solomon	W & C	"	29 Oct 1814	48.00	Widow intermarried 24 Jan 1816
1234	McConnell, William	"	"	25 Jul 1812	48.00	Widow intermarried 16 Apr 1815
1235	Miller, John	"	"	13 Nov 1813	48.00	Widow intermarried 4 Aug 1816

Ohio and the War of 1812

Nbr	Soldier	Heirs W=Widows W&C = Widows & children	Rank	Paid started (Date of death)	Per annum	Remarks
1236	Mathews, John	"	"	3 Mar 1814	48.00	
1237	Meek, William	"	"	23 Feb 1813	48.00	
1238	McAlister, Samuel	"	"	1 Sep 1812	48.00	Widow intermarried 2 May 1816
1239	McCoy, Angus	"	First Lieutenant	13 Aug 1813	180.00	
1240	Nealy, John	"	Private	15 Jun 1813	48.00	
1241	Nash, John	"	"	26 Dec 1813	48.00	Widow intermarried 24 May 1815
1242	Owen, Abraham	"	Aide de camp	7 Nov 1811	300.00	
1243	Parks, George	"	Private	28 Nov 1811	48.00	
1244	Plowman, Mesheck	"	Sergeant	3 Aug 1812	48.00	
1245	Porter, James	"	Private	17 Nov 1813	48.00	
1246	Powers, Avery	"	"	25 Jul 1812	48.00	
1247	Phillips, Enoch	"	"	18 Nov 1813	48.00	Widow intermarried 24 Oct 1815
1248	Pierce, Benoni	"	Captain	18 Dec 1812	240.00	
1249	Randolph, Henry	W & C	Private	12 Dec 1813	48.00	Widow intermarried 18 Mar 1815
1250	Reynolds, Ephaim	W	"	4 Dec 1813	48.00	
1251	Ramsey, Nathan	"	"	7 Dec 1812	48.00	
1252	Roath, Joseph	"	"	13 Jun 1814	48.00	
1253	Ross, Adam	"	"	30 Apr 1813	48.00	
1254	Ramsey, John	"	First Lieutenant	21 Mar 1813	180.00	
1255	Russell, Jeremiah	"	Private	5 Nov 1813	48.00	
1256	Reed, Benjamin	"	"	22 Jan 1813	48.00	
1257	Reeves, James	"	"	27 Nov 1813	48.00	Widow intermarried 14 Aug 1817
1258	Rambo, Tobias	"	"	8 Jan 1813	48.00	
1259	Reppy, Joseph	"	"	15 Mar 1813	48.00	
1260	Randolph, Thomas	"	"	7 Nov 1811	39.96	
1261	Sturgeon, Robert	"	"	4 Dec 1813	48.00	Widow intermarried 4 Jun 1816
1262	Spurling, Jesse	"	"	13 Jul 1813	48.00	
1263	Snider, Arnold	W & C	"	22 Jun 1813	48.00	Widow intermarried 6 Dec 1815
1264	Stout, George	W	Musician	5 Oct 1813	54.00	
1265	Salvister, James	"	Private	24 Oct 1813	48.00	
1266	Shaw, Freeman	"	"	30 Apr 1813	48.00	
1267	Smith, Henry	"	Sergeant	3 Jan 1814	66.00	Widow intermarried 17 Aug 1815
1268	Stewart, Edie	"	Private	15 Feb 1814	48.00	
1269	Spence, Peter	"	"	2 Sep 1813	48.00	
1270	Strickland, Henry	"	"	26 Dec 1813	48.00	
1271	Study-baker, John	"	"	3 Oct 1813	48.00	
1272	Skeels, Henry	"	"	2 Dec 1813	48.00	
1273	Shaw, Samuel	"	Quarter-master	13 Aug 1813	60.00	
1274	Topping, Zophar	"	Private	27 Sep 1814	48.00	

Ohio and the War of 1812

Nbr	Soldier	Heirs W=Widows W&C = Widows & children	Rank	Paid started (Date of death)	Per annum	Remarks
1275	Traverse, William	"	"	27 Jun 1813	48.00	Widow intermarried 8 Aug 1816
1276	Thompson, Archibald	"	Sergeant	18 Apr 1814	66.00	
1277	Taft, Abraham	"	Private	7 Jan 1814	48.00	Widow intermarried 1 Mar 1815
1278	Thomas, Arthur	"	Captain	1 Sep 1813	240.00	
1279	Trovinger, Jacob	"	Private	13 Dec 1813	48.00	
1280	Ulery, Henry	"	Captain	5 Aug 1812	240.00	
1281	Van Camp, Moses	"	Private	14 Dec 1813	48.00	
1282	Van Vickle, Robert	"	"	2 Jul 1813	48.00	
1283	Warden, Benjamin	"	Fifer	1 May 1814	54.00	Widow intermarried 15 Aug 1816
1284	Wilkins, Cornelius	"	"	3 May 1813	48.00	
1285	Wright, Samuel	"	"	18 Feb 1813	48.00	Widow intermarried 2 Mar 1815
1286	Wright, Robert B.	W & C	"	9 May 1814	48.00	Widow intermarried 21 Apr 1816
1287	Wirick, Jacob	"	Drummer	12 Dec 1812	43.92	Widow intermarried 21 Nov 1814
1288	Warnick, Robert	W	Private	15 Sep 1812	48.00	
1289	Woods, Charles	"	"	25 Nov 1813	48.00	
1290	Wilson, Sylvester	"	"	13 Jul 1813	48.00	
1291	Warman, Joshua	W & C	Corporal	6 Mar 1813	60.00	
1292	Watts, Henry	W	Private	22 Dec 1813	48.00	Widow intermarried 12 Feb 1815
1293	Wilson, Thomas	"	"	9 Dec 1813	48.00	
1294	Wells, Joseph	"	"	30 Oct 1813	48.00	
1295	Wells, Charles	"	"	11 Dec 1813	48.00	
1296	Wilson, Peter	"	"	9 Sep 1814	48.00	
1297	Walker, Isaac	"	Captain	5 Apr 1813	240.00	
1298	Willis, William	"	Private	1 Apr 1814	48.00	
1299	Wright, William	"	"	29 Aug 1813	48.00	
1300	Yatman, Peter	"	"	5 Dec 1813	48.00	

History of the 17th Regiment of U.S. Infantry

The 17th Regiment of U.S. Infantry was organized under the Congressional Act of 11 January 1812 as part of a ten regiment buildup of the army prior to the beginning of the War of 1812.[74] The regiment was authorized for a maximum period of five years.

The regiment was structured into two battalions of nine 110-man companies.[75] A lieutenant colonel commanded each of the battalions with a colonel serving as the regimental commander. The 1st battalion was raised in Kentucky, while the 2nd battalion was scheduled to have been raised in Ohio.

The 17th Infantry was reorganized under the Congressional Act of 26 July 1812 and restructured into ten 102-man companies.[76] One lieutenant colonel's position was eliminated. The regiment's authorized manning was set at 1,070 men. The 2nd battalion was split off to become the 19th Regiment of U.S. Infantry.

Enlistments were authorized for five years and 18-month enlistments were added on 8 April 1812. On 12 December 1812 'during the war' enlistments were approved for this regiment.

Under the Act of 3 March 1813, a second major's position was authorized along with ten 3rd lieutenants' positions and ten additional sergeants' positions.[77] This act set the new manpower strength for the regiment at 1,091 men. The additional manpower was used to supplement the regiment's recruiting efforts.

There were actually two 17th Infantries organized during the War of 1812. The first 17th Infantry was created on 11 January 1812, and it was disbanded on 12 May 1814 under the act of 3 March 1814. Previously, some of the men from this regiment had transferred into the newly created 2nd Regiment of U.S. Rifle, which had been organized under the act of 10 February 1814. This rifle regiment was raised primarily from within Kentucky, Ohio and Tennessee.

The second 17th Regiment of U.S. Infantry was authorized under the act of 3 March 1814 then the 17th and 19th Regiments of U.S. Infantry merged to form this new regiment on 12 May 1814. The "17" designation was reused for this new regiment. The new regiment was made up of men from Kentucky, Ohio, and the Territories of Indiana and Michigan.

Both 17th Infantries operated as part of the Army of the Northwest in the 8th Military District during most of the war. After the Battle of the Thames, the first 17th Infantry would be transferred to the Army of the North, and they would operate within the 9th Military District until the regiment merged with the 19th Infantry to form the new 17th Infantry.

First Organization
2 Battalions (18 Companies)

On 12 March 1812 the following men were commissioned as officers in the 17th Infantry: Colonel Samuel Wells of Kentucky; Lieutenant Colonel William McMillen of Ohio; Lieutenant Colonel John

---

[74] Heitman, Francis B., **Historical Register and Dictionary of the United States Army From Its Organization, September 29, 1789, to March 2, 1903**, Volume I, (Genealogical Publishing Company, Baltimore, Maryland: 1994), page 113, Seventeenth Regiment.

[75] Mahon, John K. and Romana Danysh, **Infantry Part 1: Regular Army**, Army Lineage Series, (Office of the Chief of Military History, United States Army, Washington, DC: 1972), page 14, History of the Organization of the Infantry: *Through the Second War with England*.

[76] Heitman, Francis B., **Historical Register and Dictionary of the United States Army From Its Organization, September 29, 1789, to March 2, 1903**, Volume II, (Genealogical Publishing Company, Baltimore, Maryland: 1994), pp. 572-573, Organization of the Army under the Act of June 26, 1812.

[77] **Ibid**, pp. 574-575, Organization of the Army under the Act of March 3, 1812.

Miller of Steubenville, Ohio; Lieutenant Colonel John B. Campbell of Kentucky; and Major George Tod of Youngstown, Ohio. Major Richard Davenport of Kentucky was commissioned on 12 April 1812.

The following captains were commissioned on 12 March 1812: Abraham Edwards of Dayton, Ohio, James Hunter of Kentucky, George Croghan of Kentucky, Richard Hightower of Kentucky, William Adair of Kentucky, David Holt of Kentucky, William Bradford of Kentucky, Robert Edwards of Kentucky, James Duncan, Junior, of Kentucky, James Meade of Kentucky, Angus Langham of Chillicothe, Ohio, Harris Hickman of the Territory of Michigan, Hugh Moore of Cincinnati, Ohio, Wilson Elliott of Warren, Ohio, James Herron of Zanesville, Ohio, and Robert Lucas of Portsmouth, Ohio.

John Chunn of the Territory of Indiana was commissioned a captain on 14 April 1812, while Richard Graham of Kentucky was commissioned on 4 June 1812, and Asabael Nearing of Connecticut was commissioned on 6 July 1812.

Lieutenant Colonel John Miller established the headquarters of the 2nd battalion at Chillicothe, Ohio, and the recruiting centers at Chillicothe and Zanesville, Ohio.

On 6 July 1812 the following officers were transferred to the 19th Regiment of U.S. Infantry: John Miller, John Campbell, George Tod, Angus Langham, Harris Hickman, Hugh Moore, Wilson Elliott, James Herron, Robert Lucas, John Chunn, Richard Graham and Asabael Nearing.

First Organization
10 Companies

Colonel Samuel Wells of Kentucky served as the regimental commander of the 17th Infantry from 12 March 1812 until he was discharged from the army on 1 June 1814. William McMillan of Ohio was the regiment's lieutenant colonel. He was commissioned on 12 March 1812, and he was discharged from the service on 1 June 1814.

The regiment had four men from Kentucky who served as regimental majors during the War of 1812. They were Richard Davenport, George Croghan, Richard Graham and Richard Oldham. Davenport was commissioned a major on 12 April 1812, and he resigned from the army on 1 February 1813. Croghan was a captain in the regiment before being promoted to major on 30 March 1813. He left the regiment on 21 February 1814 when he was promoted to lieutenant colonel and transferred to the 2nd Regiment of U.S. Rifle. Graham was a captain in the 19th Infantry, and he was promoted to major and reassigned to the 17th Infantry on 30 March 1813. He was transferred to the second 17th Infantry on 12 May 1814. Oldham was a captain in the 1st Regiment of U.S. Infantry when he was promoted to major and reassigned to the 17th Infantry. He also was transferred to the new 17th Infantry on 12 May 1814.

Ten men were commissioned captains on 12 March 1812. They were Abraham Edwards of Dayton, Montgomery County, Ohio, and the following men from Kentucky: James Hunter; George Croghan; Richard Hightower; William I. Adair; David Holt; William Braford; Robert Edwards; James Duncan, Junior; and James Meade. Charles Querry became a captain on 8 May 1812; Caleb H. Holder on 29 March 1813; William O. Butler on 5 April 1813; Martin L. Hawkins on 16 April 1813; Benjamin W. Sanders on 16 April 1813 and Charles Scott Todd on 29 May 1813.

It is doubtful that Abraham Edwards served as a company commander or even as a recruiting officer in the regiment. He was a physician who had been a surgeon's mate in the army before the War of 1812. He was the hospital surgeon under Brigadier General William Hull when the general surrendered his army to the British at Fort Detroit.[78] Edwards would later serve as a deputy quartermaster general for the army between 15 March 1814 and 15 June 1815 holding the rank of major.

Captain Richard Hightower's company participated in the first engagement at the River Raisin, Territory of Michigan, on 18 January 1813. The companies of Captains Hightower, James Meade and Robert Edwards were involved in the massacre in the second engagement of the River Raisin on 22

---

[78] Gillett, Mary C., **The Army Medical Department 1775-1818,** Army Historical Series, (U.S. Government Printing Office, Washington, D.C.: 1981), Chapter 8, Early Campaigns in the North, 1812 to 1813, page 162.

January 1813[79] Captain Bradford's and Captain Holt's companies were at the siege of Fort Meigs, Ohio, between 28 April and 9 May 1813.[80] They were attached to Colonel Miller's 19th Regiment of U.S. Infantry.

During the first assault on Fort Meigs, Colonel Miller led a counterattack with 350 men, regular troops plus militia from Kentucky, Ohio and Pennsylvania, against a British battery just east of the fort.[81] The force was composed of the companies from the 19th Infantry, men from Captains Holt and Bradford's companies of the 17th Infantry, volunteers from Major John B. Alexander's Independent Battalion from Pennsylvania and Virginia, and Captain William Sebree's Company from the Kentucky militia.[82]

The detachment surprised the enemy's artillery crew capturing 42 British artillerymen, and they succeeded in spiking the cannons. On the way back to the fort, 150 Canadian militiamen and 300 Indians attacked Colonel Miller's men. The detachment was able to hold off the attackers and make it back to the fort. The Americans suffered 30 killed and 90 wounded.

During the siege of Fort Stephenson, Ohio, on 2 April 1813, Captain Holt's Company and Captain Hunter's Company successfully stopped the British from taking the fort. These companies were under the command of Major George Croghan. Major Croghan would be brevetted a lieutenant colonel for distinguished conduct for his successful defense of Fort Stephenson.

Eleven men from the regiment volunteered to serve with the U.S. Navy as part of Commodore Perry's Lake Erie Squadron.[83] These men served on the *Scorpion, Lawrence, Trippe, Niagara* and *Tigress,* and they all participated in the Battle of Lake Erie on 10 September 1813 serving as marines.

Lieutenant Colonel Croghan and his detachment escorted 600 British soldiers and sailors captured during the Battle of Lake Erie and the Battle of the Thames to Camp Bull, Chillicothe, Ohio.[84] He had orders to leave 300 at Camp Bull and then he proceeded with the remaining prisoners to Newport, Kentucky. Major Richard Graham was ordered by the Department of War on 17 November 1813 to escort more British prisoners of war to Frankfort, Kentucky, and to turn over the prisoners to General John Mason, the Commissary General for Prisoners of War.[85]

Under the act of 10 February 1814 the 2nd Regiment of U.S. Rifle was organized in Kentucky, Ohio and Tennessee. The initial core of officers and enlisted men came from the existing regiments that were assigned to the Army of the Northwest. Among those from the 17th Infantry who were transferred were Major Croghan, who was promoted to lieutenant colonel and 1st Lieutenant Benjamin Johnson, who was promoted to captain. A number of junior officers and enlisted men were also transferred into this new regiment.

After the Battle of the Thames, part of the 17th Infantry was transferred to the Niagara Theater along with companies from the 19th, 24th and 26th Infantries. This brigade was under the command of General

---

[79] Clift, G. Glenn, **Remember the Raisin!**, (Kentucky Historical Society, Frankfort, Kentucky: 1961), pp. 174-177.

[80] Rauch, Steven J., Major, U.S. Army, **War for the Northwest**, page 29, Order of Battle at Fort Meigs.

[81] Nelson, Larry L., **Men of Patriotism, Courage & Enterprise! Fort Meigs in the War of 1812**, (Heritage Books, Inc., Bowie, Maryland: 1970), page 80.

[82] Lexington, K., **History of the Late War in the Western Country**, (Worsley & Smith: 1816), reprinted by University Microfilms, Inc., Ann Arbor, Michigan: 1966, page 268.

[83] Altoff, Gerald T., **Deep Water Sailors, Shallow Water Soldiers, Manning the United States Fleet on Lake Erie 1813**, (The Perry Group, Put-in-Bay, Ohio: 1993), 17th United States Infantry Regiment, pp. 95-96.

[84] Medert, Patricia Fife, **Raw Recruits & Bullish Prisoners, Ohio's Capital in the War of 1812**, Ross County Historical Society Publication, (Jackson Publishing Company, Jackson, Ohio: 1992), page 115.

[85] Knopf, Richard C., **Document Transcriptions of the War of 1812 in the Northwest,** Volume VII, Part 3, Letters from the Secretary of War 1812 & 1813 Relating to the War of 1812 in the Northwest, (Ohio Historical Society: Columbus, Ohio: 1961), page 164, War Department to Major Richard Graham, 17 November 1813.

Harrison and they landed at Buffalo, New York, on 24 October 1813 according to the general's letter to the secretary of war.[86]

The brigade proceeded to Fort George, Upper Canada, where they then received orders to proceed to Sackets Harbor, New York. The brigade arrived at their new post on 23 December 1813. From the officer's returns of January 1814 for Sackets Harbor, the officers from the 17th Regiment were Captain Holt, and lieutenants Craig and Sharp.[87]

In January 1814 there were 100 men from the 17th Infantry stationed at Fort Shelby, Detroit.[88] By April the detachment had been combined with elements of the 19th, 24th and 28th Infantries to form an 'ad hoc' regiment of 558 men.[89] Second Lieutenant Chesteen Scott commanded a detachment of the 17th Infantry in March 1814 at Fort Stephenson, Ohio.[90]

Another detachment from the regiment was stationed at Fort Knox, Territory of Indiana, during January 1814.[91] The detachment was part of the command of Captain Ambrose Whitlock of the 1st Regiment of Infantry, which contained a total of 151 men from the 1st, 7th and 17th Infantries.

On 12 May 1814, under the act of 30 March 1814, the regiment was consolidated with the 19th Regiment of U.S. Infantry to form the new 17th Regiment of U.S. Infantry. Captains William I. Adair, David Holt, Caleb H. Holder, Martin L. Hawkings, and Benjamin W. Sanders were retained in the second organization of the regiment. Captains William Bradford and Richard Hightower were transferred to the new 19th Infantry.

Captains James Hunter, James Duncan and Charles Querey were discharged from the army on 1 June 1814. Previously, Captain Butler had transferred to the 44th Regiment of Infantry on 3 August 1813, and Captain Scott had transferred to the 28th Regiment of U.S. Infantry on 13 August 1813.

The 17th Regiment of U.S. Infantry as organized under the act of 11 January 1812 ceased to exist when the remaining men from this regiment merged with the 19th Regiment of U.S. Infantry on 12 May 1814 forming the new 17th Regiment of U.S. Infantry.

Second Organization

The 17th Regiment of U.S. Infantry was re-organization under the same acts of Congress that established the first organization of this regiment. Enlistments were approved for five years, 18-months and during the war.

The regimental headquarters was moved from Kentucky to Chillicothe, Ohio, and two major recruiting centers were established at Chillicothe and Lexington, Kentucky. The regiment operated in both the 8th and the 9th Military Districts.

Colonel John Miller of Steubenville, Jefferson County, Ohio, became the commander of the second 17th Regiment of U.S. Infantry on 12 May 1814, and he served in this position until 17 May 1815.

---

[86] Cruikshank, Ernest, editor, **The Documentary History of the Campaign on the Niagara Frontier,** Oct. 1813 – May 1814, Volume III, (Arno Press & The New York Times, New York, New York), General Harrison to Secretary of War, 24 October 1813, page 91.

[87] **Duncan McArthur Papers**, Library of Congress, 1922, Microfilm 47, Reel 2, Volumes 4-5, 22 September 1813 – 4 March 1814, document number 699, Officers of the 8th Military District at Sackett's Harbor, 22 January 1814, Ohio Historical Society, Columbus, Ohio.

[88] **Ibid**, document number 748, Monthly Returns for Brigadier General Cass's Brigade under the command of Lieutenant Colonel Butler, January 1814, Ohio Historical Society, Columbus, Ohio.

[89] **Ibid**, document number 1383, Monthly Returns at Detroit, 30 April 1814, Ohio Historical Society, Columbus, Ohio.

[90] **Ibid**, document number 1369, Monthly returns for Lower Sandusky, Lieutenant C. Scott, 17th Regiment of U.S. Infantry, 31 March 1814, Ohio Historical Society, Columbus, Ohio.

[91] **Ibid**, Monthly Returns for the Territory of Indiana, 31 January 1814, Ohio Historical Society, Columbus, Ohio.

Colonel Miller had previously been the commander of the 19th Regiment of U.S. Infantry, and he became the commander of the 3rd Regiment of U.S. Infantry after the war.

George Tod of Youngstown,[92] Trumbull County, Ohio, was a major in the 19th Infantry. He was promoted and reassigned to the 17th Infantry on 13 March 1814 and was discharged from the army on 17 May 1815.

Major Richard Graham and Major Richard Oldham, both from Kentucky, were transferred from the original 17th Infantry into the new 17th Infantry on 12 May 1814. Both men were discharged from the service on 15 June 1815.

The following men were transferred from the first organization into the new 17th Infantry: William I. Adair, David Holt, Caleb H. Holder, Martin L. Hawkings, William Bradford and Benjamin W. Sanders. Four captains from the 19th Infantry were transferred into the 17th Infantry. They were Harris H. Hickman of the Territory of Michigan, John T. Chunn of the Territory of Indiana, James Herron and George W. Jackson, both of Zanesville, Muskingum County, Ohio. Henry Crittenden of Kentucky was commissioned a captain on 8 July 1814.

Captain Chunn and his company, newly transferred from the 19th Infantry, took part in the raid of Dover, Upper Canada, on 14 May 1814.

During the summer of 1814, it became crucial that Fort Michillimachinac on Mackinaw Island, Territory of Michigan, be taken back from the British. The fort controlled the entrance to Lake Michigan, and it was a key link of the British supply line to the upper Mississippi River valley, which was still in their hands.

A joint army-navy force left Fort Gratiot, north of Fort Detroit, on July 12th. Fort Gratiot was built by the Americans at the entrance of the St. Clair River to keep any British naval ships from sailing down the river to Detroit. The brigs, *Niagara* and *Lawrence,* plus the schooners, *Caledonia, Tigress* and *Scorpion* transported the army north to Fort Michillimachinac. Lieutenant Colonel George Croghan commanded the Americans with five companies (500 men) from the 17th, 19th, 24th and 28th Infantries and 250 men militia from Colonel William Cotgreave's Ohio Volunteer Regiment.[93] Captain Hawkings' company represented the 17th Infantry in this assault on Mackinaw Island.[94]

The Americans started their attack on the fort on July 26th but withdrew after finding that the guns of the fleet could not be raised high enough to bombard the fort. A land assault was launched on August 4th when the Americans landed on the backside of the island. The British ambushed the invading army inflicting heavy casualties on the Americans and forcing their withdrawal from the island. The fort and control of the upper Mississippi River valley would remain in the hands of the British until the end of the war.

After the Battle of Mackinaw Island, Colonel Croghan learned of the existence of a British supply depot on the Nottawasaga River at the southern end of the Georgian Bay of Lake Huron and the squadron set sail for this British base. Colonel Croghan's men attacked and destroyed the supply depot. In the process the only remaining British warship on the upper Great Lakes, the sloop *Nancy*, was destroyed by the British to avoid its capture by the Americans.

Lieutenant Colonel Campbell of the 19th Infantry was the Commander of Military at Erie, Pennsylvania. On 13 May 1814 he was ordered to take his command of 750 men, made up of regulars and militia, to Buffalo, New York.[95] This order occurred the day after the 19th Infantry merged into the 17th

---

[92] Youngstown is now in Mahoning County, Ohio.

[93] McAfee, Robert Breckinridge, **History of the Late War in the Western Country,** (University Microfilms, Inc., Ann Arbor, Michigan: 1966), originally published in 1816, Chapter X, Expedition of Captain Holmes, pp. 410-453.

[94] **Ibid.**

[95] Cruikshank, Ernest, editor, **Documents Relating to the Invasion of the Niagara Peninsula by the United States Army**, (The Niagara Historical Society, Niagara-on-the-Lake, Ontario, Canada: 1920), pp. 18-19, letter to William Jones, Secretary of the Navy, from A. Sinclair, 13 May 1814.

Infantry. Colonel Campbell's detachment would disembark at Buffalo as part of the new 17th Infantry. The remaining companies were also re-assigned to the Niagara Theater, and arrived at Buffalo on October 8th. [96]

A detachment from the regiment fought at the Battle of Lundy's Lane, Upper Canada, on 25 July 1814. The 17th Infantry along with a detachment from the 19th Infantry formed the right wing of the 21st Regiment of U.S. Infantry during this battle.[97] They were involved in a major attack on the British lines in which they captured the central British artillery battery forcing the entire British battle line to withdraw from their defensive line to a secondary position.

On 1 September 1814, Colonel Miller wrote a letter to Major Tod at Fort Malden ordering the major to gather all of the new recruits, and to proceed to Fort Erie, Upper Canada.[98] Tod was in charge of the recruiting service for the 17th Infantry, and he called all of the recruits from the recruiting stations in Kentucky and Ohio to rendezvous at Chillicothe. Two companies were formed under the command of Captain Hickman and Captain Holder.[99]

Captain Chunn's Company participated in the Battle of Fort Erie, Upper Canada, between 13 and 15 August 1814 during the first siege by the British army and in the second battle on 17 September 1814 when the British once again besieged the fort. This detachment from the 17th Infantry was attached to the 21st Regiment of U.S. Infantry.[100] Captain Chunn would be brevetted a major on 15 August 1814 for distinguished service in defense of Fort Erie, Upper Canada.

On 17 May 1815, the 17th Infantry was consolidated with the 1st, 19th, 28th and 39th Regiments of U.S. Infantry to form the new 3rd Regiment of U.S. Infantry.[101] Captains Adair and Chunn were transferred to the 3rd Regiment on 17 May 1815. Captain Jackson resigned from the army on 9 July 1814 while Captain Crittenden resigned on 25 April 1815. Captain Bradford was promoted to major on 20 August 1814 and he was reassigned to the 21st Regiment of U.S. Infantry. The remaining senior officers were discharged from the service on 15 June 1815.

---

[96] **War of 1812 – The 17th Regiment of U.S. Infantry**, Welcome of Fort Erie and the War of 1812, History, http://www.iaw.on.ca/~jsek/us17inf.htm

[97] Cruikshank, Ernest, editor, **Documents Relating to the Invasion of the Niagara Peninsula by the United States Army**, (The Niagara Historical Society, Niagara-on-the-Lake, Ontario, Canada: 1920), page 82, Memoranda of Occurrences and some Important Facts attending the Campaign on the Niagara in 1814.

[98] **George Tod Papers 1783-1834**, Western Reserve Historical Society Archives Library, Cleveland, Ohio, manuscript section, call number MS-3202, Container 1B, Folder 9, letter from Colonel Miller to Major Tod, 1 September 1814.

[99] **Ibid**, Container 1B, Folder 7, letter from Major Tod to Captain Hickman and Captain Holder, 12 October 1814.

[100] Cruikshank, Ernest, editor, **The Documentary History of the Campaign on the Niagara Frontier in 1812-14,** (Arno Press & The New York Times, New York, New York), General Brown to Secretary of War, 1 October 1814, page 215.

[101] McAfee, Robert Breckinridge, **History of the Late War in the Western Country,** (University Microfilms, Inc., Ann Arbor, Michigan: 1966), originally published in 1816, Chapter X, Expedition of Captain Holmes, pp. 410-453.

History of the 19th Regiment of U.S. Infantry

The 19th Regiment of U.S. Infantry was authorized under the Congressional Act of 26 June 1812 for a period of not more than five years.[102] The regiment was initially formed from the 2nd battalion of the 17th Regiment of U.S. Infantry. The regiment was authorized to have ten companies of 102 men each with a headquarters' staff for a total manning of 1,070 men.[103] The officers and men were recruited from Ohio and from the Territories of Indiana and Michigan.

On 6 July 1812 the following senior officers were transferred from the 17th Infantry into the 19th Infantry: John Miller, John Campbell, George Tod, Angus Langham, Harris Hickman, Hugh Moore, Wilson Elliott, James Herron, Robert Lucas, John Chunn, Richard Graham and Asabael Nearing.

Under the Act of 3 March 1813 a second major's position was authorized along with ten 3rd lieutenants' positions and ten additional sergeants' positions.[104] This act set the new manpower strength for the regiment at 1,091 men. The additional manpower was used to supplement the regiment's recruiting efforts.

Enlistments were authorized for five years and then 18-month enlistments were approved on 8 April 1812 and 'during the war' enlistments on 12 December 1812. The regimental headquarters and the main recruiting center were established at Chillicothe, Ohio.

The history of this infantry regiment is unique for there were actually two entirely different regiments raised in Ohio that were designated as the 19th Regiment of U.S. Infantry during the War of 1812. The first 19th Infantry was created on 26 June 1812, and it was disbanded on 12 May 1814 under the act of 3 March 1814 then the regiment merged with the 17th Infantry to form a new 17th Regiment of U.S. Infantry. Previously, some of the men from this regiment had transferred into the newly created 2nd Regiment of U.S. Rifle, which had been organized under the act of 10 February 1814. This rifle regiment was raised primarily within Kentucky, Ohio and Tennessee.

The second 19th Regiment of U.S. Infantry was authorized under the act of 3 March 1814 then the 26th and 27th Regiments of U.S. Infantry along with two companies from the original 17th Regiment of U.S. Infantry merged to form this second regiment on 12 May 1814. None of the officers from the first 19th Infantry were transferred to the second 19th Infantry. The 26th and 27th Regiments of U.S. Infantry were raised in Ohio under the act of 29 January 1813.

The first 19th Infantry was never fully manned, and there may have been as few as 700 men on the regiment's roster at any one time during the war.[105] The Secretary of War, James Armstrong, wrote to Major General William H. Harrison on 7 March 1813 requesting that the general promote the full recruitment of this regiment since two more infantry regiments were going to be raised in Ohio.[106] Five years, during the war and 18-month enlistments were authorized for this regiment.

The second 19th Infantry probably never had more than 500 men on its roster. Both the 26th and 27th Regiments of U.S. Infantry were created with one-year enlistees and during their one-year existence some

---

[102] Heitman, Francis B., **Historical Register and Dictionary of the United States Army From Its Organization, September 29, 1789, to March 2, 1903**, (Genealogical Publishing Company, Baltimore, Maryland: 1994), Volume I, page 116, Nineteenth Regiment.

[103] **Ibid**, Volume II, pp. 572-573, Organization of the Army under the Act of June 26, 1812.

[104] **Ibid**, Volume II, pp. 574-575, Organization of the Army under the Act of March 3, 1812.

[105] Quisenberry, Anderson Chenault, **Kentucky in the War of 1812**, (Genealogical Publishing Company, Baltimore, Maryland: 1969), page 175, Nineteenth Regiment, United States Infantry.

[106] Knopf, Richard C., **Document Transcriptions of the War of 1812 in the Northwest**, Volume VIII, Letters from the Secretary of War 1812 & 1813 Relating to the War of 1812 in the Northwest, (Ohio Historical Society: Columbus, Ohio: 1961), page 131, Secretary of War to General Harrison, 7 March 1813.

of the men re-enlisted for the duration of the war. The 26th Infantry had at its peak strength 300 men on its roster while the 27th Infantry had 700 men.

Both 19th Infantries operated as part of the Army of the Northwest in the 8th Military District during most of the war. After the Battle of the Thames most of the first 19th Infantry would be transferred to the Army of the North, and they would operate within the 9th Military District until the regiment merged with the 17th Infantry. The second 19th Infantry operated out of Fort Detroit, Territory of Michigan, and in 1814 some of its companies were also transferred to the 9th Military District.

First Organization

Colonel John Miller of Steubenville, Jefferson County, Ohio, was the regiment's commanding officer serving from 6 July 1812 to 12 May 1814. Miller had previously been the lieutenant colonel of the 17th Regiment of U.S. Infantry and in charge of the second battalion prior to commanding the 19th Infantry. He transferred back to the 17th Infantry to serve as its commander after the merger of the two regiments.

John B. Campbell of Kentucky was the regiment's lieutenant colonel. He served from 6 July 1812 to 9 April 1814. Campbell was transferred from the 17th Infantry, and he left the 19th Infantry to assume the command of the 11th Regiment of U.S. Infantry. He died from wounds that he had received on 5 July 1814 during the Battle of Chippewa, Upper Canada.

The regiment had three majors assigned to it during its existence. They were George Tod of Youngstown,[107] Trumbull County, Ohio, Thomas Sidney Jesup of Ohio, and Nathan Heald of Massachusetts. Tod served between 6 July 1812 and 13 March 1814. He had transferred from the 17th Infantry and he left the 19th Infantry to become the lieutenant colonel in the 17th Infantry. Jesup served between 6 April 1813 and 19 April 1814. He had been a captain in the 7th Regiment of U.S. Infantry before joining the 19th Infantry and he was reassigned to the 25th Regiment of U.S. Infantry. He was brevetted a lieutenant colonel for gallantry during the Battle of Chippewa on 5 July 1814. Heald served between 18 April 1814 and 12 May 1814. He had been a major in the 4th Regiment of U.S. Infantry before joining the 19th Infantry.

Five men were commissioned as captains on 12 March 1812 in the 17th Infantry, and then they were transferred to the 19th Infantry on 6 July 1812. They were Angus L. Langham of Chillicothe, Ross County, Ohio; Harris H. Hickman[108] of the Territory of Michigan; Hugh Moore of Cincinnati, Hamilton County, Ohio; Wilson Elliott of Warren, Trumbull County, Ohio; and James Herron of Zanesville, Muskingum County, Ohio.

Four more men were commissioned as captains between 14 March 1812 and 6 July 1812. They were John T. Chunn of the Territory of Indiana; Richard Graham of Kentucky; Robert Lucas of Portsmouth, Scioto County, Ohio; and Asabael Nearing of Connecticut. During 1813 four more men were commissioned captains: John Anderson of the Territory of Michigan, David Gwynne of Franklinton, Franklin County, Ohio, George W. Jackson of Zanesville, Muskingum County, Ohio, and Samuel Booker of St. Clairsville, Belmont County, Ohio. These men were assigned to the companies in which their commanders had either been transferred or had died.

When the regiment was organized in 1812 they were given linen summer uniforms to wear until their standard blue and white infantry uniforms arrived.[109] However, delays in making and then shipping the regiment's uniforms forced the War Department to issue drab wool roundabouts and overalls to the

---

[107] Youngstown is now in Mahoning County, Ohio.

[108] Captain Hickman was the son-in-law of Brigadier General William Hull according to *The Robert Lucas Journal of the War of 1812 during the Campaign under General William Hull*, edited by John C. Parish, (The State Historical Society of Iowa, Iowa City, Iowa: 1906).

[109] Kochan, James L. and David Rickman, **The United States Army 1812-1815**, Men-at-Arms Series, (Osprey Publishing, Oxford, England: 2000), pp. 11-17, Infantry Dress.

regiment in the fall of 1812. It would not be until the fall of 1813 that the regiment's standard infantry uniforms would arrive and then be issued to the men. The regiment wore the 1812 style uniform with a blue single-breasted coat, white pants and a shako (hat) made from felt.

The 19th Infantry was headquartered at the Chillicothe Barracks in Chillicothe, Ohio, beginning in March 1812 when the unit was still the second battalion of the 17th Infantry.[110] The barracks were used as a regimental recruiting and training center throughout the war. The regiment never operated with all of its companies during any battles and engagements that the regiment participated in during the war. Detachments of two to four companies would operate as a unit whenever General Harrison needed troops. At least one company was always stationed in Chillicothe; usually this was a new company that was being formed or trained.

Captain Lucas was a company commander in the Ohio militia when he was commissioned as an officer in the regular army. His company was part of Brigadier General William Hull's Army of the Northwest. While at Fort Detroit, Territory of Michigan, in the summer of 1812, Lucas learned of his appointment as a captain in the 19th Infantry, but he elected to stay with his militia company. He was captured and paroled by the British after General Hull's surrender. He was released in a prisoner of war exchange and he rejoined the Ohio militia. It is doubtful that he actually served with the 19th Infantry. He resigned from the army on 10 February 1813.

Captain Hickman was ordered to raise a company from within the Territory of Michigan. He and his recruits joined the Army of the Northwest after the army had arrived at Fort Detroit on 5 July 1812. Ensign John Whistler, Junior, of Captain Hickman's detachment was wounded during the Battle of Brownstown on 9 August 1812.

Captain Hickman and his men were forced to surrender to the British when General Hull capitulated to the enemy on 16 August 1812. It is doubtful that Captain Hickman's men were equipped and uniformed as regular soldiers at the time of their capture. It appears that they were not sent to Montreal and Quebec, Lower Canada, along with the 1st and 4th Infantries to be interned as prisoners of war. Most likely they were treated as militia and released on parole with the militiamen from Ohio.

Captain Hickman was not able to raise a full complement of men for a company in the Territory of Michigan. Once he joined the regiment in Ohio, he was placed in the recruiting service and stayed there until late in the war when he finally received command of a company.

After General Harrison and his relief forces lifted the siege of Fort Wayne, Territory of Indiana, on 12 September 1812, Captain Moore was appointed the commandant of this fort. He held this position from mid-September 1812 until Major Joseph Jenkinson from the 26th Regiment of U.S. Infantry replaced him in mid-1813. Captain James Rhea, the previous commandant from the 1st Regiment of U.S. Infantry, had been found drunk during the siege and General Harrison forced him to resign from the service. Captain Moore commanded Captain Rhea's 76-man company and a company of militia.[111] During his stay at Fort Wayne, Captain Moore rebuilt and doubled the size of the fort.[112]

On 25 November 1812 Lieutenant Colonel John B. Campbell of the 19th Infantry led a mixed force of 650 regulars and militia against the Indians along the Mississiniway River in the northern Territory of Indiana. On December 18th they defeated the Indians at the Battle of Mississiniway forcing the Delaware tribe along with some other area Indian tribes to accept peace terms with the United States. Captain Elliott's company participated in this battle and three of his men were wounded in this engagement.

---

[110] Medert, Patricia Fife, **Raw Recruits & Bullish Prisoners, Ohio's Capital in the War of 1812**, Ross County Historical Society Publication, (Jackson Publishing Company, Jackson, Ohio: 1992), page 19.

[111] Knopf, Richard C., **Document Transcriptions of the War of 1812 in the Northwest**, Volume VII Part 3, Letters to the Secretary of War 1812 Relating to the War of 1812 in the Northwest, (Anthony Wayne Parkway Board, Ohio State Museum, Columbus, Ohio: 1957), page 79, Captain Moore to Secretary of War Armstrong, 3 February 1813.

[112] **Ibid**, pp. 8-9, Captain Moore to Secretary of War Armstrong, 6 January 1813.

Captain Langham's company was part of Brigadier General James Winchester's western division of the Army of the Northwest, which was defeated at the Battle of the River Raisin, Territory of Michigan, on 22 January 1813.[113] The British captured five of his men and they were made prisoners of war. The company was attached to the 17th Infantry, which had three of its companies assigned to the western division.

After this battle Captain Langham was ordered to report to Brigadier General Simon Perkins of the 2nd Ohio Volunteer Brigade (militia) along with his company on 9 February 1813.[114] General Perkins' brigade formed the right wing of General Harrison's army, and it was posted along the Seneca River in north central Ohio.

Four companies under Colonel Miller took part in the defense of Fort Meigs, Ohio, between 28 April and 9 May 1813 against the British during the first siege of this fort. These companies were under the command of Captains Elliott, Nearing, Langham and Gwynne.[115] First Lieutenant Jonathan Rees of Captain Nearings' company was wounded on 28 April 1813 during the siege. Captain Nearing would later die of fever at Fort Meigs on 30 September 1813. Two companies from the 17th Infantry were attached to the 19th Infantry during this siege.

During the first assault on Fort Meigs, Colonel Miller, along with Major Tod, led a counterattack with 350 men.[116] The force was composed of elements from the companies under Captains Nearing, Elliott, Langham plus men from 1st Lieutenants David Gwynne and James Campbell's detachments of the 19th Infantry, men from Captains David Holt and William Bradford of the 17th Infantry, volunteers from Major John B. Alexander's Independent Battalion from Pennsylvania and Virginia, and Captain William Sebree's Company from the Kentucky militia.[117]

The detachment surprised the artillery crew capturing 42 British artillerymen and they succeeded in spiking the cannons. On the way back to the fort, 150 Canadian militiamen and 300 Indians attacked Colonel Miller's men. The detachment was able to hold off the attackers and make it back to the fort. The Americans suffered 30 killed and 90 wounded.

Major Jesup with two companies from the 19th Infantry were stationed at Cleveland during the spring and summer of 1813 protecting the village and supervising the building of boats for the upcoming invasion of Upper Canada.[118] There were 170 men in this detachment and by 24 May 1813 they had established three boat yards around Cleveland and had finished building 26 boats. The Ohio militia was also building the same type of boats at Fort Amanda in western Ohio.[119] The boats were flat bottomed and could carry 40-50 men with their baggage, arms and provisions. The boats were to be used to transport the Army of the Northwest across Lake Erie when the army invaded Upper Canada.

---

[113] Clift, G. Glenn, **Remember the Raisin!**, (Kentucky Historical Society, Frankfort, Kentucky: 1961), page 177.

[114] "Correspondence of Major George Tod, Selection No. 2 – War of 1812," **Western Reserve and Northern Ohio Historical Society,** Tract Number 17, (Fairbanks & Company, Printers: 1877), Letter from Captain Elliott to Major Tod, 29 June 1813, page 2

[115] Raunch, Steven J., Major, U.S. Army, **War for the Northwest**, page 29, Order of Battle at Fort Meigs.

[116] Nelson, Larry L., **Men of Patriotism, Courage & Enterprise! Fort Meigs in the War of 1812**, (Heritage Books, Inc., Bowie, Maryland: 1970), page 80.

[117] Lexington, K., **History of the Late War in the Western Country**, (Worsley & Smith: 1816), reprinted by University Microfilms, Inc., Ann Arbor, Michigan: 1966, page 268.

[118] Knopf, Richard C., **Document Transcriptions of the War of 1812 in the Northwest,** Volume VII Part 2, Letters from the Secretary of War 1812 & 1813 Relating to the War of 1812 in the Northwest, (Ohio Historical Society: Columbus, Ohio: 1961), page 139, Major Jesup to Secretary of War, 24 May 1813.

[119] **Ibid,** page 132, Secretary of War to Thomas Jesup, 9 March 1813.

On June 14th Major Jesup wrote to the Secretary of War stating that two British warships, supposedly the *Queen Charlotte* and the *Lady Prevost,* had laid off Cleveland the previous day.[120] Major Jesup stated that a British defector had arrived at Cleveland on the 12th and the defector had said that the British were low on supplies at Ft. Malden and that they had planned on attacking the village in order to obtain provisions. A thunderstorm and then a heavy fog appear to have prevented the British from attacking Cleveland. The major finished his letter by saying that his detachment had completed 60 boats for the invasion. By July 1st Major Jesup had 70 boats finished, and he expected to have between 80-90 boats completed the by 15th.[121]

Six men from the 19th Infantry served with the Lake Erie naval squadron under the command of Master Commandant Oliver H. Perry, and they were with him during the Battle of Lake Erie on 10 September 1813.[122] They were individually assigned to serve as marines on board the ships *Tigress, Lawrence* and *Porcupine.*

During the invasion of Upper Canada on 27 September 1813 a detachment from the 19th Infantry under Major Tod was part of the U.S. invasion force. The major was placed in command of Fort Malden, Upper Canada, in September 1813 after the western district of Upper Canada came under the control of the United States.[123]

After the Battle of the Thames, most of the 19th Infantry was transferred to the Niagara Theater along with companies from the 17th, 24th and 26th Infantries. This brigade was under the command of General Harrison, and they landed at Buffalo, New York, on 24 October 1813 according to the general's letter to the secretary of war.[124]

General Harrison proceeded to Fort George, Upper Canada, where he began to organize an expedition against the British positions at Burlington Heights, Upper Canada. But he was speedily ordered to embark with all his troops on the ships of Chauncey's naval squadron for Sackets Harbor, New York.

General Harrison left behind at Fort George a detachment from both the 19th and 24th Infantries. Fort George was later evacuated and all the American troops were ordered to Fort Niagara, New York. Both detachments participated in the Battle of Fort Niagara, New York, on 19 December 1813. The British captured 1st Lieutenant Henry Frederick and four other men from the 19th Infantry. The British made them prisoners of war.

Major Tod wrote to General Harrison on 23 December 1813 from Sackets Harbor stating that the men were still being assigned to their barracks and that everything was on schedule and that drill would commence in a few days.[125] Major Tod also said that Colonel Miller had left for Washington, D.C., on the 19th and that he was expected to return to the regiment in February. No reason for the trip was given. General Harrison had also left for Washington, D.C., and General McArthur who had accompanied the

---

[120] Knopf, Richard C., **Document Transcriptions of the War of 1812 in the Northwest,** volume VII part 2, Letters from the Secretary of War 1812 & 1813 Relating to the War of 1812 in the Northwest, (Ohio Historical Society: Columbus, Ohio: 1961), page 169, Major Jessup to Secretary of War, 14 June 1813.

[121] Knopf, Richard C., **Document Transcriptions of the War of 1812 in the Northwest,** Volume VII Part 3, Letters to the Secretary of War 1812 Relating to the War of 1812 in the Northwest, (Anthony Wayne Parkway Board, Ohio State Museum, Columbus, Ohio: 1957), page 2, Major Jessup to the Secretary of War, 1 July 1813.

[122] Altoff, Gerald T., **Deep Water Sailors, Shallow Water Soldiers, Manning the United States Fleet on Lake Erie 1813**, (The Perry Group, Put-in-Bay, Ohio: 1993), 19th United States Infantry Regiment, page 96.

[123] "Papers of the Late Elisha Whittlesey," **Western Reserve and Northern Ohio Historical Society, Tract Number 12**, (Fairbanks & Company, Printers: 1877), page 1.

[124] Cruikshank, Ernest, editor, **The Documentary History of the Campaign on the Niagara Frontier, Oct. 1813 – May 1814**, volume III, (Arno Press & The New York Times, New York, New York), General Harrison to Secretary of War, 24 October 1813, page 91.

[125] "War of 1812 Correspondence – Selection No. 8," **Western Reserve and Northern Ohio Historical Society,** Tract Number 28, (Fairbanks & Company, Printers: 1877), Letter from Major Tod to General Harrison, 23 December 1813, pp. 3-4.

brigade to New York left for Albany to be a witness against General Hull at his court martial. Major Tod was now in command of this brigade.

The monthly returns for officers during January 1814 at Sackets Harbor listed Colonel Miller, Major Tod, Captains Elliott and Chunn, two lieutenants and two ensigns.[126]

In January 1814 there were 136 soldiers from the 19th Infantry stationed at Fort Shelby, Detroit, according to the monthly returns for Brigadier General Cass's Brigade. By April the detachments from the 17th, 19th, 24th and 28th Infantries that were stationed at Fort Shelby were combined into an 'ad hoc' regiments consisting of 558 men.[127]

Under the act of 10 February 1814 the 2nd Regiment of U.S. Rifle was organized in Kentucky and Ohio. The initial core of officers and enlisted men came from the existing regiments that were assigned to the Army of the Northwest. Among those from the 19th Infantry who were transferred were 1st Lieutenant Batteal Harrison who was promoted to captain and Captain David Gwynne who was promoted to major. A number of junior officers and enlisted men were also transferred to this new regiment.

Captain Chunn returned to the northwest and in March 1814 he was in command of Fort Stephenson, Ohio, with 68 men from the 19th Infantry, 64 men from the 26th Infantry, and a battalion of Ohio militiamen.[128]

On 1 March 1814, Major George Tod, Captain James Herron, Surgeon Charles Marvin plus a lieutenant, two ensigns, the sergeant major, the quartermaster sergeant and a private were ordered to report to the recruiting service in Ohio.[129] They had all been stationed at Sackets Harbor.

Under the Act of 3 March 1814 the regiment was consolidated with the 17th Infantry to create the new 17th Regiment of U.S. Infantry. The following senior officers from the 19th Infantry were transferred to the 17th Infantry: Colonel John Miller; Captain George W. Jackson; Captain James Herron; Captain Richard Graham; Captain Hugh Moore; Captain Harris H. Hickman; and Captain John T. Chunn. The following senior officers were discharged: Major Nathan Heald, Captain Wilson Elliott, and Captain Samuel Booker. The act went into effect on 12 May 1814.

Lieutenant Colonel Campbell was the Commander of Military at Erie, Pennsylvania. On 13 May 1814 he was ordered to take his command of 750 men, made up of regulars and militia, to Buffalo, New York.[130] This order occurred the day after the 19th Infantry merged into the 17th Infantry. Colonel Campbell's detachment would disembark at Buffalo as part of the new 17th Infantry.

Captain Langham would be promoted to major on 15 August 1813 and he was transferred to the 10th Regiment of U.S. Infantry. Captain Graham would be promoted to major on 30 March 1813 and he was reassigned to the 17th Infantry. Captain Anderson was promoted to brevet major and he became a topographical engineer for the army.

The 19th Regiment of U.S. Infantry as organized under the act of 26 Jun 1812 ceased to exist when the men in this regiment merged with the 17th Regiment of U.S. Infantry on 12 May 1814.

---

[126] **Duncan McArthur Papers**, Library of Congress, 1922, Microfilm 47, Reel 2, Volumes 4-5, 22 September 1813 – 4 March 1814, document number 699, Officers of the 8th Military District at Sackett's Harbor, 22 January 1814, Ohio Historical Society, Columbus, Ohio.

[127] **Ibid**, Microfilm 47, Reel 3, Volumes 6-8, 22 September 1813 – 4 March 1814, document number 1383, Monthly Returns at Detroit, 30 April 1814, Ohio Historical Society, Columbus, Ohio.

[128] **Ibid**, Microfilm 47, Reel 3, Volumes 6-8, 22 September 1813 – 4 March 1814, document number 1128, Report of strength of detachment at Lower Sandusky, 24 March 1814, Ohio Historical Society, Columbus, Ohio.

[129] **Adjutant General's Office**, 1 March 1814, Sackets Harbor, New York, reassignment orders, manuscript section, call number MS-660, Container 1, Folder 9 Western Reserve Historical Society Archives Library, Cleveland, Ohio.

[130] Cruikshank, Ernest, editor, **Documents Relating to the Invasion of the Niagara Peninsula by the United States Army**, (The Niagara Historical Society, Niagara-on-the-Lake, Ontario, Canada: 1920), pp. 18-19, letter to William Jones, Secretary of the Navy, from A. Sinclair, 13 May 1814.

Second Organization

The 19th Regiment of U.S. Infantry was re-organized under the same acts of Congress that established the first organization of this regiment. The lengths of enlistments were approved for five years, 18-months and during the war.

Colonel George Paull of St. Clairsville, Belmont County, Ohio, was regiment's first commander under the reorganization act of 3 March 1814. He served from 12 May 1814 until he resigned from the service on 31 October 1814. He had previously served as the commander of the 27th Regiment of U.S. Infantry. The final commander of the regiment was Colonel Robert Carter Nicholas of Kentucky who served between 4 September 1814 and 17 May 1815. Nicholas had transferred from the 1st Regiment of U.S. Infantry to assume command of the regiment.

Thomas B. Van Horne of Warren County, Ohio, was the regiment's lieutenant colonel. Van Horne served from 12 May 1814 to 17 May 1815. He had been the lieutenant colonel and commander of the 26th Regiment of U.S. Infantry.

The regiment had three majors assigned to it during its existence. They were William H. Trimble of Highland County, Ohio, Thomas Rowland of Columbiana County, Ohio, and Thomas Montgomery of Maryland. Montgomery replaced Trimble when Trimble was promoted to lieutenant colonel and transferred to the 1st Regiment of Infantry. Trimble had been a major in the 26th Infantry while Rowland had been a major in the 27th Infantry. Montgomery had been a captain in the 14th Regiment of U.S. Infantry before he was promoted and reassigned to the 19th Infantry.

The following captains from the 26th Infantry were transferred to the 19th Infantry: Joel Collins, Richard C. Talbott and George Kesling. The following captains from the 27th Infantry were transferred to the 19th Infantry: William Gill, Isaac Van Horne, Junior, Henry Northup and Alexander Hill. The following captains from the 17th Infantry were transferred to the 19th Infantry: William Bradford and Richard Hightower.

Captain Hugh Moore transferred from the original 19th Infantry. Captain Northup resigned from the army on 11 November 1814 while Captain Moore resigned on 12 October 1814.

The Secretary of War John Armstrong wrote to Major General Jacob Brown, commander of the Army of the North, on 19 June 1814 stating that he had ordered General McArthur, the new commander of the Army of the Northwest, to forward his recruits from the 17th, 19th and 24th Infantries to New York.[131] They were to assemble at Detroit and then travel by ship to Buffalo, New York. In the same letter he ordered General Brown to invade Upper Canada and capture Fort Erie.

The ships *Ohio*, *Porcupine* and *Somers* were ordered to transport three companies of the 1st Regiment of U.S. Infantry under the command of Lieutenant Colonel Nicholas from Erie to Buffalo and then to return to pick up the men from the 17th, 19th and 24th Infantries being assembled at Cleveland and the mouth of the Portage River.[132]

William Baird replaced Captain Hightower on 29 June 1814. Carey A. Trimble replaced Captain Bradford on 20 August 1814. William McDonald replaced Captain Hill on 11 Nov 1814. George Will replaced Captain Van Horne on 4 August 1814. Hightower resigned his commission while Bradford was promoted to major and transferred to the 21st Regiment of U.S. Infantry. Van Horne was killed during the Battle of Mackinaw Island, Territory of Michigan.

Captain Hill and his company were stationed at Zanesville.[133] He was ordered to report with his company to Fort Detroit after the Battle of the Thames and once there he was sent to Fort Malden, Upper Canada, to assume command of that post. He was then ordered back to Zanesville and from there he was

---

[131] **Ibid**, pp. 49-50, letter from Edmond P. Kennedy to William Jones, Secretary of the Navy, 22 July 1814.

[132] **Ibid**, pp. 35-37, letter from Secretary of War to General Brown, 19 Jun 1814.

[133] Andrews, Martin R., M.A., **History of Marietta and Washington County, Ohio, and Representative Citizens**, (Biographical Publishing Company, Chicago, Illinois: 1902), pp. 557 and 564.

then ordered to the Niagara Theater along with Captain Bradford's company. This detachment was under the command of Major William Trimble.

The two companies were then stationed at Fort Erie, Upper Canada, and they were involved in the taking of the fort on 3 July 1814 and the two sieges by the British on 13-15 August and 17 September 1814.[134] While stationed at Fort Erie Captain Carey Trimble replaced Captain Bradford and Captain McDonald replaced Captain Hill after Hill resigned from the army.

The regiment also fought in the Battle of Chippewa, Upper Canada, on 5 July 1814 suffering three privates killed, two wounded and two missing.[135] The two companies from the 19th Infantry were attached to the 21st Regiment of U.S. Infantry.

Second Lieutenant Abraham Fisk was wounded during the Battle of Lundy's Lane, Upper Canada, on 25 July 1814. The regiment was once again attached to the 21st Infantry and they were involved in a major attack on the British lines in which they captured the central British artillery battery forcing the entire British battle line to withdraw from their defensive line to a secondary position. The 19th Infantry along with a detachment from the 17th Infantry formed the right wing of the 21st Infantry during this battle.[136] Captain MacDonald was promoted to brevet major on 25 July 1814 for his actions during the Battle of Lundy's Lane.

The greatest glory obtained by the 19th Infantry during the war occurred when the British stormed Fort Erie on 14 August 1814 and the 118 men of this regiment plus an artillery battery from the Corps of U.S. Artillery successful defended the fort. During this battle five privates were killed and 16 men were wounded.[137] Among the wounded were 1st Lieutenant Andrew Bushnell of Captain Chunn's company and Ensign Charles Cissna. On the following day 2nd Lieutenant Alexander Patterson of Captain Hill's company was wounded.[138]

The last battle to be fought at Fort Erie occurred on 17 September 1814 when the American forces under Major General Peter Porter attacked the British artillery batteries.[139] The 19th Infantry under the command of Major Trimble along with the 9th and 11th Infantries were a part of the Colonel James Miller's brigade. This force captured two British batteries and they were able to spike the cannons rendering the cannons useless. During the engagement both Major Trimble and Ensign Nicholas Neely were wounded.[140]

During the summer of 1814 it became crucial that Fort Michillimachinac on Mackinaw Island, Territory of Michigan, be taken back from the British. The fort controlled the entrance to Lake Michigan

---

[134] Babcock, Louis, L., **The War of 1812 on the Niagara Frontier**, (Buffalo Historical Society, Buffalo, New York: 1927), page 193, The Attack on the Fort, and pp. 212 and 223, The Period Between the Assault and the Sortie.

[135] Cruikshank, Ernest, editor, **The Documentary History of the Campaign on the Niagara Frontier, Oct. 1813 – May 1814**, Volume III, (Arno Press & The New York Times, New York, New York), report of the killed and wounded on the plains of Chippawa, 5 July 1814, Upper Canada, page 43.

[136] Cruikshank, Ernest, editor, **Documents Relating to the Invasion of the Niagara Peninsula by the United States Army**, (The Niagara Historical Society, Niagara-on-the-Lake, Ontario, Canada: 1920), page 82, Memoranda of Occurrences and some Important Facts attending the Campaign on the Niagara in 1814.

[137] Cruikshank, Ernest, editor, **The Documentary History of the Campaign on the Niagara Frontier, Oct. 1813 – May 1814**, Volume III, (Arno Press & The New York Times, New York, New York), report of the killed and wounded at Fort Erie, Upper Canada, 15 August 1814, page 151.

[138] **Ibid**, report of the killed and wounded on the plains of Chippawa, 14 August 1814, Upper Canada, page 150.

[139] Babcock, Louis, L., **The War of 1812 on the Niagara Frontier**, (Buffalo Historical Society, Buffalo, New York: 1927), page 225, Chapter VXI Sortie of the Americans.

[140] Cruikshank, Ernest, editor, **The Documentary History of the Campaign on the Niagara Frontier, Oct. 1813 – May 1814**, Volume III, (Arno Press & The New York Times, New York, New York), report of the killed and wounded at Fort Erie, Upper Canada, 17 September 1814, page 214.

and it was also part of the British supply line to the upper Mississippi River valley, which was still in their hands.

A joint army-navy force left Fort Gratiot, north of Fort Detroit, on July 12th. Fort Gratiot was built by the Americans at the entrance of the St. Clair River to keep any British naval ships from sailing down the river to Detroit. The brigs *Niagara* and *Lawrence* plus the schooners *Caledonia*, *Tigress* and *Scorpion* transported the army north to Fort Michillimachinac. Lieutenant Colonel George Croghan commanded the Americans with five companies (500 men) from the 17th, 19th, 24th and 28th Infantries and 250 men militia from Colonel William Cotgreave's Ohio Volunteer Regiment.[141] Captain Isaac Van Horne, Junior, and his company represented the 19th Infantry in this expedition.

The Americans started their attack on the fort on July 26th but withdrew after finding that the guns of the fleet could not be raised high enough to bombard the fort. A land assault was launched on August 4th when the Americans landed on the backside of the island. The British ambushed the invading army inflicting heavy casualties on the Americans and forcing their withdrawal from the island. The fort and control of the upper Mississippi River valley would remain in the hands of the British until the end of the war. Captain Van Horne was killed in action during the assault on this island.

After the Battle of Mackinaw Island Colonel Croghan learned of the existence of a British supply depot on the Nottawasaga River at the southern end of the Georgian Bay of Lake Huron and the squadron sets sail for this British base. Colonel Croghan's men attacked and destroyed the supply depot. In the process the only remaining British warship on the upper Great Lakes, the sloop *Nancy*, was destroyed by the British to avoid its capture by the Americans.

On 17 May 1815, the 19th Infantry was consolidated with the 1st, 17th, 28th and 39th Regiments of U.S. Infantry to form the new 3rd Regiment of U.S. Infantry.[142] Brevet Major MacDonald would transfer to the 3rd Infantry while the remaining senior officers of the 19th Infantry were discharged from the army on 15 June 1815.

---

[141] McAfee, Robert Breckinridge, **History of the Late War in the Western Country,** (University Microfilms, Inc., Ann Arbor, Michigan: 1966), originally published in 1816, Chapter X, Expedition of Captain Holmes, pp. 410-453.

[142] **Ibid.**

Captain George Sanderson and the Battle of the Thames

In the summer of 1813 Major General William Henry Harrison invited Governor William Shelby of Kentucky to bring his militiamen to northern Ohio to spearhead the invasion of Upper Canada. The governor brought with him 3,000 Kentuckians organized into five brigades and eleven regiments. Another Kentucky regiment of mounted troops under the command of Colonel Richard M. Johnson joined the invading army where Port Clinton, Ohio, now stands.

General Harrison's regular forces from the U.S. Army numbered well over 2,000 men, but these troops had been trained to fight against the British regulars while the militia was accustomed to fight against the Indians. General Harrison knew that the upcoming battle for supremacy in the northwest would involve the militia against the Indians. He chose Captain George Sanderson's company of 142 men as the only regular army unit for the upcoming battle.

Captain Sanderson's company was part of the 27th Regiment of U.S. Infantry, which had been raised in eastern Ohio. The regiment was organized under the Congressional Act of 29 January 1813. The captain had raised his company from the Fairfield County area.

After the army had landed on the shores of Upper Canada, General Harrison and his forces pursued the British up the Thames River valley. On October 4th the army overtook a rear guard of Indians and they defeated them at Chatham, Upper Canada. The next day General Harrison's army caught up to the main British force near Moravian Town where they crushed the British and Indians at the Battle of the Thames.

The company from the 27th Infantry had been assigned to the right most position on General Harrison's battle line. The company's mission was to capture the British artillery battery before the British were able to use their artillery against the American lines. This the company accomplished without a loss of life. The company now was in a flanking position, which prevented many of the British soldiers from escaping once the battle ended. After the battle Captain Sanderson's company guarded the British prisoners of war and escorted them back to the Detroit River. The British were from the 41st Regiment of Foot and they would eventually be interned at the Newport Barracks in Kentucky.

Captain Sanderson and many of his men took an extreme risk of life in participating in the Battle of the Thames. The year before, Sanderson had been a company commander in Brigadier General William Hull's army, which had surrendered to the British on 16 August 1812. Sanderson and many of his men in his company were still prisoners of war on parole status and had the British caught them a second time, they probably would have been invited to stand before a British firing squad.

Captain Sanderson would resign from the army the following year, and he returned home to rejoined the Ohio militia. In the years following the War of 1812 he continued to rise in rank until he became a major general in the Ohio militia.

History of the 26th Regiment of U.S. Infantry

The 26th Regiment of U.S. Infantry was organized under an Act of Congress on 29 January 1813 as the first of 19 new infantry regiments that were to be raised for one year.[143] A twentieth infantry regiment was authorized but it was converted into ten companies of rangers. The 26th Infantry was authorized to have ten 102-man companies plus a headquarters' staff for a total strength of 1,091 men.[144] The regiment would be raised from within the 1st, 2nd and 5th Divisions of the Ohio Militia, which constituted the western half of Ohio.

On 28 January 1814 the regiment's authorization was changed to five years or less. At the same time enlistments were approved for five years or during the war. The regimental headquarters and the main recruiting center were established at Chillicothe, Ohio. The regiment operated in both the 8th and the 9th Military Districts.

Recruiting the regiment proved to be a problem and only 300 men were enlisted by June 30th, 791 men short of a full complement. The regiment operated as part of the Army of the Northwest in the 8th Military District.

Colonel Duncan McArthur of Chillicothe, Ross County, Ohio, commanded the 26th Infantry from 20 February 1813 to 12 March 1813. Thomas B. Van Horne of Warren County, Ohio, was appointed the regiment's lieutenant colonel, and he held this position from 9 April 1813 to 12 May 1814. Joseph Jenkinson of Butler County, Ohio, and William A. Trimble of Highland County, Ohio, were appointed the regimental majors. Jenkinson held his position from 19 February 1813 to 12 May 1814 while Trimble served from 18 March 1813 to 12 May 1814.

On 12 March 1813 Colonel McArthur was promoted to brigadier general, and he was assigned to command one of the two regular brigades that were scheduled to be part of Major General William H. Harrison's invasion of Upper Canada. Due to the fact that the regiment was two-thirds under strength no one was appointed to replace McArthur as the regiment's colonel. Lieutenant Colonel Van Horne commanded the battalion-sized regiment after Colonel McArthur left the unit.

Ten men from Ohio were commissioned as captains on 20 May 1813. They were Samuel Swearingen of Ross County, Joel Collins of Butler County, William A. Puthuff, John McDonald, Richard C. Talbott, John Moore, George Kesling, Christopher Wood, John Lucas of Scioto County and Josiah Lockhart. The regiment was headquartered at the Chillicothe Barracks, Chillicothe, Ohio.[145]

Major Joseph Jenkinson was the commandant of Fort Wayne, Territory of Indiana, from mid-1813 to the spring of 1814. He was in command of Captain Rhea's 76-man company from the 1st Regiment of U.S. Infantry and three companies of militia.[146] Captain James Rhea had been found drunk during the Siege of Fort Wayne in September 1813 and he was forced to resign from the service by General Harrison.

Colonel McArthur had written to Ohio's Senator Thomas Worthington in a letter dated 30 June 1813 from Chillicothe, stating that 240 men from his regiment had left the previous week for northern Ohio.[147]

---

[143] Heitman, Francis B., **Historical Register and Dictionary of the United States Army From Its Organization, September 29, 1789, to March 2, 1903**, (Genealogical Publishing Company, Baltimore, Maryland: 1994), Volume I, page 125, Twenty-sixth Regiment.

[144] **Ibid**, Volume II, pp. 574-575, Organization of the Army under the Act of March 3, 1812.

[145] Medert, Patricia Fife, **Raw Recruits & Bullish Prisoners, Ohio's Capital in the War of 1812**, Ross County Historical Society Publication, (Jackson Publishing Company, Jackson, Ohio: 1992), page 19.

[146] Griswold, B. J., **The Pictorial History of Fort Wayne, Indiana**, (Robert O. Law Company, Chicago, Illinois: 1917), chapter VIII 1812-1813.

[147] Knopft, Richard C., **Thomas Worthington and the War of 1812, Volume III of the Document Transcriptions of the War of 1812 in the Northwest**, (The Anthony Wayne Parkway Board, Ohio State Museum, Columbus, Ohio: 1957), letter from Duncan McArthur to Thomas Worthington, 30 June 1813, page 208.

Major General William H. Harrison, who was preparing for his invasion of Upper Canada, had called the regiment to duty. Another 60 men had been recently recruited, and they would be soon marching to northern Ohio. Those captains, along with their lieutenants and ensigns, who had not been able to recruit a company, were retained in western Ohio as part of the recruiting service for the regiment.

One fourth of the 26th Infantry had previously been members of the Ohio militia, which had surrendered to the British the year before.[148] These men were prisoners of war on parole status and if they were captured again, they could face a British firing squad.

Carlos Norton wrote to Senator Worthington on 7 July 1813 stating the Captains Puthuff and Kessling had left Franklinton for Sandusky with two other companies.[149] He also said that the platoon officers still haven't received their confirmations for their officer appointments. The other two companies were under the commands of Captains Collins and Swearingen.

Colonel McArthur suggested to Senator Worthington that he dismiss some of his officers and have these men serve as recruiters in western Pennsylvania and western Virginia (now West Virginia). He was also hopeful that another battalion of men (approximately 500 men) could be raised in Ohio, but he felt that this would not be accomplished in time to support the upcoming invasion.

The regiment marched to Fort Seneca along the Sandusky River in northern Ohio where the unit met up with the 27th and 28th Regiments of U.S. Infantry. These three regiments drilled and prepared for the upcoming invasion of Canada. The 27th Infantry was raised in eastern Ohio and it had 700 men on its roster while the 28th Infantry came from Kentucky with 600 men.

The 26th Infantry's first combat experience was gained on 10 September 1813 during the Battle of Lake Erie.[150] Fifteen men from the regiment volunteered to serve temporarily with Commodore Oliver H. Perry's naval squadron. General Harrison had canvassed his regiments for volunteers who had previously worked on either boats or ships. These men were divided and assigned to the ships *Porcupine, Niagara, Ariel* and *Scorpion*. The men were used as marines in Commodore Perry's squadron.

On September 25th the long awaited invasion of Upper Canada began when General Harrison ordered Colonel Richard Johnson and his mounted Kentucky militia regiment to proceed to the River Raisin in the Territory of Michigan. Two days later the Army of the Northwest boarded the ships of Commodore Perry's squadron, and they landed three miles below Fort Malden in Upper Canada. General Lewis Cass and his brigade entered Amherstburg unopposed and they took Fort Malden and the naval shipyard. General Duncan McArthur and his brigade headed north towards the village of Sandwich. They crossed over the Detroit River and then occupied Fort Detroit unopposed. On September 30th Colonel Johnson's regiment entered Detroit before they crossed over to Upper Canada to join General Harrison's forces. This was the only mounted regiment with horses in the invasion force. The mounted troops, both regular and militia, that had crossed Lake Erie with General Harrison had left their horses on Catawba Island in Ohio.

After the Battle of the Thames, General Harrison was ordered to the Niagara Theater with part of his army. He took 1,300 regular soldiers leaving 400 soldiers and the militia behind to guard the western district of Upper Canada and the Territory of Michigan. The naval squadron transported the army to New York making stops at Put-in-Bay, Ohio, and Erie, Pennsylvania. General Harrison wrote to the Secretary of War from Erie, Pennsylvania, on 21 October 1813 stating that he was leaving for Buffalo, New York,

---

[148] Knopf, Richard C., **Document Transcriptions of the War of 1812 in the Northwest,** Volume VII, Part 2, Letters from the Secretary of War 1812 & 1813 Relating to the War of 1812 in the Northwest, (Ohio Historical Society: Columbus, Ohio: 1961), page 183, General Harrison to Secretary of War, 23 June 1813.

[149] Knopf, Richard C., **Document Transcriptions of the War of 1812 in the Northwest,** Volume III, *Thomas Worthington and the War of 1812*, (Anthony Wayne Parkway Board, Ohio State Museum, Columbus, Ohio: 1957), Carlos A. Norton to Thomas Worthington, 7 July 1813, page 213.

[150] Altoff, Gerald T., **Deep Water Sailors, Shallow Water Soldiers, Manning the United States Fleet on Lake Erie 1813**, (The Perry Group, Put-in-Bay, Ohio: 1993), 26th United States Infantry Regiment, page 97.

with part of General McArthur's brigade and a battalion of rifleman.[151] General Harrison's forces landed at Buffalo on 24 October 1813 according to his letter to the secretary of war dated the same date.[152] It took seven vessels to transport the greater part of General McArthur's brigade and the riflemen under Colonel Smith.

A part of the brigade and most of the baggage were left behind at Bass Island [Put-in-Bay, South Bass Island, Ohio], and they would be picked up by the returning vessels and brought to Buffalo. General Harrison was going to march his troops to Fort George, Upper Canada, and from there he would wait for further orders from the secretary of war.

General McArthur became the commander of a smaller Army of the Northwest but he accompanied his brigade to New York. General Cass was appointed the military governor of the Michigan Territory and the western district of Upper Canada. Unit the end of the war, the British were still in control of Fort Michillimachinac in northern Michigan Territory, plus the northern parts of the Territories of Illinois Territory and Missouri.

General Harrison established his headquarters in Newark, Upper Canada, outside of Fort George and he found to his dismay that only a single brigade of New York militia was defending the Niagara frontier. The regular forces had been transferred to Sackets Harbor, New York, in defense of upper New York. General Harrison's intelligence indicated that a British force was gathering at the head of Lake Ontario and that they would be attacking Fort George in the near future.

On 1 November 1813,[153] he wrote to Governor Tompkins of New York requesting additional state militia for his command and stating to the governor that he had ordered 'considerable' reinforcements from Detroit but felt that they will not arrive in time for the British attack.

Shortly after writing to the governor, General Harrison received his orders from the Secretary of War ordering him to immediately take his brigade to Sackets Harbor. This would leave the border along the Niagara River again defended by the New York militia with some regular soldiers guarding the forts. The brigade left the mouth of the Niagara River for Sackets Harbor by ship on November 16th.[154]

Major George Tod of the 19th Infantry wrote to General Harrison on 23 December 1813 from Sackets Harbor stating that the men were still being assigned to their barracks and that everything was on schedule and that drill would commence in a few days.[155] Major Tod wrote a letter to Brigadier General Smith on 22 February 1814 at Sackets Harbor requesting that he be given permission to discharge part of the 26th Infantry since some of their enlistments were expiring.[156]

There were at least two companies of the 26th Infantry stationed at Sackets Harbor. According to Private Lewis Gordon, he was transferred from Captain George Kesling's company to Captain William Puthuff's company while stationed at Sackets Harbor.[157] The officers from the regiment were sent home to the recruiting service, and the enlisted men were incorporated into the 19th Regiment of Infantry.

---

[151] Cruikshank, Ernest, editor, **The Documentary History of the Campaign on the Niagara Frontier, Oct. 1813 – May 1814**, (Arno Press & The New York Times, New York, New York), General Harrison to Secretary of War, 21 October 1813, page 87.

[152] **Ibid**, General Harrison to Secretary of War, 24 October 1813, page 91.

[153] **Ibid**, General Harrison to Governor Tompkins, 1 November 1813, pp. 116-117.

[154] **Ibid**, story from the Buffalo "Gazette," 23 November 1813, page 225.

[155] "War of 1812 Correspondence – Selection No. 8," **Western Reserve and Northern Ohio Historical Society, Tract Number 28**, (Fairbanks & Company, Printers: 1877), Letter from Major Tod to General Harrison, 23 December 1813, pp. 3-4.

[156] "Letter from Major Tod to Brigadier General Smith, 22 February 1814," **George Tod Papers 1783-1834**, Western Reserve Historical Society Archives Library, Cleveland, Ohio, container 1B, folder 9.

[157] Altoff, Gerald T., **Deep Water Sailors, Shallow Water Soldiers, Manning the United States Fleet on Lake Erie 1813**, (The Perry Group, Put-in-Bay, Ohio: 1993), 26th United States Infantry Regiment, page 144.

Meanwhile, General McArthur had written to Senator Worthington from Chillicothe on 7 December 1813 stating that he had traveled with his brigade as far as Fort George, Upper Canada, and he had seen them embark for Sackets Harbor.[158] He had taken sick at Fort Detroit before the brigade left and the voyage across Lake Erie had worsened his illness. He was recovering at his home in Chillicothe and was awaiting orders to attend the court martial of General William Hull at Albany, New York.

First Lieutenant Carey A. Trimble was captured during the Battle of Fort Niagara, New York, on 19 December 1813, and the British made him a prisoner of war. Also captured was Private Thomas Anderson of Captain Samuel Swearingen's company, who stated that he was interned in Montreal, Lower Canada, and exchanged on 15 April 1814.[159]

On 17 January 1814, Lieutenant Daniel McFarland, and his 28-man detachment, stationed at Fort Seneca, were ordered to Put-in-Bay by General Cass as part of a 200-man reinforcement to be sent to the Niagara peninsular.[160] McFarland was not a company commander but he was in command of a detachment of men from the regiment who had recovered from various illnesses and who were now fit for duty. Once they arrived at the Niagara peninsular, this detachment was merged into its parent company.

A detachment of 172 men was stationed at the Sandwich Batteries across the river from Detroit in Upper Canada in January 1814 according to the monthly returns for Brigadier General Cass's Brigade.[161] By April 1814 there were 149 men from the 26th Infantry at Sandwich serving as occupation troops.[162] First Lieutenant William MacDonald commanded a detachment of 64 men from the 26th Infantry stationed at Fort Stephenson, Ohio, In March 1814.[163]

On 1 March 1814, Captain Samuel Swearingen and Captain George Kesling plus three lieutenants and an ensign were ordered to report to the recruiting service in Ohio.[164] They had all been stationed at Sackets Harbor. Captain Swearingen resigned from the service on 9 April 1814 while Captain McDonald resigned on 7 August 1813. Captain Puthuff transferred to the 2nd Regiment of U.S. Rifles on 21 February 1814.

Under the act of 30 March 1814 the 26th and 27th Regiments of U.S. Infantry along with two companies from the 17th Regiment of U.S. Infantry consolidated and became the new 19th Regiment of U.S. Infantry on 15 May 1814.[165] Most of the officers and men from the 26th Infantry were released from

---

[158] Knopft, Richard C., **Thomas Worthington and the War of 1812, Volume III of the Document Transcriptions of the War of 1812 in the Northwest**, (The Anthony Wayne Parkway Board, Ohio State Museum, Columbus, Ohio: 1957), letter from Duncan McArthur to Thomas Worthington, 7 December 1813, page 224.

[159] Altoff, Gerald T., **Deep Water Sailors, Shallow Water Soldiers, Manning the United States Fleet on Lake Erie 1813**, (The Perry Group, Put-in-Bay, Ohio: 1993), 26th United States Infantry Regiment, pp. 120-121.

[160] Cruikshank, Ernest, editor, **The Documentary History of the Campaign on the Niagara Frontier, Oct. 1813 – May 1814**, (Arno Press & The New York Times, New York, New York), John S. Gano to William Henry Harrison, 17 January 1814 and 24 January 1814, pp. 128-129, 145-146.

[161] **Duncan McArthur Papers**, Library of Congress, 1922, Microfilm 47, Reel 2, Volumes 4-5, 22 September 1813 – 4 March 1814, document number 748, Monthly Returns for Brigadier General Cass's Brigade under the command of Lieutenant Colonel Butler, January 1814, Ohio Historical Society, Columbus, Ohio.

[162] **Ibid**, document number 1383, Monthly Returns at Detroit, 30 April 1814, Ohio Historical Society, Columbus, Ohio.

[163] **Ibid**, document number 1128, Report of strength of detachment at Lower Sandusky, 24 March 1814, Ohio Historical Society, Columbus, Ohio.

[164] **Adjutant General's Office**, 1 March 1814, Sackets Harbor, New York, reassignment orders, manuscript section, call number MS-660, Container 1, Folder 9 Western Reserve Historical Society Archives Library, Cleveland, Ohio.

[165] Mahon, John K. and Romana Danysh, **Infantry Part 1: Regular Army**, (Office of the Chief of Military History, United States Army, Washington, D.C.: 1972), War of 1812, page 14.

duty since their one-year enlistment was expiring. The men who had re-enlisted for "five years or during the war" were transferred to the 19th Infantry.

Lieutenant Colonel Van Horne, Major Trimble and Captains Kesling, Collins and Talbott were transferred into the 19th Infantry on 12 May 1814. The remaining senior officers were discharged on 1 June 1814.

Blankets for the dead [166]

Captain Wilson Elliott's company of the 19th Regiment of U.S. Infantry participated in the Mississineway Expedition under the command of Lieutenant Colonel John B. Campbell during the War of 1812. This regiment was raised in Ohio during the war and the regiment enlisted Ohioans from all corners of the state. Captain Elliott's company fought at the Battle of Mississineway River, Territory of Indiana, on 17-18 December 1812.

After returning to Ohio the soldiers were re-issued clothing, replacing items that were worn out or had been lost during the expedition. The clothing report of 25 January 1813 showed that seven soldiers were re-issued blankets because these men had given up their blankets after the battle so that the dead could be covered and buried in them.

This was a very significant act of humanity since most of the 650 men who participated in the expedition had returned to Ohio suffering from frostbite and winter related illnesses. These men were Privates Thomas Cavalu (sic), William Lysle, John Leonard, John Hall, John Shaw, Joel Thurman and Charles W. Hide.

---

[166] "Clothing issue roster for Captain Wilson Elliott's Company", 25 January 1813, **George Tod Collection**, Western Reserve Historical Society Archives Library, Cleveland, Ohio, manuscript section, call number MS-3202, container 2.

History of the 27th Regiment of U.S. Infantry

The 27th Regiment of U.S. Infantry was organized under the Congressional Act of 29 January 1813.[167] This new regiment was apart of a twenty-regiment build up of the army during the War of 1812. It was authorized for one year and all initial enlistments were for twelve months.[168]

On 28 January 1814 the regiment's authorization was changed to five years or less. At the same time enlistments were approved for five year or during the war and the one-year enlistments were eliminated. The regimental headquarters and the main recruiting center were established at Zanesville, Ohio. The regiment operated as part of the Army of the Northwest in the 8th Military District.

The army was having problems recruiting men for its regiments since the current tour of duty was for "five years or during the war" so these regiments were formed with one-year enlistees to help boost the strength of the army. The regiment was authorized to have 10 companies of 102 men each with a headquarters' staff for a total manning of 1,091 men.[169]

The Secretary of War John Armstrong wrote to Major General William Henry Harrison on 5 March 1813 informing him that he was assigning four regiments to the Army of the Northwest to support Harrison's invasion of Upper Canada.[170] Armstrong said, "Cleveland is believed to be the place best fitted for this purpose [the staging area for the invasion]. It will also be made the depot for the troops to be employed on the expedition, which will be the 24th Regt., now at Massac, -- and three of the twenty new Regts. Provided by an Act of the cession of congress which closed yesterday. Two of these will be raised in the state of Ohio, & the third in that of Kaintucky."

The 24th Regiment of U.S. Infantry had been raised in Tennessee and this regiment was stationed at Fort Massac along the Ohio River in the Territory of Illinois. The 26th Infantry was raised in western Ohio while the 27th Infantry was raised in eastern Ohio and the 28th Infantry was raised in Kentucky.

Colonel Lewis Cass of Zanesville, Muskingum County, Ohio, served as the regiment's first commander from 20 February 1813 to 12 March 1813. On March 12th he was promoted to brigadier general and was assigned to command one of the two regular brigades under General Harrison. George Paull of St. Clairsville, Belmont County, Ohio, became the 27th Infantry's second commander on 29 June 1813, a position he held until 12 May 1814. In civilian life he was a lawyer and a brigadier general in the Ohio militia.[171]

During the formation of the regiment Colonel Cass selected George Paull as his lieutenant colonel and Jeremiah R. Munson of Muskingum County, Ohio, and Robert Morrison of Belmont County as his regimental majors. After Paull become the commander of the regiment Thomas Rowland of Columbiana County, Ohio, was selected to replace Paull as the lieutenant colonel.

Ten Ohio men were commissioned as captains on 20 May 1813. They were William Gill and Absalom Martin of Belmont County; Henry Northup, Isaac Van Horne, Junior, and Joseph Cairns of Muskingum

---

[167] Heitman, Francis B., **Historical Register and Dictionary of the United States Army From Its Organization, September 29, 1789, to March 2, 1903**, (Genealogical Publishing Company, Baltimore, Maryland: 1994), Volume I, pp. 126-127, Twenty-Seventh Regiment.

[168] Mahon, John K. and Romana Danysh, **Infantry Part 1: Regular Army**, (Office of the Chief of Military History, United States Army, Washington, D.C.: 1972), War of 1812, pp. 14-16.

[169] Heitman, Francis B., **Historical Register and Dictionary of the United States Army From Its Organization, September 29, 1789, to March 2, 1903**, (Genealogical Publishing Company, Baltimore, Maryland: 1994), Volume II, pp. 574-575, Organization of the Army under the Act of March 3, 1813.

[170] Knopf, Richard C., **Return Jonathan Meigs, Jr. and the War of 1812, Volume II of the Document Transcriptions of the War of 1812 in the Northwest**, (Anthony Wayne Parkway Board, Ohio State Museum, Columbus, Ohio: 1961 Secretary of War John Armstrong to General Harrison, 5 March 1813, pp 83-84.

[171] **Western Reserve and Northern Ohio Historical Society**, Tract Number 36, January 1877, page 2, (Western Reserve and Northern Ohio Historical Society, Cleveland, Ohio), Statement of General George Sanderson of Lancaster, Ohio, April 1870.

County, Alexander Hill of Washington County, John Spencer of Licking County, George Sanderson of Fairfield County, and James Applegate and James A. Harper of Trumbull County.

Simon Perkins of Trumbull County, Ohio, had been chosen to become the second commander of the regiment.[172] He was also a brigadier general in the Ohio militia. In a letter to Ohio's Senator Thomas Worthington dated 1 June 1813, Carlos Norton informed the senator that Perkins had accepted the position but then on 8 June 1813 Colonel Cass informed the senator that Perkins had turned down the appointment. Colonel Cass then recommended Lieutenant Colonel Paull to be the next commander of the regiment.[173]

Originally the recruits for both the 26th and 27th Infantries were to rendezvous at Zanesville, Ohio, where both regiments would have been organized. Senator Worthington wrote to the Secretary of War James Armstrong on 10 April 1813 suggesting that the rendezvous point be moved to Chillicothe, Ohio, because the troops could be supplied there at one-third the cost.[174]

By 1 June 1813 the recruiters had signed up between 500 and 600 men for the regiment.[175] Colonel Cass wrote to Senator Worthington on 22 June 1813 from Zanesville stating that the 27th Infantry had received its marching orders from General Harrison.[176] The regiment was formed in Zanesville and had nearly 700 men recruited from eastern Ohio by the time the regiment joined the Army of the Northwest. The majority of the men who enlisted in this regiment were from the 3rd Division of the Ohio Militia from southeastern Ohio while the remaining men came from the 4th Division of the Ohio Militia from northeastern Ohio.

As of 7 June 1813 the uniforms for the regiment had not arrived from the army depot in Pittsburgh but General Cass had received word that 500 uniforms had been shipped to him. General Cass wrote to the Secretary of War requesting his permission to draw upon the extra uniforms that were the property of the 17th and 19th Infantries that were in storage at Chillicothe and Franklinton, Ohio, in order to outfit his troops.[177] Once all of his uniforms had arrived then he would replace the uniforms that he received from the other two regiments.

The 27th Infantry was initially issued the white summer linen uniform in the spring of 1813. The regiment would later be issued the 1813 style uniform, which consisted of a single-breasted blue coat with red cuffs and collars, white pants and a felt hat called a "shako."

Companies were organized after the recruiting service had enlisted a hundred men. The recruits were ordered to rendezvous at Zanesville, and they were organized into a company. From there the new companies marched to Chillicothe where they were to be clothed, armed, and equipped. Upon arriving at

---

[172] Knopf, Richard C., **Document Transcriptions of the War of 1812 in the Northwest,** Volume III, Thomas Worthington and the War of 1812, (Anthony Wayne Parkway Board, Ohio State Museum, Columbus, Ohio: 1957), Carlos A. Norton to Thomas Worthington, 1 June 1813, page 187.

[173] **Ibid**, page 191.

[174] Knopf, Richard C., **Document Transcriptions of the War of 1812 in the Northwest,** Volume VII, Part 2, Letters from the Secretary of War 1812 & 1813 Relating to the War of 1812 in the Northwest, (Ohio Historical Society: Columbus, Ohio: 1961), page 24, Senator Worthington to Secretary of War, 10 April 1813.

[175] **Ibid,** Volume III, **Thomas Worthington and the War of 1812,** (Anthony Wayne Parkway Board, Ohio State Museum, Columbus, Ohio: 1957), Carlos A. Norton to Thomas Worthington, 1 June 1813, page 187.

[176] **Ibid,** Volume III, **Thomas Worthington and the War of 1812,** (Anthony Wayne Parkway Board, Ohio State Museum, Columbus, Ohio: 1957), Lewis Cass to Thomas Worthington, 22 June 1813, page 202.

[177] **Ibid**, Volume VII, Part 2, Letters from the Secretary of War 1812 & 1813 Relating to the War of 1812 in the Northwest, (Ohio Historical Society: Columbus, Ohio: 1961), page 160, General Cass to Secretary of War, 7 June 1813.

Chillicothe the early companies found that their uniforms, weapons and supplies had been shipped north to Franklinton (now Columbus) and they then trekked to this village where they were outfitted.[178]

The regiment formed up at Franklinton and from there they marched to Fort Seneca, south of present day Sandusky, Ohio, where the unit met up with the 26th and 28th Infantries. These three regiments drilled and prepared for the upcoming invasion of Upper Canada.

The Quartermaster General of the Army of the Northwest, John C. Bartlett, wrote to General Cass on 22 July 1813 informing him that the British were once again besieging Fort Meigs.[179] He also stated that 500 regulars under Colonel Paull were 22 miles from General Harrison's headquarters at Fort Seneca and that they were heading towards Fort Meigs. The siege would be lifted by the time the regiment arrived at Fort Meigs.

Two companies of the 27th Infantry under the command of Major Robert Morrison were detached and sent to Cleveland in July 1813 to re-enforce Major Thomas Jesup of the 19th Regiment of U.S. Infantry who was already stationed there with two companies from his regiment.[180]

General Harrison wrote to Secretary Armstrong from Cleveland on 9 July 1813 stating that he was dismayed in finding out that both majors from the 27th Infantry and a number of the men were prisoners-of-war on parole status.[181] Many of the officers and men in the 27th Infantry had served with General Cass at Fort Detroit when General Hull surrendered his army to the British in 1812. Technically, these men were not allowed to participate in any military operations during the war until they were released in a prisoner of war exchange. If the British once again captured these men, then they could have been placed in front of a firing squad. Over 200 men from the regiment were on parole status.

Three hundred and fifty men under Colonel Paull arrived at Fort Seneca towards the end of July. Ten officers and one-third of the men who arrived at Fort Seneca were prisoners of war on parole status.

The 27th Infantry's first combat experience occurred on water not land, which is very unusual for an infantry regiment. During the summer of 1813 Master Commandant Oliver Hazard Perry did not have enough men to man his ships so he asked General Harrison if he had any men who would volunteer to serve temporarily with the navy. General Harrison canvassed his troops for volunteers who had previously worked on either boats or ships. Thirty-three men from the 27th Infantry volunteered to serve on the ships of the Lake Erie Squadron. The men were divided and assigned to the ships *Trippe, Lawrence, Niagara, Tigress, Scorpion, and Somers*. These men participated as marines in the Battle of Lake Erie on 10 September 1813.[182]

The staging area for the invasion of Upper Canada had been moved west from Cleveland to Fort Meigs, Fort Seneca, Fort Ball and Fort Stephenson in the northwestern sector of Ohio. Cleveland did not have a harbor and the village only had a small fort for its defense. The area north of the four forts along the southwestern coast of Lake Erie and within the lake's islands had many harbors that could easily be defended and used by the naval squadron. The army moved from the four forts to Catawba Island. From

---

[178] **Ibid,** Volume VII, Part 3, Letters to the Secretary of War 1812 Relating to the War of 1812 in the Northwest, (Anthony Wayne Parkway Board, Ohio State Museum, Columbus, Ohio: 1957), page 28, Captain Joseph Wheaton to the Secretary of War, 19 July 1813.

[179] Knopf, Richard C., **Return Jonathan Meigs, Jr. and the War of 1812, Volume II of the Document Transcriptions of the War of 1812 in the Northwest**, (Anthony Wayne Parkway Board, Ohio State Museum, Columbus, Ohio: 1961 J. C. Bartlett to General Lewis Cass, 22 July 1813, page 84.

[180] Knopf, Richard C., **Document Transcriptions of the War of 1812 in the Northwest,** Volume VII Part 3, Letters to the Secretary of War 1812 Relating to the War of 1812 in the Northwest, (Anthony Wayne Parkway Board, Ohio State Museum, Columbus, Ohio: 1957), page 12, General Harrison to the Secretary of War, 9 July 1813.

[181] **Ibid,** Volume VII, Part 3, Letters from the Secretary of War 1812 & 1813 Relating to the War of 1812 in the Northwest, (Ohio Historical Society: Columbus, Ohio: 1961), page 12, General Harrison to Secretary of War, 9 July 1813.

[182] Altoff, Gerald T., **Deep Water Sailors, Shallow Water Soldiers, Manning the United States Fleet on Lake Erie 1813**, (The Perry Group, Put-in-Bay, Ohio: 1993), 27th United States Infantry Regiment, pp 97-98.

Catawba Island the army moved to South Bass Island and then on to Middle Sister Island by batteaux.[183] From Middle Sister Island the army landed on the south coast of Upper Canada.

The 27th Infantry was assigned to General Cass' brigade, which on September 27th landed three miles southeast of Amherstburg, Upper Canada, as part of General Harrison's invasion force. The brigade was made up of the 26th, 27th and 28th Infantries. The brigade entered Amherstburg without any resistance and occupied the town, the fort, and the naval yard. The British had destroyed the fort and had burnt all of the public buildings in the area before they fled. All of the artillery pieces at the fort had been used to arm the ships of the British squadron, and they were now in the hands of the Americans. The British had abandoned the fort for without the artillery the fort had no military value, and it was defenseless.

General Cass' brigade traveled north to the village of Sandwich, which was across the river from Detroit. From there they occupied the former British artillery positions overlooking Fort Detroit. The brigade was assigned the duties of holding the western district of Upper Canada and to act as the reserve force when General Harrison engaged the British in battle.

Master Commandant Perry's victory over the British on Lake Erie had made General Harrison's conquest of the British far easier than he had ever hoped for. A good portion of the British regular troops and all of the artillery from Fort Malden and Fort Detroit had been used to man and gun the ships of the British squadron and they were now in American hands. The upcoming battle with the British would be fought mainly with the American militia against what was left of the British regulars and their Indian allies.

General Harrison's regular forces numbered over 2,000 men, but these troops had been trained to fight against the British regulars while the militia was trained to fight against the Indians. General Harrison chose a regiment of Kentucky mounted militia troops and five brigades of Kentucky infantry militia to engage the enemy. He then chose Captain George Sanderson's Company of 142 men as the only regular army force for the upcoming battle.[184] Both General Cass and Commodore Perry would accompany General Harrison as observers, while Colonel Paull would be in the overall command of the regulars.

Besides Colonel Paull and Captain Sanderson, Major Thomas Rowland of Columbiana County and 1st Lieutenant Abraham Shane of Tuscarawas County were apart of the detachment from the 27th Infantry.[185]

General Harrison and his army pursued the British up the Thames River valley. On October 4th the Army of the Northwest overtook a rear guard of Indians, and they defeated them at Chatham, Upper Canada. The next day General Harrison's forces caught up with the main British force near Moravian Town, and there they defeated the British and Indians at the Battle of the Thames.

The 27th Infantry had been assigned the right flank position on General Harrison's battle line. The regiment's mission was to capture the British artillery battery. The detachment was able to capture this battery before the British were able to use their artillery against the American lines. The 27th Infantry now received its first combat experience on land. The western district of Upper Canada was in control of the United States until the end of the war.

Captain Sanderson's company guarded the British prisoners of war and escorted them back to the Detroit River.[186] The British were from the 41st Regiment of Foot. They would be interned at the Newport Barracks in Newport, Kentucky.[187]

---

[183] A bateau was a large, flat-bottomed boat used to transport troops and supplies during the war. These craft were built for General Harrison's invasion of Upper Canada and they could carry 40-50 men with their baggage, arms and provisions.

[184] **Western Reserve and Northern Ohio Historical Society**, Tract Number 36, January 1877, page 2, (Western Reserve and Northern Ohio Historical Society, Cleveland, Ohio), Statement of General George Sanderson of Lancaster, Ohio, April 1870.

[185] **Shawnee's Reservation, Tecumseh's Death,** http://www.geocities.com/southbeach/cove/8286/

[186] **Report and Collections of the State Historical Society of Wisconsin for the Years 1857 and 1858**, Volume IV, (James Ross, State Printer, Madison, Wisconsin), pp. 369-374, Death of Tecumseh at the Battle of the Thames in 1813, Rev. Alfred Brunson.

After the Battle of the Thames, General Harrison was ordered to the Niagara Theater with half of his army consisting of General McArthur's brigade plus the squadron of dragoons and a battalion of riflemen totaling 1,200 men. The naval squadron under Commodore Perry transported these men to the Buffalo, New York.

General McArthur was appointed the commander of a smaller Army of the Northwest. General Cass assumed the duties of the military governor of the Territory of Michigan and the western district of Upper Canada. The British were still in control of the northern Territory of Michigan, the northern Territory of Illinois, and the northern Territory of Missouri until the end of the war. General McArthur had most of the 24th, 27th and 28th Infantries under his command.

By the end of the year there were only 400 regular soldiers and 130 Ohio militiamen stationed at Fort Detroit.[188] The army rebuilt Fort Malden and regular troops occupied this post and the battery positions at Sandwich.

Major Morrison died on 12 December 1813 probably at Detroit, Territory of Michigan, during the cholera epidemic that struck the Army of the Northwest during December 1813 and January 1814. The majority of the 700 or so soldiers who died from the disease were probably from the 27th Infantry since this was the largest infantry regiment stationed at Detroit during this time.

Even though the Americans had captured the western district of Upper Canada between Detroit and what is now London, Ontario, the Army of the Northwest firmly controlled only the Canadian lands near the Detroit River. Most of the western district became a no-man's land patrolled by both sides until the end of the war. Minor skirmishes and battles would occur in the area for the next year.

The Canadian militia near Chatham, Upper Canada, ambushed a scouting mission under the command of Lieutenant Joseph Larwill of the 2nd Regiment of U.S. Artillery on 15 December 1813.[189] Thirty-nine men were captured including Private Joseph Berry of Captain Absalom Martin's company and Private Isaac Devault. The men would be exchanged at Odelltown, New York, on 3 February 1814.

During January 1814 there were 478 men from the 27th Infantry stationed at Fort Shelby, Detroit, according to a morning report issued on the January 23rd.[190] By April 1814 there were only 374 men from the regiment at Detroit.[191]

A weekly recruiting report for the regiment issued on 15 February 1814 reported that the regiment's recruiting service had enlisted a total of 770 men.[192] This figure does not include the 57 commissioned officers assigned to this regiment. The report revealed that the regiment had 13 recruiting stations in eastern Ohio.

A raiding party under the command of Captain Andrew Hunter Holmes of the 24th Infantry began on 3 March 1814 from Fort Detroit with hopes of capturing the British military outpost at Delaware near the

---

[187] Donnelly, Colonel Joseph L., M.D., Ph.D., **Newport Barracks, Kentucky's Forgotten Military Installation**, (Kenton County Historical Society, Covington, Kentucky: 1999), Chapter III, War of 1812, pp. 19-28.

[188] Knopf, Richard C., **Document Transcriptions of the War of 1812 in the Northwest,** Volume VII, Part 3, Letters to the Secretary of War 1812 Relating to the War of 1812 in the Northwest, (Anthony Wayne Parkway Board, Ohio State Museum, Columbus, Ohio: 1957), page 95, General Cass to the Secretary of War, 21 October 1813.

[189] Altoff, Gerald T., **Deep Water Sailors, Shallow Water Soldiers, Manning the United States Fleet on Lake Erie 1813**, (The Perry Group, Put-in-Bay, Ohio: 1993), 27th United States Infantry Regiment, pp 124, 138.

[190] **Duncan McArthur Papers**, Library of Congress, 1922, Microfilm 47, Reel 2, Volumes 4-5, 22 September 1813 – 4 March 1814, document number 702, Morning Report for Fort Shelby under the command of Lieutenant Colonel Butler, 23 January 1814, Ohio Historical Society, Columbus, Ohio.

[191] **Ibid**, Microfilm 47, Reel 3, Volumes 6-8, 22 September 1813 – 4 March 1814, document number 1383, Monthly Returns at Detroit, 30 April 1814, Ohio Historical Society, Columbus, Ohio.

[192] **Ibid**, Microfilm 47, Reel 2, Volumes 4-5, 22 September 1813 – 4 March 1814, document number 853, Weekly Recruiting Report of the 27th Regiment of U.S. Infantry under Colonel Paull, 9-15 February 1814, Ohio Historical Society, Columbus, Ohio.

present day city of London, Ontario. The force of 180 men was made up from men of the 24th, 27th and 28th Infantries plus a company of the rangers and militia from the Territory of Michigan. 1st Lieutenant Samuel Shannon commanded the detachment from the 27th Infantry.[193]

The Americans defeated 300 British regulars, militia and Indians in the Longwoods forest near Delaware on March 4th. Captain Holmes was able to secure a victory since his force occupied the higher ground. He withdrew his raiding party back to Fort Detroit after the battle when he realized that he probably did not have enough men to take and hold the outpost.

Under the act of 30 March 1814 the 27th Infantry was consolidated with the 26th Infantry and two companies from the 17th Infantry to form the new 19th Regiment of U.S. Infantry on 15 May 1814.[194] Most of the men were released from duty since their one-year enlistments were expiring. Those men who had re-enlisted for "five years or during the war" were transferred into the 19th Infantry.

Colonel Paull became the new commander of the 19th Regiment of U.S. Infantry while Major Thomas Rowland became one of the regiment's majors. Captains Alexander Hill, Isaac Van Horne, Junior, Henry Northup and William Gill became company commanders in the 19th Infantry.

Captain Applegate had resigned from the army on 16 October 1813. Captain Cairns was dismissed from the service on 18 February 1814. The rest of the senior officers were discharged from the army on 1 June 1814.

---

[193] Brannan, John, **Official Letters of the Military and Naval Officers of the United States During the War with Great Britain in the Years 1812, 13, 14 and 15**, (Arno Press Inc., 1971), Letters from Lieutenant Colonel Henry Butler to Major General Harrison, pp. 40-41.

[194] Mahon, John K. and Romana Danysh, **Infantry Part 1: Regular Army**, (Office of the Chief of Military History, United States Army, Washington, D.C.: 1972), War of 1812, page 14.

History of the other Ohio army units

2nd Regiment of U.S. Light Dragoons
Lieutenant Colonel Ball's Squadron

The 2nd Regiment of U.S. Light Dragoons was authorized under the act of 11 January 1812 to serve for a period not to exceed five years. The regiment consisted of twelve companies. Enlistments were set at five years but changed to five years or 18 months on 8 April 1812. On 12 December 1812 'during the war' enlistments were authorized.

Major James V. Ball of Virginia was ordered by the Secretary of War on 16 September 1812 to report to Brigadier General William H. Harrison in order to organize a squadron of dragoons for the Army of the Northwest.[195] Captain Samuel Hopkins of Kentucky raised a company of dragoons for the 2nd Dragoons and the company was assigned to Major Ball's squadron.[196]

Various state militia companies were also attached to this squadron throughout the war. These companies were elite militia companies from Kentucky, Michigan, Ohio and Pennsylvania, which served with the squadron for either a 6-months or one-year tour of duty.

The Bourbon Blues under the command of Captain William Garrard from Bourbon County, Kentucky, served for one year. A detachment of Michigan light dragoons under Cornet Isaac Lee's company from Michigan also served for 12-months. Captain Benoni Pierce's company of light dragoons from Muskingum County, Ohio, served for six months.

Four companies of light dragoons from Pennsylvania served in Major Ball's squadron. These companies were under the command of Captain Joseph Markle, Captain James McClelland, Captain Thomas Seely,[197] and Lieutenant Thomas Warren. Markle's company served for one year while the other companies served for 6-months.

The squadron was headquartered in Franklinton (now Columbus), Ohio, during most of the war due to the availability of food for the horses. The monthly report for the squadron, dated 31 May 1813 from Franklinton, states that the unit had four troops totaling 286 men.[198] Besides Captain Hopkins' troop of 99 men there were Captain Markle's troop of 56 men, Captain Garrard's troop of 96 men and Captain McClelland's troop of 35 men.

Major Ball commanded the light dragoons at the Battle of Mississinewa River, Territory of Indiana, 17-18 December 1812. His detachment consisted of one company of regular dragoons and three militia light dragoon companies. For his actions at the Battle of Mississinewa River, Major Ball was breveted to the rank of lieutenant colonel.

Major General William H. Harrison in mid-July 1813 sent Lieutenant Colonel Ball and his squadron to build a fort along the Sandusky River. This fort was named Fort Ball and it was a part of a string of forts used for the defense of the northwest and as a supply depot.[199] The location of the old fort is now in Tiffin, Ohio. As soon as the fort was finished the squadron was ordered to Fort Stephenson to relieve

---

[195] Knopf, Richard C., **Document Transcriptions of the War of 1812 in the Northwest,** Volume VIII, Letters from the Secretary of War 1812 & 1813 Relating to the War of 1812 in the Northwest, (Ohio Historical Society: Columbus, Ohio: 1961), pp. 84-84, Secretary of War to Major James V. Ball, 15 September 1812.

[196] **Ibid,** page 77, Secretary of War to Samuel Hopkins, 2 September 1812.

[197] Rauch, Steven J., Major, U.S. Army, **War for the Northwest**, page 29, Order of Battle at Fort Meigs.

[198] **Duncan McArthur Papers**, Library of Congress, 1922, Microfilm 47, Reel 1, Volumes 1-3, 5 October 1783 – 20 September 1813, Monthly Report of Lieutenant Colonel Ball's Squadron, 31 May 1813, Franklinton, Ohio, Ohio Historical Society, Columbus, Ohio.

[199] Hartzell, Stephen J., **Fort Ball: A Bit of it's Background & History,** http://www.friendlynet.com/stevenharzell/FtBall.html

Major Croghan of his command. Along the way Indians attacked the squadron. Ball's forces defeated the Indians without losing a man.

On 28 August 1813 the *Petersburg Volunteers,* under the command of Captain Richard McRea of Virginia, was attached to Lieutenant Colonel James V. Ball's squadron. This was an infantry company.

Colonel Ball had been given the command of the legionary corps of the Army of the Northwest. This corps was made up of all of the light dragoons, artillery and U.S. Voluntary Corps companies that were assigned to this army.

Twenty men from the light dragoons served on the schooner *Caledonia* while one man served on the schooner *Ohio*.[200] The men assigned to the *Caledonia* participated in the Battle of Lake Erie on 10 September 1813.

Colonel Ball's corps landed on the shores of Upper Canada as the first wave of troops during the invasion of Upper Canada on 27 September 1813. The corps served as the rear guard for General Harrison's army when he defeated the British at the Battle of the Thames on 5 October 1813.

After the Battle of the Thames, the corps was dissolved and the light dragoons were transferred to New York. Listed in the returns for officers stationed at Sackets Harbor, New York, in January 1814 were Captain Hopkins and Lieutenant Hedges.[201]

On 12 May 1814 under the act of 30 March 1814 the regiment was consolidated with 1st Regiment of U.S. Light Dragoons to form the Regiment of U.S. Light Dragoons, and the officers and men not retained were discharged 1 June 1814.

2nd Regiment of U.S. Artillery

The 2nd Regiment of U.S. Artillery was organized under the act of 11 January 1812 to service for a period of not more than five years. The regiment consisted of two battalions of ten companies. Enlistments were set a five years, 18 mosnths and 'during the war.' On 12 May 1814, under the act of 30 March 1814, the regiment was consolidated with the 1st and 3rd Regiments of U.S. Artillery to form the Corp of U.S. Artillery.

Captain Daniel Cushing of Warren County, Ohio, was commissioned a captain on 2 July 1812. He raised a company for the 2nd Artillery from within Ohio. He recruited most of his men from western Ohio while 1st Lieutenant Joseph H. Larwill recruited the remaining men from eastern Ohio.

Cushing's Company participated in the Siege of Fort Meigs, Ohio, between 28 April and 9 May 1813.[202] Two men from Captain Cushing's Company served aboard the ship *Trippe* during the Battle of Lake Erie, 10 September 1813.[203] Captain Cushing was drowned while crossing a river in western Ohio on 24 March 1815 while he was still in the army.

---

[200] Altoff, Gerald T., **Deep Water Sailors, Shallow Water Soldiers, Manning the United States Fleet on Lake Erie 1813**, (The Perry Group, Put-in-Bay, Ohio: 1993), 2nd United States Light Dragoons, pp. 100-101.

[201] **Duncan McArthur Papers**, Library of Congress, 1922, Microfilm 47, Reel 2, Volumes 4-5, 22 September 1813 – 4 March 1814, document number 699, Officers of the 8th Military District at Sackett's Harbor, 22 January 1814, Ohio Historical Society, Columbus, Ohio.

[202] Rauch, Steven J., Major, U.S. Army, **War for the Northwest**, page 29, Order of Battle at Fort Meigs.

[203] Altoff, Gerald T., **Deep Water Sailors, Shallow Water Soldiers, Manning the United States Fleet on Lake Erie 1813**, (The Perry Group, Put-in-Bay, Ohio: 1993), 2nd United States Artillery Regiment, page 100.

1st Regiment of U.S. Rifles [204]

The 1st Regiment of U.S. Rifles was organized under the act of 12 April 1808 as the Regiment of U.S. Rifle to serve for a period of not more than five years. On 24 December 1811 the regiment became a permanent part of the U.S. Army.

Enlistments were authorized for 'five years' or 'during the war.' Recruiting headquarters were located at Shepherdstown, Virginia, and Savannah, Georgia. The regiment operated in the 6th, 8th and 9th Military Districts.

Part of the regiment was raised in Kentucky and in Ohio. James McDonald of Ohio was commissioned a captain in the rifles on 3 May 1808, a major on 1 August 1812, and then he was promoted to lieutenant colonel on 24 January 1814. He transferred to the 4th Regiment of U.S. Rifles on 17 September 1814 serving as this regiment's colonel and second commander. Lieutenant Colonel McDonald was brevetted a colonel on 17 September 1814 for actions during the Battle of Fort Erie.

Henry Richard Graham of Kentucky was commissioned a captain on 8 March 1809 while Michael C. Hays was commissioned a captain on 1 June 1811. Thomas Ramsay was commissioned a captain on 30 November 1812 after having served as a 1st lieutenant since 31 July 1810.

The companies from Ohio and Kentucky were still forming when federal troops were needed during the Indian upraising in 1811. Captain Moses Whitney's company from Rhode Island was ordered west and this company participated in the Battle of Tippecanoe. The company was ordered back to the east after the battle. Colonel Thomas A. Smith of Georgia was the regimental commander during the invasion of Upper Canada in September 1813 and the commander of 520 riflemen in the Army of the Northwest.

This battalion of riflemen was never used by General Harrison in the northwest and they were transferred to New York in late 1813. Listed in the returns for officers stationed at Sackets Harbor, New York, in January 1814 were Colonel Smith and Major McDonald.[205]

The 1st Rifle participated in many battles in New York and in the south. Under the act of 3 March 1815 the regiment was consolidated with the 2nd, 3rd, and 4th Regiment of US. Rifle to become the Regiment of U.S. Rifle. The regiment was discharged under the act of 1 June 1821.

2nd Regiment of U.S. Rifles [206]

The 2nd Regiment of U.S. Rifles was organized under the act of 10 February 1814 for a period of not more than five years. Recruiting headquarters were established at Lexington, Kentucky, and Nashville, Tennessee. Enlistments were authorized for 'five years' or 'during the war.' The regiment was assigned to the 8th Military District.

Colonel Anthony Butler of Kentucky was the commander of the regiment from 21 February 1814 to 17 May 1815. Lieutenant Colonel George Croghan of Kentucky was the regiment's lieutenant colonel between 21 February 1814 and 17 May 1815. The regimental majors were David Gwynne and William H. Puthuff of Ohio who served from 21 February 1814 to 17 May 1815.

Recruiting centers were established at Chillicothe, Ohio, Lexington, Kentucky, and Nashville, Tennessee. Five captains from Kentucky were Robert Breckinridge, Benjamin Desha, Hugh Innes, Benjamin Johnson and John O'Fallon. The captain from Ohio was Batteal Harrison.

---

[204] Fredriksen, John C., Ph.D., **Green Coats and Glory, The United States Regiment of Riflemen 1808-1821**, (Old Fort Niagara Association, Youngstown, New York: 2000), pp. 45-46.

[205] **Duncan McArthur Papers**, Library of Congress, 1922, Microfilm 47, Reel 2, Volumes 4-5, 22 September 1813 – 4 March 1814, document number 699, Officers of the 8th Military District at Sackett's Harbor, 22 January 1814, Ohio Historical Society, Columbus, Ohio.

[206] Fredriksen, John C., Ph.D., **Green Coats and Glory, The United States Regiment of Riflemen 1808-1821**, (Old Fort Niagara Association, Youngstown, New York: 2000), page 43.

The 2nd Rifle was stationed at Fort Detroit, Territory of Michigan, during the last year of the war. They saw no action during this conflict. Under the act of 3 March 1815 the regiment was consolidated with the 1st, 3rd, and 4th Regiment of U.S. Rifle to become the Regiment of U.S. Rifles on 17 May 1815.

United States Rangers

Six companies of rangers were authorized by Congress under the act of 2 January 1812 for one year to counter any threat of an Indian invasion of any state or territory of the United States.[207] Each company was made up on a captain, a 1st lieutenant, a 2nd lieutenant, an ensign, four sergeants, four corporals and sixty privates.

They were to provide their own arms, equipment and horses. They would be paid one dollar a day extra when using their horses and 75 cents per day while serving without their horses. The rangers received the same pay and rations as the infantry. The rangers were funded under the act of 20 February 1812.[208]

Ohio was assigned the raising of the first two ranger companies while Kentucky and the Territories of Indiana, Illinois and Missouri were each assigned to raise a single company. The company commanders from Ohio were James Manary and William Perry.

On 2 May 1812 Colonel William Russell, commander of the 7th Regiment of U.S. Infantry, stationed at Vincennes, Territory of Indiana, took command of the ranger companies formed in Ohio, Kentucky and the Territories of Indiana and Illinois.[209] Captain Perry's company was ordered west to Vincennes while Captain Manary's company stayed in Ohio patrolling the northwest frontier. Captain Manary's company was used to deliver dispatches between Fort Detroit and Chillicothe, Ohio, and between Fort Knox, Territory of Indiana, and Chillicothe.

On 31 March 1813 Robert Lucas of Portsmouth, Ohio, received a letter from Senator Thomas Worthington stating that he had been commissioned a lieutenant colonel in the volunteers and that he had been placed in command of the United States Rangers.[210] He was ordered to report to Brigadier General Benjamin Howard in St. Louis, Territory of Missouri.

Lucas had asked for a position in the regular infantry and was dumbfounded that he received a commission with the rangers of which he said, "**they being a band of troops that has never met my views.**" He declined the commission stating that he preferred to serve in one of the infantry regiments that were being formed in Ohio.

---

[207] **Public Statutes at Large of the United States of America**, Volume II, (Boston: Charles C. Little and James Brown, 1845), Twelfth Congress, Session 1, Chapter IX, page 670, 2 January 1812, "An act authorizing the President of the United States to raise certain companies of rangers for the protection of the frontier of the United States."

[208] **Ibid**, Chapter XIII, page 678, 20 February 1812, "An act making an appropriation for the expenses incident to the six companies of Mounted Rangers, during the year one thousand eight hundred and twelve."

[209] Knopf, Richard C., **Document Transcriptions of the War of 1812 in the Northwest,** Volume VIII, Letters from the Secretary of War 1812 & 1813 Relating to the War of 1812 in the Northwest, (Ohio Historical Society: Columbus, Ohio: 1961), page 25, Secretary of War to Governors Ninian Edwards and Charles Scott 2 May 1812.

[210] **Ibid**, Thomas Worthington and the War of 1812, (Anthony Wayne Parkway Board, Ohio State Museum, Columbus, Ohio: 1957), Robert Lucas to Thomas Worthington, 10 May 1813, page 180.

The Old Guard

Whatever happened to General Harrison's Army of the Northwest? Did you know that it still exists today as the 3rd United States Infantry Regiment?

Officially, the Army of the Northwest, also called the Northwestern Army, was a division of the U.S. Army and not an actual army. It was commanded by Major General William Henry Harrison and at its height, right after the Battle of the Thames in October 1813, the army consisted of two brigades and a legion plus militia units from various states.

The first brigade was under the command of Brigadier General Duncan McArthur, and it was made up of the 17th, 19th, and 24th Regiments of Infantry. The second brigade consisted of the 26th, 27th and 28th Regiments of Infantry and its commander was Brigadier General Lewis Cass. The legion was under the command of Lieutenant Colonel James V. Ball of the 2nd Regiment of Light Dragoons. This legion consisted of a company of light dragoons, two companies of artillery from the 2nd Regiment of Artillery, a battalion of four rifle companies from the 1st Regiment of Rifles and a number of one-year militia companies.

Besides the regular army units and one-year militia companies, the Army of the Northwest also had, at one time or another, 6-month militia regiments and companies from Kentucky, Michigan, Ohio, Pennsylvania and Virginia.

On 12 May 1814 the Army of the Northwest went through a major reorganization of its regiments. The 17th Infantry and the 19th Infantry merged to form a new 17th Regiment of U.S. Infantry while the 26th and the 27th Infantries merged to form a new 19th Regiment of U.S. Infantry.

After the War of 1812, the Act of 3 March 1815 established the peacetime army by consolidating all of the existing infantry regiments into eight new infantry regiments, a rifle regiment and two artillery regiments totaling 10,000 men.

On 17 May 1815 the act went into effect and the 1st, 17th, 19th, 28th and 39th Regiments of U.S. Infantry consolidated to form the new 3rd Regiment of U.S. Infantry. The 1st Infantry had been stationed at St. Louis, Territory of Missouri, for most of the war, while the 39th Infantry had been apart of Major General Andrew Jackson's Army of the South.

The 3rd Regiment of U.S. Infantry is now the 3rd Infantry Regiment, and it is the oldest regiment on active duty in the U.S. Army. The 3rd Infantry Regiment's lineage begins with the formation of the Regiment of U.S. Infantry on 3 June 1784, and it also has inherited the history and honors of the Army of the Northwest. The regiment is nicknamed "The Old Guard" and its mission is to "conduct ceremonies, memorial affairs, and special events to demonstrate the excellence of the United States Army to the world." The regiment is a ceremonial regiment, which conducts state funerals, honor guards, honor guards at the Tomb of the Unknown Soldier, drill teams and Fife and Drum Corps. Besides serving as a ceremonial unit, the regiment also trains for combat duty.

Some Ohio soldiers and militiamen who were captured during the War of 1812

This is a partial listing of Ohioans who were captured by the British during the War of 1812 and who were later exchanged for British soldiers. The names were taken from documents found in the *Records Relating to War of 1812 Prisoners of War* in Record Group 94 at the National Archives.

Besides raising militia brigades and regiments to serve in the war, Ohio also raised three regiments for the U.S. Army. The 19th Regiment of US Infantry was raised in 1812 from all parts of Ohio. The regiment also recruited in Indiana and Michigan. In 1813, the 26th and the 27th Regiments of US Infantry were raised. The 26th Infantry was raised in western Ohio while the 27th Infantry was raised in eastern Ohio. Some men from these two regiments were recruited in western Pennsylvania.

The manuscript number of each document along with the page numbers are included with each listing of soldiers.

An Ohio soldier from the 19th Regiment of US Infantry who was exchanged for a British soldier during the Prisoner of War Exchanged received from Quebec on 26 October 1814. (Manuscript 78, page 3)

Last Name	First Name	Rank
Thornburg	Thomas	Private

Ohio and Michigan army officers from the 19th Regiment of US Infantry who were captured at the Battle of French Town on 22 January 1813. (Manuscript 80, page 2)

Last Name	First Name	Rank	Notes
Anderson	John	Lieutenant	Now a topographical engineer (from Michigan)
Edwards	Abraham	Captain	
Hickman	Harris H	Captain	(from Michigan)
Jesup	Thomas S	Lieutenant	Now a major
Whistler	John	Ensign	(from Michigan)
Phillips	Asher	Ensign	

Ohio soldiers from the 19th, 26th and 27th Regiments of US Infantry who were exchanged for British soldiers during the Prisoner of War Exchanged on 25 April 1814. (Manuscript 82, pages 4, 5, 7, and 9)

Last Name	First Name	Rank	Regiment
Anderson	Thomas	Private	26th US Infantry
Buckover	Peter	Private	19th US Infantry
Chadwick	Thomas	Private	27th US Infantry
Dailey	John	Private	19th US Infantry
Devault	Isaac	Private	27th US Infantry
Downes	Jesse	Private	19th US Infantry
Fenton	Davidson	Private	27th US Infantry
Foens	Daniel B	Sergeant	19th US Infantry
Goodwin	James	Private	27th US Infantry
Grant	William	Private	19th US Infantry
Haynes	Carlisle	Private	19th US Infantry

Last Name	First Name	Rank	Regiment
Holdenfield	James	Private	26th US Infantry
Jennings	Edward	Private	19th US Infantry
Jones	William	Sergeant	19th US Infantry
Lacey	Fielding	Private	26th US Infantry
Leicester	Jonathan	Private	19th US Infantry
Martin	Robert	Private	19th US Infantry
Miller	Benjamin	Private	27th US Infantry
Miller	Jacob	Private	19th US Infantry
Moore	Abraham	Private	26th US Infantry
Mullen	Charles	Private	19th US Infantry
Self	Charles	Private	19th US Infantry
Sherman	Joel	Corporal	19th US Infantry
Smith	Charles	Private	27th US Infantry
Webb	Joseph	Private	26th US Infantry

Ohio militia officers who were captured on 16 August 1812 at Fort Detroit during the surrender of Brigadier General William Hull's Army of the Northwest. (Manuscript 83, pages 2 and 3)

Last Name	First Name	Rank	Regiment
Baird	Nathan	Ensign	McArthur
Barrier	George W	Captain	McArthur
Brown	Ephraim	Captain	Findlay
Cairns	Joseph	Captain	Cass
Cass	Lewis	Colonel	Cass
Cilley	Joseph	Paymaster	Findlay
Denny	James	Major	McArthur
Dent	Abner	Paymaster	Cass
Douglass	Robert	Quartermaster	McArthur
Dugan	Thomas	Quartermaster	Findlay
Estie	Charles	Surgeon	Cass
Ferris	Johns	Captain	Findlay
Findlay	James	Colonel	Findlay
Gill	William	Captain	Cass
Guthrie	William	Lieutenant	Findlay
Heckerwelder	Thomas	Ensign	Cass
Hughes		Chaplain	
Joslen	Israel	Lieutenant	Findlay
Kean		Lieutenant	Cass
Kelly	David	Ensign	McArthur
Kemper	Edward Y	Surgeon's Mate	Findlay
Kemper	Prestley	Wagon Master	Cass
Keys	William	Captain	McArthur
Kyle	Samuel B	Captain	Findlay
Lockhart	Josiah	Captain	McArthur

Last Name	First Name	Rank	Regiment
Lucas	John	Captain	McArthur
Macadine	Samuel	Surgeon	McArthur
McArthur	Duncan	Colonel	McArthur
McDonald	John	Paymaster	McArthur
McFarlane	Stephen	Lieutenant	Cass
Mcormick	Samuel	Adjutant	Findlay
Miller	Samuel	Lieutenant	Findlay
Moore	John	Lieutenant	McArthur
Moore	Thomas	Major	Findlay
Morrison	Robert	Major	Cass
Munson	Jeremiah	Major	Cass
Nelson	John	Lieutenant	Findlay
Northup	Henry	Adjutant	Cass
Pentz	John	Lieutenant	Findlay
Puthuff	William H	Adjutant	McArthur
Reynolds		Commissary	
Robinson	John	Captain	Findlay
Rose	Levi	Captain	Cass
Rupe	David	Captain	McArthur
Sanderson	George	Captain	Cass
Sawyer	William	Lieutenant	Cass
Schenck	Peter L	Clerk	Findlay
Seward	Richard	Ensign	Findlay
Sharp	John	Captain	Cass
Sheets	John	Captain	Findlay
Sloan	James W	Captain	Light Dragoons
Spencer	John	Captain	Cass
Steward	Samuel	Captain	Findlay
Trimble	William	Major	McArthur
Turner	William	Surgeon	Findlay
Van Horne	Thomas B	Major	Findlay
Walker	Christopher	Lieutenant	Light Dragoons
Wallace	Robert	Aid de camp	McArthur
Waring	William	Cornet	Light Dragoons
Warner	Winthrop	Lieutenant	Cass

A list of officers and soldiers of the Ohio militia who had been captured at Fort Detroit on 16 August 1812 and who had later enlisted or received a commission in the 27th Regiment of U.S. Infantry. These men were stationed again at Fort Detroit. (Manuscript 86, page 2)

Last Name	First Name	Rank	Last Name	First Name	Rank
Battles	Avery	Recruit	Kelly	Eua	Recruit
Blake	Henry	Recruit	Lackey	Andrew	Recruit
Blake	Rehemiah	Recruit	Lackey	Hugh	Recruit

Last Name	First Name	Rank	Last Name	First Name	Rank
Brown	James	Recruit	Lafferty	Archibald	Recruit
Butler	Asaph	Recruit	McDonald	Stephen	Recruit
Byron	John	Recruit	McFadden	Neal	Recruit
Cairns	Joseph	Captain	Morrison	Robert	Major
Cairns	Richard	Recruit	Munson	Jeremiah R	Major
Casey	Archibald	Recruit	Nixon	James	Recruit
Cass	Ira	Recruit	Northup	Henry	Captain
Delaurier	John B	Recruit	Pastor	Christian	Recruit
Dennis	Samuel	Recruit	Pettit	Joseph	Recruit
Devore	Enos	Recruit	Pigman	John G	Recruit
Dugan	John	Recruit	Post	Cornelius	Recruit
Eagan	John	Ensign	Rawl	William	Recruit
Eagan	John	Recruit	Shadley	Henry	Recruit
Edson	Luther	Recruit	Sickle	George M	Recruit
Emmit	Abraham	Recruit	Skeels	Henry	Recruit
Futhey	Isaac	Recruit	Spencer	John	Captain
Gill	William	Captain	Stadler	Joseph	Recruit
Gilman	Elias	Lieutenant	Thompson	David	Recruit
Gordon	John L	Recruit	Tucker	Frederick	Recruit
Groves	Solomon	Recruit	Van Meter	John	Recruit
Hall	John	Recruit	Van Winkle	James	Recruit
Hughes	Elias	Recruit	Warner	Winthrop	Lieutenant
Jefferies	Jonas	Recruit	Wells	John	Recruit
Johnston	John	Recruit	Winner	John	Recruit
Johnston	Samuel	Recruit	Wood	James M	Recruit

Ohio soldiers who were interned at Quebec and who were later exchanged as prisoners of war on parole. They were quartered in Charleston, Massachusetts, on 20 December 1812. These men were members of the 19th Regiment of US Infantry. (Manuscript 87, pages 6, 7, and 10)

Last Name	First Name	Rank	Notes
Dougherty	Robert	Sergeant	
Dunlap	James	Private	
Philips	Asher	Ensign	
Whistler	John	Ensign	
Wood	Michael	Private	Died in Charleston

Bibliography

Records Relating to War of 1812 Prisoners of War, 1812; (National Archives Microfilm Publication M2019); Records of the Adjutant General's Office, 1780's-1917; Record Group 94; National Archives, Washington, D.C.

List of Ohio officers in the Regular Army

A list of officers in Detachment No. 1 commanded by Brigadier General James Winchester and resident in the state of Ohio.[211]

Name	Rank	Regiment[212]	Residence
John Miller	Lieutenant Colonel	17th Infantry	Steubenville
George Tod	Major	17th Infantry	Youngstown
Robert Lucas	Captain	19th Infantry	Portsmouth
Angus L. Langham	Captain	19th Infantry	Chillicothe
Wilson Elliot	Captain	19th Infantry	Warren
James Herron	Captain	19th Infantry	Zanesville
Abraham Edwards	Captain	17th Infantry	Dayton
Hugh Moore	Captain	19th Infantry	Cincinnati
James Hedges	1st Lieutenant	2nd Light Dragoons	St. Clairsville
Samuel Booker	1st Lieutenant	19th Infantry	St. Clairsville
David Gwynne	1st Lieutenant	19th Infantry	Franklinton
James Campbell	1st Lieutenant	19th Infantry	Westminster
George W. Jackson	1st Lieutenant	19th Infantry	Zanesville
Joseph H. Larwell	1st Lieutenant	2nd Artillery	Canton
Lewis Howell	1st Lieutenant	19th Infantry	Cincinnati
Jonathan Rees	2nd Lieutenant	19th Infantry	
Charles Este	2nd Lieutenant	Artillery	
Henry Frederick	2nd Lieutenant	19th Infantry	New Lisbon
Philip Price	2nd Lieutenant	19th Infantry	Cincinnati
Timothy E. Danielson	2nd Lieutenant	24th Infantry	Marietta
Robert Morrison	2nd Lieutenant		
John D. Reeves	2nd Lieutenant	19th Infantry	Paint Creek
John Miligan	Ensign	19th Infantry	Jefferson County
Batteal Harrison	Ensign	19th Infantry	St. Clairsville
Daniel D. Armstrong	Ensign	19th Infantry	Cincinnati
Asher Philips	Ensign	19th Infantry	Dayton
John E. Morgan	Ensign	19th Infantry	Jefferson County
James Flynn	Ensign	U.S. Rangers	

---

[211] "Listing of Officers from Ohio", 1 December 1814, **George Tod Collection**, Western Reserve Historical Society Archives Library, Cleveland, Ohio, manuscript section, call number MS-3202, military papers.

[212] This column was added by the author.

Essays

Ohio and the War of 1812

The Battle of Marblehead Peninsula

One of the most obscure yet historically important battles of the War of 1812 was the Battle of Marblehead Peninsula, which was fought in northern Ohio on 29 September 1812 during the opening days of the war. This battle, a skirmish compared to the great battles of this war, involved a composite company of 72 Ohio militiamen and an Indian war party of approximately 130 braves.

After the fall of Fort Detroit on 16 August 1812 the frontier of Ohio was wide open for invasion. Most of the settlements in northern Ohio, west of the Cuyahoga River (in today's Cleveland), had been attacked or were under the threat of attack from various Indian raiding parties. Many settlers in north central Ohio had been killed or captured by the Indians in the months before the War of 1812 and these incidents increased after hostilities started.

This area of Ohio had only recently been opened for settlement. The Treaty of Greenville on 3 August 1795 had legally allowed settlement east of the Cuyahoga River in the area of Ohio called the Western Reserve. The Treaty of Fort Industry on 4 July 1805 opened the rest of the Western Reserve west of the Cuyahoga River for settlement. Included in this last treaty was the western extension of the Western Reserve called the Firelands (or Sufferer's Lands).

The Firelands, in which the Battle of Marblehead Peninsula occurred, now comprises Erie County, Huron County, Ruggles Township in Ashland County, Danbury Township in Ottawa County and the Lake Erie islands owned by Ohio. Legal settlement began in the Firelands after the townships in this reserve were sold in 1808 and surveyed the following year. Most of the legal settlers had been living in this area for less than two years.

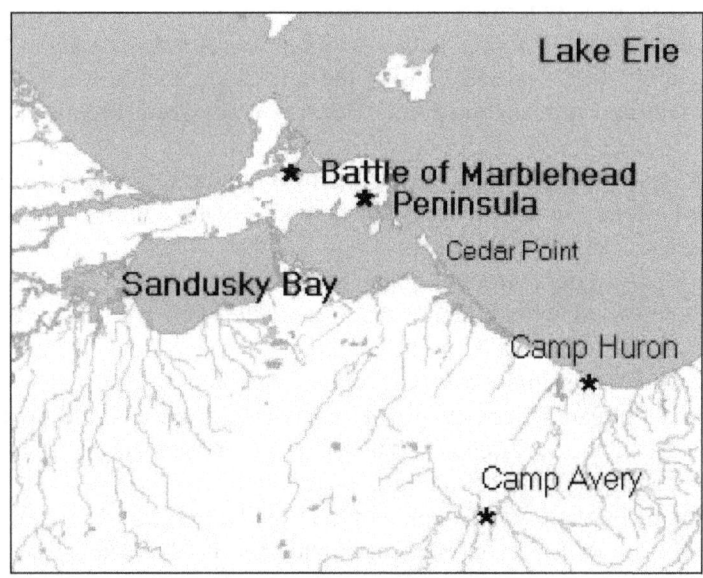

Map of the Sandusky Bay area showing the site of the battle

Two other areas of northwestern Ohio, which had legal settlements, were the 12-square Mile Reservation and the 2-square Mile Reservation. The first reservation centered on the Rapids of the Maumee River and by 1812 there were 75 families living in the area. Most of these settlers were originally French and British nationals who had settled along the Maumee River prior to 1796 when British still had control of this area of the United States. This settlement had a U.S. customs agent and a post office. Fort Meigs would be built in this reservation during the war.

The second reservation is now the City of Fremont on the lower Sandusky River. The federal Indian agent had his headquarters there plus there was also a small Indian settlement. During the war Fort

Sandusky would be built in this reservation. Both of these locations would play major roles during the war.

The final treaty, which affected settlement in Ohio prior to the War of 1812, was the Treaty of Brownstown on 25 November 1808. This treaty ceded a tract of land two miles wide from the Western Reserve connecting Cleveland and the two reservations with Detroit in the Territory of Michigan. The purpose of this treaty was to establish a post road between Cleveland and Detroit. Most of the road would only be a pathway during the war since Congress had only authorized the surveying and construction of this road in 1811 and construction had not begun by the start of the war.

Once Brigadier General William Hull surrendered his American army to the British at Detroit the whole frontier area in the old northwest came under an invasion scare. Although the British were in no position to launch a major invasion into Ohio, their Indians allies did send their war parties into the northwestern area of Ohio and the northern areas of the Territories of Indiana and Illinois raiding and pillaging many of the forts and settlements.

Ohio's governor, Return Jonathan Meigs, Junior, called out the Ohio militia in August and ordered each of his four division commanders to deal with the situation as best they could. The state militia in 1812 had 34,726 men listed on its muster rolls. The Fourth Division of the Ohio Militia, under the command of Major General Elijah Wadsworth in northeastern Ohio, could field 7,500 men but only half of the militiamen had weapons and only a tenth of them had bayonets. This division included the Western Reserve, the Firelands, and the counties of Columbiana, Jefferson, Stark and Wayne.

General Wadsworth determined to set up a defensive line running along the Huron River in the middle of the Firelands south to Wooster in Wayne County. Cleveland was chosen to be the staging area for the northern military operations and as the re-supply point for the division. Canton in Stark County would be staging area for the militia in the southern area of the division.

The Fourth division would split its forces in two with half of its men serving at Wooster and the other half serving along the Huron River. Initially, all of the militia regiments were activated but before the men had a chance to reach their rendezvous points General Wadsworth ordered that half of the men be sent home.

The general then ordered two new brigades to be organized under the commands of Brigadier Generals Reasin Beall and Simon Perkins. General Beall's forces would be made up of a composite regiment from the 1st brigade headquartered in Jefferson County and another composite regiment from his own 2nd brigade in Columbiana County. These two regiments would meet in Canton were they would be joined by a detachment from this county. Once the brigade was formed then they would move forward to Wooster.

General Perkins' forces would be made up of three composite regiments from the 3rd and 4th brigades. On August 26th, General Perkins arrived in Cleveland followed by his three regiments. Lieutenant Colonel Richard Hayes would lead his regiment from Cleveland and he would then take the lake road to the mouth of the Huron River in the Firelands. The other two regiments were under the commands of Lieutenant Colonels Jedediah Beard and William Rayen.

Two companies from Colonel Rayen's regiment left on September 15th for Huron County as re-enforcements. The rest of Colonel Rayen's regiment would stay in Cleveland guarding the military stores and protecting this area from invasions. Colonel Beard's regiment would be used as a reserve regiment. A militia camp was established in Cleveland and it was referred to as "Camp Cleveland." General Wadsworth would setup his forward headquarters in this village. Later, he would move his headquarters to Camp Old Portage in present day Akron, Ohio, along the Cuyahoga River. Colonel Beard's regiment would be stationed at Camp Portage. This camp was also called "Camp Portage."

Once General Perkins' forces had arrived in the Firelands he released the two companies of local militia that had been called out during the invasion scare. He then ordered these men were to stay home with their families, and he said that they would be called back to duty if they were needed.

General Perkins' forces constructed a fortified stockade three miles east of the mouth of the Huron River on 6 September 1812. This fort was called "Camp Huron" but to the troops it was "Fort Nonsense" since it was exposed to both a potential lake and a land attack. General Wadsworth ordered that the fort be abandoned, and General Perkins then had Camp Avery built near the present village of Milan in Erie

County, which was ten miles up the Huron River from the Lake Erie. Camp Avery was also called "Camp Huron" and "Perkins' Camp." Approximately four hundred men were stationed at Camp Avery during September.

Camp Avery was situated in Avery Township, now Milan Township in Erie County. One account said that the militia facility was three miles north of Milan while another source states that the facility was a mile and a half north of the village. There were approximately 225 inhabitants in this township at the start of the war. Many of these residents had fled east to the more protected settlements in Cuyahoga County.

General Perkins sent two expeditions to scout out the area once the camp had been established. A small detachment of militiamen under Major Austin and Lieutenant Benjamin Allen left Camp Avery for the Marblehead Peninsula and then to Cunningham's (now Kelley's) Island. While on the island, the men found a British schooner that had gone aground and the vessel was stripped and burnt. A small party of militiamen was attacked by Indians on Marblehead Peninsula on 15 September 1812 and Privates Matthew Guy and Aquilla Puntney were killed.

Major Samuel Frazier was ordered to take two militia companies west to the Sandusky River where elements of General Hull's army had built a blockhouse and stockade and then abandoned them when his army surrendered to the British. Fort Stephenson would be built at this location in 1813 by the regular army. At the blockhouse, a supply of pork and beef was found along with other food items. These were loaded onto four boats that had been left behind by General Hull's forces. Captain Clark Parker and 20 men were ordered on September 26th to row down the Sandusky River with the boats and supplies to the Sandusky Bay and then into Lake Erie. The men would follow the coastline of Lake Erie along the Cedar Point Peninsula to the mouth of the Huron River and then row up the river to Camp Avery. The rest of the men under Major Frazier remained at the stockade, which became a forward post for the division.

Captain Parker's flotilla made it as far as Bull's Island at the mouth of Sandusky Bay when they took shelter to avoid a violent storm. Bull's Island would be renamed Johnson's Island in 1852 and it would be the site of the Union Army's Confederate officer's prison and cemetery during the Civil War. The mouth of the Sandusky Bay is formed on the north by the Marblehead Peninsula and on the south by the Cedar Point Peninsula. Bull's Island is inside the bay's mouth next to the Marblehead Peninsula.

In the morning two settlers, Captain Joseph Ramsdell and his son, Valentine Ramsdell, were able to hail Captain Parker's party on Bull's Island, and they were brought over to the island in one of the boats. Captain Ramsdell was a sea captain from Massachusetts who had settled on Marblehead Peninsula the year before. Captain Ramsdell had built a small ship in western New York and had sailed to Ohio with his family. He would later build a larger ship and become a lake captain.

Ramsdell's homestead was eight miles northwest of Bull's Island at a place called Two Harbors on the north side of the Marblehead Peninsula. The Indians had raided the settlements and had driven nearly all of the settlers off the peninsula. These Indians had attacked Ramsdell and his son, and the men had fled towards Bull's Island when they saw Captain Avery's militiamen.

Ramsdell led a small party of militiamen back to his homestead where they counted 47 Indians at his cabin feasting on corn and honey. The party returned to Bull's Island and Captain Parker sent a messenger to Camp Avery. The messenger arrived at headquarters on the afternoon of September 28th. The rest of Captain Parker's party relocated to the Cedar Point Peninsula.

General Perkins ordered an expedition to be formed in order to attack and to drive the Indians off the Marblehead Peninsula. Many of the militiamen were sick with fever, and there wasn't a company at full strength at Camp Avery. Captain Joshua T. Cotton, the senior captain in the regiment, was ordered to form a new company and head for the peninsula. With 64 volunteers from five different companies, the new company left in darkness and they arrived on the northern point of Cedar Point Peninsula at 4 o'clock on the morning of September 29th.

The two militia parties joined forces and they crossed over to Bull's Island. The combined force numbered 72 men. Seven men under Corporal Coffin remained behind on Bull's Island to guard the boats after the rest of the men were put ashore on Marblehead Peninsula. Flanking guards under Sergeants Thomas Hamilton and James Root were detailed on each side of the road as the main body headed toward Two Harbors.

Within an hour after the main body of troops had left Bull's Island, the Indians attacked Corporal Coffin's party. Contrary to orders, Corporal Coffin had taken two men and landed on the peninsula in search of food. While on the peninsula they saw an Indian war party coming down the bay, and they headed back towards the island. They loaded their supplies into two of the smaller boats and headed back to Cedar Point Peninsula. They made it to safety, but the Indians destroyed the remaining two boats.

This incident was the start of the Battle of Marblehead Peninsula, which was fought during a 12-hour period on 29 September 1812. The battle became an endless pursuit by the Indians who ambushed the militia on two occasions during the day.

Meanwhile the main body of troops under Captain Cotton had reached the Ramsdell homestead where they found the remains of butchered cattle and Indian campfires still burning. The troops then headed to a wheat field about a mile west of the homestead. Captain Cotton left Sergeant Root with 11 men and ordered them to harvest the wheat. The captain and the rest of the men headed back towards Bull's Island. Once the wheat had been harvested, Sergeant Root and his detachment were to meet up with the rest of the company.

With their mission completed, Sergeant Root and his men headed back towards the island, but when they had gone only three quarters of a mile, a war party of 50 Indians attacked. Privates James Bills and John Blackman along with Valentine Ramsdell were killed in the medlee. One or two other militiamen were wounded.

The rest of the men were able to catch up with the main body of troops. Captain Cotton ordered Sergeant Aaron Rice and half the men to return to the battle site in order to bury the dead and to retrieve the wounded. The three dead militiamen were interred between two logs and covered with leaves and brush. Once the detachment returned with the wounded, Captain Cotton ordered his entire force to head back towards the landing.

As the party neared the south shore of the peninsula, they came across two Indians in the road and moments later the main body of Indians attacked the militiamen. The company was able to find cover and return fire. Whenever the Indians came within range Captain Cotton would order a bayonet charge, which would cause the Indians to disperse. The Indians tried a number of times to outflank the militiamen who were able to break up their advances each time. Hand-to-hand fighting occurred between the militiamen and the Indians. Causalities on the American side were light since the Indians had been firing their weapons wildly.

Finally, Captain Cotton ordered a retreat, and he took half of his men into an abandoned cabin while the rest of his men with six wounded militiamen rushed past the cabin to the landing. At the landing the men found the two wrecked boats, and they tried to plug the holes with clothing. Their attempts failed. Meanwhile, Sergeant Coffin on the Cedar Point Peninsula had heard the shooting, and he and his men headed back to the landing on the Marblehead Peninsula.

The wounded were loaded onto the boats and sent back to Camp Avery on the Huron River. Lieutenant Allen with 30 men returned to the cabin on October 1st to relieve Captain Cotton. There they found Captain Cotton's party still in the cabin. The Indians had broken off their assault, and they had retreated.

During the dash to the cabin, two days before, three more men were killed. Privates Daniel Mingus, Abraham Simmons and Alexander Mason fell near the cabin. Simmon's body was stripped and scalped and his was missing his right hand. Mason had also been scalped. Mingus had been picked up by his brother after he had fallen dead and carried into the cabin. All three men were buried under the floor of the cabin.

Captain Harvey Murray wrote a letter on the death of Private Mason after the battle on 13 October 1812. The captain stated, "He expired immediately, but covered with honor. He had shot one Indian dead and run (Sic) his bayonet through the vitals of another when he was fired upon."

Killed in this battle were James S. Bills, Alexander Mason, Valentine Ramsdell, Simeon Blackman, Daniel Mingus, and Abraham Simons. Wounded were Jacob Franks, James Jack, Moses Eldred, Elias Sperry, Samuel B. Tanner, John Carlton, Samuel Mann, John McMahon, Joseph Ramsdell and one civilian, a Mr. Lee, first name unknown. The Indians would later kill McMahon while he was going home on military leave.

The Indians' causalities are not known and there is no way of finding out the number of killed and wounded since the Indians were experts on retrieving their fallen members. After the war Captain Cotton did learn from an Indian chief at Fort Detroit that 40 Indians had been killed during this battle. This, of course, cannot be confirmed.

This battle was extremely important to Ohio during the early days of the war. Captain Cotton's composite company of militiamen stopped a major Indian war party before it hit the mainland of Ohio. Had they not been able to stop the Indians, the Indians could have pillaged and plundered settlements in what are now Erie and Lorain Counties, and could have threatened Cleveland in Cuyahoga County.

The Indians would have eventually been stopped some place between the Marblehead Peninsula and Cleveland, a distance of 60 miles. Although the militia regiments at Camp Avery were at less than half strength due to sickness, the two regiments under General Beall had been ordered north from the Wooster-Mansfield area of Ohio to Camp Avery. The rest of Colonel Rayen's regiment and all of Colonel Beard's regiment would have been ordered to the Huron River if they were needed.

For the remainder of the war, the Indian war parties that penetrated Ohio tended to be small in numbers, and they did not pose a major threat like the party that invaded the Marblehead Peninsula. Thousands of Indians joined the British assaults on Fort Meigs and Fort Sandusky in 1813 but they returned to their homes once these battles ended.

Close up of the two monuments within the fenced in area.

A stone monument was erected in 1857 near the site where Mingus, Simmons and Mason had died during the second skirmish of the battle. The United States Daughters of the War of 1812 placed a plaque upon this monument in 1913. Another monument has been placed beside the original monument and this stone lists the names of the two men killed on 15 September 1812 and the six men killed on 29 September 1812. The monuments are on the south side of the Marblehead Peninsula across from Johnson's Island along state route 163 in a small park honoring this battle.

Bibliography

"Abstract of the Return of the Fourth Division of the Militia of the State of Ohio," **Ohio Militia, 4th Division Records 1812-1815**, call number MS-3203a, Western Reserve Historical Society's Archives Library, Cleveland, Ohio.

Burke, Thomas Aquinas, **Ohio Lands: A Short History**, second edition, (Columbus, Ohio: Ohio Auditor of State, June 1989).

Firelands Pioneer, Volume XIV, Firelands Historical Society, (Norwalk, Ohio: Laning Company: 1902), Captain Joshua T. Cotton's Statement of the Battle on the Peninsula of Sandusky Bay, September 1812, pp. 880-884; Captain Joshua T. Cotton's Account of the Battle on the Peninsula in September 1812, pp. 886-889 and James Root's Statement of the Battle of the Peninsula in 1812, pp. 884-886.

The Fire Lands Pioneer, March 1859, (Sandusky, Ohio), Reminiscences of the Hon. F. W. Fowler of Milan, First Alarm of the Settlers, Incidents of the War of 1812, Skirmish with the Indians, pp. 3-7.

Historical Collections of the Mahoning Valley, Volume 1, (Youngstown, Ohio: Mahoning Valley Historical Society: 1876), History of the War of 1812 as given mainly by Captain Jedediah Burnham, Captain of the Kinsman Company, 1812, pp. 304-321 and Remembrances of the Skirmish with the Indians on the Peninsula in the War of 1812, pp. 321-331.

History of the Fire Lands comprising Huron and Erie Counties, Ohio, (Cleveland: W. W. Williams, 1879), Pioneers and the War of 1812, pp. 459-460

Knopf, Richard C., **Document Transcriptions of the War of 1812 in the Northwest,** Volume VIII, Letters from the Secretary of War 1812 & 1813 Relating to the War of 1812 in the Northwest, (Columbus, Ohio: Ohio Historical Society, 1961), pp. 23-24, Secretary of War to Governors of the Various States, 13 April 1812, militia strengths by states.

Roster of Ohio Soldiers in the War of 1812, Adjutant General of Ohio, (1916, reprinted by Heritage Books, Inc., Bowie, Maryland: 1995).

Waggoner, Clark, **History of the City of Toledo and Lucas County, Ohio**, (New York, New York: Munsell & Company, 1888), chapter II, Civil Government Established, page 285.

Western Reserve and Northern Ohio Historical Society, Number 51, December 1879, (Cleveland, Ohio), Gen. Wadsworth's Division, War of 1812, pp. 115-123.

Gunboats on the Cuyahoga: Lake Erie's Lost Squadron

One of the mysteries of the War of 1812 is that Cleveland, Ohio, built a squadron of gunboats for the U.S. Navy and that these tiny warships served in the Lake Erie Squadron under Master Commandant Oliver Hazard Perry. Many of the early histories of Cleveland claim such a fact, but it is well documented that the four gunboats used by the navy during the Battle of Lake Erie were all built in Erie, Pennsylvania, and that they were all rigged as two-mast schooners. These vessels were the U.S. Schooners *Porcupine*, *Tigress*, *Scorpion*, and *Ariel*.

The navy had been in the gunboat business for many years, and it had 143 gunboats stationed along the Atlantic and the Gulf of Mexico coastlines in 1810, and more would be built during the war. The U.S. Navy would also build gunboats on Lake Champlain and Lake Ontario. All of the gunboats were built as a defensive measure to protect our ports and harbors.

There were two types of gunboats being built, one having a full deck and the other having no deck but with one or two gun platforms at either end of the vessel. This second type of gunboat was called a row galley or barge. All of these types of gunboats were ideal for a low budget navy. They had a shallow draft with a keel, and they were propelled by oars and sails. The smaller row galleys carried at least one cannon while the larger row galleys carried two cannons.

In James Wallen's *Cleveland's Golden Story*,[213] he states, "the shipwrights of Cleveland had the honor of constructing two noble ships of Perry's fleet. The "Porcupine" and the "Portage" were built on the Cuyahoga River and provisioned and equipped with sails in Cleveland." In *A History of Cleveland*[214] by Samuel P. Orth, it states, "It is surprising to learn that in 1813 two of the boats in Commodore Perry's fleet on September 10, 1813, were built on the Cuyahoga river, some fifteen or twenty miles above its mouth. It was at 'Old Portage,' a prominent frontier place at that time. After these boats were launched they were floated down to 'the pineries,' where their masts were put in place. These boats were probably provisioned and equipped with sails at Cleveland."

According to the *Dictionary of American Naval Fighting Ships*, an official publication of the Department of the Navy, there are no records that any gunboat was ever built for the navy in the Cleveland area during the war.[215] A report entitled the *Conditions of the Navy and the Progress made in Providing Materials and Building Ships*,[216] which was issued by the Department of the Navy on 18 March 1814, showed that no gunboats or barges were built for the navy on Lake Erie during 1813. The four gunboats built at Erie, Pennsylvania, were listed with the other schooners in the section on the vessels stationed on this lake.

This basically ends any notions that the U.S. Navy built any gunboats on Lake Erie other than those rigged as schooners, but this doesn't end this story. The U.S. Army did build a fleet of bateaux (boats) in three boatyards on the Cuyahoga River and on the Grand River in Ohio for its invasion of Upper Canada, which occurred on 27 September 1813. The Secretary of War John Armstrong appointed Major Thomas Sidney Jesup of the 19th Regiment of U.S. Infantry on 9 March 1813 to command the invasion operations

---

[213] Wallen, James, **Cleveland's Golden Story,** (Cleveland, Ohio: William Taylor, Son and Company, April 1920), Chapter III, Taming the Wilderness, page 21.

[214] Orth, Samuel P., **A History of Cleveland**, Volume 1, (Chicago-Cleveland; S. J. Clarke Publishing Company, 1910), The War of 1812, pp. 304-306.

[215] **Dictionary of American Naval Fighting Ships,** Department of the Navy, Naval Historical Center, Washington Navy Yard, Washington, D.C.

[216] **American State Papers,** Documents, Legislative and Executive, of the Congress of the United States, 1789-1819, (Washington, D.C.: Gales and Seaton, 1832), Naval Affairs, Conditions of the Navy and the Progress made in Providing Materials and Building Ships, 18 March 1814, page 309.

in Cleveland.[217] By July 1st Major Jesup had 70 boats finished, and he expected to have between 80-90 boats completed by July fifteenth.[218]

In all of his correspondences, Major Jesup never stated where his three boatyards were located, but evidence does suggest that at least one boatyard was located in Cleveland while another boatyard was located further up the Cuyahoga River in what is now Cuyahoga Falls in Summit County. The boatyard at Cuyahoga Falls was called the Old Portage Boatyard. Another facility at Peninsula in Summit County was called the 'pinery,' which was down the river from the boatyard. At the 'pinery' is where the boats were installed with masts and spars.

Another location where some of the bateaux may have been built was on the Grand River, east of Cleveland in today's Painesville in Lake County. On 27 March 1813 Captain Jesup wrote to the secretary asking for regular troops to protect both Cleveland and the Grand River in order to protect the boats.[219] The mouth of the Grand River was also used as one of the staging areas for the provisions being gathered for the invasion of Upper Canada. The main re-supply center for both the army and the navy was located at Cleveland.

A civilian shipyard was operating on the Grand River at a place called the Painesville Flats in Painesville.[220] Another shipyard on the Chagrin River just west of Painesville was where the merchant schooner *Cuyahoga Packet* had been built in 1805. The British at Amherstburg, Upper Canada, captured this vessel shortly after the war had been declared.

Map of the Cleveland-Akron Area of Northeast Ohio

Cleveland had been in the shipbuilding business for many years. The merchant schooner *Ohio* was built in this village in 1810, and the navy purchased this ship in 1812 and converted it for military use.

---

[217] **Ibid,** Military Affairs, Correspondences between the Secretary of War and Major General Harrison, 9 March 1813, page 452.

[218] Knopf, Richard C., **Document Transcriptions of the War of 1812 in the Northwest,** Volume VII Part 3, Letters to the Secretary of War 1812 Relating to the War of 1812 in the Northwest, (Anthony Wayne Parkway Board, Ohio State Museum, Columbus, Ohio: 1957), page 2, Major Jessup to the Secretary of War, 1 July 1813.

[219] **Ibid**, page 198, Captain Jesup to the Secretary of War John Armstrong, 27 March 1813.

[220] **Here is Lake County, Ohio**, Lake County Historical Society, (Cleveland, Ohio: Howard Allen Publishing, 1964), Shipbuilding, pp. 73-74.

The ship became the U.S. Schooner *Ohio,* and it was used as a re-supply vessel in Master Commandant Perry's squadron. The village did not have a sawmill, so lumber would have to be hauled into the village from a sawmill located at Newburgh, which was a little way up the river from Cleveland.

The key to whether gunboats were built along the Cuyahoga River depended on the ship building facilities located at each of the boatyards. Bateaux were built on flat ground and constructed upside down. The ribs of the boat were assembled first and then planked over and caulked. Once completed, the boats were carried into the river, flipped over and then finished.

At least 65 bateaux may have been built at the Old Portage Boatyard.[221] They were 50 feet long by 10 feet wide and were powered by sail and oars. There was a large steering oar mounted on the stern. One man standing operated the steering oar and at least six men paddled, three on a side. They could carry 40 to 50 soldiers with their equipment. True gunboats were built on stocks, up right, and then they were launched into a river or lake.

Cleveland could have built some of these gunboats during the war on the shores of the Cuyahoga River, and these boats would have to be slid into the river upon completion. The village had constructed a number of schooners and sloops before the war and it would build two private merchant schooners in 1814. This suggests that the boatyard in Cleveland was active throughout the war.

In his book *Old Portage*, C. R. Quine states that during the 1930's the remnants of two dry docks were found at the site of the boatyard in Cuyahoga Falls.[222] "There is good evidence that a boat yard existed at a point six-tenths of a mile east of the Portage Tree," he continues, "at this point there remain the outlines of two long pits connecting with the river. An excavation was made there in the 1930's during a period of low water on the river and at the bottom of the pits heavy planks were found. It is considered that these planks formed the floor of the dry docks."

Quine quoted a number of local historians from the 1800's who had gathered information on the boatyard and who had interviewed a number of men who had built these gunboats. Three companies of Ohio militiamen had assisted in the boat building by felling trees and dragging the logs to a sawmill, which was located near the boatyard.

Arthur Blower, a historian for the Summit County Historical Society in 1940, researched the possibility that gunboats were built on the upper Cuyahoga River during the War of 1812.[223] Local legends had persisted for over 100 years that two gunboats were built at the Old Portage Boatyard and that they were part of Perry's naval squadron.

On the site of the old boatyard, Blower found two depressions 150 feet by 75 feet and three feet deep that had been connected to a channel ending at the Cuyahoga River. The old timers in the area had said that the depressions had been eight feet deep in the late 1800's and that constant flooding by the river had filled in much of the depressions with silt.

Blower found no evidence that the U.S. Navy had built gunboats for the Lake Erie squadron on the Cuyahoga River. He had written to the Department of the Navy in 1913, and he had received a reply signed by Franklin D. Roosevelt, acting Secretary of the Navy, stating that the navy had no records of any gunboats built for the navy during the war except the four built at Erie, Pennsylvania.[224] Blower then dismissed the idea that naval gunboats were built on the upper river, but he concluded that a couple of large vessels were built there around the time of the War of 1812.

Quine quoted William Coggeswell of Bath Township who said, "I was employed with others to float the boats down to the lake with instructions that when we got to the pinery near Peninsula we should

---

[221] **Crossroads RC & D**, Crossroads Resource Conservation and Development Council, Inc., New Philadelphia, Ohio, January 2002, Volume 10, Number 1, page 3, NE Ohio Wood Helped Win the War of 1812!

[222] Quine, C. R., **Old Portage**, (1953), "The Boat Yard at Old Portage," pp. 20-23.

[223] Blower, Arthur H., **The Shipyard on Old Portage, a survey of all available information on this subject**, (Akron, Ohio: Summit County Historical Society, 1942).

[224] **Ibid**, page 7.

furnish each boat with mast and spars. When we got to Cleveland, the boats were examined by many and the general opinion was that they were the kind needed. These boats at once went into commission and did good service in the Battle of Lake Erie." This is a direct reference to vessels that were larger than bateaux, which could engage the British naval squadron in battle.

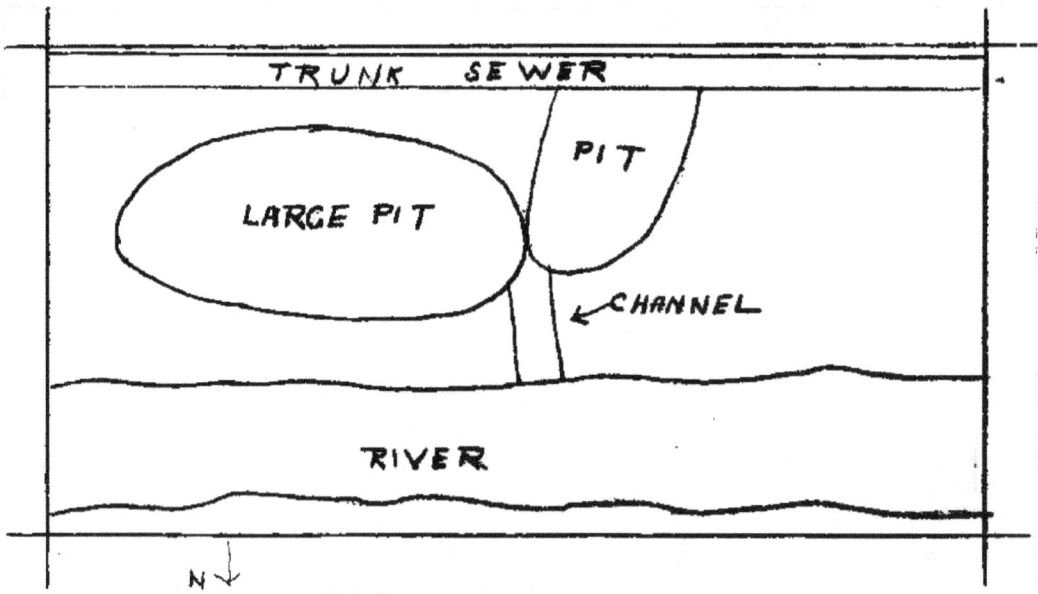

Drawing from Arthur Blower's book showing the dry docks

At least three gunboats were built at the Old Portage Boatyard, and they were named the *Portage*, the *Porcupine* and the *Hornet*. Once built, they were floated down the Cuyahoga River to the 'pinery' where each was outfitted with spars and masts. Quine said that at some points on the river a team of oxen was needed to drag the boats over the shallow areas.

These vessels were not built and paid for by the U.S. Navy but they were built for the U.S. Army. The main question now is why the army needed to have gunboats when the navy was building a squadron of warships at Erie. The second question is that if these vessels were rigged as sloops (single mast vessels) or schooners (two-mast vessels), where did the army find the men to operate them? The navy had a terrible time finding enough men to man its own squadron at Erie.

America had two fleets on Lake Erie during the War of 1812. The navy operated the warships of the Lake Erie Squadron while the army operated the invasion fleet to transport the army to the shores of Upper Canada. Both fleets had their own purpose and mission. The men who had built the invasion fleet could have manned the gunboats. Most of these men were from the Pittsburgh, Pennsylvania area and they probably knew how to sail and operate the vessels that they built.

There is no evidence that these gunboats were armed in the Cleveland area. Cannons could have been brought overland from the army's arsenal at Pittsburgh, but all available cannons had been used to gun Fort Meigs in western Ohio and to arm the naval squadron at Erie. Cleveland did have one or two cannons at Fort Huntington in this village, but it is doubtful that these cannons would have been used for the gunboats until the lake was secure and in American hands.

Probably the primary reason why the army needed gunboats was that it had to have vessels capable of transporting two companies of artillery with field cannons from Fort Meigs to Upper Canada. Bateaux could have carried one or two cannons, but these vessels were needed to transport troops as they were designed. Bateaux could carry the larger cannons but only as cargo.

If the American squadron had not been able to gain control of Lake Erie, General Harrison had a secondary invasion plan. The Army of the Northwest would have marched to Detroit while the bateaux would have carried the supplies and provisions for the army. Gunboats would have been needed to protect these bateaux on their dash to Detroit. This, of course, hinged on whether the gunboats and bateaux could have made it to Fort Meigs from Cleveland without being molested by the British and then be able to slip past Fort Malden, Upper Canada, on their way to Detroit.

The Bateaux

The bateau (plural: bateaux) is French for 'boat' and this type of vessel had been used in America and Canada for over a hundred years by the time that the war had started. These boats were flat-bottomed, shallow-drafted crafts with pointed ends and no true keel. They were propelled by oars, poles or sail. These boats were modified by length, width and draft for the rivers and waterways where they operated. Major Jesup referred to these crafts as 'transports' in all of his letters to the Secretary of War.

Bateaux had been the mainstay of the inland shipping industry in America, and they had been used heavily by the French, British and American armies to transport troops and supplies throughout the American and Canadian colonies. The different types of bateaux were named after the location where they were first built or for who had originally designed the boats.

The Durham Boat was designed by Robert Durham of Reiglesville, Pennsylvania, in 1757, for use on the Delaware River.[225] The largest boats were 65 feet long by 8 feet wide, and they could carry 20 tons of iron ore or 150 barrels of flour. A captain and a crew of six men operated these vessels. George Washington had used these boats during his crossing of the Delaware River on the night of 25 December 1776.

The Albany Boats and the Schenectady Boats were originally built in New York for shallower waters.[226] Both boats were named after the villages in which they were first built. The Albany Boat was 24 feet long by 3 feet wide while the Schenectady Boat was wider and up to 45 feet long. The Schenectady Boat could carry 40 to 50 soldiers, and these were the boats that were built along the Cuyahoga River and the Grand River during the War of 1812.

The Gunboats

Gunboats were keeled vessels that were built upright on land in a frame and then slid into the river or lake when completed. These boats could also have been constructed in a dry dock and then floated out into the river or lake to be finished. Gunboats had a full deck, and they could be mounted with different cannon configurations. The gunboats in Perry's squadron were armed with one or two cannons on swivel mounts, which could be fired from either side of the boat. In addition some gunboats had cannons firing through gun ports in the ship's hull similar to the larger warships.

The *Porcupine* and the *Tigress* measured 60½ feet long on deck and 50 feet at the waterline. They were 17 feet wide with a draft of 5 feet.[227] The *Scorpion* and the *Ariel* measured 68½ feet long on deck and 60 feet at the waterline. They were 17 feet wide with a draft of 5 feet. The first two gunboats displaced 52 tons of water while the others displaced 75 tons. These types of vessels were probably too large to have been constructed on the upper Cuyahoga River because of their five-foot drafts.

---

[225] **Durham Boats…**, http://www.10crucialdays.org/htm,l/durham.htm

[226] Meany, Joseph F. Jr., Ph.D., **Bateaux and 'Battoe Men': An American Colonial Response to the Problem of Logistics in Mountain Warfare**, New York State Military Museum and Veterans Research Center, New York State Division of Military and Naval Affairs, http://www.dmna.state.ny.us/historic/articles/bateau.htm

[227] Malcomson, Robert, **Warships of the Great Lakes 1754-1834**, (Annapolis, Maryland: Naval Institute Press, 2001), Chapter 6, 'Only required for one battle' Lake Erie 1812-1814, pp. 87, 90.

Row galleys, however, were flat-bottomed, keeled boats which had no decks. They used a rudder for directional control. In the bow and the stern there was a platform which mounted a single cannon on a swivel which could be aimed approximately 45 degrees left or right of the boat's center line.

The smaller row galleys were 50 feet long by 12 wide and the hull depth was 3½ feet, almost identical to a bateaux.[228] They drew only 22 inches of water and they were propelled by 26 oars with a single sail. They displaced 40 tons of water and mounted a single cannon. The larger row galleys were 75 feet long and 15 wide with a depth of 4 feet. They were propelled by 40 oars and two sails. The larger row galleys also drew 22 inches of water. They displaced 70 tons of water and mounted two cannons.

Both types of row galleys had a standard rudder, and they used ballast to right the craft. These vessels looked very similar to a bateau but they were wider. The gunboats that were built on the Cuyahoga River were probably not decked over and they were most likely modified to transport the artillerymen, cannons, shots, powder and equipment of the two artillery companies.

The gunboats built on the Cuyahoga River for the U.S. Army were probably constructed from plans obtained from the U.S. Navy and then altered to fit the needs of the army. The navy had approved plans for all of the types of ships in its inventory. Local builders often modified these ships because of the availability of material and for local conditions in which these vessels operated.[229]

The Invasion

During the actual invasion of Upper Canada the navy and the army operated as a single team. The naval vessels carried the officers, Indians and guests of the Army of the Northwest, while the army's enlisted personnel rowed the bateaux across Lake Erie. The naval ships were fully gunned and the former merchant vessels in the squadron were probably also carrying the army's ration barrels within their cargo hauls.

Robert Dodge in his book entitled the *Battle of Lake Erie* states that Major Eleazer Wood of the regular army's engineers had six bateaux mounted with one cannon, loaded and ready to fire during the invasion.[230] This statement is probably in error due to the fact that the cannons were mounted on army carriages and not naval carriages. The cannons would have been off loaded immediately after the invasion fleet had beached on Canadian soil and moved into position to support the army. The cannons were probably not loaded with shot and powder while on the row galleys since the main battle fleet had enough firepower to support the landing. Naval carriages were designed to operate on ship's decks and not to follow the army into battle.

Samuel Brown was one of the thousands of men who rowed across Lake Erie during the invasion. He wrote a book after the war in which he described the invasion of Upper Canada on 27 September 1813.[231] He said, "It was a sublime and delightful spectacle to behold 16 ships of war and 100 boats filled with men, borne rapidly and majestically to the long sought shores of the enemy."

In his battle orders for the invasion, Major General William Henry Harrison had given instructions on how he wanted his artillery to be deployed.[232] He had fully expected that once his army had set foot on

---

[228] Ansley, Norman, **Vergennes, Vermont, and the War of 1812,** (Severna Park, Maryland: Brooke Keefer Limited Editions, 1999), page 42, Gunboats of the United States Navy.

[229] Malcomson, **Warships of the Great Lakes 1754-1834**, chapter 8, 'Every man to do his duty' Lake Champlain 1812-1814, pp. 125-126.

[230] Dodge, Robert J., **The Battle of Lake Erie**, (Fostoria, Ohio: Gray Printing Company, 1979), chapter 5, Transporting Harrison's Army, pp. 31-33.

[231] Brown, Samuel R., **Views of the Campaigns of the North-Western Army,** (Philadelphia, Pennsylvania: Griggs and Dickinson, Printers, 1815), page 60.

[232] **William Henry Harrison battle orders**, Filson Special Collection, Henry Family Papers, Library of Congress, Washington, D.C., page 2.

Canadian soil the British and the Indians would attack his forces. The general said, "A detachment of artillery with a six pounder, four pounder and howitzer will land with the advanced light corps, the rest of the artillery will be held in reserve & landed at such point as Major Wood may direct." Major Eleazer Wood, U.S. Engineers, was the beach master for the invasion, and he was in charge of the landing of troops and off-loading of equipment and supplies.

Since the army landed on a beach, it is extremely doubtful that the gunboats carrying the artillery were the standard type gunboats. Due to their rounded hulls and draft, it would have been difficult to beach these crafts and then to keep them upright. The boats in question had to be the keeled, flat-bottom row galleys, which could be beached and off loaded.

The gunboat flotilla was divided into two divisions with the first three boats landing with the invasion force while the second three boats were held off shore in reserve. The left wing of the invasion force was made up of the regular army while the center section consisted of a legionary corps. This corps was made up of field artillery, dismounted light dragoons, friendly Indians, and the militiamen from the U.S. Voluntary Corps. The right wing contained the Kentucky militiamen under the command of Kentucky's Governor Isaac Shelby. The reserve artillery could have landed at any point on the invasion line giving direct gun support to either wing.

It appears that each row galley had only one cannon on board. Since the main purpose of the artillery was to be used on land and not from the lake, the boats would have had to carry all of the cannon balls, powder and equipment for each gun plus the men to operate the guns. There would also have to be a gun carriage and a caisson (or wagon) for the ammunition and equipment. Extra men may have been assigned to the artillery crew since horses were not brought along on the invasion, and these men would have been used to move the cannons and the caissons into position wherever they were needed.

Although not stated in the battle plans, the reserve artillery probably had the same configuration of cannon and equipment. Dodge said that there were six bateaux equipped with cannons in the fleet but he probably mistook the row galleys as bateaux.

Prior to the invasion, General Harrison had ordered Brigadier General Duncan McArthur, the commander of Fort Meigs, on 20 September 1813, to send the gunboats to Put-in-Bay.[233] General Harrison's headquarters was at Camp Portage where the troops were being embarked for Put-in-Bay so the gunboats were still at Fort Meigs being loaded with cannons, ammunition and artillery equipment when General Harrison wrote this letter.

The Mystery solved?

Row galleys in the navy were given names or boat numbers to identify them. Bateaux were not numbered or named. Since the builders named the three vessels that were built at the Old Portage Boatyard, it can be assumed that they were not bateaux. The army probably did not keep the names for these gunboats; however, the boats were probably numbered for identification purposes.

The local population during the war knew the difference between a bateau and a gunship. Bateaux were a common sight along the lakeshore and inland on the rivers in Ohio. The army and the Ohio militia had used these boats since the beginning of the war to transport supplies from Cleveland to the forts and posts in northwestern Ohio.

Another clue that row galleys were used in the invasion of Upper Canada is the number of warships that Brown had seen in the fleet. He counted 16 warships, but this number was too high for the number of known ships available for this invasion. The Americans had 10 ships in its squadron, but the US Brig *Lawrence* was too badly damaged and it was still anchored in the Put-in-Bay harbor during the invasion.

---

[233] **Duncan McArthur Papers**, Library of Congress, 1922, Microfilm 47, Reel 1, Volumes 1-3, 5 October 1783 – 20 September 1813, document number 584, letter from Major General William H. Harrison to Brigadier General Duncan McArthur, 20 September 1813, Ohio Historical Society, Columbus, Ohio.

The British had six ships in its squadron but the HM Brigs *Detroit* and *Queen Charlotte* were also heavily damaged and sitting in the harbor. The available ships would have numbered 13, not, 16 as counted by Brown.

Brown could have mistaken three of the row galleys for bateaux since a smaller version of this vessel had the same basic appearance as a bateau depending on the sail configuration. Three of these vessels were probably the enlarged version, which had two masts, and they had a very similar appearance to a schooner.

After the invasion the naval squadron sailed up the Detroit River to Detroit where they weighed anchor. The naval warships probably towed a number of these bateaux up the river, and these boats were used to ferry troops between Detroit and Sandwich on the Canadian side of the river.

Row galleys had been built in all of the military theaters during the war including Lake Ontario and Lake Champlain. So it is totally reasonable to assume that these vessels were also constructed on Lake Erie. After the invasion of Upper Canada, the army did not need the bateaux and the row galleys and they were probably disposed of in a public sale or simply abandoned. The navy also had more than enough ships in its squadron, and the navy began to sell some of its warships soon after the invasion. The navy did not need the army's gunboats.

It can now be seen that the army did build gunboats for its invasion of Upper Canada. The smaller gunboats known as row galleys seem to have been built at the Old Portage Boatyard while the larger row galleys may have been built at Cleveland and at Painesville. Army contract records for this period need to be researched to see exactly what was built along the shore of Lake Erie for the invasion of Upper Canada.

Making sense of the Roster of Ohio Soldiers in the War of 1812

In 1916 the Adjutant General of Ohio published the *Roster of Ohio Soldiers in the War of 1812* [234] *(Roster)*. This is a listing of all of the militia companies and headquarters' staffs that were activated for state or federal military duty during the war and that had submitted a personal roster and an equipment status report to the adjutant general's office. The book states that there are 1,759 officers and 24,521 men listed. This book is not a complete listing of men who lived in Ohio and who were veterans of this war.

The actual number of men listed in the *Roster* is far less than the 26,280 men that are found within the pages of this book. Many men in this book are listed more than once with many of these men having multiple enlistments in a number of different companies or headquarters' staffs. The actual number of men may be as low as 15,000 due to these multiple enlistments. Many of the missing company rosters can be found listed in the various county history books that were produced in the later part of the 1800's and in early 1900's. Many of the archival libraries that are located in Ohio also have the rosters of Ohio's companies that are not found in the *Roster*.

The *Rolls and Inspection Returns for 1812* that were submitted to the War Department in Washington, D.C., by the Ohio's Adjutant General stated that there were 34,726 men in the Ohio militia in 1812.[235] This number would have increased yearly throughout the war. Men were called up to serve by the governor for military duty with either the state's army or with the federal army. The state maintained a picket line of forts and blockhouses from Sandusky to Mansfield through Mount Vernon to Columbus and onwards to Dayton and finally west to the state line. This line of defense was used to check any Indian attacks. Ohio's companies on federal duty served with the Army of the Northwest in northwestern Ohio and in the Territories of Indiana and Michigan.

The *Roster* is very misleading for it groups the majority of the 473 listed militia companies into the 1st, 2nd or 3rd Ohio Regiments. This is a total of 249 companies. By law Ohio's militia regiments were made up of between four and eight companies. Nearly all of the companies that were called up for state or federal duty were organized into brigades consisting of at least two regiments. Officially, the state's volunteer brigades were called 'detachments' but this term was rarely used. Another term used instead of brigade by the state officials and militia leaders was 'quota', as in the '1st Ohio Quota'. The *Roster* labels the volunteer detachments as the '1st Brigade, Ohio Militia' or the '1st Regiment, Ohio Militia'. This makes no distinction as to whether the detachment was called up for federal duty or state duty. This book groups the brigade and regimental staffs together and the companies under these commands separately. It is impossible to reconstruct the actual brigades and regiments that served during the war using the *Roster*.

Following in line with the designation adopted by the other states and territories, Ohio's detachments should have been called the '1st Ohio Volunteer Brigade' or the '1st Ohio Volunteer Infantry'. The term regiment is not needed on the "1st Ohio Volunteer Infantry" since normally the smallest infantry unit that was called up for military duty by the federal government was a regiment. The term 'volunteer infantry', with a state's name in front of the term, was used during the War of 1812, the Mexican War, the Civil War, and the Spanish-American War. Before World War I the National Guard (militia) was reorganized into infantry divisions using the same designations as the regular army and the term 'volunteer' ceased to be used.

---

[234] **Roster of Ohio Soldiers in the War of 1812**, The Adjutant General of Ohio 1916, (Heritage Books, Inc., Bowie, Maryland: 1995).

[235] Knopf, Richard C., **Document Transcriptions of the War of 1812 in the Northwest, volume VIII**, Letters from the Secretary of War 1812 & 1813 Relating to the War of 1812 in the Northwest, (Ohio Historical Society: Columbus, Ohio: 1961), pp. 23-24, Secretary of War to the Governors of the Various States, 15 April 1812.

Numbering of the Units

The federal Militia Act of 1792 [236] required the states and territories to number their militia units. Most states sequentially numbered their units so that they had only one 1st brigade and only one 1st regiment. As each brigade and regiment was formed, they received that next highest number according to that type of unit. Ohio, on the other hand, did not sequentially number its units but reused the numbers within its militia hierarchy. Ohio had five divisions in 1813 and each division had a 1st brigade and each brigade in turn had a 1st and 2nd regiment. Some brigades had as many as six regiments. Ohio's 1st division had two brigades, the 2nd division had five brigades, the 3rd division had four brigades, the 4th division had four brigades, and the 5th division had two brigades. With Ohio's numbering system it had five 1st brigades and eighteen 1st regiments and eighteen 2nd regiments.

Ohio followed the letter of the law, but its numbering system would cause confusion for the next 200 years. In most cases the regiments would be referred to by the name of its colonel, that is, Colonel Charles Miller's Regiment (Coshocton County) instead of its numeric designation, the 2nd Regiment of the 4th Brigade of the 3rd Division, Ohio Militia.

Federal Duty

Surprisingly, the governor could not call out the existing brigades and regiments during a time of crisis but he was allowed to demand a detachment from each division for militia duty. He was required to specify the number of men needed and the time and place of rendezvous. He could call out all or part of the militia.

Ohio's militia call-ups were based on a quota system determined by the federal government, which had set Ohio's quota at 5,000 volunteers who could serve with the United States Army. Either the War Department or Major General William Henry Harrison would ask Ohio's governor for a quota of men to serve with the Army of the Northwest. If the request were for 1,000 volunteers, then the governor would ask for the volunteers from Ohio's divisions in order to form a new brigade for federal duty. The adjutant general of the state would then decide how many men from each division would be needed to make up the 1,000 men for the call up. Each division would determine how many men from each of its brigades would be needed to fill its quota.

The commanding officer for each detachment was selected according to earliest date of commission for the rank needed in the call up, that is; the officer with the earliest commission would be the commander. If a regimental size detachment were being called up then the oldest colonel and the two oldest majors from within the brigade would assume command of the detachment.

When the men rendezvoused at the preset location, they would then form themselves into new companies of 50 to 80 men and then would elect their officers. Companies would then form into battalions, battalions into regiments, etc., and then officer elections occurred for each of the command levels. Officers who were called up for state or federal military duty accepted a state commission in the militia. These commissions lasted for a five years.

Determining the Type of Duty

Determining whether a company was called up for federal duty or for state duty will involve some research. There are many county history books and other books on the War of 1812 listing a company or companies as to where they served and to what regiment to which they were attached. A pension application from one of the members of the company may list the regiment and places of service. If your ancestor was in the militia and received a land bounty in the 1850's or his wife received a widow's

---

[236] Von Steuben, Frederick William Baron, **Baron von Steuben's Revolutionary War Drill Manual**, (Dover Publications, Inc., New York, New York: 1985), appendix, <u>Militia Act of 1792</u>.

pension. then he had served with his company on federal duty. The State of Ohio did not award its militiamen land or pensions for service during the war.

The *Roster* for the most part does list the muster-in-date for each company and the muster-out-date when militiamen complete their tour of duty. Normally those companies that performed less than 90 days of military duty served with the state, while federalized companies normally served for either six months or for a year. Many companies were released early from their tour of duty.

Another problem with the *Roster* is that it tries to identify each company as to its county of origin. All of the companies listed in this book were regimental, brigade or divisional companies, which were made up of men from a number of different counties. In most cases the names of the county listed in the book are actually the counties from where the commanding officer lived and not where the majority of the men lived. However, most of the regimental companies were probably formed from men within the same county. Some regiments did cross county lines.

Companies that were called up to serve on the state's picket line tended to be formed with men from the same regiment, battalion or company. Isaac Evans from Coshocton County was elected captain of a company formed from the 2nd battalion of the 2nd regiment for service at Mount Vernon in 1812. The men came from the 1st through 4th infantry companies of this battalion. The same battalion also had a rifle company under the command of Adam Johnston. Part of his company was activated and sent to Mount Vernon with Johnston as its commander. The remaining men still maintained the original four infantry companies and the rifle company within the borders of Coshocton County while the other men were stationed at Mount Vernon.

Isaac Meredith from Coshocton County was the commander of a company that served on federal duty in late 1812. This was a brigade company made up volunteers from Coshocton, Guernsey, Muskingum and Tuscarawas Counties. The company was formed in Zanesville, Ohio, and the men elected Meredith as their captain.[237]

Many researchers will find their ancestors listed in a company that was from a county in which they know that their ancestors never lived. Checking the table of brigades and counties at the end of this article may help to identify ancestors who were members of a company formed from within a brigade. Some of the companies, which served in late 1814 and early 1815, were made up of men from the same division and therefore consisted of men from a multitude of counties.

Definitions

The *Roster* lists the rosters of 432 infantry companies, 25 mounted infantry companies, 13 cavalry troops, two mounted spy companies and one artillery battery. Five additional infantry companies that are listed in this book were recruited for the regular infantry regiments.

Many of the infantry companies are mislabeled for they were actually mounted infantry companies. Another name for a mounted infantry is 'dragoons.' You will find cornets, saddlers and furriers listed in some of these infantry companies. These ranks are unique to cavalry type troops and not for the standard infantry companies. Mounted infantry companies are not true cavalry units. They were foot soldiers that used horses for transportation. Once on the battlefield the men dismounted and fought on foot. The companies listed as cavalry units in the book were probably actually mounted infantry. Since each man supplied his own arms and equipment, few men could afford to purchase the arms and equipment necessary to form a true cavalry unit. Due to the heavily wooded areas of the northwest, traditional cavalry units were not used during the war. Cavalry units were designed to fight other cavalry units and to charge infantry positions.

---

[237] **Pension application of Elijah Collins**, War of 1812, SO-2235, SC-1161, BLW 8176-160-50, Served in Captain George Richardson's Company and Captain Isaac Meredith's Company, Ohio Militia, Declaration of Surviving Soldiers for Pension, (National Archives and Records Administration, Washington, D.C.)

Light dragoons were lightly armed cavalry units whose mission was to disrupt the enemy behind their lines by raiding supply lines and to involve the enemy in minor skirmishes. They were also used as dispatch riders and as military escorts. Spy companies were used as reconnaissance units. They were sent behind enemy positions in order to gather information on the enemy. The regular army called these companies 'rangers'. Both spy and rangers companies were normally mounted.

Regular Army

The *Roster* lists five Ohio companies that were raised for three regular army regiments. Two companies were part of the 27th Regiment of Infantry while two were part of the 19th Regiment of Infantry. The 26th Regiment of Infantry had one company listed. Ohioans also served in the 1st Regiment of Infantry, the 7th Regiment of Infantry, the 17th Regiment of Infantry, the 24th Regiment of Infantry and the 28th Regiment of Infantry. Two other federal regiments that were partially formed with men from Ohio were the 1st and 2nd Regiments of Rifle. The 7th, 17th and 28th regiments were primarily raised in Kentucky while the 19th regiment was raised in Ohio and in the Territory of Michigan. The 24th Regiment of Infantry was raised in Tennessee and the Territory of Mississippi. The 26th regiment was raised in western Ohio from within the 1st, 2nd and 5th Militia Divisions while the 27th regiment was raised in eastern Ohio from within the 3rd and 4th Militia Division.

Ohioans were also recruited to serve in the light dragoons, ranger and artillery companies in the regular army plus many served with Commodore Perry during the Battle of Lake Erie. Approximately 2,500 men from Ohio served in the regular army during the War of 1812 (this figure my be higher). Many militia companies, primarily mounted infantry companies, were attached to regular army units and they served their entire enlistments with the regular army. These companies were armed and equipped by the federal government.

Conclusion

The *Roster of Ohio Soldiers in the War of 1812*, although it is a unique genealogical treasure, must be treated as a partial listing of the men from Ohio who served during the War of 1812. Probably less than half of the men who served during the war are listed among its pages. This book should be used in conjunction with the other genealogical sources that are available for researchers. These sources include the pension and land bounty claims available through the federal government, local published county histories and cemetery listings, and family sources. Just because your ancestor is not listed in the *Roster* it does not mean that he did not serve in the War of 1812 as a resident of Ohio.

Many Ohioans have not been credited with service in the War of 1812 because they were never activated into federal or state service. These men served a very important function guarding their counties and training for the possibility of being activated for service with the state or federal units. In Warner's *History of Tuscarawas, County, Ohio*,[238] it is told that Captain Alexander McConnell and six of his cavalrymen captured three armed Indians on a small island near Goshen in the Tuscarawas River on 2 April 1813. This cavalry company, actually a mounted infantry unit, patrolled the northern and western borders of the county looking for Indian penetrations throughout the war. Although the unit was never activated for militia duty these men were unpaid volunteers who had a mission to perform.

The exact number of men who served during the war from Ohio may never be known but the number may reach as high as 50,000 men. This number represents the men who served in the regular army, the state regiments serving a tour of duty, and in local county units.

In 1809 the Ohio Assembly passed a militia act, which divided the state into four divisions and fifteen brigades. Each county was assigned to a brigade. This act was replaced in 1813 by another militia act,

---

[238] **The History of Tuscarawas County, Ohio**, (Warner, Beers, and Company, Chicago, Illinois: 1884), Chapter XII, Tuscarawas County in the Wars of 1812 and 1846, pp. 407-409.

which further divided the state into five divisions and eighteen brigades. The realignment also added the new counties that were created between 1809 and 1813.

Example: If you know that an ancestor of yours was living in Hamilton County in 1812 but you find that his name was included in a company roster from Clermont County, this may be correct. Ohio's Governor Return Meigs normally asked each of his brigade commanders to send a company of volunteers during a call up of the militia. In this case the volunteers from both Clermont and Hamilton Counties would have rendezvoused at a set place and time and then elected their officers. Most of the companies from these two counties listed in the *Roster* were probably made up of men from both of these counties.

Note: The boundaries of most of the counties in 1809 and 1813 were larger than they are today. You will need to consult the published county history books in order to research the formation of the county in which your ancestor was living during the War of 1812.

Breakdown of the Ohio Militia - 14 February 1809 [239]

Division	Brigade	Counties
First	First	Clermont, Hamilton
	Second	Warren
	Third	Butler
	Fourth	Greene, Champaign
	Fifth	Darke, Miami, Montgomery, Preble
Second	First	Adams, Highland
	Second & Third	Ross, Scioto
	Fourth	Delaware, Franklin, Knox, Richland
Third	First	Athens, Gallia, Washington
	Second	Fairfield, Licking
	Third	Belmont
	Fourth	Muskingum, Tuscarawas
Fourth	First	Jefferson
	Second	Columbiana, Stark, Wayne
	Third	Ashtabula, Cuyahoga, Geauga, Portage, Trumbull

Breakdown of the Ohio Militia - 9 February 1813 [240]

Division	Brigade	Counties
First	First	Clermont, Hamilton
	Second	Warren, Clinton
	Third	Butler

---

[239] **Acts Passed by the Seventh General Assembly of the State of Ohio Begun and Held in the Town of Chillicothe, December 5th, 1808; and in the Seventh Year of Said State,** The Reports of the Auditor and Treasurer of State, Volume VII, (J. S. Collins & Company, Chillicothe, Ohio: 1809), Chapter I, An act for disciplining the militia, Section 3, organization of the Ohio militia, pp. 4-5.

[240] **Acts Passed by the Eleventh General Assembly of the State of Ohio Begun and Held in the Town of Chillicothe, December 7th, 1812; and in the 11th Year of Said State,** The Reports of the Auditor and Treasurer of State, Volume XI, (Nashee & Dennti, Chillicothe, Ohio: 1812), Chapter XXXIX, An act for disciplining the militia, Section 2, organization of the Ohio militia, pp. 100-102.

Second	First	Adams, Highland
	Second & Third	Ross, Scioto, Fayette
	Fourth	Delaware, Franklin, Madison
	Fifth	Pickaway
Third	First	Athens, Gallia, Washington
	Second	Fairfield, Licking, Knox, Richland
	Third	Belmont, Guernsey (eastern tier of townships)
	Fourth	Coshocton, Guernsey (rest of county), Muskingum, Tuscarawas
Fourth	First	Jefferson, Harrison
	Second	Columbiana, Stark, Wayne
	Third	Trumbull
	Fourth	Ashtabula, Cuyahoga, Geauga, Huron, Medina, Portage,
Fifth	First	Champaign, Greene
	Second	Darke, Miami, Montgomery, Preble

The case of the missing records:
What really happened when the British captured Washington, D.C.?

One of the most frustrating aspects of genealogy when researching the time period during the War of 1812 and before, is for someone to tell you that "those records don't exist. They were all burnt when the British destroyed Washington."

Most people don't realize that the British didn't burn Washington, D.C., to the ground on the night of 24 August 1814. The British troops set fire only to the governmental building and a few private dwellings. Two buildings, however, the post office and the patent building, were saved from destruction by returning American forces. The U.S. Navy did destroy the naval yard in Washington to prevent its capture and to keep valuable war materials from falling into the hands of the British.

The *American State Papers*, the published documents of early Congresses, contains the letters requested by the House of Representatives from the various governmental department heads in Washington, D.C., outlining what was lost from their departments during the burning of Washington. These letters were received during the months of September through December 1814.

Surprisingly, very few public records were lost due to the torching of our nation's capital. The lack of transportation prevented the total removal of all public records. The army had previously commandeered most of the wagons and carriages in and around Washington, D.C., in order to transport the army's baggage to the front lines in preparation for confronting the British invaders.

The worst hit of all of the government offices was Congress itself, losing many important documents and the Library of Congress. Congress was not in session during the invasion, and the clerks working in the capitol building had been activated with their militia companies for the defense of Washington, D.C.

Once it was realized who these militiamen were, they were furloughed and permitted to return to the capital in order to begin saving the public documents. By the time they returned to the capital there wasn't a wagon or carriage left in order to be used to save all of the documents and books. The men saved what they could by moving records into the General Washington House near the Capitol Building. The British would later burn this house to the ground. In their letter to Congress, the clerks stated that if they had wagons available to them, they could have saved all of the official papers and the Library of Congress.

Missing from the *American State Papers* were any letters from the judicial branch of the government. This would include the Supreme Court of the United States and the federal district courthouse in Washington.

The Clerk's Office of the House of Representatives reported that the manuscript records of the Committees of Ways and Means, Claims and Pensions, and Revolutionary Claims were lost in the fire. Also lost were the secret journals of Congress plus the private papers and vouchers that were in the desks of the Senators and Representatives. The flames consumed the 3,000-volume Library of Congress. After the war the Congress purchased the personal library of Thomas Jefferson, which probably more than replaced most of the books that had been lost in the fire.

The offices of the government reporting no lost of records were the General Post Office, the Navy Department, the Navy's Accountant's Office, Comptroller's Office of the Treasury Department, the Auditor's Office of the Treasury Department, the Treasurer's Office of the Treasury Department, and the Revenue Office of the Treasury Department. The Treasury Department itself lost no important records although unimportant documents were destroyed. The Register's Office of the Treasury Department reported that all essential books were removed to safety but many records were lost. A detailed inventory of those destroyed records were printed in the *American State Papers*.

The General Land Office stated that all maps and necessary papers were saved but destroyed in the fire were military warrants, some land patents, and the monthly returns from the land offices located in the various parts of the country. The Department of State saved the important records although some other records were destroyed.

The War Department reported that it lost no records to the fire. The Army Pay Office for the City of Washington lost recruiting accounts and vouchers but the office stated that duplicates that had been sent to the Treasury Department could replace all of their lost documents.

The Accountant's Office of the War Department, however, reported that only the important records were saved. Destroyed from this office were part of the papers and army accounts pertaining to the Revolutionary War. Most of the army's Revolutionary War papers had previously been destroyed in a fire in the War Department, which occurred on 8 November 1800. The burning of Washington destroyed only a fraction of the original Revolutionary War's documents.

Both the Army's Superintendent General of Military Supplies and the Ordnance Office reported that all records were saved. The Adjutant and Inspector General's Office lost the muster rolls, inspection, garrison, monthly and recruiting returns up to and including 1813.

Also saved were the paintings, the art works and the historically important documents of the revolution. Not saved were furniture and office equipment. There was some looting by both the British troops and some local residents after the papers were removed and the government buildings had lain vacant.

Although the Congressional records that were lost in the fire probably had no importance to modern day genealogists, the records from the Adjutant and Inspector General's Office are another matter. The muster rolls and the other returns are important in genealogy but most of these records were replaceable. The army clerks who prepared the monthly musters for the companies, forts, garrisons and recruiting districts actually made more than one copy of all of their reports. A copy of a report stayed with a clerk and then he filed copies with his regiment (or command) and with the Adjutant General's Office in Washington. Theoretically, when the regimental, garrison and recruiting records from the field were sent to the office after the war, these copies should have replaced most of the lost records.

The problem lies in trying to locate some of these missing documents. Some of these documents may have not have been turned in after the war, and they may be found in the personal papers of the army commanders whose collections of papers were donated to various libraries and institutes throughout the country.

The last area of concern is what happened to the early federal census records. The first nine federal censuses were conducted by the United States Marshals who were assigned to each of the federal court districts within the United States. Up until 1830 each federal courthouse kept their copies of the 1790 through 1820 censuses at their facilities. They only sent the census summaries to Washington, D.C., for each census.

In 1830 Congress passed a law requiring each of the federal courthouses to send their copies of the 1790 through 1820 censuses to the federal government. Many returns from the various federal courthouses were probably lost or destroyed prior to 1830 or the clerks simply ignored the law since there are many missing state and territories returns missing prior to 1830.

The only census records destroyed during the burning of Washington were probably the census returns for the area over which the district court had jurisdiction, that is, the District of Columbia. The other early census returns may still be found in the archives of each of the federal courthouses in the eastern United States.

When the British set fire to government buildings in Washington, D.C., on 24 August 1814 they did not destroy the seat of government of the United States. The seat of government is not a collection of buildings but the people who we elected to run this government. All of these officials returned to the capital after the British retreated in order to begin its reconstruction.

Most of the documents and official papers of this government were saved from the inferno and many of the lost items were replaceable. In the past 200 years many more documents are now 'lost' but to mismanagement and not to a match. Many items have been stored and forgotten in the archives of our government. The War of 1812 is not to be totally blamed for the lost records of our government. Instead, we need to give credit to a group of government employees who saved countless boxes of official documents from the British torches.

Bibliography

American State Papers, Documents, Legislative and Executive, of the Congress of the United States, 1789-1819, (Washington, D.C.: Gales and Seaton, 1832), Miscellaneous Volume I, 13th Congress, 3rd Session, Number 371, Books and Papers of the House of Representatives and the Library of Congress Lost by the Conflagration of the Capitol in 1814, pp. 245-246.

American State Papers, Documents, Legislative and Executive, of the Congress of the United States, 1789-1819, (Washington, D.C.: Gales and Seaton, 1832), Miscellaneous Volume I, 13th Congress, 3rd Session, Number 374, Books and Papers of the Several Executive Departments Destroyed by the Conflagration in 1814, pp. 248-252.

American State Papers, Documents, Legislative and Executive, of the Congress of the United States, 1789-1819, (Washington, D.C.: Gales and Seaton, 1832), Miscellaneous Volume I, 13th Congress, 3rd Session, Number 377, Books and Papers of the House of Representatives and Libraries of Congress Lost by the Conflagration in 1814, and the State of the Contingent Fund pp. 253-255.

American State Papers, Documents, Legislative and Executive of the Congress of the United States, volume 1, military affairs, (Washington, D.C.: Gales and Seaton, 1832), Capture of the City of Washington, page 524-599.

Heritage Quest Magazine, July-August 1998, number 76, (Heritage Quest, Bountiful, Utah), pp. 8-15, 107-110, Census Facts and Figures: Things You Don't Know Because You Never Asked, by William Dollarhide.

War Department Collection of Revolutionary War Records, (Record Group 93) 1709-1915, US National Archives and Records Administration, College Park, Maryland.

Everything you ever wanted to know about obtaining service records

One of the biggest frustrations when conducting genealogical research on ancestors who served in the War of 1812 is trying to find their pensions and service records. The one basic fact is that very few men received pensions after this war compared to the number of pensions issued after the Civil War. In fact, more widows received widow's pensions for the War of 1812 than the veterans who received military pensions. Likewise, consolidated service records for individuals, whether that person was a member of the army or navy or the militia, DO NOT exist for the War of 1812.

Service records for individuals were created after the Civil War to facilitate researching the large number of pension applications that the War Department had to process after this conflict. Regimental records were broken down and transcribed onto preprinted 3 ½ by 8 ½ inch forms for each soldier and then placed in an individual folder for each veteran. When you receive the service records for your relative from the Civil War you are actually receiving copies of the original regimental records pertaining only to your relative. Enlistment and discharge papers were also included in these folders.

True service records for a military member are a product of the 20th century. These records are created once a person joins a military organization and documents are added to this person's folder throughout that person's military career. Military records were generated for every member of the army, navy and militia during the War of 1812 but these records were never consolidated into a single source or folder. The military records for an individual can be found and a service record for that individual can be created. You may have to use some creative genealogical research in order to find some of these military records.

Organizational Records

The War of 1812 generated the same type of military records that the Civil War generated. The biggest difference between the Civil War and the War of 1812 is that the federal government had complete control over all of the men who served in the Union Army. All men who volunteered, who were drafted, and whose National Guard units were activated, served in the U.S. Army. During the War of 1812 those militia units who were called up to serve with the U.S. Army remained a part of the state or territorial militia. Many of the state militia units were called up by the state and fought in the war separately from the federal forces.

The National Archives in Washington, DC, has the rosters of the militia companies that served with the army during the War of 1812. These rosters are a part of the Adjutant General's Office records, 1780's-1917 (Record Group 94 - Orders, muster rolls, and returns). You will not receive these records from the National Archives when submitting NATF Form 86 when requesting military service records. These records have been microfilmed and you can rent the films from the National Archives. Check the National Archives' website for the list of record groups and for the information on how to order the films. Many states also have copies of these militia rosters and you can find these records either in the state library, the state archives or the state historical society.

Ancestry.com has produced a compact disc (CD) entitled, *Military Records: War of 1812 Muster Rolls*. This is an index of approximately 580,000 militiamen who served during this war. The National Archives' roll box number and roll record number are included with the information on each of the veterans.

In both the War of 1812 and the Civil War, army companies were required to maintain a personnel roster, a descriptive roster and a clothing roster. All of these types of reports are collectively called "returns." On the last day of even number months, muster was required, and these assemblies generated "muster returns." These documents are a two-month historical snapshot for each company. The muster returns contain the names of all of the men, their ranks, enlistment information, and the status of each man during that two-month period. The status included those men who were fit for duty, who were sick or wounded, who had died or were killed, who were on leave, who were serving on duty but detached from the company, who were missing, who had deserted, and who were prisoners of war.

The descriptive roster contained the names of the men, their ranks, their ages, height, skin and eye colors, birthplace, and place of enlistment. During the War of 1812 the descriptive roster also contained information on the bonuses for each man. Clothing returns list the name and rank of an individual and what military clothing was issued to that man. Although a clothing report may seem trivial, if you can't find a muster or a descriptive return then this type of report may be the only proof you have that you ancestor was a member of a particular company. On the last day of odd numbered months, a monthly return was required during the war. This report listed the number of men by ranks who were fit for duty, sick or wounded, and on detached duty away from the company. The report only listed the men by name who were not physically present with the company when the report was filled out.

Organizations above a company (battalions, regiments or brigades) were required to maintain an orders (or orderly) book and a record book. Regiments were also required to maintain payroll records. The orders book contained all of the general and special orders that the organization received regulating their day-to-day duties. The record book contains copies of all of the returns and correspondences generated by that organization. The payroll return can be a separate document or included as part of a muster return. The army was paid on the last day of even numbered months. The problem with the War of 1812 was that many men were not paid for months at a time, so some of these returns where for a multitude of pay periods. Payroll reports contain the name and rank of each soldier, enlistment information, their signatures and their counter signatures, to verify that the soldier received his pay. All of these types of returns and books were also required in each of the state or territorial militia organizations during the war.

The last "return" of any real importance was the muster out report, which ended the military service of an individual. All back pay was issued at this time, and the remaining bonuses were paid for the war service. The individual at this time turned in any U.S. government issued equipment he had signed for and he paid for any lost or damaged equipment incurred through his neglect. Besides companies and regiments, depots, forts, recruiting facilities, hospitals and other military installations also generated these same types of books and reports.

When requesting service records from the National Archives for army veterans you will receive a page from the Records of the Men Enlisted in the U.S. Army Prior to the Peace Establishment, May 17, 1815. 241 These records are not service records but they are the consolidated enlistment rosters from all of the regiments in the U.S. Army that served during the war. A page from this book will be sent to you, and it will contain the name and rank of your ancestor, his regiment, his company commander's name, his regimental commander's name, a physical description of your ancestor plus his peacetime occupation, his birthplace (county and state, or country), place of enlistment, and the period of enlistment, and additional remarks. If you are lucky, all of the columns will be filled in. This book doesn't include army officers or militiamen.

For army officers you need to find a copy of the first volume of the Historical Register and Dictionary of the United States Army From Its Organization, September 29, 1789, to March 2, 1903. 242 This book will list each commissioned officer by name, place of birth, place of residence, commissioning date, date of each promotion, dates assigned to each regiment in which the officer served, and his discharge date. Many entries also include when the officer died.

The Type of Service

---

[241] **Records of the Men Enlisted in the U.S. Army Prior to the Peace Establishment, May 17, 1815**, Record Group Number 94, (National Archives and Records Administration, Washington, D.C.).

[242] Heitman, Francis B., **Historical Register and Dictionary of the United States Army From Its Organization, September 29, 1789, to March 2, 1903**, Volume I, (Genealogical Publishing Company, Baltimore, Maryland: 1994), part I, Complete Alphabetical List of all Commissioned Officers of the Army, pp. 147-1069.

A major misconception concerning the War of 1812 is that all of your relatives served in the militia. Official army records reveal that approximately 60,000 men served in the army during the war while another 471,622 men were called up from the militia to fight in this conflict.[243] The army suffered 1,300 killed and 2,985 men wounded while the militia suffered 577 killed and 1,015 wounded. These casualty figures do not include the thousands of men who died from sickness or disease. Militiamen served a 'tour of duty' and not an enlistment. Many militiamen served more that one 'tour of duty' during the war so the actual number of individual militiamen who served in this war is less than the 471,622 listed by the army.

The Adjutant General's Office in the War Department required each state and territory to submit a yearly return showing the number of men in each militia organization.[244] The returns for 1812 show that there were 703,249 men serving in the states' militia. The letter from the War Department to the various state governors dated 13 April 1812 does not include the number of men from the territorial militia, these being Michigan, Indiana, Illinois, Missouri, Mississippi and Louisiana. The number of men serving in the territorial militia could be as high as 50,000. One hundred thousand militiamen were tasked to serve with the U.S. Army during the war. The 1812 Ohio state militia rolls had 34,726 men listed, while Ohio's quota for militiaman to serve on federal duty was set at 5,000 men by the federal government.

With the wartime population of the United States at approximately 7,500,000 people, one-tenth of the population was serving in either the army or the militia. Of that one-tenth only about half of the men actually saw service during the War of 1812.

Land Bounties

As part of the regular army's enlistment package a soldier (who finished his enlistment) was entitled to a $16 dollar enlistment bonus, three months extra pay and 160 acres of federal land. Later in the war the bonus was increased to $128 and the acreage to 320 acres. The recruit received half of his bonus upon enlisting and the remaining sum when he was discharged.

Military land was set aside in Illinois, Missouri and Arkansas for the purpose of honoring the land warrants earned by the men in the regular army. Warrants were issued to each soldier if he had enlisted for five year or for 'during the war'. He could redeem his warrant for a land deed at a federal land office in one of these states. Many men sold their warrants to land speculators or to the officers in their regiments. Very few men actually settled on the land that they received from service in this war.

In the 1850's, land bounties were given to army officers and militiamen who served with the regular army. Those militiamen who served tours of duty only with their state or territory militia were not eligible for these bounties. The militiamen received on an average of 40 acres of land per man. If your relative received 160 or 320 acres, then he probably served in the army and anything less than 160 acres service was probably performed in the militia while on federal duty. The militiamen could apply for any federal land in the United States.

The War of 1812 Bounty Lands in Illinois [245] contains for information from the warrants that were issued to the men receiving land bounties in Illinois. Each entry has the date of the patent, warrant number, name, rank, regiment, section number, township number, range number, to whom delivered, and when delivered. If the 'name' column and the 'to whom delivered' column are not the same, then veteran probably sold his warrant to the person listed in the 'to whom delivered' column.

---

[243] **Ibid,** Part II, Strength of the Army and Losses in the Several Wars, etc., War with Great Britain, June 18, 1812, to February 17, 1815, page 281.

[244] Knopf, Richard C., **Document Transcriptions of the War of 1812 in the Northwest,** Volume VIII, Letters from the Secretary of War 1812 & 1813 Relating to the War of 1812 in the Northwest, (Ohio Historical Society: Columbus, Ohio: 1961), pp. 23-24, Secretary of War to Governors of the Various States, 13 April 1812.

[245] Volkel, Lowell M., **War of 1812 Bounty Lands in Illinois**, (Heritage House, Thompson, Illinois: 1977).

Pensions

The federal government issued two types of pensions for service during the War of 1812. The first pension was called the "Old War" pension, and these were given to men who were wounded or disabled and to the families of those veterans who had died or were killed during the war. The majority of these pensions were issued to the men (or to their families) who served in the regular military.

In the 1870's pensions were given to militiamen who were still living or to their widows if the widows had not remarried. By the 1870's there were very few veterans of the war who were still alive, so the majority of these pensions were given to their widows. The letter prefix on pension application numbers determined the type of pensions. If the letter was a "W" then the pension was for the widow and if the letter was a "S" then it was for a survivor of the veteran, not necessarily the widow. If the pension application number had no letter prefix then this was a service pension for a veteran. The Index to War of 1812 Pension Files [246] lists all of the known pensions that were issued for service in this war.

The *Report from the Secretary of War in Obedience to the Resolutions of the Senate of the 5th and 30th of June, 1834, and the 3rd of March, 1835, in Relation to the Pension Establishment of the United States* [247] (or simply called the Pension Roll of 1835) lists all of the veterans of the Revolutionary War, the Indian Wars of the 1790's, and the War of 1812 who were on the pension rolls prior to 1835. This book is organized by state and then by county showing the name and rank of the pensioner, his annual allowance, total sums received to date, description of service, when he applied for the pension and what date his pension started, the laws under which each pension was authorized and additional comments. A second section under each county includes those families who elected to receive five-years half pay in lieu of the land bounties that their deceased veterans had earned while in the army. This listing shows the name and rank of the deceased, description of service, date of death, heirs, annual allowances, total sums received, how long on the pension rolls, and the start and ending dates for the five years.

The "description of service" column indicates service for the different wars. Units marked with "U.S.", as in the "7th U.S. Infantry", denotes service in the War of 1812. Militiamen were also included in this Pension Roll of 1835 if the veteran served on federal duty and was wounded, injured, died or killed in the line of duty. Researchers need to check all of the states and counties in which their relatives lived after the war in order to see if their relatives received a pension.

Records for Ohio Veterans

Militia records and regular army records can be found within the borders of Ohio. Ohio has many fine historical societies and public libraries, which have books, documents and records pertaining to the War of 1812. Some of these facilities have musters and rosters for both the militia and the regular army. Historical libraries are not public facilities so you may have to pay an entrance fee and a parking fee.

The records of the Adjutant General's Office for the Ohio militia have been given to the Ohio Historical Society (OHS) in Columbus and these records are available for public research. The records of the militia companies are not as complete as they should be for the War of 1812. One area of research that is often overlooked by family researchers is the personal collections of papers that military men and their families have donated to these institutions. The Duncan McArthur collection at the OHS contains 20 reels of militia and regular army rosters, musters, reports and documents pertaining to the Army of the Northwest. McArthur became the commander of this army after Major General William Henry Harrison resigned. These reels are organized by dates but they are un-indexed and a page-by-page search is

---

[246] White, Virgil D., **Index to War of 1812 Pension Files**, (National Historical Publishing Company, Waynesboro, Tennessee: Revised Edition, 1992).

[247] **Report from the Secretary of War in Obedience to the Resolutions of the Senate of the 5th and 30th of June, 1834, and the 3rd of March, 1835, in Relation to the Pension Establishment of the United States** (1835 Pension Rolls), (Duff Green, Washington, D.C.: 1835).

required to find needed documents. Other collections include the Henry Clay papers, the James Denny papers, and the Joseph Larwill family papers, to mention just a few collections. Most Ohioans, whether in the army or the militia, served in Ohio during the war as part of the Army of the Northwest or with the state forces.

The keystone collection at the OHS is the militia musters and payroll rosters that make up the *Roster of Ohio Soldiers in the War of 1812*.[248] When the book was first published in 1916, most of the genealogical information contained in these returns were left out of the book. On the two reels of rosters you will find the name and rank of your ancestor, his company and regiment, his company commander and regimental commander names, his beginning tour of duty date and his ending tour of duty date, the company's county of origin and any additional comments. These comments include if the ancestor had been killed or had died, had been sick, on leave, or had deserted. Most of the companies have the complete information.

The final set of document worth mentioning at the OHS pertaining to the War of 1812 is the *Document Transcriptions of the War of 1812 in the Northwest*.[249] These documents are the selective papers of William Henry Harrison, Return Jonathan Meigs, Junior, Thomas Worthington, and others, with additional information on the naval actions on Lake Erie.

Cleveland hosts the Western Reserve Historical Society (WRHS). The archive library at this facility has many collections pertaining to the War of 1812 particularly northeastern Ohio. The militia records for the 4th division of the Ohio militia can be found here. The 4th division covered the Western Reserve plus Wayne County, Stark County, Columbiana County, Harrison County and Jefferson County. The library also has the brigade record book of Brigadier General Reasin Beall (Columbiana, Stark and Wayne Counties), the regimental record book of Colonel John Campbell (Portage County), and the record book of the 2nd battalion of the Coshocton County militia.

Among its collections are the papers from William Allen Trimble and George Tod. The George Tod collection contains the recruiting records of the 17th and 19th Regiments of U.S. Infantry. These two federal regiments recruited in Ohio. The library also has militia rosters for Massachusetts and Vermont. There is a paper copy of the musters and rosters that makes up the *Roster of Ohio Soldiers in the War of 1812* stored in this library. This copy contains more information on each militiaman than is found in the book.

The *Robert Lucas' Diary* is a book that gives a day-by-day account of Brigadier General William Hull's army while at Fort Detroit. The Ohio Genealogical Society library in Mansfield has the early acts of the State of Ohio, which includes the militia laws for the state. The Cincinnati Historical Society has a collection of William Henry Harrison papers. Most large cities and counties in Ohio have a historical society, and it may be worth your time to see what collections and material these institutes are holding.

Many libraries, public or private, have collections of papers and documents pertaining to William Henry Harrison, and many other men who were leaders during the War of 1812. Most of these libraries will have the same papers and documents. Orders and letters were normally hand written and then copied by aides and clerks and distributed up and down the chain of command. Many of the documents are labeled as "copy" and many are not. Most of the clerks and aides signed their leader's names to these documents, so you will probably not be viewing an actual signature from one of these leaders.

Off the Wall Research

---

[248] **Roster of Ohio Soldiers in the War of 1812**, The Adjutant General of Ohio 1916, (Heritage Books, Inc., Bowie, Maryland: 1995).

[249] Knopf, Richard C., **Document Transcriptions of the War of 1812 in the Northwest,** four volumes, (Anthony Wayne Parkway Board, Ohio Historical Society, Columbus, Ohio: 1957).

Other sources of information can be found on Ohio's militia and soldiers who served in the U.S. Army where you least aspect it. The *Kentucky Soldiers of the War of 1812* [250] contains the muster rosters of the 7th, 17th and 28th Regiments of U.S. Infantry. These regiments were the responsibility of Kentucky to raise but these regiments recruited not only in Kentucky but also in Ohio, Michigan, Indiana, and Tennessee. Colonel John Miller of Steubenville was the last commander of the 17th infantry. Lieutenant Colonel George Tod of Youngstown was the last deputy commander of this regiment. Captain Harris H. Hickman of the 17th infantry was from Michigan while Captain John T. Chunn was from Indiana and Captains James Herron and George W. Jackson were both from eastern Ohio. Many of the enlisted men were also from Ohio.

The book *Remember the Raisin!* [251] has a partial listing of the members of Captain Angus L. Langham's Company of the 19th Regiment of Infantry. This company was raised in Ohio and it participated in the Battle of the River Raisin. The *Deep Water Sailors, Shallow Water Soldiers, Manning the United States Fleet on Lake Erie 1813* [252] contains the list of all of the soldiers and sailors who served on Lake Erie and who participated in the Battle of Lake Erie. Among the list of soldiers are many from Ohio particularly from the 19th, 26th and 27th Regiments of Infantry. The *Historical Register and Dictionary of the United States Army From Its Organization, September 29, 1789, to March 2, 1903* [253] also has the list of all army officers who were killed, wounded or taken as prisoners. Again, many of these men were from Ohio. The *Known military dead during the War of 1812* [254] has many Ohioans from both the militia and the regular army who had died or who were killed during this conflict.

Conclusion

As stated earlier, the service records for all of the veterans of the War of 1812 DO NOT exist but with a little help you can find the military records of your ancestors. The National Archives does have the land bounties and pension records for those militiamen who qualified for these benefits but remember; most militiamen did not qualify for bounties and pensions.

If your ancestor was in the militia and served from another state then you must contact the Adjutant General's Office in that state to see if that record still exists. The National Guard Bureau has replaced most of these offices and the bureaus normally don't maintain the old militia records. In Ohio the Adjutant General's records are stored at the Ohio Historical Society. In other states you may have to contact the state library, the state archives or the state historical society in order to find these military records. Most of the state libraries, archives and historical societies have websites where you can browse an on-line catalog and do preliminary research.

In many cases the military records stored at these institutes are not indexed, and you will either have to view the records yourself or hire a researcher. If your ancestor lived in Maine, then you will need to research in Massachusetts since Maine was part of Massachusetts during the war. Also, Alabama was part of Mississippi and Arkansas was part of Missouri during this same period of time.

If your ancestor was in the army during the war, you can extract his military records from the National Archives. Military records are stored in "record groups." Record Group 98 contains the regimental order books from the war while Record Group 94 (Adjutant General's Office) contains the orders, musters,

---

[250] Wilder, G. Glenn, **Kentucky Soldiers of the War of 1812**, (Clearfield Company, Inc., Baltimore, Maryland: 1995).

[251] Clift, G. Glenn, **Remember the Raisin!**, (Kentucky Historical Society, Frankfort, Kentucky: 1961), page 177.

[252] Altoff, Gerald T., **Deep Water Sailors, Shallow Water Soldiers, Manning the United States Fleet on Lake Erie 1813**, (The Perry Group, Put-in-Bay, Ohio: 1993).

[253] Heitman, Francis B., **Historical Register,** Volume II, Alphabetical list of officers of the regular army killed, wounded, or taken prisoner in action, 1789 to 1903, pp. 13-42.

[254] Peterson, Clarence Joseph, **Known Military Dead During the War of 1812**, (Baltimore, Maryland: April 1955).

returns, recruiting reports, desertion reports and prisoner of war reports. As stated before, these records have been microfilmed and you can rent the films from the National Archives or FamilySearch.

Here is a list of military records that you will need in order to construct a service record for you ancestor:

a. A recruiting station's weekly report showing the name of your ancestor at the time of his enlistment.
b. The recruiting contact signed by your ancestor. Boys 14 to 18 could join the army with the permission of their fathers, guardians or masters. The father, guardian or master must have signed a paper giving permission for the enlistment.
c. A muster roll for every two months that your ancestor served.
d. A descriptive roll that was maintained by the company in which your ancestor served.
e. A yearly clothing report, new uniforms and equipment were supposed to be issued yearly.
f. A clothing report issued after a battle or expedition to replace those items lost or damaged.
g. Any hospital, garrison, fort, court martial proceedings, or prisoner or war listing that may have the name of your ancestor listed.
h. Any transfer papers to another company or regiment.
i. A payroll report for every two months that your ancestor served. Some units were paid infrequently.
j. The final descriptive roll or muster out report showing that your ancestor had received all of his back pay and bonuses.
k. A land bounty warrant issued to your ancestor entitling him to federal land for his service during the war. If you know that he settled on his land after the war, then the local county courthouse at the time he received his land should have a copy of his land deed. Land bounties were issued right after the war and again in the 1850's.
l. Old War pensions that were issued right after the war if your ancestor was wounded or injured during the war. These pensions were also issued to widows and survivors for those men had died or were killed during the war.
m. Service pensions that were issued in the 1870's if your ancestor was still alive.
n. Widow pensions that were issued in the 1870's if the widow was still alive and had not remarried.
o. Survivor's pensions that were issued in the 1870's for survivors of your ancestor.

Hits and Helps

1. It is extremely important that you know if your ancestor served in the militia or in the army before you request military records. You will find some ancestors who first served in the militia and then later enlisted in the army.
2. It is very helpful to know if you ancestor was an officer or an enlisted man.
3. If you are not sure if your ancestor was in the army or the militia when requesting records from the National Archives, then submit two sets of NATF Forms 85 and 86. In box 8 of NATF Form 86 (Kind of Service) mark "volunteer" for militia and then on the other form 86 mark "regular" for army service. On NATF Form 85 in box 9 (Kind of Service) mark "volunteer" for militia and then on the other form 85 mark "regular" for army service. This may open up a few more doors for you.
4. State's names are not associated with the names of army regiments. Army regiments are referred to as the '1st Regiment of Infantry' or the '1st Regiment of U.S. Infantry'. Army regiments were not numbered beyond "48". Militia regiments are normally referred to by the name of their commanders, that is, 'Colonel Charles Miller's Regiment' although all of these regiments were numbered.
5. If your ancestor received 160 or 320 acres of land through a land bounty, then he was probably in the regular army. Acres less than 160 normally indicate that the ancestor was in the militia.
6. If he was issued a land bounty between 1815 and 1819 he probably served in the army and not the militia. Land bounties that were issued after 1850 were for army officers and militiamen.
7. Many militiamen were not called up to serve in the war but each state should still have the militia records of all of the companies that were formed before and during the war. All able-bodied men were required by federal, state and territorial laws to serve in the militia. Of the men who were called up to serve, most served with the state forces and not the federal government.
8. If your ancestor was an officer and he held the rank of first, second or third lieutenant then he was in the regular army. The militia, by federal law, only had a lieutenant's position.

9. An ensign was the lowest officer's rank in the army, the navy and the militia. "Ensign" doesn't mean that your ancestor was in the navy only that he held the lowest officer's rank.
10. Cornet was the lowest officer's rank in a light dragoon or dragoon company (cavalry).
11. Saddlers, farriers, trumpeters, sword masters, and forage masters were ranks within cavalry units.
12. Gunners, artificers, bombardiers, drivers, and matrosses were ranks within artillery units.
13. Militia maintained mount infantry or dragoons units while the army called its cavalry units 'light dragoons'.
14. The army had ranger companies while the militia called these units: rangers, mounted rangers, spies or mounted spies.
15. A muster return, whether it is for an army company or a militia company, is a two-month snapshot in time for a company. If you find a return and your ancestor is not on this document, don't despair. It only means that your ancestor was not serving in this company during that two-month period. You will probably have to find the other company returns in order to locate your ancestor. Companies produced six returns per year and names of the men were added and dropped from these documents every two months. Don't be satisfied in finding only one muster return for your ancestor. If he had served in the army for two years then there should be twelve company muster returns listing his name. You may be missing some genealogical information if you haven't obtained all of the muster returns.
16. A muster out return should contain the names of all of the men who served in a company during the war (if the company was being disbanded).
17. Some descriptive returns were used as muster out returns. The men on these documents all had the same discharge date, but they may have been from different companies and regiments.

Forts, Stockades and Blockhouses

The Department of War and the 8th Military District operated a number of forts, camps and barracks in Kentucky, Ohio, and the Territories of Illinois, Indiana, Michigan and Missouri throughout the War of 1812.[255]

Forts were normally large enclosed fortifications made of stone or brick with a moat, ditch or some sort of earthworks surrounding the enclosure. Forts were designed to house troops and to survive a major assault by the enemy. These facilities were designed to last many years, and they were expensive to build. If a civilian village was located within the enclosure, then the fortification would be labeled as a fortress. There were no true forts built in the northwest before or during the war.

Forts in the northwest were usually a series of log blockhouses connected by palisades made of vertical logs imbedded in the ground. These facilities were actually fortified stockades. Surrounding some of these facilities were earthworks designed to slow down the enemy. Moats, ditches and rivers were also used as protection. Stockades could withstand a minor siege.

Stockades were inexpensive to build as long as you had the manpower and tools needed to construct these facilities. They were designed to last for the duration of the war, and then most were abandoned once hostilities ended.

Fort Detroit in the Territory of Michigan was an exception to the rules. This facility was an enlarged wooden stockade with earthworks that lasted nearly 50 years. It was always in the state of being repaired or improved. It had originally been built by the French and rebuilt by the British before the fort was taken over by the Americans.

This stockade fort had the earthworks that were designed for a true fort, and it was connected to a palisade that surrounded the civilian village of Detroit. In essence this facility was a wooden fortress.

Camps were small facilities enclosed by wooden palisades. The houses within the camps were built against the walls, and the men used the roofs of the building to fire their weapons over the walls. Camps were designed to protect the men from the elements and from Indian attacks. They could not survive a major assault by the British. Most of these camps were called forts.

Military bivouac areas were also called 'camps'. These camps were not fortified but sites were selected that would offer some protection from attack. Many were built near rivers or on top of hills. Pickets (or guards) were stationed near the camps while patrols roamed the areas away from the camps. These facilities were short-lived. Many stockades and blockhouses started out as bivouac areas before more permanent facilities were constructed.

The most common military facility in the northwest was the simple blockhouse. This was an enlarged two-story log cabin with the second level wider than the first level. The militia and the pioneers used them for protection against Indian raids. Many of the blockhouses built in the northwest section of Ohio during the war were used as small supply depots or as guard facilities along the military roads. Most of these structures were also called forts. Many stockades started out as a single blockhouse and then enlarged during the war.

Barracks were military buildings located within a village or city, which had no palisades for protection. These facilities were used for headquarters, hospitals, supply facilities, recruiting and training centers, and for housing troops. These facilities were also called 'posts'. Barracks were also buildings that were located within a fort that housed enlisted personnel.

The Army of the Northwest operated three forward operating bases, which were used as headquarters facilities and as jumping off points for military operations. These three facilities were located at Fort Knox at Vincennes, Territory of Indiana, and facilities at Urbana and Franklinton, Ohio.

---

[255] **North American Fortifications,** Forts and Fortresses, Frontier Posts and Camps, Blockhouses and Seacoast Batteries in the United State and Canada, Ohio, http://www.geocities.com/naforts/forts.html

The army operated barracks at Chillicothe, Franklinton and Zanesville, Ohio, and Newport, Kentucky. The army used these facilities as recruiting and training centers, posting of companies, headquarters for the regiments, and as temporary prisoner of war camps.

The Army of the Northwest operated in Kentucky, Ohio and the Territory of Michigan. After the Battle of the Thames River in October 1812, the army would extend its operations into the western district of Upper Canada. The army-controlled forts in Ohio were turned over to the Ohio militia after this battle. This situation lasted until 1 June 1815 when the army withdrew its troops from Upper Canada under the provisions of the Treaty of Ghent.

In Ohio, the army maintained Fort Meigs, Fort Ball, Fort Stephenson, Fort Seneca, Fort Ferree, Fort Huntington, Fort Ball, Fort Winchester and a series of minor forts or blockhouses stretching across central and northwestern Ohio. In the Territory of Michigan the army maintained Fort Detroit and Fort Gratiot.

In Upper Canada the army controlled Fort Malden, Fort Hope, the Sandwich Battery, and Camp Covington (also called Fort Covington). Fort Hope was a small fort that supported the Sandwich Battery across the river from Detroit while Camp Covington was the main billeting facility for troops stationed in Upper Canada. This facility was located outside of Amherstburg about a mile south of the village.

Upon evacuating the Detroit River military facilities, the British army had destroyed Fort Amherstburg and Fort Detroit plus the lesser fortifications. The American army had to rebuild Fort Detroit and in the process the facility was renamed Fort Shelby in honor of the governor of Kentucky. Fort Malden was built on the site of Fort Amherstburg. Fort Hope and the Sandwich Batteries, in present day Windsor, Ontario, were repaired and manned. Camp Covington was built near Amherstburg as a new billeting facility for the army.

In early 1814 Fort Gratiot was built at the mouth of Lake Huron in present day Port Huron, Michigan. The purpose of this fort was to keep any British naval ships from attacking Detroit from the north.

The Army of the Northwest operated Fort Wayne in the Territory of Indiana for a good portion of the war and troops were stationed at Erie, Pennsylvania, later in the war to protect the naval facilities.

The Special Command operated Fort Knox and Fort Harrison in the Territory of Indiana and Fort Russell and Fort Massac in the Territory of Illinois. In Missouri the command had Fort Buffalo, Fort Howard, Fort Belle Fontaine and Fort Osage while in Wisconsin they maintained Fort Shelby until the British took control of the fort. From 1808 to 1813 the command operated Fort Madison in what is now Iowa.

Fort Belle Fontaine was the Special Command's headquarters, staging area and supply depot for operations into the upper Mississippi River valley. There were also hundreds of small stockades and blockhouses built by the militia in the area controlled by the 8th Military District. Many fortifications were built by the militia regiments that were on duty with the Army of the Northwest. Most military facilities were shared by both the army and the militia.

Amanda, Fort [256]
1813-1815, Wapakoneta, Auglaize County

A Kentucky militia regiment under the command of Lieutenant Colonel Robert Pogue built Fort Amanda as a wooden stockade with four blockhouses and barracks in the fall of 1812. In the spring of 1813, Captain Daniel Hosbrook's Company of the Ohio militia doubled the size of the fort and added an additional blockhouse. The fort was a major re-supply base in the northwest. The fort was named after Colonel Pogue's daughter, Hannah Amanda Pogue.

Ball, Fort [257]
1813-1815, Tiffin, Seneca County

---

[256] Heidler, Davis S., and Heidler, Jeanne T., **Encyclopedia of the War of 1812**, (ABC-CLIO, Inc., Santa Barbara, California: 1997, page 8, Fort Amanda.

[257] Hartzell, Stephen J., **Fort Ball: A bit of It's Background & History**, http://www.friendlynet.com/steveharzell/FtBall.html

Fort Ball was a wooden stockade with three blockhouses built in July 1813 by Lieutenant Colonel James V. Ball's squadron of the 2nd Regiment of U.S. Light Dragoons. This fort was used as a supply depot and as one of the staging areas for the invasion of Upper Canada.

Colonel Ball and his troops skirmished with the Indians near the fort shortly after its completion. The Americans suffered no causalities while the Indians lost 17 braves.

Barbee, Fort [258]
1812-1816, St. Mary's, Auglaize County

Colonel Joshua Barbee, who was a commander of a regiment of Kentucky militia, built the fort in the fall of 1812.

Brown, Fort
1812-1815, near Melrose, Paulding County

Fort Brown was a wooden stockade.

Bull, Camp [259]
1813-1814, Chillicothe, Ross County

Camp Bull was operated between October 1813 and July 1814 as a military prison. The facility was used to intern the British sailors captured during the Battle of Lake Erie. The officers and enlisted men from the 41st Regiment of Foot, who were captured at the Battle of the Thames River, were initially housed at Camp Bull before being sent to Newport Barracks, Kentucky.[260] The British army officers were sent to the state prison at Frankfort, Kentucky.

Chillicothe Barracks [261]
1813-1815, Chillicothe, Ross County

The Chillicothe Barracks was the headquarters for the 1st Recruiting District in Ohio for the U.S. Army. Companies from the 17th, 19th and 26th Regiments of U.S. Infantry were organized there. The facility was also the headquarters for the 19th and 26th infantries and for the 17th infantry in the later part of the war. The barracks was located at the corner of 2nd and Walnut Streets in Chillicothe.

Cleveland, Camp [262]
1812-1813, Cleveland, Cuyahoga County

A militia camp was established at Cleveland in August 1812 and operated by the 4th Division of the Ohio Militia until the army built Fort Huntington in the spring of 1813.

A militia regiment of 500 men was stationed at this camp. In September 1812 the camp consisted of two areas. The first area had nine tents which housed the staff of Major General Elijah Wadsworth of the 4th Ohio Division and of Brigadier General Simon Perkins, the commander of the militia in northern Ohio.

---

[258] Lossing, Benson J., **Pictorial Field Book of the War of 1812**, Chapter XVI, War with the British and Indians in the Northwest, (Harper & Brothers, Publishers, New York, New York: 1868).

[259] Medert, Patricia Fife, **Raw Recruits & Bullish Prisoners, Ohio's Capital in the War of 1812**, Ross County Historical Society Publication, (Jackson Publishing Company, Jackson, Ohio: 1992), page 115.

[260] Donnelly, Colonel Joseph L., M.D., Ph.D., **Newport Barracks, Kentucky's Forgotten Military Installation**, (Kenton County Historical Society, Covington, Kentucky: 1999), Chapter III, War of 1812, pp. 19-28.

[261] **Chillicothe, Ohio, 1796-1996, Ohio's First Capital**, (Ross County Historical Society, Chillicothe, Ohio: 1996), Chapter 4, Military History, pp. 107-110.

[262] "Quartermaster's report of Quartermaster King," 11 September 1812, Camp Cleveland, **4th Division Ohio Militia, War of 1812, collection of papers 1810-1820**, call number 3133, Folder 1, Western Reserve Historical Society's Archives Library, Cleveland, Ohio.

The second area consisted of 23 tents for the regiment of Colonel William Rayen. The actual location of the camp is not known but it was probably near where Fort Huntington was built.

Ferree, Fort [263]
1812-1815, Upper Sandusky, Wyandot County

Fort Ferree was a wooden stockade with four blockhouses and barracks built by the brigade under the command of Brigadier General Richard Crooks of the Pennsylvania militia. It would become an important re-supply post for the U.S. Army.

Findlay, Fort [264]
1812-1815, Findlay, Hancock County

Fort Findlay was a wooden stockade with four blockhouses used as a supply depot. It was built by Colonel James Findlay's Ohio militia regiment during Brigadier General William Hull's army's march to Fort Detroit in 1812. The fort was named after Colonel Findlay.

Franklinton Barracks
1810's, Columbus, Franklin County

The general headquarters for the Army of the Northwest was moved to Franklinton, after General Harrison became the commander of the army. Two to three thousand soldiers were stationed there at any one time during the war.[265]

The facility was the major staging area for operations into north central Ohio and for the invasion of Upper Canada. It was the main re-supply point for Fort Meigs, Fort Stephenson, Fort Ball, Fort Seneca and Fort Ferree.

The commissary department for the U.S. Army was located at Franklinton. The barracks also was a training camp, supply depot, hospital, recruiting station and a rendezvous point for the many military expeditions that were launch during the war.[266]

A report from the hospital at Franklinton, dated 4 March 1814, showed that there were 37 patients at the facility of which four were fit for duty, 14 were sick and 19 were prisoners of war.[267]

Hamilton, Fort
1791-1797, Hamilton, Butler County

Fort Hamilton was a wooden stockade with four blockhouses that was built by Major General Arthur St. Clair in September 1791. The army had abandoned the fort around 1797.

The grounds of the old fort were used as a bivouac area for troops moving between Kentucky and northern Ohio during the War of 1812.

---

[263] **History of Wyandot County**, (Leggett, Conaway & Company, Chicago, Illinois: 1884), Chapter XII, The County's Military Record, pp. 438-439.

[264] **Ohio Archaeological and Historical Publications**, Volume III, (Columbus, Ohio: Fred. J. Heer, publisher: 1895), "The Military Posts, Forts, and Battlefields within the State of Ohio", page 309, Fort Findlay.

[265] **Franklin County at the Beginning of the Twentieth Century**, (Historical Publishing Company, Columbus, Ohio: 1901), Columbus, page 115.

[266] Moore, Opha, **History of Franklin County, Ohio**, Volume 1, (Historical Publishing Company, Topeka, Kansas, and Indianapolis, Indiana: 1930), War of 1812, page 114.

[267] **Duncan McArthur Papers**, Library of Congress, 1922, Microfilm 47, Reel 3, Volumes 6-8, 22 September 1813 – 4 March 1814, document number 981, Barrack's hospital, Franklinton, 4 March 1814, Captain John Moore, 26th Regiment of U.S. Infantry, Ohio Historical Society, Columbus, Ohio.

Harrison, Camp [268]
1813, Cleveland, Cuyahoga County

In July 1813 Major General William H. Harrison traveled to Cleveland in order to review and organize the village defenses. He had Fort Huntington built at the foot of Ontario Street in the early spring and then his own camp, called Camp Harrison, at the foot of Seneca Street. Both facilities overlooked Lake Erie.

Camp Harrison would be used as the billeting facility for Fort Huntington and as a supply depot for the war material and rations for the invasion of Upper Canada.

Huntington, Fort
1813-1815, Cleveland, Cuyahoga County

In May 1813 Fort Huntington was built overlooking Lake Erie as protection for the village of Cleveland. The army also had a small hospital, supply depot, paymaster's office, recruiting post and a bulleting facility called Camp Harrison. Cleveland was the main army facility in northeastern Ohio.

Also along the Cuyahoga River were three boat yards, which were used to construct bateaux. These large, flat-bottomed boats were used to transport troops and supplies during the war. These craft were built for General Harrison's invasion of Upper Canada and could carry 40-50 men with their baggage, arms and provisions.

Cleveland had initially been chosen as the jumping off point for the invasion of Upper Canada but because of a lack of a harbor this site and the distance to Fort Amherstburg the site was moved to the mouth of the Portage River. Cleveland continued to be a major supply facility receiving materials from Pittsburgh and then transporting these items either by wagon to Fort Meigs or by bateaux on Lake Erie.

Fort Huntington was built at the foot of Ontario Street.[269] It was a stockade armed with two cannons and commanded by Major Thomas L. Jesup of the 19th Regiment of U.S. Infantry. The fort would be the home to four infantry and one artillery companies from the U.S. Army during the war. Two Ohio militia companies on 6-month federal duty were also stationed at this fort.

Jennings, Fort [270]
1812-1815, Fort Jennings, Putnam County

Fort Jennings was a blockhouse built by Colonel William Jennings and his Kentucky militia regiment in September 1812.

Loramie, Fort
1750?, 1769-1798, 1810's, Fort Loramie, Shelby County

Originally, a British trading post until 1782, the site was known as Peter Loramie's Post. The facility was rebuilt in 1793 by Major General Anthony Wayne and used until 1798. The fort was destroyed during the War of 1812.

Manary's Blockhouse
1812, Bellefontaine, Logan County

This blockhouse was built by Captain James Manary's company of the U.S. Rangers as a base of operations during the early part of the war.

McArthur, Fort
1812-1815, Kenton, Hardin County

---

[268] **Western Reserve and Northern Ohio Historical Society**, Tract Number 36, January 1877, Cleveland, Ohio, <u>Cleveland, War of 1812</u>, page 4.

[269] **Ibid**.

[270] Lossing, Benson J., **Pictorial Field Book of the War of 1812**, Chapter XVI, War with the British and Indians in the Northwest, (Harper & Brothers, Publishers, New York, New York: 1868).

Fort McArthur was a stockade with two blockhouses, which guarded the main supply road between Urbana and Fort Detroit. It was built by Colonel Duncan McArthur's Ohio militia regiment during Brigadier General William Hull's army's march to Fort Detroit.

Meigs, Camp (1)
1812, Urbana, Champaign County

This was the rendezvous site for Brigadier General William Hull's army. The three militia regiments from Ohio and the 4th Regiment of U.S. Infantry bivouacked at Camp Meigs before starting their march to Fort Detroit.

Meigs, Camp (2)
1813, Perrysburg, Wood County

Camp Meigs was a blockhouse and a bivouac area for Major General Harrison's troops at the rapids of the Maumee River. Fort Meigs would be built upon this site.

Meigs, Fort [271]
1813-1815, Perrysburg, Wood County

Known as the "Gibraltar of the Northwest", Fort Meigs was attacked twice by the British, but never fell. Several British siege batteries were located along both sides of the river. It was the largest fort built in Ohio during the war.

Fort Meigs enclosed 10 acres of land and it contained seven blockhouses, five artillery ramparts, and internal traverses. The British twice besieged the fort, from 1-10 May 1813 and again on 21 June 1813.

The fort was also called Camp Meigs. After the Battle of the Thames, the fort was rebuilt into a small wooden stockade with four blockhouses. The original fort was designed and built by Captains Charles Gratiot and Eleazer Wood of the U.S. Army engineers.

Necessity, Fort
1812-1817, near Williamstown, Hancock County

Fort Necessity was a wooden stockade with blockhouses. Colonel James Findlay's Ohio militia regiment built the fort during Brigadier General William Hull's army's march to Fort Detroit.

Piqua, Fort
1794-1795, 1810's, Piqua, Miami County

Fort Piqua was an U.S. Army supply post.

Portage, Camp
1813, Port Clinton, Ottawa County

Camp Portage was located at the mouth of the Portage River where Port Clinton, Ohio, now stands. It was the major staging area for the Army of the Northwest during its invasion of Upper Canada in September 1813.

After the invasion, the camp was used as a supply depot for material arriving from the Franklinton Barracks and from Cleveland. From Camp Portage these materials were shipped over Lake Erie to Detroit.

Portage, Fort (1)
1812-1813, Grand Rapid, Wood County

Fort Portage was located 18 miles south of Fort Meigs on the Maumee River, two miles northeast of Grand Rapid. It was partially destroyed in 1812, but was later rebuilt.

---

[271] Heidler, Davis S., and Heidler, Jeanne T., **Encyclopedia of the War of 1812**, (ABC-CLIO, Inc., Santa Barbara, California: 1997, page pp. 343-344, Fort Meigs.

Portage, Fort (2)
1812, Portage, Wood County

Fort Portage was a stockaded camp for disabled and invalid soldiers under Brigadier General William Hull.

Put-in-Bay [272]
1813-1815, Put-in-Bay, Ottawa County

After September 1813 Put-in-Bay, South Bass Inland,[273] became an army-navy facility with either barracks or a tent area, a small supply depot, a small hospital, temporary prisoner of war facilities and facilities to support the naval squadron operating on the Upper Great Lakes. The facility became the western headquarters of the American naval squadron.

Companies of Ohio militia were initially used to guard the prisoners of war taken during the Battle of Lake Erie and Battle of the Thames until they were transferred to southern Ohio and Kentucky.

During the winter of 1813-1814 Put-in-Bay was used as a winter-over facility for some of the damaged ships during the Battle of Lake Erie. The U.S. brigs *Niagara* and especially the *Lawrence* were repaired at Put-in-Bay and then they were sent to winter orders in Erie, Pennsylvania.[274] The captured H.M.S. ships *Detroit* and *Queen Charlotte* remained at Put-in-Bay for repairs. They were sent to Erie in May 1814 they were laid up for the rest of the war.

The navy maintained a communication and supply line between Detroit and Buffalo with stopping off points at Put-in-Bay and Erie, Pennsylvania. Cleveland was also a port of call for the navy.

St. Mary's, Fort
1784-1796, 1813-1818, St. Mary's, Auglaize County

Fort St. Mary's was built as the headquarters and supply depot for General Josiah Harmar and used by both Generals Wayne and Harrison. It was rebuilt in 1794. It was used by the regular army and militia as a staging area for raids into northern Indiana and to support Fort Wayne.

Sandusky, Camp [275]
1812, Fremont, Sandusky County

A wooden stockade with two blockhouses was erected by the militia companies under Captain John Campbell of Portage County and Captain Joab Norton of Delaware County as a supply depot for material arriving from Cleveland that was being shipped to Fort Detroit and General Hull's army. The facility would also be able to defend the federal Indian agency that was located near the site.

The stockade was abandoned after the fall of Fort Detroit but in the fall of 1812 the site was taken over and operated by the Ohio militia. In 1813 the facility was enlarged and renamed Fort Stephenson by the regular army.

Scioto, Camp
1813-1814, Chillicothe, Ross County

---

[272] Heidler, Davis S., and Heidler, Jeanne T., **Encyclopedia of the War of 1812**, (ABC-CLIO, Inc., Santa Barbara, California: 1997, page 435, Put-in-Bay.

[273] The Bass Islands in Lake Erie are made up of three main islands and a number of smaller islands. At the time of the War of 1812 North Bass Island was called St. George's Island while Middle Bass Island was called Le Fleur Island and South Bass Island was called Bass Island.

[274] **Warships to Workboats**, Volume 1, Number 3, Fall 2003, Brig Niagara – A Metamorphosis (Part 1), by Joel B. Sanbron, page 6.

[275] **Western Reserve and Northern Ohio Historical Society**, Tract Number 51, December 1879, Cleveland, Ohio, Gen. Wadsworth's Division, War of 1812, page 117.

Camp Scioto was a bivouac facility used by the Ohio militia who were on federal duty guarding the British prisoners at Camp Bull.

Seneca, Fort [276]
1813-1815, Old Fort, Seneca County

Fort Seneca was a wooden stockade with blockhouses and earthworks built by Lieutenant Colonel James V. Ball's squadron of the 2nd Regiment of U.S. Light Dragoons. This fort was used as a supply depot and as one of the staging areas for the invasion of Upper Canada.

Stephenson, Fort [277]
1812-1815, Fremont, Sandusky County

Fort Stephenson was a wooden stockade with three blockhouses and earthworks. The site was originally called Camp Sandusky. Captain Eleazer Wood of the U.S. Army engineers rebuilt this facility.

Major George Croghan of the 17th Regiment of U.S. Infantry commanded two companies from this regiment, which successfully defended the fort against a British attack on 2 August 1813.

This fort was used as a supply depot and as one of the staging areas for the invasion of Upper Canada.

Urbana Barracks
1812-1815, Urbana, Champaign County

Urbana served as the first headquarters of the Army of the Northwest.[278] After General Harrison became the commander of the army he moved the headquarters to Franklinton. Franklinton is now apart of Columbus, Ohio.

Urbana contained a commissary, quartermaster depot, hospital, blacksmith and wagon shops, harness and saddler shops and an artificer shop.[279] The facility also had a federal paymaster and an army recruiter.[280] It was used as a staging place or rendezvous point for military operations into the northern and eastern part of the Territory of Indiana and northwestern Ohio. It was also a re-supply facility for the forts and posts in the same area of the Territory of Indiana and in Ohio.

The facility also had temporary quarters for the troops that were being assembled there and there was a permanent party of troops that were stationed there to protect the facility. During the first part of the war in the west all federal troops and militia on federal duty were assembled and equipped at Urbana.

Winchester, Fort
1813-?, Defiance, Defiance County

Fort Winchester was a wooden stockade built on the site of Fort Defiance by Brigadier General James Winchester. It was used as a supply depot.

---

[276] **History of Seneca County, Ohio**, (Warner, Beers & Company, Chicago, Illinois: 1886), Chapter IX, Military History, page 330.

[277] Heidler, Davis S., and Heidler, Jeanne T., **Encyclopedia of the War of 1812**, (ABC-CLIO, Inc., Santa Barbara, California: 1997, pp. 489-490, Fort Stephenson.

[278] Middleton, Judge Evan P., **History of Champaign County, Ohio**, Volume 1, (B. F. Bowen & Company, Inc., Indianapolis, Indiana: 1917), Chapter XXIX, Urbana as Military Headquarters, pp. 678-679.

[279] **Ibid**, Chapter XXIX, Military Annals, Number of Troops in Urbana, pp. 677-678.

[280] **History of Champaign County, Ohio,** (W. R. Beers & Company, Chicago, Illinois: 1881), page 264.

Zanesville Barracks [281]
1812-1815, Zanesville, Muskingum County

The Zanesville Barracks was the headquarters for the 2nd Recruiting District in Ohio for the U.S. Army. Companies from the 27th Regiments of U.S. Infantry were organized there while men recruited for the 17th and 19th infantries from eastern Ohio rendezvoused here before marching to the Chillicothe Barracks. The facility was also the headquarters for the 27th infantry.

Zanesville's Prisoner of War Camp [282]
1813, near Zanesville, Muskingum County

A temporary prisoner of war camp was established outside of Zanesville, which housed eleven British officers and unknown number of enlisted men. The officers were transported to Frankfurt, Kentucky, while the enlisted men were sent to Newport Barracks, Kentucky.

British fort

Miamis, Fort
1764-1796, Maumee, Lucas County

Fort Miamis was a British fort taken over from the French after the end of the French and Indian War. The British rebuilt the facility in 1785 and then abandoned it after the Jay Treaty went into effect in 1796. The American army occupied the fort for the next two years before they abandoned it. The British reoccupied the ruins of the old fort during the first and second sieges of Fort Meigs in 1813.

---

[281] Carskadden, Jeff and James Morton, **Where the Frolics and War Dances are Held, The Indian Wars and the Early European Exploration and Settlement of Muskingum County and the Central Muskingum Valley**, (Gateway Press, Inc., Baltimore, Maryland: 1997), Prisoner-of-War Camp at Zanesville, page 462.

[282] **Ibid**.

Ohio's militia laws during the War of 1812

Little has been written on the organization of the Ohio militia during the War of 1812. Understanding how the militia was organized will help made sense on how the militia was used during this war. Surprisingly, the Ohio's militia was actually a peacetime force, which devoted itself to training. Once the governor issued a call to arms, men from the existing militia units were used to form new regiments and companies, which became, by law, the "state's army". This army was under the direct control of the governor. Other men were called up for federal duty. These men were also organized into new regiments and companies that served with the Army of the Northwest under Major General William Henry Harrison. In the meantime, the existing militia force was still operating but with reduced manpower.

The Ohio militia was empowered by the federal Militia Act of 1792 [283] and the 1802 Constitution of the State of Ohio. The initial state military laws were based upon the militia acts passed by the government of the Territory Northwest of the Ohio River (Northwest Territory). Ohio was formed from this territory. The state passed a number of militia acts during the 1800's, which directly governed and controlled the militia.

The federal Militia Act of 1792 gave the President of the United States the power to call up the state militias in order to repel an invasion or to put down an insurrection. The militia could be called up involuntarily for not more than three months in any one year and once called to active service they would be subject to the same military law, pay and allowances as set forth for the regular army. No militia units were ever involuntarily called up during the war. The federal government always asked the states and territories for volunteers.

Every able-bodied male between 18 years of age and under 45 years of age was automatically enrolled into the militia. Each man was required to have his own weapons, ammunition, and equipment necessary to sustain himself during his enlistment. The militiaman was also "exempted from all suits, distresses, executions or sales, for debt or for the payment of taxes" after they had been called up to serve. The act also exempted from military service the Vice President, most of the executive, judicial and legislative branches of the government along with customs and post office employees, stage coach drivers who transported the mail and all ferryman on a post road, export inspectors, merchant marine, and river and harbor pilots.

One of the first acts passed by Ohio after it became a state was the act that created and regulated the state militia. During the early years of statehood, the Ohio Assembly passed additional militia acts and amendments to these acts almost yearly. The Militia Act of 1809,[284] which was passed on 14 February 1809, was the most important act passed prior to the War of 1812 since it set the tone for the state militia during the first year of the war. The Militia Act of 1813,[285] which was passed in February of that year, regulated the militia until the end of the war. Ohio's militia acts went into far more detail than the federal Militia Act of 1792.

---

[283] Von Steuben, Frederick William Baron, **Baron von Steuben's Revolutionary War Drill Manual**, A Facsimile Reprint of the 1894 Edition, (Dover Publications, Inc., New York, New York: 1985), appendix, Militia Act of 1792.

[284] **Acts Passed by the Seventh General Assembly of the State of Ohio Begun and Held in the Town of Chillicothe, December 5th, 1808; and in the Seventh Year of Said State also, The Reports of the Auditor and Treasurer of State**, Volume VII, (J. S. Collins & Company, Chillicothe, Ohio: 1809), Chapter I, An act for disciplining the militia, pp. 3-43.

[285] **Acts Passed by the Eleventh General Assembly of the State of Ohio Begun and Held in the Town of Chillicothe, December 7th, 1812; and in the 11th Year of Said State also, The Reports of the Auditor and Treasurer of State**, volume XI, (Nashee & Dennti, Chillicothe, Ohio: 1812), Chapter XXXIX, An act for disciplining the militia, pp. 99-157.

Militia Act of 1809

The 1809 act that governed the state militia was called "an act for disciplining the militia". There were 48 sections contained in this act, and only the highlights are included in this review. The first section states that every able-bodied white male between 18 and less than 45 years of age was enrolled in the militia. When a male turned 18 years of age or when a male had moved into a new area within the state, the local militia captain had twenty days in which to enroll that person. The new militiaman then had twelve months in which to secure a good musket, fusee [286] or rifle, a knapsack, two spare flints, a pouch, a box, which would contain not less than 24 cartridges, and a powder horn. Officers were required to have a sword or similar weapon. Those men who were called to military duty were exempted from all suits, distresses, executions or sale for debt, damages or the payment of taxes.

Exempted from military duty were all ministers of the Gospel, judges, presidents of common pleas courts, jailors, customhouse officers and clerks, postal employees, and ferrymen on postal roads in addition to those men already exempted by federal law. Any person who was a conscientious objector could receive from the regiment a certificate exempting that person from militia duty after a yearly fee of $3.50 had been paid. This is usually considered as a religious exemption. Persons wishing to be excused from militia duty due to a physical limitation would first see the surgeon of the regiment in which he belongs. If the person was found to be unfit for militia duty by the surgeon, then a certificate was issued to that person excusing him from service.

The militia was divided into four divisions, which covered the whole area of the state. Most counties in 1809 were far larger in size than their current political boundaries.

Division	Brigade	Counties
First	First	Clermont, Hamilton
	Second	Warren
	Third	Butler
	Fourth	Greene, Champaign
	Fifth	Darke, Miami, Montgomery, Preble
Second	First	Adams, Highland
	Second & Third	Ross, Scioto
	Fourth	Delaware, Franklin, Knox, Richland
Third	First	Athens, Gallia, Washington
	Second	Fairfield, Licking
	Third	Belmont
	Fourth	Muskingum, Tuscarawas
Fourth	First	Jefferson
	Second	Columbiana, Stark, Wayne
	Third	Ashtabula, Cuyahoga, Geauga, Portage, Trumbull

Each division consisted of between two and four brigades,[287] while each brigade consisted of between two and six regiments. Each regiment was divided into two battalions of between four and eight

---

[286] A fusee was a small musket normally used by an officer for protection.

[287] This appears to be an error that was corrected in the militia amendment of 1811. The 1st division was setup with five brigades although the law stated that a division could be made up of between two and four brigades. The amendment readjusted the size of a division from between two and six brigades.

companies each. Each company had 64 privates. Local circumstances could adjust the number of privates in a company from 40 and to 80 men. "Odd battalions" were unattached battalions, which acted independently of regiments.[288] These were short-lived battalions that were created when a county did not have a sufficient number of men to organize a full regiment either as an initial regiment or an additional regiment. Once the number of militiamen increased to the point that another battalion could be formed then the "odd battalion" and the new battalion would merge to form a new regiment.

Provisions were included in this act to empower the division and brigade commanders to create new brigades or regiments within their organizations as the population grew and as new counties were formed. The following is the manpower strength for each of the units authorized by this militia act.

Division	Regiment	Company
1 Major General	1 Colonel	1 Captain
2 Aids-de-camps (rank of colonel)	1 Adjutant (rank of colonel)	1 Lieutenant
1 Quartermaster General (rank of colonel)	1 Quartermaster (rank of colonel)	1 Ensign
	1 Clerk (rank of lieutenant)	4 Sergeants
	1 Paymaster (rank of lieutenant)	4 Corporals
	1 Surgeon (rank of captain)	1 Drummer
Brigade		
1 Brigadier General	1 Surgeon's Mate	1 Fifer
1 Brigade Inspector (rank of major)	1 Sergeant Major	64 privates
1 Brigade Major (rank of major)	1 Quartermaster Sergeant	
1 Quartermaster (rank of major)	1 Drum Major	
	1 Fife Major	
	1 Major per battalion	

Previously to this act, a lieutenant colonel had been the commander of a regiment. This act gave the governor the power to promote the regimental commanders to the rank of colonel. The act limited the commanders' positions to citizens of the United States and required newly elected commanders to take an oath of office in which he states that he will support the constitutions of both the United States and of Ohio. Officers in each regiment would furnish the flag for each battalion, and the officers of each company would secure a drum and fife (or bugle horn) for their companies.

One artillery company and one troop of horse[289] could be raised and equipped in each regiment, and one company of riflemen, light infantry or grenadiers could be raised and equipped in each battalion. These additional companies could be raised only if the number of privates in each of the infantry companies did not fall below 40 men each. Also, the age of the men within these specialized companies must be between 18 and 40 years of age. This section also standardized the uniform for each company. By majority vote, the company could choose their own uniforms.

The manpower strengths of the specialized companies were:

---

[288] The provisions to create an 'odd battalion' was left out of this act although it was a part of the Militia Act of 1805. The amendment of 1811 will rectify this situation.

[289] Although "troop of horse" seems to refer to a cavalry type unit, in most cases these units were actually dragoons or mounted infantry. Mounted infantry used horses for transportation but once on a battlefield the men would dismount and fight on foot. Many of these units were used as dispatch riders during the war. Traditional cavalry units were not used in War of 1812.

Artillery Company	Troop of Horse [290]	Company of Grenadiers, light infantry and riflemen [291]
1 Captain	1 Captain	1 Captain
2 Lieutenants	2 Lieutenants	1 Lieutenant
4 Sergeants	1 Cornet	1 Ensign
4 Corporals	4 Sergeants	4 Sergeants
6 Gunners	4 Corporals	4 Corporals
6 Bombardiers	1 Saddler	1 Drummer
1 Drummer	1 Farrier	1 Fifer
1 Fifer	1 Trumpeter	30-64 Privates
20-30 Matrosses (privates)	30-60 Privates	

One piece of artillery was assigned to each artillery company. Artillery officers and sergeants were to arm themselves with a sword while each matross was to be equipped with a fusee, bayonet and cartridge box. Each member of the troop of horse furnished his own horse and saddle. They were also required to have a pair of boots with spurs, two pistols, and a saber.

Company musters occurred on the first Saturday of April and September. The men would meet at a predestinated location with their weapons and equipment. At 11 a.m. the men would assemble and at 11:15 a.m. a roll call would be taken and those men not present would be listed. After roll call an inspection of equipment would be conducted. The men must have with them a weapon, a bayonet, a cartridge box, a powder horn and a pouch. Any man missing from the muster or any man not having all of his required equipment would be fined. The act set the forfeitures and penalties found during a muster. Personal property could be confiscated and sold in order to pay for the fines occurred by a militiaman. Fathers were liable to pay the fines that their sons, under 21 years of age, had occurred during a muster.

Infractions	Fines	Infractions	Fines
Neglect of duties		**Privates**	
division commanders	$20-$200	Failure to attend a battalion or regimental muster	$1.00
brigade commanders	$15-$150	Failure to attend a company muster	$0.75
regiment commanders	$10-$100	Attending a battalion or regimental muster without a weapon	$0.50
battalion commanders	$8-$80	Attending a company muster without a weapon	$0.375
company commanders	$5-$50	Attending any muster without a pouch	$0.125
other company officers	$4-$40		
commander-in-chief staff	$10-$100		
division staff	$8-$80		
brigade staff	$4-$40		
regiment staff and sergeants	$2-$20		

---

[290] Cornet was the equivalent rank to an ensign, the lowest officer's position. Saddlers maintained the saddles and harnesses while a farrier was a blacksmith.

[291] Grenadiers were originally men who threw grenades or bombs, but by the War of 1812, they were shock troops made up of the biggest and strongest men from within a regiment. Riflemen and light infantry had the same functions but the riflemen were armed with rifles while the light infantry used muskets. These units covered the advances and retreats of a regiment and in battle were used as flank units, which tried to attack the enemy along the enemy's sides. Riflemen were also used as sharpshooters.

The federal government did issue one-half cent coins between 1793 and 1857. If any man was unable to furnish or equip himself, as by law, then the officers of the company could exempt that person from the fines imposed by this act.

The 1st Battalion of the 1st Regiment met on the second Tuesday of April while the 2nd Battalion of the 1st Regiment met on the second Thursday of April. The 1st Battalion of the 2nd Regiment met on the second Saturday of April while the 2nd Battalion of the 2nd Regiment met on the third Tuesday of April. Regiments, brigades and division could conduct musters as needed. Officer and staff musters occurred once a year. Officer musters started at 10 a.m. on the day of the meeting and ending at 3 p.m. on the succeeding day. This act also established Baron von Steuben's Revolutionary War Drill Manual as the day-to-day instruction guide for the militia.

This act gave the company officers the power to appoint the sergeants and corporals within their companies and to give each sergeant and corporal a ranking. The ranking was a seniority rating. The sergeant with the most experience would be given the most responsibility and then given the title of 1st Sergeant. The second most experienced sergeant would be titled the 2nd Sergeant, and so forth. Corporals were ranked accordingly.

Company officers were required to hold a Court of Enquiry at 10 o'clock on the Saturday following the September muster in order to assess the fines. Two copies of the assessment report would be made with one copy being posted at the meeting place of the court and the other one sent to the next regimental Court of Enquiry. Battalion officers were required to hold a Court of Enquiry on the Saturday following a battalion muster in order to assess the fines. The regimental clerk was required to attend and record the proceedings of the court. Two copies of the assessment report would be made with one copy posted at the meeting place of the court and one sent to the next regimental Court of Enquiry.

The regimental officers would hold a Court of Enquiry on the Friday following a regimental muster in order to assess the fines and to hold a court of appeals. The regimental clerk was required to attend and record the proceedings of the court. Two copies of the assessment report would be made with one copy posted at the meeting place of the court and one sent to the next regimental Court of Enquiry. The regimental Court of Enquiry also tried those officers from within the regiment who were charged with neglect of duty.

Every officer accepted a five-year commission in the militia. An officer would lose his commission either through a voluntary resignation or through a conviction in a court martial. An officer had the power to arrest those officers under him. The arresting officer must notify the officer being arrested in writing and must include the grounds of the arrest, his suspension from command, and the time and place of trial. The arresting officer must notify the next officer in the chain of command of the arrest and appoint him to assume the duties of the arrested officer.

The governor could not call out the existing brigades and regiments during a time of crisis, but he was allowed to demand a detachment from each division. He was required to specify the number of men needed and the time and place of rendezvous. He could only call out the whole militia during an actual invasion or extreme emergency.

When called into service the captain of a company would assemble his unit and march them to rendezvous. He gave the names of men in his company to the adjutant of the regiment with the rank of the officers and non-commissioned officers and the names of the privates. When the regiment had been completely formed, the several adjutants completed the roll for the entire detachment. Two copies were made, one for the adjutant general and the other for the brigade inspector.

Any man called to a tour of duty could appoint a substitute provided that the captain of the company approved the substitute. If the substitute was called into service himself, then the original man had to serve for that substitute or find a second substitute.

Once a detachment reached rendezvous, the commander appointed three persons to appraise the arms, accoutrements, horses and equipage. The three appraisers gave a certificate to each militiaman stating the appraised property and the amount of appraisement, and turned a copy over to the Office of the Secretary of State. If the property was lost, the owner was to be reimbursed by the state treasury.

The commander of each regiment could procure by impressment, for each company, a wagon, team and driver or a sufficient number of pack horses; six axes, six camp kettles or pots of convenient size, all to be delivered to each company commander. The treasurer of state reimburse the owner of the equipment after an appraisement was conducted and a certificate issued to the owner. The equipment becomes the property of the state and the officer in charge was held liable if the property was lost.

Once a detachment of militia had been called to either state or federal duty and was organized into a company of from 50 to 80 men, the men elected their officers by ballot. The company officers elected the battalion officers, battalion officers elected the regimental officers, and regimental officers elected the brigade officers.

If any bystander, at any muster or meeting of officers, insults or otherwise molests any officer or soldier, the commanding officer may order such person to be put under guard, not exceeding six hours. The State of Ohio did not execute deserters. Privates who deserted and were then caught were fined $100 and sent back to duty. Sergeants were fined $200 for desertions, demoted to private, and required to serve another tour of duty.

All previous militia laws were repealed when this act when into effect. This act was amended on 30 January 1811 with the Militia Act of 1811.[292] The size of a division could now range from two to six brigades. Provisions for the formation of 'odd battalions,' which were left out of the 1808 act, were included in this amendment. Additional instructions were given for officer elections, officer duties, and the handling of court cases.

Militia Act of 1813

The Ohio General Assembly passed the Militia Act of 1813 on 9 February 1813, replacing the Militia Act of 1809 and the amended Militia Act of 1811. It contained 73 sections. This act was an updated version of the 1809 militia act. The act divided the state into five militia divisions. The 1st division was split into two divisions with the new division becoming the 5th division. The counties created since 1809 were added to the division hierarchy.

Division	Brigade	Counties
First	First	Clermont, Hamilton
	Second	Warren, Clinton
	Third	Butler
Second	First	Adams, Highland
	Second & Third	Ross, Scioto, Fayette
	Fourth	Delaware, Franklin, Madison
	Fifth	Pickaway
Third	First	Athens, Gallia, Washington
	Second	Fairfield, Licking, Knox, Richland
	Third	Belmont, Guernsey (eastern tier of townships)
	Fourth	Coshocton, Guernsey (rest of county), Muskingum, Tuscarawas
Fourth	First	Jefferson, Harrison
	Second	Columbiana, Stark, Wayne
	Third	Trumbull
	Fourth	Ashtabula, Cuyahoga, Geauga, Huron, Medina, Portage,

---

[292] Bowman, Mary L., **Abstracts and Extracts of the Legislative Acts and Resolutions of the State of Ohio: 1803-1821**, (Ohio Genealogical Society, Mansfield, Ohio: 1994), ninth session of the General Assembly, an act to amend the act entitled "an act for disciplining the militia," pp. 134-135.

Fifth	First	Champaign, Greene
	Second	Darke, Miami, Montgomery, Preble

Free franking privileges were granted to the state's adjutant general, the major generals of each division and the brigadier generals of each brigade. This right of receiving mail, free of postage, was passed by an act of Congress on 13 April 1810.

Musters would be conducted in April and September for the following units:

Unit	April	September
Companies	1st Friday	1st Friday
1st Battalion of 1st Regiment	2nd Tuesday	
2nd Battalion of 1st Regiment	2nd Thursday	
1st Battalion of 2nd Regiment	2nd Saturday	
2nd Battalion of 2nd Regiment	3rd Tuesday	
Odd Battalion	3rd Thursday	
1st Regiment		2nd Tuesday
2nd Regiment		2nd Thursday
3rd Regiment		2nd Saturday
4th Regiment		3rd Tuesday
5th Regiment		3rd Thursday
6th Regiment		3rd Saturday

Artillery, horse, rifle, light or grenadier companies could be raised and formed if the manpower strength of each company did not fall below 45 men. The age of these men in the specialized companies was set between 18 and 44 years of age. Those men wishing an exemption from military duty on account of a disability must first make an oath before a justice of the peace and then present a copy of the oath to the regimental surgeon before being approved by a regiment's court of enquiry.

New infractions and adjustments in fines were approved in this act:

Infractions	Fines
Officers	
Field officers without a weapon	Up to $5.00
Company officers without a weapon	Up to $4.00
Staff officers without a weapon	Up to $4.00
Privates	
Failure to attend a regimental muster	$1.50
Failure to attend a battalion muster	$1.00
Failure to attend a company muster	$1.00
Attending a regimental muster without a weapon	$0.375
Attending a battalion muster without a weapon	$0.375
Attending a company muster without a weapon	$0.25
Attending any muster without a pouch	$0.125
Attending a regimental muster without equipment	$0.25
Attending a any other muster without equipment	$0.125

The governor had the right to exempt the militiamen in the frontier areas of the state from being called into service if the safety of that area was in question. He also had the right to further protect these areas as he saw fit. In an actual invasion, these exempted militiamen might still be required to serve as spies on the frontier.

When a detachment was called into service without the proper provisions, the commandant may appoint a purchasing commissary who had the power to purchase supplies through a contractor or a military commissary. He must submit to the auditor of state an account of all purchases along with the receipts. The treasurer of state will then be ordered to pay the bills. The commandant may also appoint an commissary officer.

Privates who deserted and were apprehended would be fined not less than $100, or more than $200 and then placed back on duty in the next tour of duty. Non-commissioned officers who deserted and were apprehended would be fined not less than $150, nor more than $250, reduced in rank to private and then placed back on duty in the next tour of duty. If a non-commissioned officer or private refused to march with his company on a tour of duty, he would be fined $20 for each month that his unit was in service.

The Militia Act of 1813 was amended on 11 February 1814.[293] This amendment updated the existing militia laws giving more instructions on the duties of the various commanders and staff officers, handling of elections, fines and penalties for neglect of duty and disobediences. The Militia Act of 1813 was replaced by the Militia Act of 1815 [294] on February 14th. This act incorporated the 'lessons learned' during the War of 1812, and this act would survive into the 1820's.

---

[293] Bowman, Mary L., **Abstracts and Extracts of the Legislative Acts and Resolutions of the State of Ohio: 1803-1821**, (Ohio Genealogical Society, Mansfield, Ohio: 1994), twelfth session of the General Assembly, an act to amend the act entitled "an act for disciplining the militia," pp. 175-176.

[294] **Ibid,** thirteenth session of the General Assembly, an act to amend the act entitled "an act for organizing and disciplining the militia," pp. 192-194.

A War of 1812 roster which has a unique tie to history

Researching can have many rewards. Whether you are researching a family, finding material for a book or an article, or just gaining additional knowledge on a certain subject, you may come across something that is unique and worth sharing with others.

Recently I was helping a Canadian prepare an article, which involved the War of 1812. She needed information on an Ohioan who had served during the War of 1812 and who had moved to Canada after the hostilities had ended. This ex-soldier was the subject of her article.

Out of courtesy, she sent me a copy of a document containing a list of American military officers who were held as prisoners of war in Canada during the War of 1812. She had seen this list in the Library and Archives Canada (the equivalent to our National Archives) and she had thought that I might be interesting in having a copy.

After first reading this list of names, I found that both of my eyebrows had risen a couple of inches above my forehead. The list not only included Ohioans, but it also included some very prominent Americans who would mold the U.S. Army after the War of 1812. It also included men who would have an impact on both American and Ohio politics between the War of 1812 and the American Civil War. If one or any of these men on this list had died in a British prisoner of war camp in Canada, the course of American history could have been altered.

The list of Americans included the names of twenty-two militia and regular army officers who had been captured after the fall of Fort Detroit and during the Battle of Queenston in 1812. The first year of the war went extremely poorly for the Americans, who had many more defeats than victories on the battlefield.

One of our victories occurred when Captain David Porter of the U.S. Frigate *Essex* captured the British transport *Samuel and Sarah* on 24 June 1812 on the Atlantic Ocean. This transport was bringing part of a battalion of the 1st Royal Scots Regiment of Foot to fight for the Canadians. This single act set the stage for a British-American prisoner of war exchange on 17 September 1813.

The twenty-two officers were being exchanged for 159 British soldiers from the 1st Royal Scots. This may seem a little lop-sided, but the exchange system was based upon a point value. A private was worth one point, a captain six points and a brigadier general twenty points. Each military rank was assigned a certain number of points.

The Americans on this list were one brigadier general, three colonels, four lieutenant colonels, one major, ten captains and three lieutenants for a total of 185 points. The British on their list had three lieutenants, nine sergeants, six corporals, two drummers and 139 privates for a total of 185 points. The men were exchanged on paper. Most of the officers had been paroled after their capture, and they had been sent home to their regiments.

The four Ohioans were Duncan McArthur of Chillicothe, James Findlay of Cincinnati, Lewis Cass of Zanesville and Robert Lucas from the Portsmouth area.

Colonel Duncan McArthur was the commander of the 2nd Ohio Volunteer Regiment under Brigadier General William Hull, and he was also a major general in the Ohio Militia. After his release, he was promoted to brigadier general in the U.S. Army and he would take command of the Army of the Northwest upon the resignation of Major General William Henry Harrison in 1814. McArthur would become the 11th governor of Ohio.

Colonel James Findlay was the commander of the 1st Ohio Volunteer Regiment under General Hull, and was also a brigadier general in the Ohio militia. He had been the mayor of Cincinnati before the War of 1812, and he would become a U.S. Congressman after the war.

Colonel Lewis Cass was the commander of the 3rd Ohio Volunteer Regiment under General Hull and also he was a brigadier general in the Ohio militia. After his release, he was promoted to brigadier general in the U.S. Army. He would resign from the army in late 1813 to become the 2nd governor of the Territory of Michigan. Later, he became an American ambassador to France, a U.S. Senator from Michigan, a Secretary of State and a Secretary of War. He ran for president of the United States in 1848.

Captain Robert Lucas was also a brigadier general in the Ohio militia. After the war, he would become a major general in the Ohio militia, the 12th governor of Ohio, and later, the first governor of the Territory of Iowa.

The other prominent men on the list of twenty-two were William Hull, Abraham Hull, James Miller, Winfield Scott, John Whistler, Josiah Snelling, Thomas Sidney Jesup, and Henry Brevoort.

Brigadier General William Hull was the commander of the Army of the Northwest, and he surrendered his army to the British on 16 August 1812 at Fort Detroit without a fight. He is considered to be the "Benedict Arnold" of the War of 1812. Hull was the uncle to Commodore Isaac Hull, the noted commander of the U.S. Frigate *Constitution*.

Captain Abraham Fuller Hull was the son and aide-de-camp to General Hull. He would be assigned to the 9th Regiment of U.S. Infantry after his return to the United States. He would be killed during the Battle of Lundy's Lane on 25 July 1814. He has a marked grave on this battlefield in Ontario, Canada.

Lieutenant Colonel James Miller was the acting commander of the 4th Regiment of U.S. Infantry under General Hull. He had fought in the Battle of Tippecanoe in 1811 and he would become the commander of the 21st Regiment of U.S. Infantry. He would lead this regiment in the Battle of Lundy's Lane. After the battle, he was promoted to brigadier general in the army. He would be elected as a U.S. Representative and later became the first governor of the Territory of Arkansas.

Lieutenant Colonel Winfield Scott served in the U.S. Army for 47 years. He was the commanding general of the U.S. Army during his last 20 years in the army. He commanded the U.S. forces during the Mexican-American War and served as the military governor of Mexico City. He ran for the presidency in 1852.

Scott molded the Union strategy during the American Civil War when President Lincoln adopted his Anaconda Plan. This plan called for the U.S. Navy to blockade the Southern ports and the U.S. Army to advance down the Mississippi River to split the Confederacy in two. The plan worked!

Captain John Whistler's story is very interesting. A native of England, he enlisted in the British Army and served under Major General John Burgoyne during the American Revolution. He fought at the Battle of Saratoga and then immigrated to the U.S. after the war. He is the father of James Whistler, the famous American artist.

Captain Josiah Snelling would end his military career as a colonel is the U.S. Army. He is noted for building Fort Saint Anthony on the upper Mississippi River. This fort would protect the early settlers in the area that would become Minnesota.

First Lieutenant Thomas Sidney Jesup would become the "Father of the Modern Quartermaster Corps" for the U.S. Army. He served in the army from 1808 to 1860 rising to the rank of brigadier general. He had an Ohio connection! He was transferred to Ohio's 19th Regiment of U.S. Infantry after his release and he was in charge of building the small boats needed by General Harrison for his invasion of Upper Canada in late 1813. He was stationed in Cleveland, Ohio.

Captain Henry B. Brevoort of the 2nd Regiment of U.S. Infantry would command the marine detachment on the U.S. Brig *Niagara* during the Battle of Lake Erie on 10 September 1813.

This list of twenty-two American military officers has been known for two hundred years. The list is available to anyone through the British, the Canadian or American national archives. What makes this list interesting is to have been able to research each officer to see what that officer contributed in the War of 1812 and afterwards.

This once mighty army

What happened to this once mighty army which dared to cross the swamp lands of northwestern Ohio in order to protect Fort Detroit during the early days of the War of 1812? Much has been written on the failures of Brigadier General William Hull's army which, he surrendered to the British on 16 August 1812 at Detroit, but little has been written on the successes of this army and almost nothing on the dispersement of his men after the surrender.

The Army of the Northwest, or the Northwestern Army as it is also called, actually had more successes than failures, but the final failure far out weighed all of the successes, and that is what the historians remember. The original War Department plan called for a three-pronged attack against Canada with General Hull launching his invasion from Detroit and Major General Henry Dearborn launching his invasion forces across the Niagara frontier and up the Lake Champaign valley. The failure of the War Department to coordinate this plan and the lack of preparation on the part of General Dearborn was the direct cause of the failure of the Army of the Northwest at Detroit.

General Dearborn's slowness in recruiting and organizing the Army of the North in northern New York gave the British sufficient time to defend themselves against any attacks from the United States during the early days of the war. Both generals were given their orders in April 1812, but it would not be until October that General Dearborn had readied his forces for action. When his army did go into battle, they were defeated at the Battle of Queenston Heights on 13 October 1812. The failure of this battle was due in part to the lack of coordination between the army and the militia.

It took General Dearborn nearly six months to launch his attack. While at Detroit, General Hull was waiting for army dispatches informing him of the success of General Dearborn's army, but little did he know at time that the Army of the North was only a "paper army."

General Hull's first success was the organizing and launching of his invasion of Upper Canada within weeks of receiving his orders. Praise must also be given to Ohio's Governor Return Jonathan Meigs, Junior, who actually organized the 1,500 Ohio militiamen and rendezvoused them at Urbana, Ohio, within the timeframe given him by the War Department. Praise must also be given to Lieutenant Colonel James Miller who brought the 4th Regiment of U.S. Infantry to Urbana on time and ready for action.

The second success of the army was the crossing of northwestern Ohio by building a military road through the wilderness and the Great Black Swamp plus the construction of forts and blockhouses to protect this road. General Hull had established his own line of communication and supply and had stationed a company of militiamen at each of the forts and blockhouses along the road.

The first failure for the Army of the Northwest was the lack of good communications from the War Department. No news was not good news for General Hull. He had no idea what was going on in the east, and originally he did not know that he was in a sink-or-swim situation. Supplies and reinforcements from the south were extremely slow in coming. The War Department came through with the war materials needed to equip General Hull's army, but the department was slow in providing war materials for additional troops.

The Territory of Michigan had a population of 5,000 civilians in 1812 and when the army arrived at Detroit this swelled the population to 7,500, which taxed the resources of this territory. Politics and the lack of funds doomed the Army of the Northwest from the start.

Before General Hull had taken over the Army of the Northwest, he was in Washington, D.C., as the governor of the Territory of Michigan, pleading for help from the federal government in order to protect his territory. He asked for naval assistance in order to gain control of the upper Great Lakes. The army had purchased a brig, and it was being outfitted near Detroit as a warship with six guns. This brig was named the *Adams*. Naval help would not be initiated until the following year and his ship became a prize of war when Detroit fell. The U.S. Army Brig *Adams* would become the H.M. Brig *Detroit* and it would be used against the Americans. This was another failure on the part of the federal government.

General Hull conducted the first successful invasion of Canada and held on to this territory in the Western District of Upper Canada along the Detroit River for a month. His forces successfully skirmished against the British on a number of occasions, and they conducted foraging raids deep into British controlled areas. Even though the American forces out-numbered the British army, one of the deciding factors in this campaign was the number of allied Indians that the British had available. If used right, the Indians would tip the balance of power in the northwest.

When the British landed troops south of Detroit out flanking the Americans, General Hull was forced to withdraw his regiments from Canada and to go on the defensive protecting Detroit. In a brilliant bluff, the outnumbered British army forced General Hull to surrender without a fight. General Hull had literally lost his nerve during the final days of the American occupation of Detroit.

The British had professionally trained army officers which was a deciding factor in this fiasco at Detroit. Even if the Americans had had a better trained commander than General Hull, the lack of support from the federal government would no doubt have ruined any commander.

Another failure for the Americans was the lack of intelligence needed to conduct a truly successful invasion. General Hull did not know the actual strength of the British army and its militia. The general had no maps of the Western District, and he had to rely on friendly Canadians to aid him.

The history books simply state that after the surrender, the regular American army troops were sent to Montreal and Quebec as prisoners of war. In October, they were released by the British on parole status and then sent to Boston where they remained until the following year when they were exchanged and sent back to the front. The 4th Regiment of U.S. Infantry would be re-assigned to the Army of the North and the regiment would have a distinguished war record during the War of 1812.

Besides the 4th Infantry, General Hull also had two companies of soldiers from the 1st Regiment of U.S. Infantry and a company of artillery from the Regiment of U.S. Artillery. The militia forces consisted of a brigade of Ohio Militia made up of three infantry regiments plus a mounted infantry company and an artillery company totaling 1,500 men. The Territory of Michigan fielded two infantry regiments and a legion made up of mounted infantry and riflemen. This force consisted of around 500 men. It is to be noted that the Ohio militia at Detroit were volunteers who had enlisted for one year in the army. They were not under state control but federal control while serving their tour of duty at Detroit.

With the militia, the history books simply state that the Ohio militia was transported by ships to Cleveland, Ohio, and from this location the men made their way home. Usually, there is no mention of the Michigan militia. These men from Michigan were disarmed, and they were permitted to return to their homes.

The British Royal Navy did not exist on the Great Lakes until 1813 when this navy absorbed the Provincial Marine of the Province of Upper Canada. At the time of the fall of Detroit, the Provincial Marine had two warships, the 20-gun Queen Charlotte and the 12-gun General Hunter. This defense force had also contracted the 2-gun schooner Caledonia from the Canada's North West Company (a fur company).

It was impossible to transport the entire Ohio brigade in one sailing on the existing ships of the Provincial Marine. Most of the Great Lakes vessels during this time period were single deck, sailing ships without sleeping quarters and kitchens. The ships normally sailed during the day light hours. They put into protected harbors at night in order to prepare meals and to sleep. Most of the hulls of these vessels were used to store cargo and ship supplies. The majority of the militiamen would have stayed on the decks of the vessels. A few men may have been forced to use the cargo hole on the larger ships.

The British pressed into service as many civilian vessels as possible to transport the brigade back to Ohio. From evidence obtained from three diaries, it appear that the British were able to deliver the militiamen back to Ohio in one sailing. Captain Robert Lucas in his diary claimed that he was transported on the *Maria of Presque Isle*, which was loaded with furs. There were 230 prisoners on board this vessel when it sailed to Ohio. It is also known that the *Caledonia* was loaded with furs.

The convoy of vessels left Amherstburg in Upper Canada on 20 August 1812, and it stopped at Put-in-Bay in the Lake Erie islands to prepare meals. From this anchorage the vessels arrived at the mouth of the Black River, present day Lorain, Ohio, where a number of militiamen were dropped off. The vessels then proceeded to Cleveland were they disembarked the rest of the brigade. The men who had been left at the

Black River arrived on foot at Cleveland on 24 August 1812 the day after the brigade had arrived at this village.

Once the militiamen had rested and were cared for by the citizens of Cleveland, they headed south towards their homes. From Cleveland to Canton the men traveled on a postal road. At Canton, two companies from Scioto County headed east to the Ohio River where they purchased two boats in which they sailed down the river to Portsmouth. The rest of the brigade continued south on the postal road to New Philadelphia and then onwards towards Zanesville. From Zanesville the brigade dispersed to all corners of southern Ohio.

The Rev. Benjamin Mortimer was a missionary of a Christian Indian settlement called Goshen, which was located outside of New Philadelphia. In his diary of 1812, he witnessed the brigade passing through his mission on their way home.

The first of the militiamen arrived on August 27th at New Philadelphia. The next day some of the men from Hull's army took breakfast at Goshen. They warned the Indians at Goshen that they were in "great danger of their lives from their incensed comrades, and warned us in a friendly manner to take great care or harm would easily befall them."

Hundreds from Hull's army passed by Goshen on August 29th. "They came along as beggars, and were in general treated everywhere with much hospitality." Colonel Duncan McArthur of the Ohio militia and other principal officers passed through the mission on this day. Another group of militiamen passed the mission on September 1st. Colonel James Findlay's regiment made their appearance on September 8th and 9th. The last of the brigade continued on to their homes.

Almost a year after this once mighty army had returned to Ohio, there were still militiamen from the brigade living in Cleveland. A number of men had been left behind at Detroit and Amherstburg because they were too sick to travel. As the health of these men improved, they were shipped to Cleveland.

One of the most touching stories coming out of the War of 1812 was about the kindness and humanity that Captain Stanton Sholes showed to a group of General Hull's militiamen who were recovering from illnesses and wounds in Cleveland during the spring of 1813. Captain Sholes was from Beaver County, Pennsylvania, and he was a captain in the 2nd Regiment of U.S. Artillery. He raised his artillery company primarily from Beaver County and on 3 May 1813 he was ordered to take his company to Cleveland as part of the defensive force being formed for this village by the regular army. His company arrived in Cleveland on May 10th.

In a letter to the Cuyahoga County Historical Society (Cleveland), dated July 1858, Sholes stated, "At my arrival I found a number of sick and wounded who were of Hull's surrender, sent from Detroit, and more coming. These were crowded into a log cabin, and no one to care for them. I sent one or two of my soldiers to take care of them, as they had no friends. I had two or three good carpenters in my company, and set them to work to build a hospital. I very soon got up a good one, thirty by twenty feet, smoothly and tightly covered, and floored with chestnut bark, with two tier of bunks around the walls, with doors and windows, and not a nail, a screw, or iron latch or hinge about the building. Its cost to the Government was a few extra rations. In a short time I had all the bunks well strawed, and the sick and wounded good and clean, to their great joy and comfort, but some had fallen asleep." Eventually, the wounded and injured militiamen from Hull's army recovered and returned home or they were laid to rest in Cleveland.

Only four militiamen from the brigade were exchanged and permitted to return to duty. These men were the three regimental commanders, Colonels Lewis Cass, Duncan McArthur and James Findlay plus Captain Robert Lucas. Lucas was a brigadier general in the Ohio militia who enlisted as a private in Hull's army and who was later given a staff position and the rank of captain. Right before Lucas left to join Hull's army, he was notified that he had also obtained a captaincy in the U.S. Army.

Cass would accept a colonel's rank in the U.S. Army, and he would raise the 27th Regiment of U.S. Infantry in eastern Ohio. McArthur also accepted a colonel's position in the army, and he would raise the 26th Regiment of U.S. Infantry in western Ohio. Both men would be promoted to brigadier generals and command a brigade under Major General William Henry Harrison.

As for the rest of the officers and men of General Hull's army, most would violate their parole and either rejoin their militia units or enlist in the U.S. Army. Half of the men in the 26th and 27th Infantries were members of Hull's army. Many militiamen from Michigan would escape south and join the 19th Regiment of U.S. Infantry, and there was one dragoon company from this territory which served in the volunteer corps for a year.

This once mighty army made its presence felt throughout the War of 1812. General McArthur's brigade retook Detroit after General Harrison's invasion of Upper Canada in September 1813. One company of General Cass's brigade participated in the Battle of the Thames River in October of that year, and they captured the British artillery detachment during this battle. Hull's army had come full circle. Their revenge was sweet.

Bibliography

Lucas, Robert, **The Robert Lucas Journal of the War of 1812**, originally printed by the State Historical Society of Iowa in 1906, reprinted by Arthur W. McGraw in 2000.

Malcomson, Robert, **Warships of the Great Lakes 1754-1834**, (Annapolis, MD: Naval Institute Press, 2001).

Mortimer, Rev. Benjamin, "*The Ohio Frontier in 1812, Diary of the Indian Congregation at Goshen on the River Muskingum for the Year 1812,*" **Ohio Archaeological and Historical Publications**, Volume XXII, (Columbus, Ohio: Fred. J. Heer, publisher: 1913).

Sholes, Stanton, "*A Narrative of the Northwestern Campaign of 1813*," **The Mississippi Valley Historical Review**, March 1929, Volume XV, Number 4, (Mississippi Valley Historical Association, Lincoln, Nebraska).

Regimental reorganizations during the War of 1812

One of the most confusing aspects of the War of 1812 was the United States Army's reorganization of its regiments under four different Congressional Acts on 26 June 1812, 3 March 1813, 30 March 1814 and 3 March 1815. The 1812 and 1813 acts actually standardized the structure and manpower strengths of each of its regiment while the next two acts downsized and reorganized the regiments, which prepared the army for its peacetime mission following the end of the war.

Although the Congress had created 48 infantry regiments for service during the war, few people realize that four of these regiments were deactivated in 1814 and two new regiments were created reusing the numeric designation of two of the deactivated regiments. Furthermore, two other existing infantry regiments were renumbered in 1814 using the designation of the remaining two deactivated regiments.

Thus, there were two different 17th, 19th, 26th and 27th Regiments of Infantry created during the war. These four regiments were disbanded on 12 May 1814, and those men retained from these regiments were organized into a new 17th and 19th Regiments of Infantry. On the same day, the 47th Regiment of Infantry was re-designated as the new 27th Regiment of Infantry while the 48th regiment became the new 26th regiment. The reorganization and renumbering of these infantry regiments kept the sequential numbering system of the infantry regiments between 1 and 46.

The Congressional Act of 26 June 1812 [295]

At the outbreak of the war, the army had 17 infantry regiments authorized by three different acts of Congress which set up three different manpower strengths based upon the authorization date of each regiment. The 1st and 2nd Regiments of Infantry had been reorganized in 1802, and they consisted of ten companies of 76 men for a total manning of 806 men.[296] By 1808 another war with Great Britain seemed a distinct possibility so Congress authorized the creation of the 3rd through the 7th Regiments of U.S. Infantry and the Regiment of Rifle consisting of 849 men each in ten companies of 80 men.[297] Under the Act of 11 January 1812 Congress authorized 10 more infantry regiments, the 8th through the 17th Regiments of Infantry.[298] These regiments were organized with 18 companies of 110 men arranged in two battalions.

The act of 26 June 1812 re-established the manpower strength of all infantry regiments at 1,070 men in companies of 102 men each. The officers' positions included a colonel, a lieutenant colonel, a major, an adjutant, a quartermaster, a paymaster, a surgeon, two surgeons' mates, ten captains, ten 1st lieutenants, ten 2nd lieutenants and ten ensigns.[299] The enlisted personal included a sergeant major, a quartermaster sergeant, two principal musicians, 40 sergeants, 60 corporals, 20 musicians, and 900 privates. The Regiment of Rifle had one less surgeons mate than the infantry regiments plus 20 fewer corporals and only 680 privates. The manpower strength of the rifle regiment was set at 829 men. The rifle regiment and each of the infantry regiments were divided into ten companies with a headquarters staff.

---

[295] Heitman, Francis B., **Historical Register and Dictionary of the United States Army From Its Organization, September 29, 1789, to March 2, 1903**, (Genealogical Publishing Company, Baltimore, Maryland: 1994), Volume II, pp. 572-573, Organization of the Army under the act of June 26, 1812.

[296] **Ibid**, Volume II, page 569, Organization of the Army under the act of March 16, 1802.

[297] **Ibid**, Volume II, pp. 570-571, Organization of the Army under the act of April 12, 1808.

[298] **Ibid**, Volume I, pp. 96-115, Infantry, 8th Regiment of Infantry through the 17th Regiment of Infantry.

[299] In the dragoon companies the rank of cornet was equivalent to the rank of ensign. In the Middle Ages the cornet was the person who played the bugle or similar instrument while an ensign carried the regiment's colors or flag. Over the years these positions became junior officer ranks.

The army in 1812 also had two regiments of light dragoons and four regiments of artillery. The 1st Regiment of Light Dragoons had 672 men in eight companies while the 2nd Regiment of Light Dragoons had 1,006 men in 12 companies. Included in these regiments were riding masters and sword masters in the officers' ranks and saddlers, farriers and blacksmiths in the enlisted ranks. These regiments did not have sergeant majors, quartermaster sergeants or musicians. The cornet rank replaced the ensign's positions.

The Regiment of Light Artillery had 919 men while the Regiment of Artillerists had 1,588 men and the 2nd and 3rd Regiments of Artillery each had 1,874 men. The Regiment of Artillerists became the 1st Regiment of Artillery. These regiments did not have ensigns in the officers' ranks, but they had artificer's positions in the enlisted ranks. The Regiment of Light Artillery had authorizations for drivers of artillery positions since they were a mobile regiment. The light artillery had ten companies while the remaining three artillery regiments had twenty companies each.

The act of 26 June 1812 also added 'during the war' enlistments for new enlistees. Later in the war, eighteen-month and one-year enlistments were authorized in order to fill the ranks of the army's regiments. These shorter enlistments did not qualify the men for the bonuses and land bounties that the government offered its soldiers for a full enlistment. Many men would later change their enlistments from 'five years' to 'during the war' in order to qualify for the bonuses and bounties.

The 18th through the 25th Regiments of Infantry were authorized on 26 June 1812 with the manpower strength of each of these regiments set at 1,070 men in companies of 102 men.[300]

The Congressional Act of 3 March 1813 [301]

Under the act of 3 March 1813 a second major's position was authorized for an infantry regiment plus ten 3rd lieutenants and ten additional sergeants. This set the manpower strength of an infantry regiment up to 1,091 men. The Regiment of Rifes gained a second surgeon's mate, ten 3rd lieutenants and ten sergeants. This increased the manpower strength of the rifle regiment to 850 men.

Prior to 3 March 1813 twenty cadets from the military academy had been assigned to each of the infantry regiments and the rifle regiments. Four cadets were assigned to the engineers, 60 to the artillery regiments and 16 to the light dragoons. These cadets received their schooling at West Point and their practical education in the regiments in which they were assigned. By 1813 it was decided to keep the corps of cadets together as a unit, and the cadets were no longer attached to any of the regiments for training.

The ten 3rd lieutenant's positions that were added by this act to each of the regiments were designed to help bolster the recruiting efforts of the regiments. Each regiment maintained its own recruiting service during the war. Not all of the company grade officers and non-commissioned officers were assigned to companies during the war. Many were on temporary or permanent duty recruiting men for their regiment.

Either one of the regiment's majors or a captain was in charge of the service center. These men would send their recruiting officers and sergeants to the cities and villages enlisting men. Once the number of recruits reached 100 then would be organized into a company and sent to the regiment in the field. From the recruiting service pool the recruiting superintendent would be selected a captain, first lieutenant, second lieutenant, ensign and the sergeants needed to command and control this new company.

The 1st Regiment of Light Dragoons gained a major's position and eight 3rd lieutenants' positions plus eight sergeants and four blacksmiths. This increased the size of this regiment to 689 men. The 2nd Regiment of Light Dragoons gained twelve 3rd lieutenants and twelve sergeants. This increased the manpower strength for this regiment to 1,030 men.

The Regiment of Light Artillery gained a major's position, ten 3rd lieutenants and ten sergeants to increase the size of this regiment to 940 men. The Regiment of Artillerists gained twenty 3rd lieutenants

---

[300] Heitman, **Historical Register**, Volume I, pp. 125-137, Infantry, 26th Regiment of Infantry to the 44th Regiment of Infantry.

[301] **Ibid**, Volume II, pp. 578-579, Organization of the Army under the act of March 3, 1815.

and twenty sergeants, which set the manpower strength at 1,628 men. The remaining two artillery regiments also gained twenty 3rd lieutenants and twenty sergeants setting their strength at 1,914 men.

On 29 January 1813 Congress created twenty more infantry regiments but only the 26th through 44th Regiments of Infantry were raised while the last regiment became ten companies of United States Rangers.[302] This last regiment would have been the 45th Regiment of Infantry under this act but the '45th' designation would be used in the next batch of regiments that would be created in 1814. Initially, these newer regiments were to be raised for only one year with one-year enlistments. Most of these regiments were switched from 'five years' to 'during the war' enlistments and the regiments were then continued until the end of the war.

The Congressional Act of 30 March 1814 [303]

Sweeping changes occurred in the organization of the army through the act of 30 March 1814, which went into effect on 12 May 1814. Three artillery regiments were combined into the Corps of Artillery. The new artillery corps had a manpower strength of 5,916 men arranged into 48 companies. The two regiments of light dragoons were combined into a single regiment called the Regiment of Light Dragoons. This unit had 979 men divided into eight companies. The infantry and rifle regiments plus the Regiment of Light Artillery had no changes in their authorized manpower or structure.

New to this year's army organizational charts were ten companies of rangers. Seven ranger companies were authorized in 1812 and ten more companies in 1813, but the manpower breakdown was not included in the previous two acts.[304] The ten companies authorized in 1813 were continued through 1814 and their manpower strengths were added to 1814's organizational chart for the army. The rangers were disbanded in 1815.

The ranger companies consisted of a captain, a 1st lieutenant, a 2nd lieutenant, a 3rd lieutenant, an ensign, five sergeants, six corporals and 90 privates. There were no field grade officers appointed over these companies and they were not organized into any form of a regiment. Ranger companies were attached to infantry regiments or to a military district as needed.

Also showing up in this year's organizational chart were ten companies of sea fencibles. These were basically "coast guard" companies of local men who guarded the ports and harbors along the seacoast and who were not subject to overseas duty. These companies were made up of a captain, a 1st lieutenant, a 2nd lieutenant, a 3rd lieutenant, ten boatswains, 60 gunners, 60 quarter-gunners [305] and 900 privates. The sea fencibles were unique since they were made up of army officers and naval enlisted men. The strengths of the rangers were set at 1,060 men while the sea fencibles had 1,070 men authorized.

Four more infantry regiments and three regiments of rifles were authorized on 30 March 1814. These units were the 45th through the 48th Regiments of Infantry and the 2nd through the 4th Regiments of Rifle.

On 12 May 1814 the Army of the Northwest, under the command of Major General William H. Harrison, went through a major reorganization of its regiments.[306] The 17th regiment (minus two companies) and the 19th regiment merged to form the new 17th Regiment of Infantry. The remaining two companies from the 17th regiment plus the 26th and the 27th regiments merged to form the new 19th Regiment of Infantry. The 26th and 27th regiments were initially made up of one-year enlistments and those men who had re-enlisted were transferred to the 19th regiment.

---

[302] **Ibid**, Volume I, pp. 115-125, Infantry, 18th Regiment of Infantry through the 25th Regiment of Infantry.

[303] **Ibid**, Volume II, pp. 576-577, Organization of the Army under the act of March 30, 1814.

[304] **Ibid**, Volume I, page 141, Rangers.

[305] Quarter-gunner was a petty officer who assisted the gunner.

[306] Adjutant and Inspector General's Office, **General Orders, Washington, May 18, 1814**, copy at the Western Reserve Historical Society's Archives Library, Cleveland, Ohio, call number 660, manuscripts.

On the same date the 48th Regiment of Infantry was re-designated as the new 26th Regiment of Infantry, while the 47th Regiment of Infantry became the new 27th Regiment of Infantry. The new 26th regiment was labeled as 'light infantry,' and the regiment was issued rifles and the uniforms of a rifle regiment.[307]

The following is a list of regiments reorganized under the act of 30 March 1814:

17th Regiment of Infantry –17th Regiment of Infantry (minus two companies) plus the 19th Regiment of Infantry
19th Regiment of Infantry – two companies of the 17th Regiment of Infantry plus the 26th and 27th Regiments of Infantry
26th Regiment of Infantry – formerly the 48th Regiment of Infantry
27th Regiment of Infantry – formerly the 47th Regiment of Infantry

Regiment of Light Dragoons – 1st and 2nd Regiments of Light Dragoons

Corps of Artillery – 1st, 2nd and 3rd Regiments of Artillery

The Congressional Act of 3 March 1815 [308]

After the War of 1812, the act of 3 March 1815 established the peacetime army by consolidating all of the existing infantry regiments, artillery regiments, the light dragoon regiment and rifle regiments into eight new infantry regiments, a rifle regiment and two artillery regiments. This act went into effect on 15 June 1815.

The designations of the new infantry regiments were based upon the seniority of its commanding officer. The new 1st Regiment of Infantry was so designated because its commanding officer was the senior most colonel in the army; the 2nd regiment had the second most senior colonel; and so forth through the 8th regiment.

The following is a list of the new regiments formed in 1815 and the older regiments that were consolidated to form these new regiments:

1st Regiment of Infantry - 2nd, 3rd, 7th and 44th Regiments of Infantry
2nd Regiment of Infantry - 6th, 16th, 22nd, 23rd and 32nd Regiments of Infantry
3rd Regiment of Infantry - 1st, 17th (new), 19th (new), 24th, 28th and 39th Regiments of Infantry
4th Regiment of Infantry - 12th, 14th and 20th Regiments of Infantry
5th Regiment of Infantry - 4th, 9th, 13th, 21st, 40th and 46th Regiments of Infantry
6th Regiment of Infantry - 11th, 25th, 27th (new), 29th and 37th Regiments of Infantry
7th Regiment of Infantry - 8th, 10th, 36th and 38th Regiments of Infantry
8th Regiment of Infantry - 5th, 18th and 35th Regiments of Infantry

Regiment of Rifle - 1st, 2nd, 3rd, 4th Regiments of Rifle

Regiment of Light Artillery - 15th, 26th (new), 30th, 31st, 33rd, 34th and 45th Regiments of Infantry, Regiment of Light Artillery

Corps of Artillery – Corps of Artillery, Regiment of Light Dragoons, 41st, 42nd and 43rd Regiments of Infantry

The new infantry regiments and the rife regiment contained ten companies of 78 men each for a total manpower strength of 820 men. In 1821 the 8th regiment and the rifle regiment would be disbanded. The infantry structure of the army after 1821 would remain constant until the Mexican War. Between these two wars, the Corps of Artillery would once again be broken into individual regiments and a dragoon

---

[307] Kochan, James L. and David Rickman, **The United States Army 1812-1815**, Men-at-Arms Series Number 345, (Osprey Publishing, Oxford, England: 2000), page 20, Rifle Uniforms.

[308] Heitman, **Historical Register**, Volume II, pp. 578-579, Organization of the Army under the act of March 3, 1815.

regiment, and a cavalry regiment would be formed. The Regiment of Light Artillery had 799 men while the Corps of Artillery had 3,944 men.

By the act of 3 March 1815 the rank of ensign and its counterpart, the rank of cornet, were eliminated from the army. Under the act of 2 March 1821, the rank of 3rd lieutenant was eliminated although this rank was brought back for one year in 1832.[309]

The Military Districts [310]

In June 1810, the army divided the country into two military sections called the Northern Department and the Southern Department. On 19 March 1813 the War Department re-divided the country into nine military districts in which the army was to operate. Each military district was the responsibility of a general officer who had under his control various infantry regiments and supporting artillery, dragoons, rifle and rangers units as needed. The various state and territorial militia within each district would also be a part of this command structure.

The purpose of these districts was to have an organized defense for each area of the country. On 2 July 1814 the secretary of war created a tenth district centering on Washington, D.C., and the surrounding area. This district would be short-lived, and would be eliminated in January 1815.

Following is a list of the military districts and the states, districts and territories assigned to each military district:

1st Military District - Massachusetts, District of Maine, New Hampshire
2nd Military District - Rhode Island, Connecticut
3rd Military District - Lower New York, eastern New Jersey
4th Military District – Western New Jersey, Pennsylvania, Delaware
5th Military District – Maryland, Virginia
6th Military District – North Carolina, South Carolina, Georgia
7th Military District – Louisiana, Tennessee, Territory of Mississippi
8th Military District – Kentucky, Ohio, Territories of Michigan, Indiana, Illinois and Missouri
9th Military District – Upper New York, Vermont
10th Military District - Washington DC, parts of Virginia and Maryland surrounding Washington, DC

These military districts were abolished on 17 May 1815, and ten military departments divided evenly between the North Division and the South Division replaced them.

The Strengths of a Regiment

The army used three basic terms to describe the combat readiness of a regiment. They were the authorized strength, actual strength and effective strength. The effective strength was the most important since this showed the actual number of men who were fit and ready for combat. Congress established the authorized strength of a regiment by limiting the number of men that a regiment could enlist. The actual strength is the number of men who were recruited into a regiment. This strength fluctuated by deaths, transfers, enlistments and discharges.

Musters were used to determine the effective strength of a regiment. These rolls showed the number of men fit for duty against those who were sick, hospitalized, on detached duty, on command duty, on extra service, on furlough, in captivity, missing, deserted or dead. Rarely was the complement of a regiment ever at its authorized strength. Most of the regiments during the war operated at half or even less of their authorized strength.

---

[309] **Ibid**, Volume II, pp. 580-581, Organization of the Army under the act of March 2, 1821, and pp. 582-283, Organization of the Army under the acts of April 2 and June 15 and 28, 1832.

[310] **Records of the United States Army Commands 1784-1821**, Record Group 98.2.2 Records of Military Districts, War of 1812, (National Archives and Records Administration, Washington, D.C.)

The regiments of artillery, rifle and light dragoons never operated as a single unit during the war. The rifle and light dragoons were divided between the three major areas of conflict, the Old Northwest, northern New York and the southwest. The artillery regiments operated as independent companies assigned to each of the major forts and fortifications around the nation. The light artillery regiment operated as an elite infantry regiment.

For the most part, all of the infantry regiments operated as a single unit in all of the commands except in the 8th Military District. With the numerous forts and fortifications stretching across Ohio and the Territories of Indiana, Illinois and Missouri, about half of the companies in each of the eight infantry regiments assigned to the 8th Military District were used to man these facilities.

Conclusion

The War of 1812 was extremely important to the growth and character of the United States Army. The army had entered the conflict as a small, untrained professional army wearing a European style ornamented uniform and using an outdated 1791 French drill manual for training. Within two years the army had turned farm boys into an effective military organization that was beating the British regulars on the battlefields. Many of these British soldiers had over six years of combat experience gained during the Napoleonic Wars, and most of them were career soldiers.

The war was also a real boost for the U.S. Military Academy, which had only been commissioning officers only since 1802.[311] This was the academy's first real test as a military institution, and it passed with flying colors. By the time the war had started most of these graduates were junior officers in the army's regiments. Since the early academy was primarily an engineering school, many of these young officers served with the engineers or in the artillery corps. A total of 89 men had graduated by the time the war started, and a total of 159 officers had graduated by the end of 1815. The bulk of the new officers entered the artillery profession totaling 105 men while only 25 were engineers. Another 20 men became company grade officers in the infantry.

At the conclusion of the war, the army was once again downsized to a peacetime force. Gone was the ornate uniform, which was replaced by a plainer and simpler design. Gone were the untrained officers and the political appointments. The war forced the academy to turn out more effective officers especially for the infantry.

The revolution may have been the birthplace of the army, but the War of 1812 saw the army mature into adulthood.

---

[311] Heitman, **Historical Register**, volume I, (Genealogical Publishing Company, Baltimore, Maryland: 1994), pp144-145, the military academy.

The Invasion of Upper Canada: Harrison's Amphibious Assault

Major General William Henry Harrison has the distinction of conducting the only successful invasion of Canada by the armed forces of the United States. Other Americans had tried to invade Canada during the Revolutionary War and failed, while some others succeeded for short periods of time during the War of 1812 before they were forced to withdraw. General Harrison captured the Western District of Upper Canada in September-October 1813, and he and his successor held on to this territory until the treaty of peace ending the war restored the boundaries of Canada and the United States to their pre-war national borders.

The Western District of Upper Canada is now in the Canadian province of Ontario. The district comprised of the counties of Essex and Kent, south of the Thames River, between what is now Windsor and just west of London, Ontario. The Americans totally controlled the western half of Essex County along the Detroit River while the rest of this county and Suffolk County became a no man's land between the American and British-Canadian forces. Fort Amherstburg was the main British fort located at the mouth of the Detroit River besides the village of Amherstburg. The Americans called this fort, Fort Malden.

What is unique about his invasion is that General Harrison accomplished this feat with a handful of small lake vessels and approximately 100 large rowboats (called bateaux). The rowboats had been built near Cleveland, Ohio, and they were rowed to what is now Port Clinton, Ohio, a distance of approximately 65 miles. From this point the rowboats were rowed to Put-in-Bay, Ohio, on South Bass Island then to Middle Sister Island in Canada, and finally to a beach called Barclay's Point just south of Amherstburg. With the total distance approaching 120 miles, this makes this invasion one of the greatest amphibious assaults by rowboats ever conducted by the United States, yet it is almost totally forgotten today.

The assumption in most publications on this war is that the naval squadron of Master Commandant Oliver Hazard Perry transported the army across Lake Erie to the shores of Upper Canada. This is true in part for the squadron did carry the army officers, their guests and the friendly Indians, but the enlisted personnel of over 4,000 soldiers rowed behind the squadron in their bateaux. It would have been physically impossible to transfer the entire army in one sailing using the naval squadron. If the squadron had carried the troops, it would have taken days to accomplish this feat and the element of surprise would have been lost after the first landing. Likewise, most of the vessels in the squadron were single decked and if the decks were crowded with men then the vessels' cannons could not have been used in support of this invasion.

Planning for the Invasion

The invasion and capture of Canada had been in the planning stages long before the War of 1812 had even started. The War Department had formed the Army of the Northwest under Brigadier General William Hull in the spring of 1812 centering around one regular army infantry regiment and an Ohio militia brigade. This sizeable force was sufficient enough to capture and hold onto the Western District of Upper Canada long enough until reinforcements arrived from the south.

The expedition under General Hull was a "comedy of errors." The British in Amherstburg had received the news that the United States had declared war against Great Britain before General Hull had been informed. The British captured an American packet boat containing the battle plans, muster rolls, hospital supplies, musical instruments, personal baggage and many other items from the Army of the Northwest.

The American army lacked the proper military intelligence needed to defeat the British. They did not know the enemy's strengths and weaknesses, they did not have strong Indian allies, they did not know the terrain of the Western District of Upper Canada and they did not have the maps needed to carry out a successful invasion. Had the Americans attacked Fort Malden in July 1812 they would have probably defeated the British ending the war in the west a year earlier than what actually happened. General Hull surrendered his army on a British bluff on 16 August 1812. As a result, it would take another year and another army to defeat the British in the west. The British would invest in building a naval squadron in order to control the upper Great Lakes, thereby forcing the Americans into a naval arms race.

General Harrison was chosen to form and lead a new Army of the Northwest in September 1812. He wrote a letter to James Madison, the acting Secretary of War, on 6 January 1813 outlining his three plans for invading Upper Canada.[312] The first plan was totally winter related, and it depended on Lake Erie being frozen over with ice solid enough so that an army could walk across the surface of the lake to attack Fort Amherstburg from the south.

His second plan mirrored General Hull's disastrous attempt to take Fort Amherstburg six months earlier. This time General Harrison would throw more men, supplies and provisions into the attempt. Once at Fort Detroit, the force would build boats in order to cross the Detroit River and then attack Fort Amherstburg from the north.

The third plan was to build a naval force capable of taking control of the Upper Great Lakes and large enough to transport his army across the lake with all of its supplies and provisions. The general felt that it would probably be more cost effective to transport the supplies and provisions on the lake rather than to try to bring these items across the muddy roads of Ohio. The army would land on the north shore below Fort Amherstburg and then commence operations against both this fort and Fort Detroit.

After the conquest of lower Michigan and Canada's Western District by the American army, the combined army-navy force would then sail north into Lake Huron and attack Fort Mackinaw. The force would then take control of both the entrances to Lake Michigan and Lake Superior cutting off the British re-supply route to the upper Mississippi River valley where the British army still had control.

The first plan failed to materialize after General Harrison sent a small military expedition across the lake in early 1813 in order to attack and destroy the British warships while the ships were in their winter quarters at Amherstburg. The expedition had to returned to Fort Meigs in Ohio after finding open water in the middle of the lake. This plan was then abandoned. It should be noted that in an age when most armies went into winter quarters, General Harrison's army operated throughout the winter of 1812-1813.

The problem with the second plan was that the army's main supply line was still crossing the swamplands in northwestern Ohio and that this road would only be opened during certain times of the year. Another road would be built farther east connecting Franklinton (Columbus), Ohio, and Fort Stephenson, near the lake. The military force would also be in greater risk of Indian attacks and the element of surprise would be gone because the British would most likely have known when the Americans were coming. This plan would still be an option if the United States did not gain control of Lake Erie.

British intelligence would have known when General Harrison's army was on the move, and the British army would have been waiting for the Americans at either the River Raisin or at Brownstown in the Territory of Michigan. To the west of the British lines would have been a sizeable force of Indians and on the east would be the British naval squadron in the Detroit River, both ready for a battle. If General Harrison had won this hypothetical battle during his land invasion, it would have been a costly victory.

The new Secretary of War John Armstrong had decided in early 1813 that Cleveland, Ohio, was the best place to launch an invasion of Upper Canada. The boats for this invasion would be built in this village and military supplies would be delivered from Pittsburgh, Pennsylvania. There was an improved road between Cleveland and Pittsburgh, which could accommodate the transfer of the large quantity of supplies and materiel needed for the invasion. He recommended that all of the troops, provisions, artillery and stores currently within the Army of the Northwest should be moved to Cleveland. This all hinged on when the American naval squadron gained control of Lake Erie.

---

[312] Knopf, Richard C., **Document Transcriptions of the War of 1812 in the Northwest, Volume I, Harrison and the War of 1812,** (Anthony Wayne Parkway Board, Columbus, Ohio: 1957), pp. 69-73, letter from Major General Harrison to acting Secretary of War James Monroe.

Only the two American brigs, the *Niagara* and the *Lawrence*, would have sleeping quarters built within their hulls. The other ships of the squadron only had a main deck and a cargo hole. The schooners and sloops built on the Great Lakes during this period traveled only during daylight hours. All cooking and sleeping were done at stops along the shoreline of the lakes.

The ships of the naval squadron could not accommodate nor would even have been able to carry the 4,500 men in the invasion force. The ships, however, would carry the officers, senior enlisted and guests including the Indians during the actual invasion while the enlisted men rowed across the lake in rowboats that would be built in Cleveland. Leaving Cleveland as the secretary suggested would force the enlisted personnel to row an additional 65 miles to the Lake Erie islands and from there row another 50 miles to the British side of the lake.

In a letter to General Harrison, dated 5 March 1813,[313] Secretary Armstrong said, "What remains for us to do is, to keep our present ground till the lake opens, and then to approach our object [Fort Malden] by water, and under convoy of the vessels of war building at Presque Isle. There will be afloat and ready to operate by the middle of May. By the same time boats for the transportation of the troops, a train of artillery, baggage, etc. may be constructed. Cleveland is believed to be the place best fitted for this purpose. It will also be made the depot for the troops to be employed on the expedition."

The secretary then wrote to Captain Thomas Sidney Jesup of the 19th Regiment of U.S. Infantry on 9 March 1813 appointing him to command the invasion operations in Cleveland.[314] The secretary told Jesup that; "the Government have the intention of building a number of boats on Lake Erie, for the purpose of transporting the troops on that lake. Cleveland is the point farthest west, where any portion of these can be made with sufficient expedition. If the whole could be made there the better. These boats will be of the kind known by the name of Schenectady boats, narrow, and sharp a-head, and flat-bottomed. They will carry from forty to fifty men each, with their baggage, arms, and accoutrements, and provision for the voyage. It is proposed to commit the superintendence of this service to you, and to bestow upon you, pro hac vice (SIC), the staff appointment of Deputy Quartermaster General. If workmen cannot be found at Cleveland and other places on the lake, you will take them from Pittsburg. Such materials as you may want, other than those produced by the country itself, you will provide at Pittsburg, and have sent on without delay." Jesup would be promoted to rank of major in the following month.

General Harrison wrote back to the Secretary of War on 17 March 1813 objecting to the secretary's invasion plan.[315] He stated that although the plan was sound, but if the naval squadron could not gain control of the lake then his army would be in the wrong place for a land invasion. The general had already been assembling troops and materiel for the invasion at Fort Meigs, and they were in better position to march towards Fort Detroit at this location instead of from Cleveland.

The general was already having boats built on the Auglaize River and the St. Mary's River in western Ohio, and these boats would be floated down to the Maumee River and then to Fort Meigs to take on the artillery, heavy baggage, material and provisions for the invading army. By March 1813, the general's personal invasion plan was already in motion.

The secretary countered the general's objections in a letter dated 8 May 1813, and he laid out a compromise.[316] He said, "I never meant that you, or your artillery, or stores for the campaign, now collected at Fort Meigs, should be brought back to Cleveland for embarkation. My intention was that the boats built there should move along the coast, in the wake of the fleet, to Sandusky, or to the very foot of the rapids, if that were practicable and expedient, taking in, on the route, what was wanted. The boats

---

[313] **American State Papers,** Documents, Legislative and Executive, of the Congress of the United States, 1789-1819, (Washington, D.C.: Gales and Seaton, 1832), Military Affairs, Correspondence between the Secretary of War and Major General Harrison, 5 March 1813, page 452.

[314] **Ibid**, 9 March 1813, page 452.

[315] **Ibid**, Correspondences between Major General Harrison and the Secretary of War, 17 March 1813, pp. 452-453.

[316] **Ibid**, Correspondences between the Secretary of War and Major General Harrison, 8 May 1813, page 454.

being built by Major Jesup are not decked, but strong and high sided, and very competent to the navigation of the lake, particularly between the chain of islands and the west shore."

The troop staging area for the invasion of Upper Canada was then moved west from Cleveland to Fort Meigs, Fort Seneca, Fort Ball and Fort Stephenson in the north central sector of Ohio. Cleveland would remain as the center for staging military supplies and for the building of the transports.

Preparing for the invasion

Secretary Armstrong wrote to Major Jesup on 6 March 1813 stating that $10,000 had been deposited in Pittsburgh for the purchasing and building of boats on Lake Erie and that more money was available if he needed it.[317] On 27 March 1813 Major Jesup wrote to the secretary asking for regular troops to protect Cleveland and the Grand River, just east of Cleveland.[318] He said, "The enemy could easily land and destroy the transports before a militia force sufficient to repel him could be collected." He also stated that he had found a contractor who could build 65 boats for $125 a piece. By 24 May 1813 there were three boat yards established, and twenty-six boats had been constructed.

Two companies of soldiers from the 19th Regiment of U.S. Infantry were sent to Cleveland.[319] An artillery company from the 2nd Regiment of U.S. Artillery was assigned to Cleveland during the spring of 1813 and two additional infantry companies from the 27th Regiment of U.S. Infantry were also sent to Cleveland.

By July 1st Major Jesup had 70 boats finished, and he expected to have between 80-90 boats completed the by the fifteenth.[320] By 15 July 1813, 77 boats had been built and 69 accepted by the government.[321] Major Jesup informed the Secretary of War that "Gen'l Harrison set out for Lower Sandusky to day. He has ordered all my transports thither, where, I understand the army is concentrating. I shall have a sufficient number of transports for from three to four thousand men." Seventy-eight (78) boats had been inspected and received by 1 August 1813.[322]

---

[317] "Letter from the Secretary of War John Armstrong to Captain Thomas S. Jesup," 6 March 1813, Special Collections, Orrin W. June War of 1812 Collection, Document Number 29, Oberlin College Library, Oberlin, Ohio.

[318] Knopf, Richard C., **Document Transcriptions of the War of 1812 in the Northwest, Volume VII Part 1, Letters to the Secretary of War 1812 Relating to the War of 1812 in the Northwest,** (Anthony Wayne Parkway Board, Ohio State Museum, Columbus, Ohio: 1957), page 198, Captain Jesup to the Secretary of War John Armstrong, 27 March 1813.

[319] **Ibid,** Volume VII, part 2, Letters from the Secretary of War 1812 & 1813 Relating to the War of 1812 in the Northwest, (Ohio Historical Society: Columbus, Ohio: 1961), page 139, Major Jesup to Secretary of War, 24 May 1813.

[320] **Ibid,** Volume, VII Part 3, **Letters to the Secretary of War 1812 Relating to the War of 1812 in the Northwest,** (Anthony Wayne Parkway Board, Ohio State Museum, Columbus, Ohio: 1957), page 2, Major Jesup to the Secretary of War, 1 July 1813.

[321] **Ibid,** Volume VII, Part 1, **Letters to the Secretary of War 1812 Relating to the War of 1812 in the Northwest,** (Anthony Wayne Parkway Board, Ohio State Museum, Columbus, Ohio: 1957), Captain Jesup to the Secretary of War John Armstrong, 15 July 1813.

[322] **Ibid,** Volume VII, Part 3, **Letters to the Secretary of War 1812 Relating to the War of 1812 in the Northwest,** (Anthony Wayne Parkway Board, Ohio State Museum, Columbus, Ohio: 1957), page 51, Captain Jesup to the Secretary of War John Armstrong, 1 August 1813.

Obtaining the provisions

General Harrison ordered 200,000 rations on 18 August 1813 from Major Peter G. Voorhies, the agent for the military contractor of Benjamin G. Orr and Aaron Greely.[323] The rations were to be used to feed the troops during the invasion of Upper Canada, and the rations were to be prepared in northern Ohio with Cleveland as the principal site to store the rations until they were transported to western Ohio.

Greely wrote back to General Harrison on 25 August 1813 stating that his firm can meet the deadline for delivering the rations but that he will fall short by 30,000 rations of salted pork.[324] He then asked the general if he could substitute the salted pork with salted beef. Greely further wrote that he had contracted some local bakers to produce 50,000 biscuits, which would keep for a year.

The contractors assembled at Cleveland 513 barrels of pork, 761 barrels of flour, 1,933 gallons of whiskey, 2,000 pounds of soap, 350 pounds of candles, 1,100 gallons of vinegar and 65 barrels of salt.[325] Deposited at the mouth of the Huron, Grand and Vermilion Rivers in northern Ohio were an additional 31 barrels of pork, 202 barrels of flour, 3,066 gallons of whiskey, and 10 barrels of salt.

The Invasion Force

For nearly a year, General Harrison had been raising a sizeable military force made up of regular soldiers, volunteer militia and state militia. The general divided his regular army into two brigades and a legion of mixed troops. The first brigade was under command of Brigadier General Duncan McArthur, and it consisted of the 17th, 19th and 24th Regiments of U.S. Infantry. This brigade was stationed at Fort Meigs. The second brigade under Brigadier General Lewis Cass was stationed at Fort Stephenson, Fort Ball, and Fort Seneca. The 26th, 27th and 28th Regiments of U.S. Infantry formed this brigade.

Lieutenant Colonel James V. Ball would command the legion made up of the all non-infantry troops. Included in this legion were Colonel Ball's squadron from the 2nd Regiment of U.S. Light Dragoons (dismounted), two companies from the 2nd Regiment of U.S. Artillery, and a battalion of riflemen made up of the Chillicothe Guards and the Petersburg Volunteers (Virginia) from the U.S. Voluntary Corps. A battalion of riflemen from the 1st Regiment of U.S. Rifles was scheduled to participate in this invasion, but they arrived too late and were instead used as occupation troops at Amherstburg. There was also a force of 260 friendly Wyandot, Shawnee and Seneca Indians attached to Ball's legion.[326]

The cavalry arm of the army consisted of Colonel Richard M. Johnson's Kentucky Mounted Volunteer Regiment and Captain John Payne's Light Dragoons Troops, both from the U.S. Voluntary Corps.[327] These troops were billeted near Fort Meigs.

The state militia forces consisted of six-month militia from Kentucky, Pennsylvania, and Ohio. There were 11 regiments of Kentuckians organized into five brigades under the command of Governor Isaac Shelby of Kentucky as an acting major general. This force of over 4,000 men was camped near Fort Stephenson.

---

[323] **American State Papers**, Documents, Legislative and Executive, of the Congress of the United States, 1789-1819, (Washington, D.C.: Gales and Seaton, 1832), Military Affairs, Correspondences between Major General Harrison and Major Peter G. Voorhies, 18 August 1813, page 653.

[324] **Ibid**, Correspondences between Aaron Greely and Major General Harrison, 25 August 1813, page 653.

[325] **Ibid**, Return of provision now deposited at different places on the shores of Lake Erie, for the use of the northwestern army, by Benjamin G. Orr and Aaron Greely, contractors, 25 August 1813, page 654.

[326] Lossing, Benson J., **The Pictorial Field-Book of the War of 1812**, (New York, New York: Harper and Brothers, Publishers, 1869), Chapter XXVI, Harrison's Invasion of Canada.

[327] Quisenberry, Anderson Chenault, **Kentucky in the War of 1812**, (Frankfort, Kentucky: The Kentucky Historical Society, 1915), Johnson's Regiment, Kentucky Mounted Volunteer Infantry, pp. 185-186.

The 147th Pennsylvania Militia Regiment[328] was under the command of Colonel Rees Hill. This was a provisional regiment made up of militiamen mainly from western Pennsylvania who initially helped guard the naval facility at Erie, Pennsylvania. Thirty-five militiamen from this regiment were on detached duty with the Lake Erie naval squadron of which 15 men participated in the Battle of Lake Erie.[329]

The regiment was ordered to Cleveland, and they helped bring the approximately 100 boats that were built at Cleveland for the invasion of Upper Canada to the mouth of the Portage River in western Ohio. The regiment refused to participate in the invasion of Upper Canada citing their rights under the federal Militia Act of 1792 of only serving within the borders of the United States. However, one officer and eleven men did volunteer, and they joined the invasion force.[330] The regiment was then used to guard the British naval prisoners that were being moved to Camp Bull in Chillicothe, Ohio, and later they were used as occupation troops at Detroit.

The Ohio militia was not invited to participate in General Harrison's party, however, depending on the source. There were approximately six thousand troops at Upper Sandusky waiting to be called into action. These militiamen had responded to help lift the second siege of Fort Meigs, but they had arrived too late to be of any aid. The militiamen continued to pour into Upper Sandusky during the summer months.

On August 29th all except 2,000 men were released from duty and sent home. The others were kept for 40 days longer. This force encamped about a mile north of Fort Ferree, which is in present day Upper Sandusky, Ohio. This encampment was called the "Grand Camp of the Ohio Militia." Another brigade of Ohioans was called into play and they replaced the regular army troops at the four main forts in northern Ohio.

The Invasion is on

General Harrison's invasion plan was one of the most ambitious invasion plans ever designed by the U.S. military up until this time. The outcome of a successful invasion and the annihilation of the British forces during the recapture of the Territory of Michigan and the capture of the lower part of Upper Canada. It would force many of the warring Indian tribes to sue for peace, secure the former Northwest Territory for the United States, and force the British to withdraw from the upper Mississippi valley. Finally, a victory would place a sizeable American army behind the right wing of the British army in eastern Upper Canada jeopardizing the British hold on all of Upper Canada.

However, the whole scenario depended on whether or not the U.S. Navy could gain and keep control of the upper Great Lakes. Had the U.S. Navy been defeated at the Battle of Lake Erie, a land invasion could have occurred only if the navy had inflicted serious enough damage on the British forcing them to retire to Amherstburg after the battle. A water invasion would need most of the navy vessels intact in order to transport the supplies and provide gun support for the landing.

As it turned out, the Battle of Lake Erie was a brilliant victory for a young master commandant. The victory temporarily put out of commission the flagship *Lawrence* and two of the largest British vessels. The combined squadron of the U.S. and former British vessels were significant enough to support the invasion.

Once the American naval squadron arrived in western Ohio, the general met with Master Commandant Perry in Sandusky Bay to finalize the invasion plan, and then the general ordered the mobilization of

---

[328] Montgomery, Thomas Lynch, **Pennsylvania Archives**, 6th Series, Volume VIII, (Harrisburg Publishing Company, State Printers, Harrisburg, Pennsylvania: 1907), Pennsylvania Volunteers, War of 1812-1814 Soldiers, Part I, Troops commanded by Colonel Rees Hill, pp. 45-135.

[329] Altoff, Gerald T., **Deep Water Sailors, Shallow Water Soldiers, Manning the United States Fleet on Lake Erie – 1813**, (The Perry Group, Put-in-Bay, Ohio: 1993), Chapter I Eastern Lake Erie, pp. 15-16.

[330] Montgomery, Thomas Lynch, **Pennsylvania Archives**, 6th Series, Volume VIII, (Harrisburg Publishing Company, State Printers, Harrisburg, Pennsylvania: 1907), Pennsylvania Volunteers, War of 1812-1814 Soldiers, Part I, Troops commanded by Colonel Rees Hill, pp. 136-137.

troops and supplies to the two staging areas for the invasion, Fort Meigs and the mouth of the Portage River. The invasion plan had been set into motion.

General Harrison's invasion routes

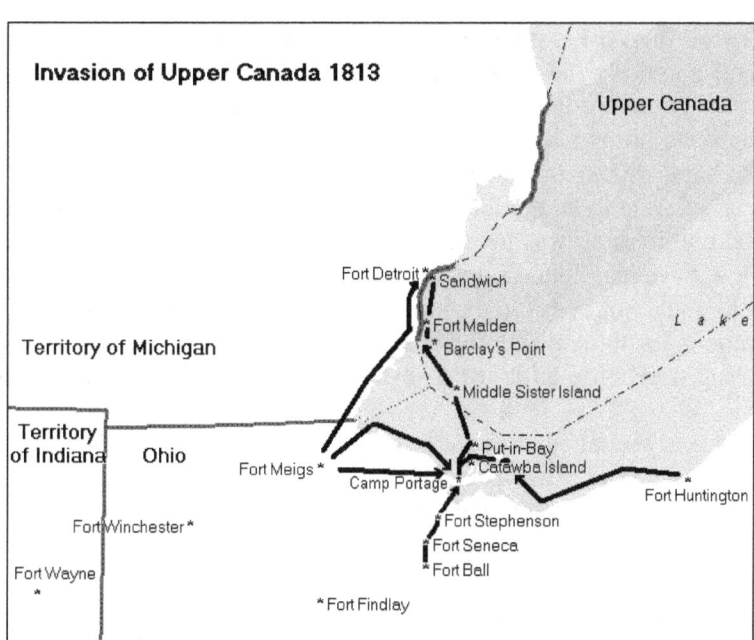

This map shows the invasion routes of the Army of the Northwest in September 1813. All troops, supplies, boats and provisions were ordered to Camp Portage (now Port Clinton, Ohio) and then they were transported to Put-in-Bay from which the invasion was launched. Colonel Johnson and his mounted troops left Fort Meigs and headed north towards Fort Detroit.

Captain Stanton Sholes of the 2nd Regiment of U.S. Artillery, stationed at Cleveland, received his marching orders from General Harrison on 8 September 1813 two days before the Battle of Lake Erie occurred.[331] Captain Sholes along with his artillery company was ordered to bring all of his boats and stores to Fort Meigs to obtain their cannons and ammunition. The rest of the regular forces and the Pennsylvania militia regiment would take their boats and provisions to the mouth of the Portage River.

The captain left with his command on the eleventh and arrived at Fort Meigs late the next day. In the meantime, the troops stationed at the four forts in northern Ohio started to move down to the Portage River and on the 13th of September then began to cross over to Put-in-Bay on South Bass Island. The transfer of the troops, supplies, and provisions would be completed on September 20th.

General Harrison arrived at the mouth of the Portage River on September 13th along with part of General Cass's brigade.[332] Camp Portage was constructed at the mouth of the river to accommodate the billeting of troops and the storage of supplies and rations. General Cass arrived with the remainder of his brigade on September 15th. Governor Isaac Shelby along with his Kentucky militia arrived at the camp on the same day. Two days later General McArthur arrived with his brigade from Fort Meigs.

---

[331] **The Mississippi Valley Historical Review**, Volume XV, Number 4, March 1929, Mississippi Valley Historical Association, Lincoln, Nebraska, pp. 519-525, A Narrative of the Northwestern Campaign on 1813 by Stanton Sholes.

[332] Knopf, Richard C., **Letters to the Secretary of War 1812 Relating to the War of 1812 in the Northwest,** volume VII, (Columbus, Ohio: Ohio Historical Society, 1961), page 952, letters from Harrison to Armstrong, 15 September 1813.

Colonel Johnson had been ordered to take his mounted regiment from Fort Meigs to Detroit on September 26th.[333] The 1,200-man force would also take four 6-pound cannons with them. This regiment would travel north paralleling the invasion force on the lake. Colonel Johnson's mission was to engage any enemy forces at either the River Raisin or at Frenchtown and then to form a battle line just south of Detroit to prevent the enemy from escaping from Detroit when the main body from the Army of the Northwest attacked Detroit from the east after crossing the Detroit River.

The American naval gunboats, the *Somers,* the *Porcupine* and the *Tigress* arrived at Fort Meigs on September 18th, and they began loading military stores on board. The vessels' mission was to carry the extra arms, ammunition and military supplies for the army. The *Porcupine* and the *Tigress* would later follow the Army of the Northwest as they made their way up the Thames River in Upper Canada.

Put-in-Bay had been selected to be the forward operating base for both the army and the navy. Due to conditions on the lake, the invasion was not able to begin until September 26th. The time was spent on training the men on how to embark and disembark from the boats in battle order. Much of the regimental and personal equipment could not be taken during the invasion. Every man carried what he needed in his backpack including rations for three days. The rest of the items including the regimental pots, pans and tents were stored in a log warehouse built at Put-in-Bay during the six days that the invasion force spent on the island.

The *Lawrence* was quickly repaired after the Battle of Lake Erie and then loaded with the sick and the wounded from the squadron before it was sent to Erie, Pennsylvania.[334] The vessel arrived at this port on September 23rd. The British ships *Detroit* and the *Queen Charlotte* had lost their masts and remained at Put-in-Bay during the invasion. These three vessels would not participate in the invasion of Upper Canada.

On September 26th the largest American fleet used during the War of 1812 left Put-in-Bay for Middle Sister Island. The fleet total 116 vessels and over 5,000 men made up of the combined American-British naval squadrons and the 100 bateaux of General Harrison's transport squadron.[335] Middle Sister Island was just south of Amherstburg on the Canadian side of Lake Erie. The invasion force spent the night on this Canadian soil. The fleet left the island the next day at 10 a.m. and arrived just south of Amherstburg at 5:30 p.m.

The Battle Orders

The initial invasion plans had been drawn up by Major Eleazer Derby Wood of the U.S. Army Corps of Engineers, a West Point graduate. General McArthur would be in charge of the land forces, both regular and militia, while Major Wood would be the beach master. Major Wood's responsibilities included the offloading of both troops and supplies onto the beach. His main job was to get the supplies off the vessels and to deliver the supplies where they were needed by the troops.

The troops would land in three waves with the regular forces on the left wing and the Kentucky militia on the right wing.[336] Colonel Ball's legion would be the first wave of troops whose mission was to secure and hold the beach for the second wave. Once the legion had landed, the volunteer riflemen would swing right and establish a skirmish line on the other side of the sand dunes. Colonel Ball's dismounted light

---

[333] **McAfee, Robert Breckinridge McAfee Papers, 1813-1859,** A\M113, Journal of Captain McAfee's Mounted Company from 18 May 1813 to 21 May 1814, Filson Historical Society, Louisville, Kentucky.

[334] Dodge, Robert J., **The Battle of Lake Erie**, (Fostoria, Ohio: The Gray Printing Company, 1979), page 31, Transporting Harrison's Army.

[335] Brown, Samuel R., **Views of the Campaigns of the North-Western Army,** (Philadelphia, Pennsylvania: Griggs and Dickinsons, Printers, 1815), page 60.

[336] **William Henry Harrison's Battle Orders,** Filson Special Collections, Henry Family Papers, Filson Historical Society, Louisville, Kentucky.

dragoons would swing left and establish another skirmish line. A company of artillery with three pieces would form on the beach in order to provide fire support for the skirmish lines. The artillery consisted of a 4-pound cannon, a 6-pound cannon and a howitzer.

The First Invasion Wave

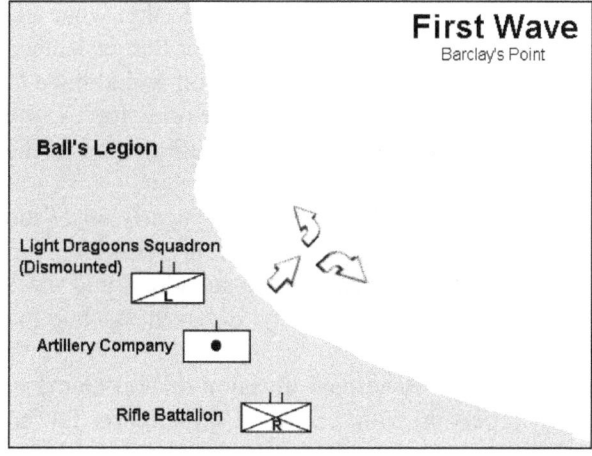

Colonel Ball's legion was the first American unit to land on the beach, where they established a skirmish line to protect the second wave when they landed.

The Second Invasion Wave

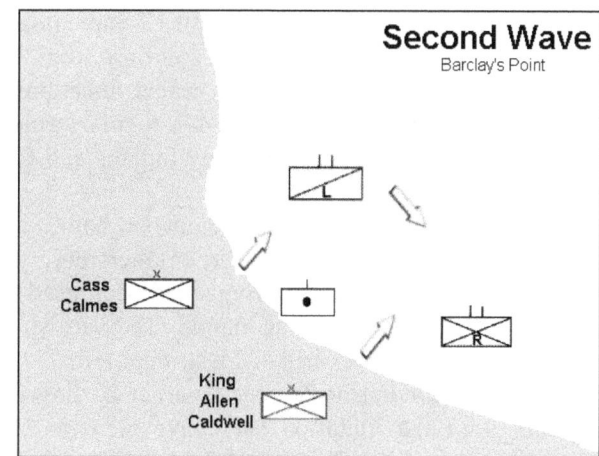

Once the regular army brigade under General Cass formed up on the beach they moved north. Colonel Ball's light dragoons (dismounted) withdrew towards the rear.

The Third Invasion Wave

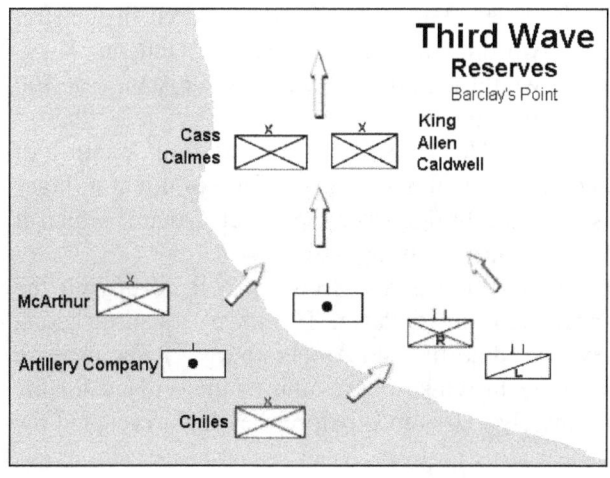

Symbols

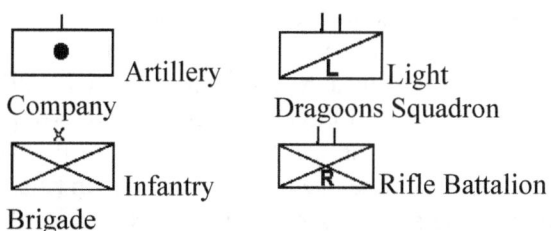

After the beach was secured, then the second wave would land on the beach. General Cass's regular brigade, once on shore, would form into battle lines ready to engage the British regulars while Brigadier General Marquis Calmes' Kentucky militia brigade would position themselves to engage any Indian or militia force. Governor Shelby would then lead the brigades of Brigadier Generals George King, James Allen and Samuel Caldwell of the Kentucky militia onto the beaches.

The third wave would be the reserve wave, which could be used any where along the beach. They could land behind the second wave or in a flanking move, land behind any British opposition. This wave consisted of General McArthur's regular brigade and Brigadier General David Chiles' Kentucky militia brigade. Also in this wave was the remaining regular artillery company with their cannons.

The Invasion

Before the Battle of Lake Erie, on 10 September 1813, General Harrison fully believed that when his invasion force landed on Canadian soil they would be met with fierce resistance. Whether that resistance would be during the water landing near Amherstburg or south of Detroit in a land invasion would have to play out. Although he knew that his regular army troops outnumbered the British regular forces, the deciding factor would be how many Indians and Canadian militia troops the British could muster in the defense of the Western District.

Once the smoke cleared after the naval battle, it was found that the British had used nearly all of the cannons at Fort Detroit and Fort Amherstburg in order to arm the naval squadron. Also, a good percentage of British regular troops had been used as sailors and marines to man the squadron, and these men were now in American hands. The British western frontier was virtually defenseless, but the remaining British forces still had a stringer left.

Master Commandant Perry had earlier in the year participated in American invasion of Fort Georgia, Canada, on Lake Ontario. This gave General Harrison a person with excellent experience for an amphibious assault. The general's invasion plans called for a naval officer, appointed by Master Commandant Perry, to be in charge of the actual landing.[337] The naval squadron would also provide firepower support during the landing.

The first and second waves landed without any opposition. With the Battle of Amherstburg never materializing, the third wave landed behind the second wave. Most of the supplies were left aboard the vessels and bateaux as they were not needed during the beach assault. The vessels unloaded their cargo at Amherstburg and Detroit once these ports were secured.

The Army of the Northwest formed up into two lines for the march to Amherstburg. The first line consisted of General McArthur's and General Calmes' brigades. The second line consisted of General Cass' brigade and General Chiles' brigade. Following the two lines were the brigades of Generals King, Allen and Caldwell in a single line. Colonel Ball's legion would lead the columns by a distance of 300 yards in a skirmish formation. Major Woods would control the movement of the artillery.

At 7:30 p.m. on 27 September 1813 the Army of the Northwest arrived and took control of Amherstburg. Phase one of the invasion plan had been completed without the loss of life or direct military action. General Cass's brigade was ordered north to secure the bridge over the River Canard, which it succeeded in capturing as the retreating British forces tried to burn the bridge.

The next day the Army of the Northwest moved into position across from Detroit occupying the former British artillery battery located at Sandwich, now Windsor, Ontario. The naval squadron along with the rowboats had paralleled the army forces as they moved north from Amherstburg. The boats were now used to ferry the regular troops over to Detroit in order to retake possession of this village for the United States. The British had burnt the fort and approximately 150 homes before they had evacuated the village. Phase two of the invasion was now complete.

On 30 September 1813, Colonel Johnson and his mounted troops arrived at Detroit, and the next day they crossed over into Canada.[338] General Harrison would lead his Kentucky troops, Colonel Johnson's mounted infantry, a company of regular soldiers and the friendly Indians up the Thames River valley

---

[337] **Ibid**.

[338] **McAfee, Robert Breckinridge McAfee Papers, 1813-1859,** A\M113, Journal of Captain McAfee's Mounted Company from 18 May 1813 to 21 May 1814, Filson Historical Society, Louisville, Kentucky.

where, outside of the Moravian Indian village, they would defeat the British at the Battle of the Thames River on 5 October 1813.

Phase three of the battle plan would not take place in 1813. The capturing of Fort Mackinaw would be delayed until the following year, and it would be unsuccessful. The winter season had come early that year ending the sailing season.

Secretary Armstrong in one of the greatest blunders of the war ordered General Harrison and half of his army to New York where they went into winter quarters at Sackets Harbor. General McArthur was placed in command of the remaining troops at Fort Detroit, now called Fort Shelby, and they too went into winter quarters.

Had Secretary Armstrong kept the Army of the Northwest intact, General Harrison could have crossed lower Upper Canada and captured Burlington Heights, the headquarters of the British army in Upper Canada. This would have caused the collapse of the British army positions along the Niagara River and opened the opportunity for an American army to retake York, the capital of Upper Canada. From York, the army could have threatened Kingston, the main British naval base. With the fall of Kingston, Lake Ontario and Upper Canada would have been in American hands.

U.S. Control of Upper Canada

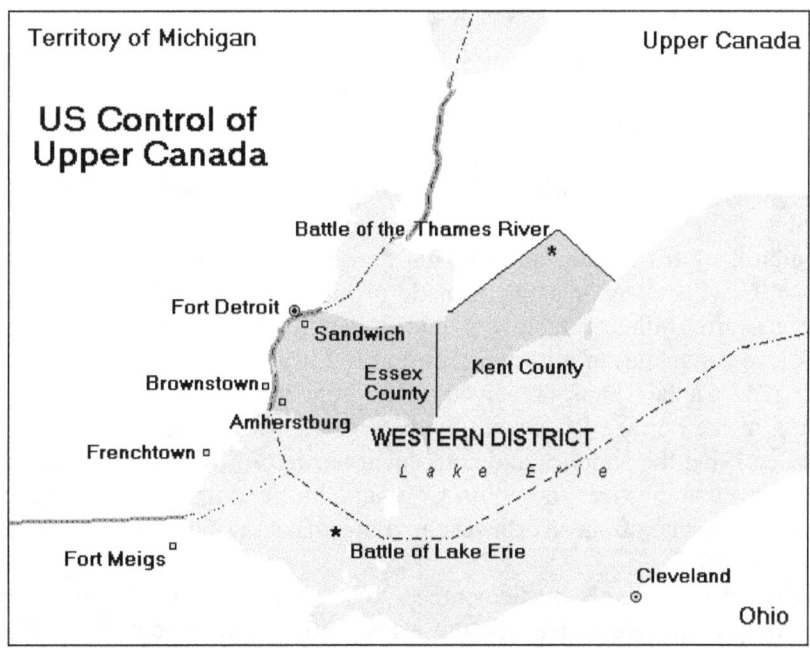

The Army of the Northwest controlled the Western District of Upper Canada from 27 September 1813 until the provisions of the Treaty of Ghent went into effect in July 1815. In the fall of 1813 Brigadier General Lewis Cass was appointed the military governor of the Western District, a position he held until he resigned from the army on 1 May 1814 to become the Territorial Governor of Michigan. He is the first American to have been appointed governor over captured enemy territory.

Captain Stanton Sholes and the Ohio Militia

One of the most touching stories coming out of the War of 1812 was the kindness and humanity that Captain Stanton Sholes showed to a group of Ohio militiamen who were recovering from illnesses and wounds in Cleveland, Ohio, during the spring of 1813.

Stanton Sholes of Beaver County, Pennsylvania, was commissioned a captain in the 2nd Regiment of U.S. Artillery on 2 July 1812, and he was discharged from the U.S. Army on 15 June 1815. He raised his artillery company primarily from Beaver County. On 3 May 1812, he was ordered to take his company to Cleveland, Ohio, as part of the defensive force being formed for this village. His company arrived in Cleveland on May 10th.

In a letter to the Cuyahoga County Historical Society, dated July 1858, Sholes stated, "At my arrival I found a number of sick and wounded who were of Hull's surrender, sent from Detroit, and more coming. These were crowded into a log cabin, and no one to care for them. I sent one or two of my soldiers to take care of them, as they had no friends. I had two or three good carpenters in my company, and set them to work to build a hospital. I very soon got up a good one, thirty by twenty feet, smoothly and tightly covered, and floored with chestnut bark, with two tier or bunks around the walls, with doors and windows, and not a nail, a screw, or iron latch or hinge about the building. Its cost to the Government was a few extra rations. In a short time I had all the bunks well strawed and the sick and wounded good and clean, to their great joy and comfort, but some had fallen asleep."

The captain had been tasked by the army to build a fortification in Cleveland, but he took the time to have his company take care of a group of Ohio militiamen who had been left behind in Cleveland after Brigadier General William Hull had surrendered his army to the British the year before. The British had paroled the Ohio militiamen, and they were released at Cleveland. These militiamen had been forgotten for nearly a year, and they were probably only surviving because of the kindness and generosity of the people of Cleveland.

The captain then built a fortified stockade on a bluff overlooking Lake Erie just north of Public Square in today's downtown Cleveland. A breastwork made of logs was placed in front of the fort facing the lake. The fort and a nearby billeting facility would house Stanton's company and four companies of regular infantry and two companies of militiamen during 1813.

On 8 September 1813 Captain Sholes received orders from Major General William Henry Harrison to proceed to the mouth of the Portage River with the bateaux (rowboats) that had been built in Cleveland. The boats would be carrying the supplies and equipment needed for the invasion of Upper Canada. The fleet of small boats arrived at the river (now Port Clinton, Ohio) and then the next day the bateaux began task of transporting the Army of the Northwest to Put-in-Bay, South Bass Island. The transfer was completed on September 20th.

The army then rowed the bateaux on September 26th to Middle Sister Island where they spent the night. The next morning the rowboat fleet left the island and landed three miles south of Amherstburg, Upper Canada. On the 29th the American naval squadron arrived at Detroit, and part of the U.S. Army occupied the fort and that village while the remaining troops secured the Canadian shore.

After the Battle of the Thames, Captain Sholes' company was stationed in Detroit until the end of the war. The company's first task was to rebuild the fort and to re-install the cannons that the British had used from the fort to gun their naval squadron. The fort had been burnt to the ground by the British army when the evacuated the Territory of Michigan. The new fort was named Fort Shelby after the governor of Kentucky.

U.S. Schooner Ohio

One of the least known and almost totally forgotten naval vessels of the War of 1812 was the U.S. Schooner *Ohio*. This warship served in Master Commandant Oliver H. Perry's Lake Erie squadron but she was on a re-supply mission when the Battle of Lake Erie occurred on 10 September 1813. Less than a year later the *Ohio* would be captured by the British and renamed the H.M. Schooner *Huron*.

The *Ohio* was built in Cleveland, Ohio, in 1810 as a merchant schooner of 60 tons. She was purchased by the United States Navy in 1812 and converted to a warship by Henry Eckford at the Black Rock Naval Yard outside of Buffalo, New York. The *Ohio* was commissioned in the navy prior to 13 June 1813. The schooner was part of what is known as the "Black Rock Fleet." Five vessels were outfitted at this naval base in 1812-1813. Besides the *Ohio*, three other schooners were purchased and refitted. These ships were the *Somers*, the *Tigress* and the *Trippe*. The fifth vessel was the *Caledonia,* which had been captured from the British on 8 October 1812.

The *Ohio's* tonnage was increased to 62 tons during the conversion. She was armed similarly as the *Trippe* with a 24-pound long cannon on a pivot mount so that the weapon could be fired from either side of the ship. The cannon fired a 5.82 inch ball. Sailing Master Daniel Dobbins was her captain and she had a crew of 35 men. A schooner is a sailing vessel with two masts rigged with triangular sails in front of and in back of each mast.

The five ships remained at Black Rock through the early part of June 1813 because of the British blockade at the mouth of the Niagara River. Fort Erie on the British side of the river had prevented the American ships from entering Lake Erie. Under the cover of darkness and fog Master Commandant Perry had the five ships towed to Lake Erie where the vessels set sail on June 15th for the Erie Naval Yard at Erie, Pennsylvania, and they joined the rest of the Lake Erie Naval Squadron.

The summer months were spent patrolling the waters of Lake Erie keeping an eye on the British squadron and waiting for the brigs *Niagara* and *Lawrence* to be finished. The brigs were brought over the sand bars near the port of Erie on August 4th and the final outfitting of these two vessels began. On 16 August 1813 the American squadron set sail for Sandusky Bay in western Ohio so that Master Commandant Perry could meet with Major General William H. Harrison, the commander of the Army of the Northwest. There the two men planned for the destruction of the British naval squadron and for the invasion of Upper Canada.

While the squadron headed for the Canadian side of the lake to challenge the British squadron, the *Ohio* set sail for the Erie Naval Yard on August 17th to take on provisions and stores for the other ships. She returned to the squadron on September 3rd and immediately set sail once again for the naval yard. Three days after the Battle of Lake Erie, the *Ohio* entered Put-in-Bay, South Bass Island, with sorely needed meat and fresh vegetables thus missing the famous battle, both squadrons (now one) were anchored off Put-in-Bay.

The *Ohio* probably participated in the invasion of Upper Canada on September 27th as part of the invasion fleet made up of the undamaged ships of the Lake Erie squadron and approximately 100 bateaux which carried the 4,500 men of General Harrison's army to the shores of Canada. The bateaux were flat-bottom boats, which could carry 40-50 men with three days of supplies. It took eight days to row these craft across Lake Erie. These bateaux had been built in Cleveland and rowed to the Lake Erie islands for the invasion.

During the winter of 1813-1814 the *Detroit* and the *Queen Charlotte* were left at Put-in-Bay because they still hadn't been totally repaired. The *Ariel, Trippe, Chippewa* and *Little Belt* began their wintering at Buffalo, New York. The rest of the fleet including the *Ohio* wintered at the Erie Naval Yard. These ships were the *Niagara, Lawrence, Caledonia, Scorpion, Porcupine, Somers, Tigress, Lady Prevost* and *Hunter*. A British raiding party destroyed the four ships at Buffalo in December 1813.

Once the ice had melted on Lake Erie in early 1814, the *Ohio* began patrolling between Long Point, Upper Canada, and the Erie Naval Yard to intercept any British activities by water. In May she assisted in convoying the *Detroit* and *Queen Charlotte* from Put-in-Bay to the Erie Naval Yard.

During the summer of 1814 the Americans had captured Britain's Fort Erie, across from Buffalo. Throughout August and into September the fort was under siege by the British. The *Ohio*, *Somers* and *Porcupine* had been assigned to give direct firepower support to the fort.

On the night of 11-12 August 1814, a British boarding party of 75 Royal Marines captured the *Ohio* and the *Somers* as they lay anchored off the coast near Fort Erie. The two ships now manned by the British began firing on Fort Erie. The return fire from the fort damaged the *Somers* and set her afire. The ship was abandoned, and she went aground on Grand Island in the Niagara River. The *Porcupine* managed to escape capture and she was forced to fire upon her former sister ships.

The *Porcupine* was armed with a 32-pound cannon on a pivot mount, heavier and more deadly than the *Ohio's* 24-pound cannon. The ship was able to silence the *Ohio's* cannon, but in a freak accident the *Porcupine's* cannon exploded killing one man. The *Ohio*, although damaged, was able to escape to the west. The *Ohio* was now flying the British flag as the H.M. Schooner *Huron*. She served in the British navy until 1817 when she was placed in ordinary (retired from service). The *Somers* was repaired and she served in the British navy until 1817 as the H.M. Schooner *Sauk*.

The naval action on the night of 11-12 August 1814 can be described as the Second Battle of Lake Erie, and it was the last naval battle to be fought on the Great Lakes. Although small in comparison to the first battle the year before, it was a very important battle for the British who were still trying to regain control of the Upper Great Lakes. The Americans lost one seaman killed and three officers and four seamen wounded while the British suffered two men killed and four wounded. The *Ohio* was finally able to fire its gun in anger but sorry to say against her former sister ship.

Bibliography

The Dictionary of American Naval Fighting Ships, volume 5 N-Q, Defense Department Staff, Navy, Naval History Division, (Washington, D.C.: United States Government Printing Office).

Dodge, Robert J., **The Battle of Lake Erie**, (Fostoria, Ohio: The Gray Printing Company, 1977).

List of Vessels Employed on British Naval Service on the Great Lakes, 1755-1875, compiled by Ken R. Macpherson. (originally published in *Ontario History*, volume 55, pp. 173-79), http://www.hhpl.on.ca/GreatLakes/Documents/shiplists/macpherson.htm

Lossing, Benson J., **Pictorial Field-Book of the War of 1812**, Chapter XXVI, Harrison's Invasion of Canada and Chapter XXXVI, War of the Niagara Frontier in 1814, (New York: Harper & Brothers, Publishers, 1868).

Whittlesey, Colonel Charles, **Early History of Cleveland, Ohio**, (Cleveland: Fairbanks, Benedict & Company, 1867), Early Lake Craft, page 461, Schooner Ohio.

How many men served in America's land forces during the War of 1812?

One of the questions that always comes up when discussing the War of 1812 is now many men served in the U.S. Army and the militia during this conflict.

Ancestry.com has a CD containing the index of militiamen who are listed of the muster rolls from this war and it claims that there were approximately 580,000 service records. This represents 580,000 possible militiamen. The actual records are stored at the National Archives in Washington, D.C.

This number of records does not represent the total number of men who served in the militia. Many men served more that once so they would have multiple service records at the archives. These records also contain the names of the men who were drafted and who found a substitute to take their places. Eliminating the extra records of the men who served more than once and those who found substitutes could probably knock off a couple hundred thousand records.

One gauge to determine the number of men who served in the War of 1812 can be found in the three acts of Congress, which authorized the call up of militia forces and the funding of these troops.

Congress created the United States Voluntary Corps under the Act of 6 February 1812. This corps was made up of militiamen who would serve a one-year enlistment with the U.S. Army. These volunteer militiamen were totally under federal control, and they did not report to any state or territorial militia organization. The president had the power to accept 50,000 militiamen into this corps. The Voluntary Corps lasted for two years, and the remaining men after those two years were given the chance to re-enlist in the army as part of the 45th through 48th Regiments of U.S. Infantry.

The second Congressional Act was passed on 10 April 1812, and it authorized the call up militia units based upon a quota of men from each state and territory not to exceed 100,000 militiamen. These militia units were raised by the states and territories, and these governments had limited control over their militia. These militiamen, by law, could serve up to six months with the army.

The final bill, entitled the *Apportionment of a Detachment of 80,000 Militia*, was passed on 12 November 1814. This act replaced the previous act, which authorized the President to call up 100,000 militiamen for service with the army and which had a two-year limitation.

Adding up the number of men authorized by the three acts showed that Congress would only pay the salaries of 230,000 militiamen who were called to duty throughout the entire war. This number seems very low, but it may be closer to the actual figure for those that served.

The Military Policy of the United States by Emory Upton contains the year by year strength reports for the army and the militia during the War of 1812. These records were consolidated from the militia and military records obtained from the War Department, the Auditor's Office and the Pension Office.

The regulars, as the book calls the men who served in the army, totaled 56,032 men who were commissioned or who enlisted in the army. This total also includes the approximately 5,000 sailors and marines who served with the army. The figure leaves out the 3,049 who served with the rangers. The rangers were part of the army but were listed separately in these strength reports. Adding to the total number of men plus the rangers and subtracting the naval personnel leaves 54,081 men who served in the army.

Upton lists 10,110 men serving with the volunteers and 458,463 men serving with the militia for a total of 468,573 in the militia forces. This brings the total number of men who served in the army, the volunteers and the militia during the War of 1812 to 522,654 men.

The second set of figures that Upton provides in his book is the terms of service for the men who served during the war. Those men serving for 12 months or more numbered 63,179. Men serving between six months and a year totaled 66,325. There were 124,643 men who served at least three months. Between one month of service and three months of service were 125,307 men. Finally, 147,200 men served less than one month during the war.

You can not break down these figures of actual military service by men in the army, volunteers or the militia. A good percentage of militiamen where called to duty only to be discharged early after it was determined that they were not needed. Even though the army had a minimum of a one-year enlistment for some regiments, men actually served less than one year if they had been killed or died, or were given medical discharges due to wounds or illnesses.

The military records of the men who served in the War of 1812 were never consolidated into individual service records. Actual service records are a product of the 20th century when a file was kept on each individual soldier from the time that he enlisted to the time that he was discharged from the service. All military records for that individual were included in his file.

To facilitate the pension approval process in the issuance of service pensions during the 1870's for the veterans and their widows of the War of 1812, the militia regimental records from this war were broken down into individual service records. If a man served twice in two different regiments at different times during the war, then he would have two service records at the National Archives. The army drew heavily from the militia forces to fill the ranks of existing and newly created regiments during the war. Many men would have service records with both the militia and the army.

The best and probably the only way to determine how many times a veteran served during the war is through his pension application, including those applications that were rejected for one reason or another. But this depends on whether the veteran or his widow recorded all tours of duty on the application.

Upton's figure of 54,081 men serving in the army is probably a pretty good estimate since the army kept far better records of their men than the various militia units. The actual number of militiamen who served during the war is probably closer to 230,000 men than the 468,573 men listed by Upton. Many states and territories called out their militia in support of the army, and they were dismissed by the army because they were not needed. Since this was a declared war, the federal government was forced to pay the salaries of these unneeded troops thus the number of militiamen authorized by Congress to serve passed the 230,000 limitation. The actual militia figure will never be known, but the total of all individual militiamen who served during the War of 1812 is probably around 350,000 men.

Ohio's militia figures for the War of 1812 are as confusing as the federal government's militia figures. According to the two Congressional Acts, Ohio would provide 5,000 men under the act authorizing 100,000 men and 3,965 men under the act authorizing 80,000 men for a total of 8,965 militiamen. Ohio supplied approximately 2,500 militiamen for the U.S. Voluntary Corps and probably another 3,000 men for the U.S. Army. This brings the total of Ohioans serving in the war to 11,765 men according to the above figures.

The *Roster of Ohio Soldiers in the War of 1812* which was originally published in 1916 by the Adjutant General's Office in Columbus, Ohio, states that there were 1,759 officers and 24,521 enlisted men listed within its pages. The total number of men is 26,280. Many of the men in this book are listed more than once with many of these men having multiple 'tours of duty' in a number of different companies or headquarters' staffs. The actual number of men may be as low as 15,000 men because of these multiple tours of duty. The book contains the muster rolls from both the volunteers and the militia and there are a number of known missing rosters.

The *Ohio Statesmen and Annals of Progress* by William A. Taylor gives a lower number of militiamen who served from Ohio during the war. This book has a summary of each legislative session of the Ohio Assembly from 1788 to 1900, and it contains militia information. Prior to 1803 the summary is for the government of the Northwest Territory, which predates the State of Ohio.

Taylor states that Ohio furnished 23,951 soldiers for the war out of a male population of 64,814 who were over twenty-one years of age in 1815. This represents 33% of the male population and 50% of those subject to military duty. What is interesting is that Taylor's work does not state that this figure represents only militiamen, and it may include also those men who served in the U.S. Army. The 23,951 figure is probably very close to the number of Ohioans who served in the U.S. Army, the volunteers and the militia during the War of 1812.

Dictionary of the War of 1812

Abatis
A barricade made of felled trees with the sharpened branches pointing outwards in the direction of an attacker.

Accoutrements
Accoutrements are equipment other than clothes or weapons that were carried by soldiers, including belts, blanket rolls, caps, cartridge boxes, canteens, mess kits, and backpacks.

Aide-de-camp
Aides-de-camp are members of the personal staff of a general officer, acting as his confidential assistants. They are employed in representing him, in writing orders, in carrying them in person if necessary, in communicating them verbally upon battlefields and other fields of maneuver.

Adjutant
An adjutant is a staff officer who is in charge of and responsible for the administrative functions within a regiment, including correspondence and record keeping. He maintains the regimental orderly book. There was one adjutant assigned to a regiment, and he held the rank of colonel.

Adjutant General (US Army)
The active duties of adjutants general consist in establishing camps; visiting guards and outposts; mustering and inspecting troops; inspecting guards and detachments; forming parades and lines of battle; the conduct and control of deserters and prisoners; making reconnaissance; and in general discharging such other active duties as may be assigned them.

Adjutant General (Militia)
The adjutant general of the state shall distribute all orders from the commander in chief (the governor) to each to the divisions. He shall attend all public reviews with the commander in chief. He was in charge of conducting the yearly returns, which outlined the strengths of the state militia.

Ammunition
Ammunition is a term, which comprehends gunpowder, and all the various projectiles and pyrotechnical compositions and stores used in the service.

Apothecary General (US Army)
The apothecary general performs the duties of a quartermaster general and a paymaster general in the Medical Department.

Army
The largest tactical unit of the United States Army is called an army. An army is divided into one or more divisions.

Arsenal
An arsenal is a building or establishment for manufacturing, storing, repairing, and issuing arms and ammunition.

Artificer
Military workman assigned to a company of artillery who prepares the shells, fuses and grenades. He holds the rank of private.

Artillery (US Army)
Artillery consists of all guns of larger caliber and longer range than a musket or rifle. **See Light Artillery, Foot Artillery, Heavy Artillery and Horse Artillery.**

Artillery (Militia)
A militia artillery company had one piece of artillery assigned to it. Artillery companies were assigned to militia infantry regiments.

Barracks
(1) A military building used to house soldiers within a fortification.
(2) A small, unfortified military post with a permanent party of soldiers usually made up of more than one building.

Bastion
A triangular projection of a fortification used to mount artillery.

Bateau (plural bateaux)
A bateau was a large, flat-bottomed boat used to transport troops and supplies during the war. These craft were built for General Harrison's invasion of Upper Canada. They could carry 40-50 men with their baggage, arms and provisions.

Battalion
(1) A regular army infantry unit made up of nine companies and a headquarters that was

commanded by a lieutenant colonel. Two battalions made up an infantry regiment. The infantry regiments that were authorized on 11 January 1812 used this type of military unit but they were eliminated on 26 June 1812 during the army reorganization of its regiments.

(2) An ad hoc military unit made up of two or more companies and commanded by a lieutenant colonel or major during the War of 1812. This unit was temporary and was used to perform certain missions.

(3) A militia unit made up of between four to eight companies and a small headquarters staff. A major is normally a commander of a battalion. Two battalions made up a regiment. A battalion could have one rifle, light infantry or grenadier company attached to it. **See Odd Battalion**

Battery

A group of guns, mortars, artillery pieces, etc., placed under one tactical commander in a certain area is called a battery.

Battle

A hostile meeting of two opposing forces, usually with a predefined objective, is called a battle. **See Skirmish**

Battle Honor (British)

An award given by the British Crown for distinguished service of a regiment during a war is called a battle honor.

Bayonet

A short sword that is attached to the end of a musket or rifle barrel making the combination of the two items a defensive and an offensive weapon. Early bayonets were attached to the weapon by a socket at the end of the bayonet. Modern bayonets have a knife handle making the bayonet a more versatile weapon.

Blockhouse

Blockhouses were enlarged two-story log cabins with the second level wider than the first level. The militia and the pioneers used them for protection against Indian raids. Blockhouses were also constructed on the corners of military forts.

Bombardiers

Bombardiers were artillerymen who were in charge of bombs and fuses.

Bonuses and Land Bounties (US Army)

On 6 May 1812 Congress passed a law giving bonuses and land bounties for the men who enlisted in the regular army for 'five years or during the war.' The men would receive a total of $16 and 160 acres of land when they had completed their service. $8 dollars of the bonuses were issued when recruited and the balance when discharged. The Act of 10 December 1814 increased the land bounty to 320 acres and the bonus to $128.

Brevet Commissions (US Army)

An honorary rank given to an officer during the War of 1812 for valor in combat that was one or more ranks above an officer's actual rank for which he was paid. An officer might be given a single brevet, that is, a captain being breveted to a major. He was entitled to be addressed by his highest brevet rank, yet in actual authority and pay he remained a captain.

Brigade

A brigade was a military unit made up of a headquarters' staff and at least two regiments. A brigadier general commanded this unit.

Brigadier (British)

A senior colonel who was in charge of more than one regiment in the field was given the title of Brigadier. Today, this is a rank in the British Army, which is equivalent to a brigadier general in the U.S. Army.

Brigadier General

A brigadier general is an officer's rank before a major general and above a colonel. A brigadier general is normally a commander of a brigade.

Brigade Inspector

The brigade inspector is the chief inspector in a brigade who attended all officer's, regimental and battalion musters. He inspected all arms and equipment, noting delinquents and reporting back to each regimental commander. He delivered the general orders of the brigade commander and made out the returns for the brigade. He held the rank of major. The brigade inspector would also perform the duties of the brigade major during the war.

Brigade Major
The brigade major assisted a brigadier general with all of his duties. He held the rank of major. The duties of the brigade major were assigned to the brigade inspector during the war.

Cadet (US Army)
A student assigned to the United States Military Academy who will be commissioned as an ensign in the United States Army upon graduation.

Caliber
The diameter of a projectile or of a bore of a gun or cannon is called a caliber.

Camp
(1) A temporary area in the field where military units bedded down for the night.
(2) A small temporary fort usually constructed during an expedition.

Campaign
An organized troop movement into enemy territory with a mission and a purpose is called a campaign. Campaigns were normally lengthy and may involve a number of battles.

Captain
A captain is an officer's rank below a major and above a first lieutenant. A captain is normally a commander of a company.

Carriage
A small vehicle, usually with two wheels, on which a cannon is mounted making the artillery piece mobile.

Cashiered
An officer who had been convicted in a general or regimental court martial and who had been forced to leave the military has said to been cashiered.

Cavalry
Cavalry regiments were trained to fight on horseback against the enemy's cavalry and to charge the enemy's battle lines disrupting the infantry. They were also called 'heavy horse' since they used a heavier horse than the dragoons or light dragoons. Their weapons were designed to be used from horseback. Their muskets and pistols could be reloaded from the saddle. Cavalry units were very rare in the army prior to the Civil War, and they were not used during the War of 1812 by the American army. **See Dragoons, Light Dragoons and Mounted Infantry.**

Chaplain
A chaplain is a minister of the gospel or priest who was commissioned in the army. A chaplain was normally assigned to a brigade.

Class (Militia)
A company was divided into eight classes of eight men each. Militiamen were 'classed' twice a year, meaning that they were given a number and assigned to one of the eight classes. Two classes plus a sergeant and a corporal made up a squad.

Clerk
A clerk maintained the regimental books and took the minutes in all regimental court proceedings. He held the rank of lieutenant.

Colonel
A colonel is an officer's rank below a brigadier general and above a lieutenant colonel. A colonel is normally a commander of a regiment.

Colors
A regimental flag carried by ensigns while marching or in formation. Infantry and artillery had a buff colored flag with a scroll containing the name of the unit on it while rifle regiments used a flag with a green background. Light Dragoon regiments did not carry colors.

Commissary
(1) A store or storehouse handling food and merchandise at a military post, camp, or station.
(2) An officer at a military post, who was assigned the additional duty as a commissary officer (often called simply the commissary); was in charge of that post's commissary supplies and storehouse.

Commission
Commissions were written authority given to an individual who became an officer in the army or militia. Commissions normally established the rank

of that individual, and it could specify duties and responsibilities.

Congressional commissions were established by act of Congress while presidential commissions were given to men in the U.S. Voluntary Corps.

Company (US Army)

A company was a military unit of approximately 100 men commanded by a captain. Companies were made up of four squads and ten companies made up a regiment.

Company (Militia)

A military unit commanded by a captain. Companies were made up of eight classes and between four and eight companies made up a battalion. There were 64 privates in a company.

Company Grade Officers

Company grade officers are captains, lieutenants and ensigns (or cornets).

Cornet

A cornet is the lowest officer's rank in a company of cavalry, dragoons, light dragoons or mounted infantry. Corresponds to the rank of ensign in an artillery or an infantry company.

Corporal

A corporal is an enlisted rank below a sergeant and above a private. He was an assistant to the sergeant who was in charge of a squad. Corporals were also in charge of instructing the privates on performing sentinel (guard) duties.

Corps

A specialized section of the army, which supports the combat units in a battle zone, such as, the Corps of Engineers or the U.S. Volunteer Corps.

Court Martial

A court martial is a military court to try military offenses.

Court of Enquiry

A court of enquiry is a military court held after each muster of a company, a battalion or a regiment. It was used to levy fines for the infractions of the militia laws that occurred during a muster. The court also handled appeals. All officers within the unit were required to attend.

Debt

All non-commissioned officers, artificers, privates, and musicians enlisted in the actual service of the United States were exempt, during their term of service, from all personal arrests for any debt or contract. No non-commissioned officer, musician, or private shall be arrested or subject to arrest, or be taken in execution for any debt under the sum of twenty dollars, contracted before enlistment, nor for any debt contracted after enlistment.

Defeat

To lose in battle to the opposing side is called a defeat. Many battles during the 1700's in which the American forces lost were called defeats, such as, Harmer's Defeat.

Department

A specialized section of the army, which supports one aspect of army life, that is, pay, substance, legal, etc. Departments are non-combatant units of the army.

Depot

A military supply post is called a depot.

Descriptive Book

A book that was maintained by the first sergeant of a company containing the name and physical description of every man in the company, his trade or occupation, place of birth and residence, when, where and for what term he was enlisted, and bounty, clothing or equipment assigned to him. Also included in this book were all furloughs, discharges and casualties, that is, deaths and sickness.

Detachment (Militia)

By law, any group of militiamen who were called to serve in the state's army or with the federal army was called a detachment. Those detachments that were assigned to federal units were also called "quotas."

Detachment (US Army)

Detachments were any group of soldiers or units used to perform a certain function for a given amount of time. Detachments were used to escort convoys of prisoners or supplies, or guarding forts or posts, or for an expedition against the enemy.

Discharge rolls

A roster very similar to a description roll, which was used when a group of men were being discharged from the army. Besides having the information that was found on a description roll, the discharge roll would show the last day of regular pay and any remaining bonuses, and a listing of clothing that was issued to each man.

Division

A division was the first major sub-division of an army. A major general commanded a division. Each division was divided into two to six brigades.

Dragoons

Dragoons were mounted infantries who were trained to fight on horseback when necessary. The army's mounted units were called 'dragoons' while most of the state militia mounted units were called 'mounted infantry'. The regular army had no dragoons during the War of 1812.

Drill Manual

The army had been using Baron von Steuben's drill manual since the Revolutionary War. This manual not only instructed the troops on how to march but also on how to conduct themselves in combat. It also set forth the duties and responsibilities for each rank within the army, both officers and enlisted.

In 1812 Colonel Alexander Smyth of the rifle regiment (and later the inspector general of the army) published his *Regulations for the Field Maneuvers, and Conduct of the Infantry of the United States; Drawn Up and Adapted to the Organization of the Militia and Regular Troops*. This book replaced Baron von Steuben's drill manual. This new manual adopted the French tactics of Napoleon first published in 1805 and it went into effect on 30 June 1812 as the standard manual for the army.

Drummer

A musician in a company of artillery, infantry, grenadier, light infantry or rifle who used a drum is called a drummer. He issued directions to the troops from his commander.

Engineers (US Army)

Engineers were soldiers trained and employed for engineering duties, including road and bridge building, construction, demolition, surveying, etc.
See Topographical Engineer

Enlistment

Enlisted personnel signed a contract to become a member of the army for a given amount of time. Enlistments at the beginning of the War of 1812 were for five years. Once the war started 'during the war' enlistments were approved as were 18-month enlistments and one-year enlistments.

Ensign

An ensign is the lowest officer's rank in an infantry or an artillery company. Corresponds to the rank of cornet in a cavalry-type company. He was in charge of the cleanliness of the company. He also took turns carrying the flags (colors) of the regiment when the unit was on the march or in battle. This rank was eliminated after the war.

Epaulets

An epaulet is a shoulder decoration made of stiff gold, silver, red or blue braid worn on officers, non-commissioned officers and corporal's uniforms in order to distinguish ranks.

Espontoon (or Spontoon)

An espontoon was a type of thrusting weapon that was sometimes called a half-pike because it was about six feet long, or roughly half the length of a medieval pike. It was made of wood, with a double-edged blade at the cutting end and an iron tip at the other.

Infantry officers carried the espontoon as a symbol of rank, and as a sort of baton, or signaling device, for use in directing their men. It was an officer's primary weapon, since it allowed him to keep his eyes on the battle. Furthermore, his signals could be seen from a distance in the din and disorder of the battlefield, when voice commands might be indistinguishable.

Exchange

Prisoners of war were normally traded by an agreement between two warring parties usually as a one-to-one exchange based upon the rank of the individuals.

How soldiers were to be repatriated was normally set forth by an agreement between two sides during a conflict.

Expedition
An expedition is an enterprise undertaken either by sea or by land against an enemy, the fortunate termination of which principally depends on the rapidity and unexpected nature of its movements.

Farrier
A farrier was a soldier who shod horses and treated their diseases. Farriers were authorized in regiments that used horses for transportation, that is, cavalry and artillery units.

Fatigue or Fatigue Duty
Any duty performed by a soldier other than military duty or training, usually involving manual labor is called fatigue duty.

Fatigues
Fatigues were a work uniform worn by soldiers who were performing fatigue duty.

Fencibles
Fencibles were military personnel who were raised from the local population and who were not subject for overseas duty. The British raised many Canadian regiments for the army as fencibles. These troops could only used in British North America.
The Sea Fencibles were raised to protect our major harbors while Rangers were to be used only in the Old Northwest. They could only be used for this purpose.

Field Gun
A cannon attached to a carriage that can be transported and used on a field of battle. Field guns were usually of a smaller caliber than the cannons used in a fort.

Field Grade Officers
Field grade officers are colonels, lieutenant colonels and majors.

Fifer
A fifer was a musician using a fife or flute that served in a company of artillery, infantry, grenadier, light infantry or rifle.

First Sergeant
The highest enlisted rank in a company is the first sergeant.

Flag of Truce
A white flag used to communicate a desire to open a dialog between two warring parties.

Foot Artillery
Foot artillery is a term not a type of company. The light artillery companies in the War of 1812 were used as elite infantry in lieu of equipping these companies with artillery pieces thus the name 'foot' artillery.

Forage
The hay, corn, fodder, and oats required for the subsistence of the horses of an army is called forage.

Forage Master
A forage master was an officer who was assigned the duties of obtaining food for the horses or mules.

Fort
A fortified facility designed to withstand a military siege is called a fort. Most of the forts in the northwestern area of the country were made from blockhouses that were connected by wooden palisades. A more permanent facility was made of stone or brick and had earthen ramparts.

Furlough
The term 'furlough' is usually applied to the absence with leave of non-commissioned officers and soldiers.

Fusee
A fusee was a small musket normally used by an officer for protection.

Gaiters
Gaiters were shin-high leather or cloth leg coverings worn in conjunction with low boots or shoes.

Garrison
A garrison designates the troops employed in a strong place for its security, and it is also applied to the place itself when occupied by troops.

General Grade Officers

General grade officers are major generals and brigadier generals. The highest officer rank during the War of 1812 was a major general.

General Orders

General orders are official orders that were issued in writing by a headquarters that related to the entire command.

General Staff - See Staff

Grenadiers

Grenadiers were originally men who threw grenades or bombs but by the War of 1812 they were shock troops made up of the biggest and strongest men from within a regiment.

Guardhouse

A building near the main gate of a fortification used by soldiers detailed for sentinel duty. The guardhouse usually had a prison cell to confine garrison prisoners.

Gunners

Gunners were artillerymen who operated the guns or cannons that were assigned to their companies.

Half Pay

Survivors of a soldier who was killed or who had died while in the service of the United States could receive half pay for five years in lieu of receiving land bounties. Half pay was based on the current rank of the fallen soldier.

Hanger

A hanger was a short sword with a blade length of approximately 20 inches, also called a hunting sword.

Heavy Artillery

Heavy artillery companies operated the forts and fortifications during the War of 1812. They normally had artillery pieces of larger caliber than the light or horse artillery and these were not easily transportable.

Heavy Horse - See Cavalry

Horse Artillery

Horse artillery companies were light artillery companies designed to follow light dragoon or cavalry units. All personnel in these companies traveled on horseback. These companies were not used during the War of 1812.

Hospital Mates (U.S. Army)

Hospital mates were responsible for dressing all wounds, administrated prescriptions, and keeping a casebook on each patient.

Hospital Surgeon (U.S. Army)

The hospital surgeon is the chief medical officer in an army hospital.

Hospital Steward (U.S. Army)

The hospital steward acted as the quartermaster within a hospital.

Hot Shot

A cannon ball that had been heated red hot and fired into an enemy's position. Used to set forts and fortifications on fire.

Howitzer

An artillery piece with a short barrel used to fire artillery shells in a high trajectory.

Independent Company – See Odd Company

Infantry

Infantry are soldiers who traveled and fought on foot. The infantry regiment fought European style, that is, they formed lines facing the enemy who were also arranged in the same type of formation. The infantrymen were trained not to think but to follow orders. The closest line to the enemy fired their muskets on order, straight ahead without aiming, and then while they were reloading the second line fired their muskets. After a number of volleys were exchanged between the two sides then a bayonet charge would occur. Either the enemy fled the battlefield or hand-to-hand combat determined the winner of the battle. **See Light Infantry, Riflemen, Rangers and Spies.**

Inspector General

There were two inspectors general in the U.S. Army who held the rank of colonel. Assistant adjutants general are exofficio assistant inspectors general.

Invalids (British)
British invalid regiments were made up of men who had retired from the army and who were collecting pensions. These regiments were used as garrison troops in the British Isles freeing up line regiments for overseas duty.

Judge Advocate
The judge advocate prosecuted in the name of the United States He was also a counsel for prisoners. The judge advocate administered the prescribed oaths to the court and its witnesses.

Land Bounty
See Bonuses and Land Bounties

Laundresses
Laundresses were camp women, sometimes the wives of soldiers, employed to wash soldiers' clothing. The Army authorized four laundresses for each company. They received rations, bedding straw, and medical care, as well as a set payment for their work.

Legion (or Legionary Corps)
An ad hoc military unit made up of more than one company from at least two of the various army branches. Legions were normally regimental size consisting of infantry, artillery and cavalry companies. Regular army regiments were organized this way in the early 1790's while the various state and territorial militias were actually legions during the War of 1812. See Regiment (Army and Militia)

Lieutenant (US Army)
1st Lieutenant – An officer's rank below captain and above a second lieutenant. This officer was second in command of a company.
2nd Lieutenant – An officer's rank below first lieutenant and above a third lieutenant.
3rd Lieutenant – An officer's rank below second lieutenant and above an ensign. This rank was created during the War of 1812 for the regimental recruiting service. This rank was eliminated after the war.

Lieutenant (Militia)
A lieutenant is an officer's rank below the rank of captain and above an ensign. This officer was second in command of a company. He attended to the general care of the men and made the duty assignments within the company.

Lieutenant Colonel
A lieutenant colonel is an officer's rank below a colonel and above a major. This officer was second in command of a regiment. In some of the earlier US army regiments this officer was a battalion commander.

Light Artillery
Light artillery companies were attached to infantry regiments providing firepower during battles. The artillery pieces were placed on two wheeled carriages with an accompanying caisson. The light artillery companies were used as elite foot artillery during the War of 1812.

Light Dragoons
Light Dragoons were designed for reconnaissance, screening missions and for transporting official messages. They were also used to disrupt the enemies supply lines, and they could skirmish with the enemy on horseback. They fought with lighter muskets that could be reloaded on horseback. The standard weapons were the pistol and saber. There were also called 'light horse' or 'light cavalry'. These were the only true cavalry units used during the War of 1812 by the regular army.

Light Horse - See Light Dragoons

Light Infantry
Light infantry were made up of men who were taught to think and to shoot at targets of the own choosing. They did not form battle lines but operated as a unit with each man a yard or two apart. They used natural cover when they advanced minimizing themselves as targets. These units were used to screen the advance or retreat of the regular infantry companies. While the regular infantry was fighting in the battle lines, the light infantry would be used to flank the enemy attacking them from their sides. When companies of light infantry were attached to infantry regiments they were called 'flank' companies.

Line Officers (US Army)
The U.S. Army lists all active duty army officers by rank and date of promotion. The list is

used for promotions and for command positions assignments when they became available. Officers are considered to be line officers if they are in the infantry, artillery, or cavalry.

Line Regiments (US Army)
Regiments capable of being used in combat and who could perform their duties overseas were called line regiments.

Lower Canada (Canada)
Lower Canada, British North America, is now the Province of Quebec, Canada.

Magazine
A magazine is a structure where ammunition or explosives are stored.

Major
A major is an officer's rank below lieutenant colonel and above a captain. A major normally commanded a battalion in the militia.

Major General
A major general was the highest officer's rank during the War of 1812. This rank was above a brigadier general, and he was usually a commander of an army.

Maritime Provinces (Canada)
During the War of 1812 the Maritime Provinces consisted of the Colonies of Cape Breton, Nova Scotia, New Brunswick and Prince Edward Island.

Master Musician (US Army)
The senior fifer and the senior drummer in a regiment were called master musicians.

Matross
Matrosses were artillerymen who assisted the gunners in loading, firing and sponging the cannons. They carried weapons and guarded the store wagons when marching. These men had the rank of private.

Military Academy (US Army)
The military school at West Point, New York, which was used to train and commission officers for the United States Army, was called the military academy. Founded in 1802, the early mission of the school was to train young officers to become artillery or engineering ensigns.

Military District
The country was divided into nine military areas commanded by a general officer who was in charge of the defense of that portion of the country. He was in charge of all military units, both regular and militia, that were on federal duty. A tenth district was created for a short time in 1814 centering on Washington, D.C.

Militia
Congress passed the basic militia law in 1792 that called for the individual states and territories to organize citizen militias, with each militiaman providing his own arms and munitions.

Miner
A soldier in the Corps of Engineers who handled mines and the setting off of mines. Mines were usually set off in tunnels under an enemy's fortification.

Mounted Infantry
Mounted infantry were not a traditional cavalry unit, but they were light infantries that used horses for transportation. Once on a battlefield they would dismount and fight on foot. Another name for mounted infantry was 'dragoons'. The regular army used the term 'dragoons' while the militia would use either 'mounted infantry' or 'dragoons'.

Musicians (Militia)
One fifer and one drummer were assigned to each company as musicians.

Musicians (US Army)
One fifer and one drummer were assigned to each company and one fife major and one drum major to each regiment. By the end of the war these men were organized into a regimental band and not assigned to an individual company.

Musket
A musket was the standard weapon for most of the soldiers during the War of 1812. The musket fired a solid round shot through a smooth bore, and it needed to be reloaded after every firing.

Muster Roll
A bi-monthly roster of all men in a company showing their names, rank, date of enlistment,

duration of enlistment, and any comments pertaining to each man was called a muster roll. Monthly reports were required in between months which showed the total number of men in a company by rank and by name who was missing and why. Muster rolls were completed during a muster of the company by the commanding officer. Musters were performed on the last day of February, April, June, August, October and December while monthly reports were due on the last day of the other months.

Non-Commissioned Officers

Non-commissioned officers hold the rank of sergeant, which includes sergeants, sergeant majors, first sergeants, and quartermaster sergeants.

Odd Battalion (Ohio Militia)

When a new county did not have enough men to form a regiment then an 'odd' battalion could be formed. Odd battalions operated as a regiment having a regimental headquarters staff but only half the number of companies that would have been assigned to a regiment. A major commanded an odd battalion.

Odd Company (Ohio Militia)

An odd company was an independent company, which was not attached to a battalion.

Old Northwest

The area of the United States that contains the current states of Indiana, Illinois, Ohio, Michigan, Wisconsin and the eastern part of Minnesota. The area was originally known as the Territory North of the Ohio River or the Northwest Territory.

Orders (or Orderly) Book

A book maintained by a military unit, which contains the general and special orders that were issued by the commanding generals, colonels and majors.

Ordnance

Ordnances are all types of combat weapons, with their ammunition, equipment, and accessories, including repair tools and machinery.

Palisades

Palisades were strong pickets, six or seven inches broad on each side, having about one foot of their summits sharpened in a pyramidal form. They are frequently placed at the foot of slopes, as an obstacle to the enemy.

Palisades were also used as walls of fortifications. They were made of logs 9 to 10 feet in length that were imbedded in the ground side by side. Usually a fortification had a minimum of four walls made from palisades and at the corners a blockhouse was constructed.

Parade Grounds

The center section of a fort or fortification, which serves as a drill and assembly area for the garrison, is called the parade grounds.

Parole

Prisoners of war who were on parole status were given permission to return to their homes if they signed an agreement not to take up arms until they were exchanged.

Enemy officers were at times granted another type of parole in which they agreed not to escape and in turn they were permitted to walk freely around a town or a given area.

Pay Rolls

A pay roll was a roster from a company listing each of the men and having a place for their signatures or "X"s. These rolls were used to issue pay.

Paymaster

A paymaster was an officer in a regiment assigned the task of procuring monies for the payroll and to dispense the monies on payday. Paymasters had the rank of lieutenant.

Physician and Surgeon General

The Physician and Surgeon General is the chief medical officer in the U.S. Army and the head of the army's Medical Department.

Picket

Soldiers who were performing guard duty away from the main camp or fort were called pickets. They provided advance warnings of an approaching enemy. A string of soldiers on picket duty would form a picket line.

Pioneers
Pioneers were soldiers whose primary function was to cut roads through forests and to perform other construction jobs as needed. They were lightly armed, and they could defend themselves.

Pistol
A small hand held musket with a short range, which was used by officers as a defensive weapon and by cavalry troops as an offensive weapon was called a pistol.

Platoon
A platoon was an ad hoc military unit used during the War of 1812. Companies were divided into two platoons when marching or in formation. The captain would command one of the platoons while the first lieutenant (or lieutenant) would be in charge of the second platoon.

Post
A post was a military facility with a permanent garrison.

Prisoner of War
Soldiers who had been captured by an enemy and confined until either exchanged or paroled were classified as prisoners of war. **See also Parole and Exchange.**

Private
The lowest enlisted rank in the army was the private.

Provost Marshal
1) An officer appointed in the field to secure prisoners confined on charges of a general nature.
2) Each president of a court martial proceeding appointed a provost marshal whose duty it was to summon all witnesses, to execute the orders of the court, and to keep bystanders from disrupting the court.

Quartermaster
A quartermaster was a regimental or post staff officer, usually with the rank of lieutenant, who looked after the assignment of quarters, the provision of clothing, forage, fuel, and all other quartermaster supplies. During deployments he was in charge of encampments. Quartermasters on the brigade level held the rank of major while regimental quartermasters held the rank of lieutenant.

Quartermaster Sergeant
Quartermaster sergeant assists the regimental quartermaster. It is his responsibility to see that the regiment's tents and camp equipment are properly loaded on the wagons while the regiment is on the march.

Quartermaster General
A quartermaster general is the senior quartermaster in a division, holding the rank of colonel.

Quota
Militia detachments that were called up for federal duty were called "Quotas," as in, the 1st Ohio Quota.

Raid
An organized assault into enemy territory with an objective to capture or destroy an enemy's supply or fortifications.

Rangers
Rangers were light infantries that were used as scouts in the forest, spying and harassing the enemy. They gathered intelligence and normally operated behind enemy lines. Rangers operated as independent companies attached to a military district or to a regular infantry regiment. They were not organized into regiments. These companies were used in the northwest during the War of 1812 and they normally operated as mounted units. Many of the state's ranger companies were called 'spies' or 'mounted spies'. **See also spies.**

Reconnaissance
Reconnaissances are warlike operations for the purpose of procuring information on the positions and strength of corps of the enemy.

Record Book
A book maintained by military units, which contained copies of the musters, class rolls, officer commissioning reports, court minutes and other types of documents pertaining to that unit.

Recruit

A recruit was a newly enlisted member of the U.S. Army who hadn't joined his regiment in the field.

Redoubt

A redoubt is the strongest part of a fortification, which is able to withstand direct assaults from the enemy. It is usually square with outflanking defenses.

Regiment (US Army)

A regiment was a military unit made up of a headquarters' staff and 10 infantry companies. A colonel commanded this unit. Rifle, artillery and light dragoon regiments varied in the number of companies assigned to their regiments.

Regiment (Militia)

A regiment is a militia unit made up of a headquarters' staff and from 8 to 16 infantry companies divided into two battalions. A colonel commanded a regiment.

A regiment could have one company of artillery and one company of cavalry attached to its organization. A company of riflemen, light infantry or grenadiers could be attached to each battalion in the regiment. Two to six regiments made up a brigade.

The U.S. army had separate regiments for the infantry, artillery and light dragoons units while the militia regiments were consolidated units made up of infantry, artillery and cavalry-type units.

Regular Army

That part of the U.S. Army that is always on active, full-time military duty is called the regular army.

Return

A monthly roster or report was called a "return." A report that was required to be filled out and returned to a higher headquarters.

Riding master

A riding master was an officer in charge of teaching horsemanship.

Rifle

Rifles were muskets, which had a spiral groove inside its barrels. This increased the distance that a bullet could travel and greatly improved its accuracy; thus, rifles had a longer range than a musket. Rifles also had a slower rate of fire.

Riflemen

Rifle regiments used rifles instead of the standard musket. The men is these regiments were also used as sharpshooters who targeted British officers and non-commissioned officers during battle.

Rendezvous

(1) A place where militiamen met to form companies, regiments and battalions for federal or state military duty.
(2) A place where regular army units met to form a detachment to be used in an expedition against the enemy.
(3) A place where recruits met to be formed into companies.

Saber

A saber was a curved sword used by men assigned to cavalry-type units.

Saddlers

A saddler was a soldier in a cavalry-type unit whose job it was to repair saddles.

Sapper

Sappers were soldiers who were used in building fortifications. There was only one company of sappers organized during the war and they were employed by the army in New York.

Scout

A soldier who served as a guide leading other troops. Also called a pathfinder or guide.

Sea Fencibles

Fencibles were regular army troops that were raised and served in a particular region of a country and who were not subject to overseas duty. Sea fencibles were raised at all of our major seaports to defend these cities and harbors from attack. Officers received the uniform, pay, and rations of the army, while the balance of each company, the boatswains, gunners and privates, received the uniform, pay, and rations of the navy.

Senior Hospital Surgeon (U.S. Army)

The senior hospital surgeon is the chief medical officer in an army or a military district.

Sergeant

A sergeant was an enlisted rank below sergeant major and above a corporal. Sergeants were in charge of a squad with a corporal assisting. They were also in charge of training recruits.

Sergeant Major

The sergeant major was the highest enlisted rank in a regiment who assisted the adjutant. He was also responsible for the conduct and behavior of all of the non-commissioned officers within the regiment.

Shako

A tall, stovepipe hat used as basic head covering for soldiers in the U.S. Army during the war. The initial shakos were made of felt while the later issues were made of leather.

Siege

To surround an enemy's fort or fortification to deny them outside assess in order to a force surrender.

Skirmish

Normally a small battle without an objective, usually a chance meeting between two opposing forces. **See Battle**

Sortie

A sortie is an attack launched while under siege in order to break up an enemy's position. An objective would have been to capture an enemy's artillery or to break a whole into the enemy's lines.

Squad

A squad was a subdivision of a company, four squads made up a company. A sergeant and a corporal were assigned to each squad.

In the militia, squads were made up of two classes with a sergeant and a corporal in charge.

Squadron

A cavalry unit containing more than two troops is called a squadron.

Special Orders

Special orders were written orders issued by a headquarters pertaining to or concerning certain individuals or elements within a command.

Spies

(1) Spies are persons who gather military intelligence to assist their country's military.
(2) Militia rangers were called spies, mounted spies, rangers or mounted rangers.

Spike

To render useless an enemy's artillery by plugging the vent hole of a cannon preventing it from being fired.

Staff

(1) The general staff consisting of adjutants general and assistant adjutants general; aides-de-camp; inspectors general and assistant inspectors general. The functions of these officers consist not merely in distributing the orders of commanding generals, but also in regulating camps, directing the march of columns, and furnishing to the commanding general all necessary details for the exercise of his authority. Their duties embrace the whole range of the service of the troops, and they are hence properly styled general staff-officers.
(2) Staff corps, or staff departments. These are special corps or departments, whose duties are confined to distinct branches of the service.

Staff Officer

An officer assigned to a staff or headquarters and not to a military unit was called a staff officer.

Standard

A regimental flag representing the nation was called a standard. It was carried by an ensign when the unit was marching or in formation. The flag was normally dark blue with an American eagle and a scroll with the name of the regiment printed on it.

Stockade

Historically, a military facility in which a palisade of strong and closely planted timbers constituted the principal defense. If necessary, a stockade can be strengthened by ditch and abatis, and flanked by blockhouses. This was a normal defense against an Indian attack. Most of these structures were called forts.

Subalterns
The officer ranks below a captain are collectively called subalterns, that is, lieutenants and ensigns (cornets).

Substitute
A 'substitute' was a militiaman who was serving a tour of duty for another militiaman who had been drafted.

Supplies
The U.S. Army maintained four supply department throughout the war. These were:
(1) The Ordnance Department, which provides ordnance and ordnance stores.
(2) The Quartermaster's Department, which furnishes quarters, forage, transportation, clothing, camp and garrison equipage.
(3) The Subsistence Department, which furnishes subsistence.
(4) The Medical Department, which provides medicines and hospital stores.

Surgeon
A surgeon was the chief medical officer in a regiment who had been trained as a physician or a surgeon in civilian life. He held the rank of captain.

Surgeon's Mate
The surgeon's mate was an assistant to a surgeon in a regiment. Regiments could have one or two surgeon's mates depending on the type of regiment.

Sutler
A sutler was a trader who sold drinks and provisions to the troops. Beginning in 1812, a civilian was appointed to serve as the sole licensed merchant operating on a military post or appointed to accompany a regiment in the field during wartime.

Sword
A sword is a weapon with a handle and a long blade normally carried by officers and non-commissioned officers both as a weapon and a symbol of their rank. **(see Saber and Hanger)**

Sword master
A sword master was an officer who was in charge of teaching swordsmanship.

Topographical Engineer
An engineer whose duties included conducting surveys for the defense of the frontiers, positions for fortifications, military roads, map making, routes of communications, and places for bridges. They were also in charge of all civil works.

Troops
A collective term for uniformed soldiers was 'troops'.

Trumpeter
A trumpeter was a musician in a cavalry-type unit who used a trumpet or bugle.

Tour of Duty
When a militiaman volunteered or was drafted for duty with either the state's army or the federal army, his period of enlistment was called a 'tour of duty.'

Upper Canada (Canada)
Upper Canada, British North America, is now the Province of Ontario, Canada.

Wagon Master
A wagon master was an officer or contractor who was in charge of one or more wagons that were used to transport supplies for the army.

Waiter
A waiter was a private who was assigned to an officer to serve as his personal aide.

Ward Master (U.S. Army)
Ward masters were in charge of general cleanliness in hospital wards and of the patients. He supervised the nurses and attendants in his ward.

Washerwomen - See Laundresses

Western District (Canada)
The Western District of Upper Canada contained the Counties of Essex and Kent (south of the Thames River). The county seat of Essex County was Amherstberg while the seat of Kent County was Chatham.

Bibliography

Thompson, Erwin N., **Defender of the Gate, The Presidio of San Francisco, A History from 1846 to 1995**, National Park Service, military dictionary,
http://www.nps.gov/prsf/history/hrs/thompson/thompson.htm

Scott, Colonel H. L., **Military Dictionary comprising Technical Definitions; information of raising and keeping troops, including makeshifts and improved materiel; and law, government, regulation, and administration relating to land forces**, (D. Van Nostrand, New York, New York: 1861).

Smyth, Colonel Alexander, **Regulations for the Field Maneuvers, and Conduct of the Infantry of the United States; Drawn Up and Adapted to the Organization of the Militia and Regular Troops,** (Philadelphia, Pennsylvania: 1812).

Von Steuben, Frederick William Baron, **Baron von Steuben's Revolutionary War Drill Manual**, a facsimile reprint of the 1794 edition, (Dover Publishing Company, Mineola, New York: 1985).

The Canadian Military History Gateway, Glossary,
http://www.cmhg.gc.ca/html/gl-ga/index-eng.asp.

Charts

Militia divisions as organized under the Federal Militia Act of 1792

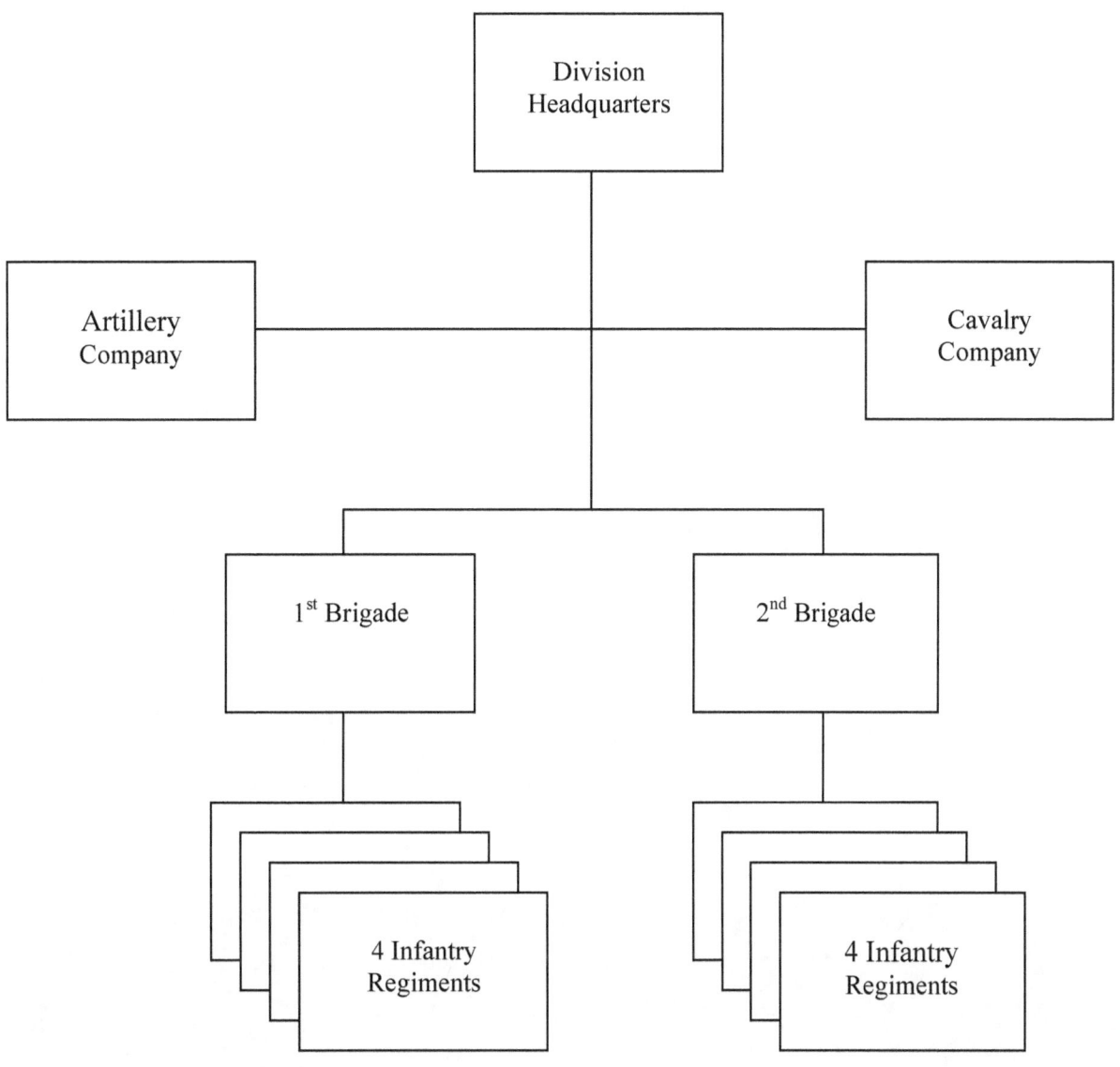

Militia regiments as organized under the Federal Militia Act of 1792

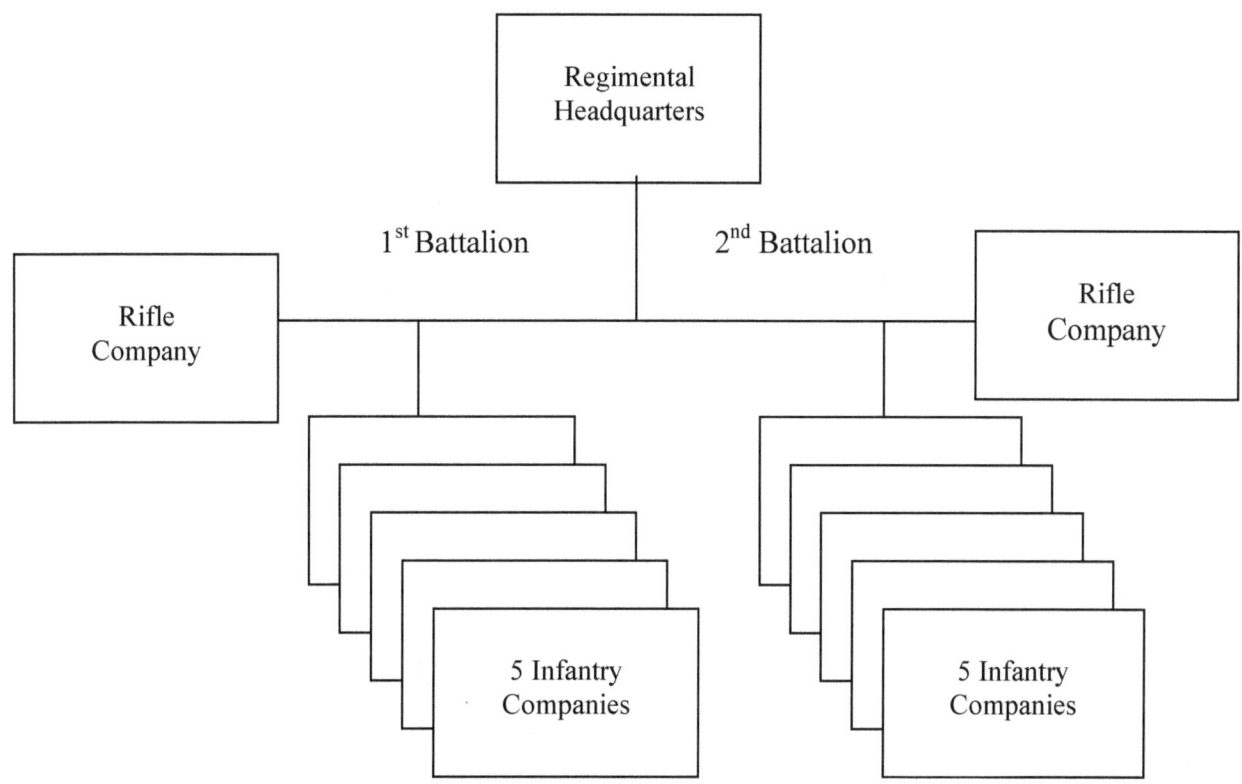

Ohio Militia Regiments as organized during the War of 1812

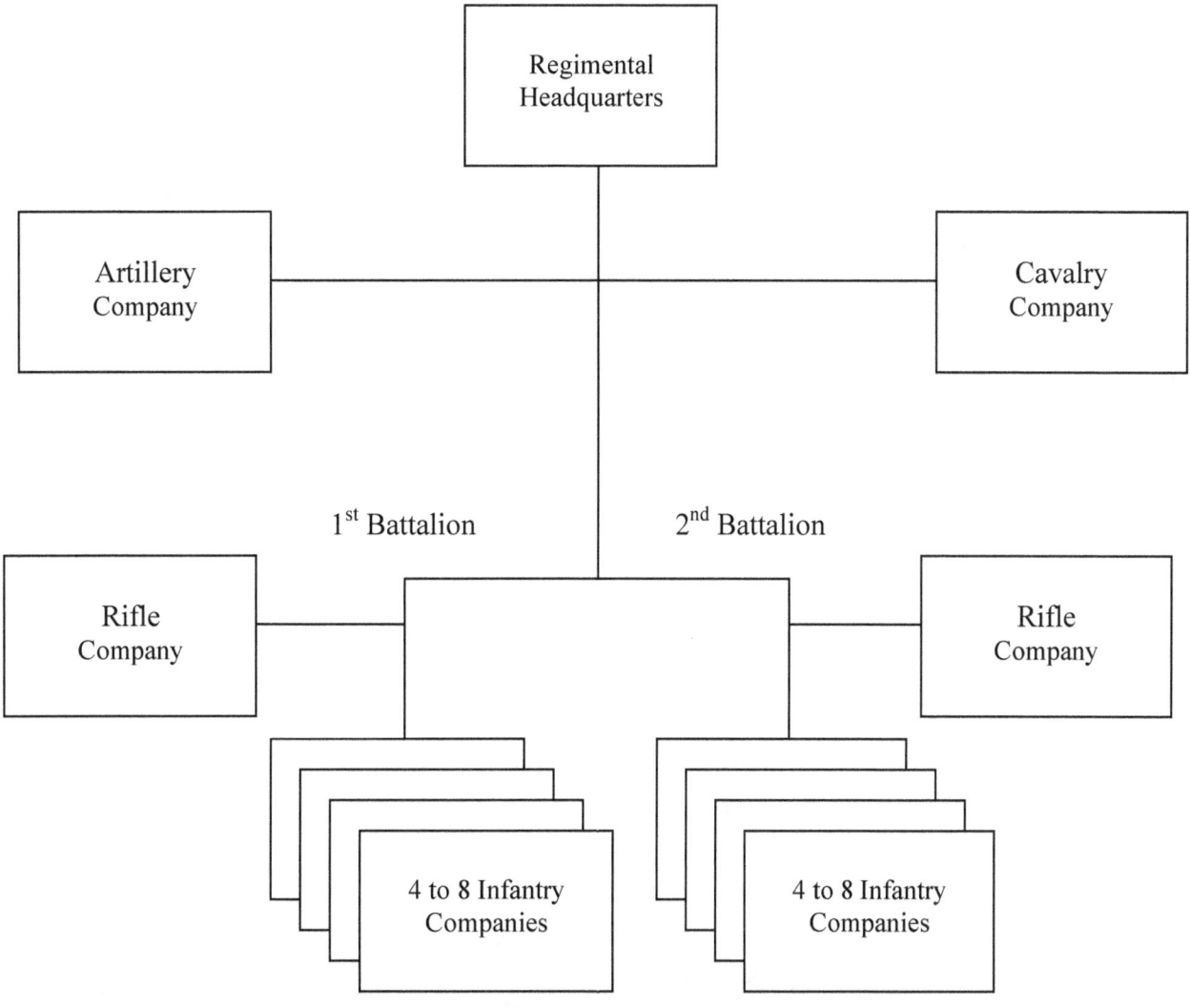

One artillery company and one cavalry company could be raised by a regiment while one rifle company could be raised by each battalion. The minimum configuration for a militia regiment would be eight infantry companies, while the maximum configuration would be 16 infantry companies, two rifle companies, one artillery company and one cavalry company.

Ohio Militia Odd Battalions as organized during the War of 1812

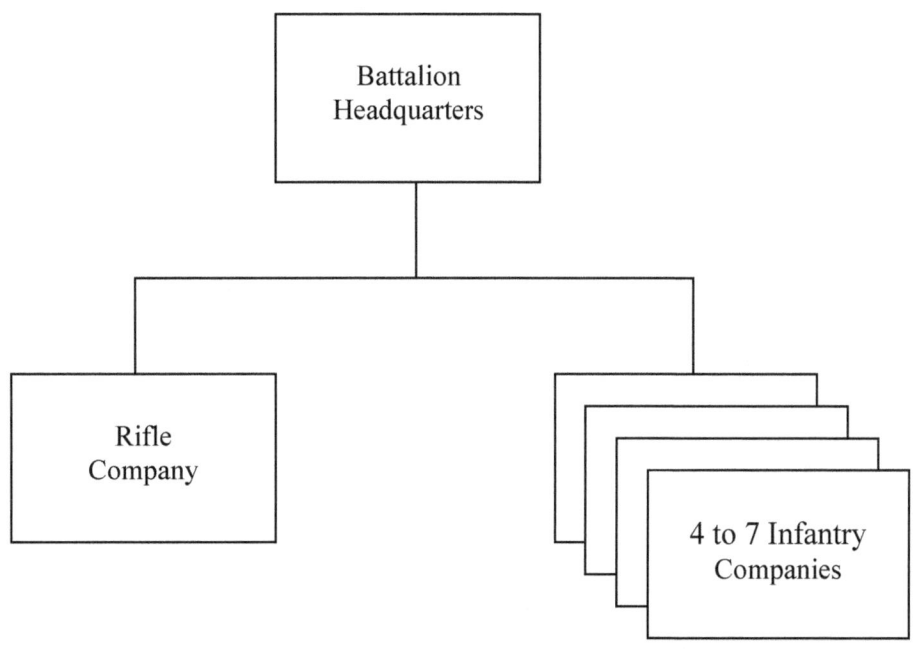

Odd Battalion Staff:

1 major
1 adjutant
1 quartermaster
1 clerk
1 paymaster
1 surgeon
1 surgeon's mates
1 sergeant major
1 quartermaster sergeant
1 drum major
1 fife major

One rifle company could be raised by each odd battalion. When an odd battalion was close to reaching in maximum strength, the battalion would have been converted to a regiment.

Ohio's Regular Army Infantry Regiments Lineage

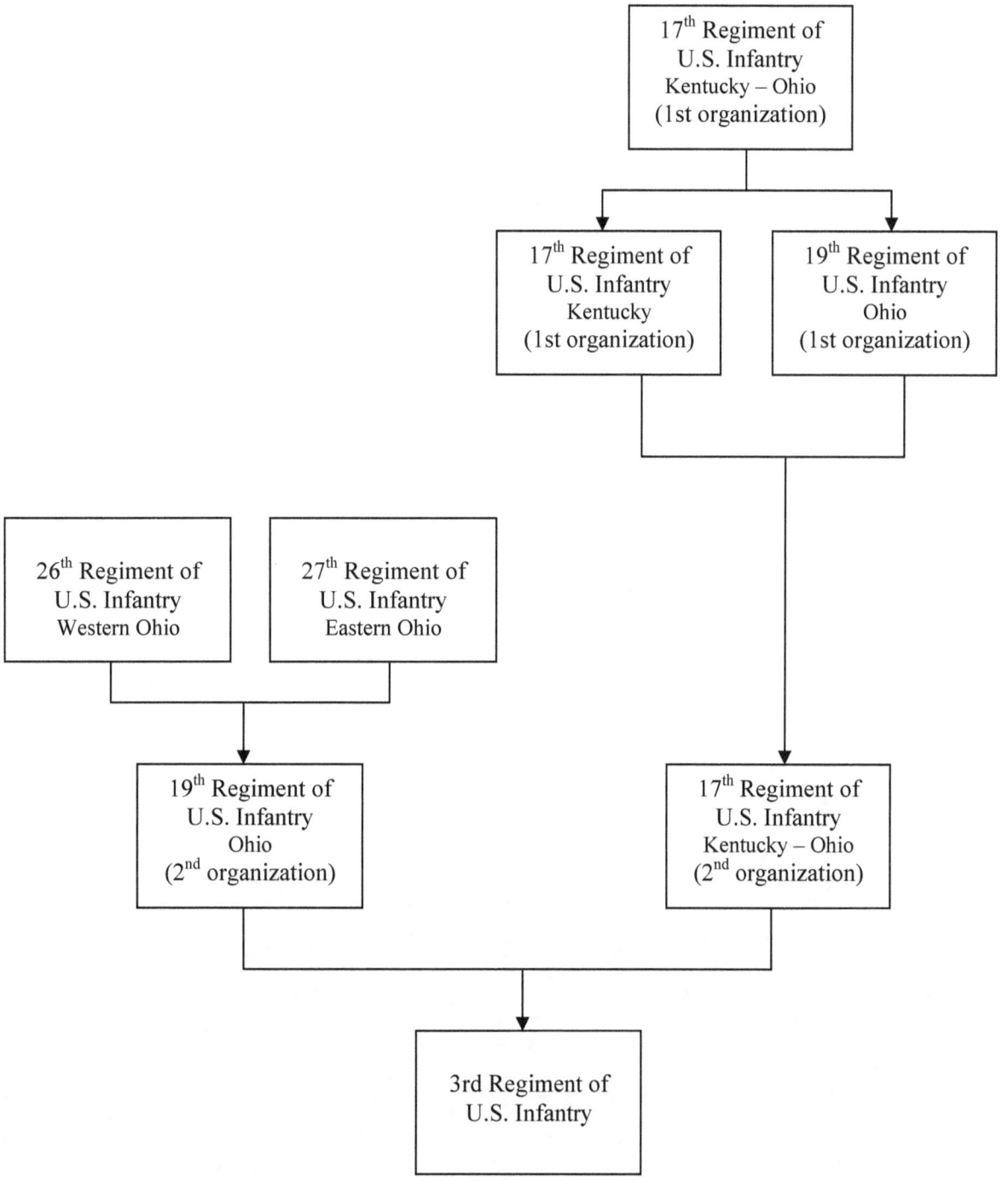

The 3rd Regiment of U.S. Infantry was formed from the 1st, 17th, 19th, 24th, 28th and 38th Regiments of U.S. Infantry which served during the War of 1812.